AF606024

The *Commentaries* of Pope Pius II (1458–1464) and the Crisis of the Fifteenth-Century Papacy

EMILY O'BRIEN

The *Commentaries* of Pope Pius II (1458–1464) and the Crisis of the Fifteenth-Century Papacy

UNIVERSITY OF TORONTO PRESS
Toronto Buffalo London

Toronto Buffalo London
www.utppublishing.com
Printed in the U.S.A.

ISBN 978-1-4426-4763-3

Printed on acid-free, 100% post-consumer recycled paper with vegetable-based inks.

Toronto Italian Studies

Library and Archives Canada Cataloguing in Publication

O'Brien, Emily, author
The commentaries of Pope Pius II (1458–1464) and the crisis of the fifteenth-century papacy / Emily O'Brien.

(Toronto Italian studies)
Includes bibliographical references and index.
ISBN 978-1-4426-4763-3 (bound)

1. Pius II, Pope, 1405–1464. Commentarii rerum memorabilium.
2. Pius II, Pope, 1405–1464. 3. Church history–Middle Ages, 600–1500–Historiography. 4. Popes–Biography–History and criticism.
5. Self-perception. 6. Autobiography. 7. Renaissance–Italy. I. Title.
II. Series: Toronto Italian studies

BX1308.O27 2015 282.092 C2015-903581-3

This book has been published with the help of a grant from the Federation for the Humanities and Social Sciences, through the Awards to Scholarly Publications Program, using funds provided by the Social Sciences and Humanities Research Council of Canada.

University of Toronto Press acknowledges the financial assistance to its publishing program of the Canada Council for the Arts and the Ontario Arts Council, an agency of the Government of Ontario.

Canada Council for the Arts
Conseil des Arts du Canada

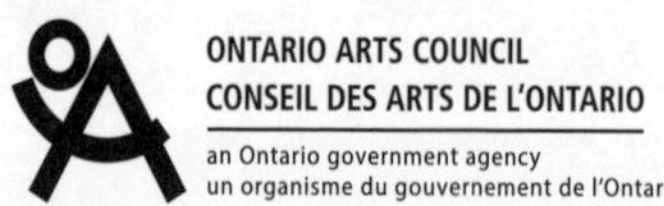

Funded by the Government of Canada
Financé par le gouvernement du Canada

To my Mother and my Father

Contents

Acknowledgments

This book was built on the generous support and guidance of many people. Chief among them are the two scholars I consider my mentors: Anthony Molho and Riccardo Fubini. They, more than anyone else, taught me the historian's craft and equipped me with the tools necessary to tackle this project. From them I learned what it means to scrutinize a document; how to listen for conversations among humanist texts; and why historical context is so important to unlocking their meaning. For the patient, thoughtful, and expert guidance of these two scholars, I am deeply grateful. I hope this book stands as a testament to the valuable lessons they have taught me.

The example of good scholarship alone did not fuel this book. My project would not have been possible without the support of grants and fellowships from several institutions. At various stages, the research and writing of this book were funded by the Fulbright Foundation, by the Social Sciences and Humanities Research Council of Canada, and by Simon Fraser University. A grant from the Canadian Federation for the Humanities and Social Sciences has aided its publication.

The ideas in this book were nurtured by many libraries and their skilful staffs. For several years, the Biblioteca Apostolica Vaticana was my intellectual home as I worked on this project. I am indebted to the librarians and other staff members there who helped me to get my bearings and who made working there one of the most rewarding and enjoyable experiences of my career. I am particularly grateful to the former prefect, Leonard Boyle, who made the library so welcoming to young scholars and who generously assisted me in my investigations. I would also like to thank the staff and librarians of the American Academy in Rome, Houghton Library at Harvard University, and the Thomas Fisher

Rare Book Library at the University of Toronto. Finally, special thanks are due to the exceptionally resourceful interlibrary loan librarians at Simon Fraser University. They have worked tirelessly on my behalf to bring Renaissance Italy to the shores of British Columbia.

While writing and revising this book, I have benefited greatly from the insights and suggestions of a host of fellow scholars. I am especially grateful to Anthony D'Elia and Thomas Izbicki, who offered thoughtful and careful readings of drafts of the book. Christopher Celenza, Joanna Drell, Gary Ianziti, and Timothy Kircher also gave me expert advice on both the book's arguments and its structure. A much broader community of scholars has contributed more indirectly to the development of this project. They are the colleagues who have inspired me through their own accomplishments and who, in various ways, have offered support, friendship, and frequent reminders of the worth of our scholarly labours. Everyone mentioned to this point belongs in this group. So do Nancy Bisaha, Scott Blanchard, Gerald Christianson, Una Roman D'Elia, Frances Gage, Kenneth Gouwens, Anne Leader, Liza McCahill, Margaret Meserve, David Mirhady, Susanne Saygin, Simonetta Serra, Marcello Simonetta, Saundra Weddle, and Leah Whittington.

To the University of Toronto Press and my two editors, Ron Schoeffel and Suzanne Rancourt, I, in turn, owe many thanks. When I first submitted my manuscript for review, Ron was the editor of the Italian Studies Series. I was incredibly fortunate to have such an expert as my guide; and I am deeply grateful for all he did to shepherd me through the review process. Suzanne has been an invaluable resource in the later stages of the book's production and generous above all with her patience. I must also thank my copy editor, Kate Baltais, for her careful reading of the manuscript and for her thoughtful suggestions.

Finally, I thank my friends and my family for the myriad ways they have contributed to this book. I am especially grateful to Ilaria Brancoli Busdraghi Broucke, Willeen Keough, Katie Johnson, Carmen O'Brien, David O'Brien, Michael Owler, Meg Penner, Jane Rosenzweig, Julie Rosenbaum, Ligaya Temperatura, and most of all, Joanna Drell. In so many ways, her friendship has been the anchor of this book. To my husband, Paul Garfinkel, my gratitude is boundless. As a fellow historian, he patiently read numerous drafts of the manuscript, offered expert advice, and was always there to give me the encouragement and perspective that I needed. He also gave me the gift of time by keeping our son Michael happily entertained on the many days I worked downstairs at my desk. Without him, writing and completing this book would have been, quite simply, impossible. In his own important way, little Michael also contributed to this book. The sound of his feet overhead was the music by which I wrote; and his hugs, smiles, and zest for life have been my greatest source of energy and inspiration.

My deepest debt is to my parents, Anne and Michael O'Brien. It was they who first introduced me to Italy, who taught me their love of language, who kindled my interest in Renaissance history, and who, as academics themselves, inspired me to follow in their footsteps. They were my greatest champions and my best friends; and their presence is everywhere in this book. I cannot know the joy of showing it to them, but I do have the honour of dedicating it to their memory.

The *Commenta*
(1458–1464) ar
Fifteenth-Cent

Abbreviations

Baldi	Barbara Baldi, *Pio II e le trasformazioni dell'Europa cristiana (1457–1464)* (Milan: Edizioni Unicopli, 2006).
Commentarii	Aeneas Silvius Piccolomini, *I Commentarii*, ed. and trans. Luigi Totaro, 2 vols. (Milan: Adelphi, 1984).
Defensorium	*Defensorium Obedientiae Apostolicae et Alia Documenta*, eds. Heiko Oberman, Daniel E. Zerfoss, and William J. Courtenay (Cambridge, MA: Belknap Press of Harvard University Press, 1968).
De gestis	Aeneas Silvius Piccolomini, *De gestis concilii Basiliensis commentariorum, libri II*, eds. Denys Hay and W.K. Smith (Oxford: Clarendon Press, 1978).
Dialogus	Aeneas Silvius Piccolomini, *Dialogus*, ed. Duane R. Henderson. (Hannover: Hahnsche Buchhandlung, 2011).
Germania	Aeneas Silvius Piccolomini, *Germania*, ed. Maria Giovanna Fadiga (Florence: Sismel-Edizioni del Galluzzo, 2009).
In minoribus	Carlo Fea, ed. *Pius II Pont. Max. a calumniis vindicatus.* (Rome, 1823).
Opera Omnia	Aeneas Silvius Piccolomini, *Opera Omnia* (Basel, 1551).
Orationes	Aeneas Silvius Piccolomini, *Pii II. P.M. olim Aeneae Sylvii Piccolominei Senensis orationes politicae et ecclesiasticae*, ed. J.D. Mansi, vol. 1 (Lucca, 1755–59).
Pentalogus	Aeneas Silvius Piccolomini, *Pentalogus*, ed. Christoph Schingnitz (Hanover: Hahnsche Buchhandlung, 2009).
Wolkan	*Der Briefwechsel des Eneas Silvius Piccolomini*, ed. Rudolf Wolkan, in *Fontes Rerum Austriacarum*, ser. 2, vols. 61, 62, 67, 68 (Vienna, 1909–18). Cited as Wolkan 1 for vols. 61 and 62; Wolkan 2 for vol. 67; and Wolkan 3 for vol. 68.

Introduction

> The deceitful tongue that did not spare so many of Christ's vicars, nor Christ himself, will not spare Pope Pius II. While he lives among us, Pius II is accused and condemned. When he is dead, he will be praised ... [T]he truth will come forth again, and Pius will be counted among the illustrious popes.[1]

The author of this bold and confident prediction was none other than Pope Pius II himself. The words appear in the preface to his *Commentarii rerum memorabilium quae temporibus suis contigerunt* (1462–64), the thirteen-book account of his life, his pontificate, and the age in which he lived. Pius casts himself in this passage as the victim of vicious persecution, and through his parallel to Jesus, a persecution from which, in time, he is destined to be saved. "In the meantime," he goes on to say, "we will write the history of his papacy."[2] Pius's words here suggest that he sees himself participating in this process of salvation: it is through the *Commentaries*, in other words, that "the truth" about Pope Pius II will at last begin to "come forth." Historians continue to view the *Commentaries* as one of the most important humanist texts of Renaissance Italy, but they have grown more wary of it as "truth." Rather than an objective account, they now categorize the text as an apology or defence, as propaganda, and as a carefully calculated work of self-promotion. What purpose this defence serves, how it is constructed, and how we should understand its larger significance, both historically and historiographically, are the driving questions of this book.

What makes these questions worth answering is, in part, the author himself. Aeneas Silvius Piccolomini – Pius II, as pope – was one of the most accomplished humanists and influential public figures in fifteenth-century Europe, and long before he took the papal throne. Born in 1405 in the village of Corsignano, and into a noble but impoverished Tuscan family, he trained in law and letters at the University of Siena. An accomplished diplomat and statesman, he served as secretary, ambassador, and close adviser to several cardinals, three popes, an anti-pope, and the Holy Roman emperor. After taking orders late in his career (1446), he rose swiftly through the ecclesiastical hierarchy as bishop (1447–56), cardinal (1456–58), and eventually pope (1458–64).

In these various capacities, he participated in some of the most pivotal events in European politics, both secular and ecclesiastical. He was a prominent figure at the Council of Basel (1431–49), a powerful and controversial assembly that deposed the sitting pope and precipitated a decade-long schism in the Western Church. Pius, then Aeneas, played a pivotal role in resolving that schism and, in so doing, helped to shape the religious landscape of Europe on the eve of the Reformation. He also stood at the forefront of the European response to one of the defining events of the century: the fall of Constantinople to the Ottoman Turks in May 1453. A vocal proponent of the crusade, Aeneas spent much of his career as cardinal and bishop exhorting popes, princes, and the Holy Roman emperor to unite in launching such an expedition. He continued those efforts relentlessly during his pontificate (1458–64) and made his own leadership of a crusade one of the central aims of his papacy. Ultimately, Pius exercised his most powerful and lasting influence through what he wrote more than what he did. His vast corpus of humanist writings includes orations, treatises, dialogues, poetry, a novella, a comedy, numerous historical works, and an extensive epistolary. Most of them, including the *Commentaries*, engage directly or indirectly with the turbulent political and ecclesiastical worlds in which he played out his career. In his own day, Pius earned a reputation for his incisive and incomparable eloquence. In ours, he ranks alongside Petrarch, Lorenzo Valla, Leonardo Bruni, and Poggio Bracciolini as one of the most distinguished and influential humanists of his age. Studying the *Commentaries*, then, promises to illuminate a truly towering figure of Renaissance culture and politics.

It also promises to do something much broader in scope: to elucidate a pivotal moment in the history of the papacy. Pius's pontificate and his pre-papal career coincided with a period of profound crisis, change, and uncertainty for the papal monarchy.[3] Like their medieval predecessors, the popes of the mid-fifteenth century still claimed sovereignty over a universal church, but their formidable titles masked a very different reality. A new system of states was coalescing across Europe and effectively replacing the *respublica christiana* as the defining framework of the West. The concurrent changes in spiritual topography were just as substantial. The rulers of these states were rapidly assuming control in their territories over what had traditionally been papal prerogatives – judicial, fiscal, and administrative; and as they did, they were sharply curtailing the power, influence, and very relevance of the pope as a universal monarch.

Still more dangerous to papal sovereignty was the different and corporate model of ecclesiastical government that was threatening to transform the institution from an absolute to a limited monarchy. Conciliar doctrine located ecclesiastical sovereignty not in the pope, but instead in the church as a whole as represented by a general council. When Pius's papacy began, the conciliar movement was more than just an abstract threat. Through a series of legal instruments, it restricted papal authority in practice; and by drawing on a formidable array of theoretical weapons, it continued to erode papal claims to sovereignty. With its powerful following, moreover, and, in the eyes of many, with the best remedy for solving the problems of the contemporary church, the conciliar model left the future of the papal monarchy uncertain.

The instability and uncertainty of papal authority also extended into its temporal realm. The hallmark of the fifteenth-century papacy was the development of the Papal States into a powerful principate, but when Pius took the throne, that transformation was only just underway. Its progress to date had been uneven and its successes tenuous. As princes of the Papal States, the popes of mid-century struggled to subdue rebellious communes and *signori* protective of their own independence; and despite their efforts to take the lead in Italian diplomacy, they remained vulnerable to the territorial ambitions of neighbouring states. Even the papacy's claims to temporal authority remained insecure, in large part because many questioned the value and viability of a pope who would also be prince.

In short, the institution that stands at the centre of Pius's *Commentaries* was immersed in an unprecedented crisis of authority, legitimacy, and identity. Studying this text allows us to open a window onto that crisis, and an extraordinary window at that. Penned by the very man who sat on the papal throne, the *Commentaries* afford a view from within the eye of the storm. At the same time, this text tells us something about how the papacy responded to that crisis: it shows us how one pope sought to construct his own self-portrait when the papacy's very identity was under fire.

As a case study of papal imagery, Pius's *Commentaries* are no less valuable. What was a turning point in the history of the papacy has also been identified as a watershed moment in how the papacy envisioned and represented its authority. In his now magisterial *Il sovrano pontefice*, Paolo Prodi distils from existing scholarship an important claim: that beginning in the mid-fifteenth century, the papacy began drawing on the language, imagery, and ideals of temporal politics to conceptualize both its spiritual and its temporal authority. As a result, the Renaissance popes in both their literary and artistic representations began to take on the appearance of contemporary Italian *signori*.[4] For many reasons, Pius's *Commentaries* are crucial to exploring and understanding this significant shift in papal imagery. Written when these developments were in their early stages, the text offers us the opportunity to investigate both the initial causes of this transformation and its earliest substantial expressions. What makes the *Commentaries* still more valuable for such a study is that they reflect the views not just of the papal curia but of the very man occupying the papal throne.

While the *Commentaries* intersect with significant developments in papal imagery, they also belong to an equally dynamic and important period in Western historiography. Traditionally, the fifteenth century, and in Italy especially, has been hailed as the dawn of a new critical approach to writing about the past and the birthplace of "modern" historical methods.[5] While these views continue to shape current understandings of Renaissance historiography, recent scholarship has illuminated a more complex picture of how historians in this period constructed the past. Their methodology, it has been argued, was in many ways more akin to that of their medieval predecessors; and in many cases, their new critical methods were shaped primarily by political forces and turned to political ends.[6] A careful study of the *Commentaries*, Pius's most important historical work, will help to situate their author in the context of these important developments, and, at the same time, will do something more. As one of the most prolific and influential historians of his age, Pius II occupies an important position in the landscape of Renaissance historiography; and scholars today concur that his *Commentaries* are among the most important historical works of this period. Studying this text, therefore, affords us an opportunity to learn about more than just Pius the historian: it will also help us to understand the broader historiographical contours of his age.

Given their considerable significance, both historical and historiographical, how is it that the *Commentaries* still require further study? Until a few decades ago, the main reasons were practical and logistical. While scholarship on the work's manuscript tradition grew in the first half of the twentieth century, it was not until the mid-1980s that the first modern edition of the Latin text appeared. Until then, most historians were forced to rely on a heavily censored *editio princeps* from the sixteenth century, the partial publication of its missing fragments, and Italian and English translations.[7] Further complicating the study of the text was the similar fate suffered by Pius's other writings: most were accessible only in early, often unreliable printed editions or in manuscript form. Perhaps the greatest challenge to studying the *Commentaries* as an apology, however, has been an incomplete understanding of the context from which it emerged. To be sure, Ludwig von Pastor's richly detailed account of Pius's pontificate (and of the fifteenth-century papacy more generally) provides an indispensable foundation for such an investigation. For all its wealth of archival material, however, *The History of the Popes* is limited, in particular, by one of its chief non-archival sources: for Pastor, as for Jacob Burckhardt before him and for biographers of Pius writing well into the twentieth century, the *Commentaries* themselves serve as a principal fount of information. Classifying the text as a set of memoirs or a diary, these scholars tend to treat the work in the way Pius himself suggests in his preface: as a reliable record of historical fact.[8]

If scholarship has handicapped the study of the *Commentaries* as an apology, so in some sense has the text itself. To even the most seasoned scholar of Italian humanism, Pius's text is a formidable work. Running twelve books in length with a fragment of a thirteenth, its size alone is daunting.[9] Still more so is its scope. As the full title suggests, the *Commentaries on Memorable Things that Happened in [Pius's] Age* is meant to be more than simply the *res gestae* of his papacy. The events and accomplishments of Pius's pontificate and his pre-papal career remain the text's primary focus; but they are positioned in a detailed and wide-reaching narrative of temporal and ecclesiastical politics. This narrative, moreover, often takes centre stage: the account of Pius's papacy yields frequently to often lengthy *excursus* – geographical, historical, ethnographic, or biographical in nature. Particular attention is given to chronicling the dynastic struggles of recent and contemporary European princes and to describing in detail the chronic wars that ravaged the continent. Structurally, therefore, the *Commentaries* is a challenging text to navigate, while substantively it can be overwhelming. Just how – or if – its various components fit together into an organic whole, let alone into a unified apology, is a complicated problem to resolve.

The building blocks and composition of the *Commentaries* only add to its complexity. Pius's source base was both textual and documentary. To construct the account of his papacy, he depended in part on the records of the papal chancery, but he also drew on historical, literary, and geographical writings; on verse as well as prose; on ancient and medieval authors; and on the works of contemporary humanists – including his own. Indeed, Pius's vast corpus of writings (and his letters, orations, and histories in particular) served as one of the most important sources for his account. Identifying these varied documents and texts, and listening to the *Commentaries'* often subtle conversations with them, is a formidable task. Nor is it the only way that the text's composition complicates its interpretation. Pius's work is a contemporary history: he shaped his record of events only shortly after they had transpired and, in many cases, while they were still happening. Writing under these conditions is challenging for any historian, but Pius's circumstances made it particularly so: he was constructing an apology for his pontificate without knowing how it would end. Years earlier, when composing a history of the Council of Basel, Pius had explicitly noted the challenge of writing contemporary history. "I must change many things," he reports in 1450, in a letter to Cardinal Juan de Carvajal, "because things didn't turn out the way I thought they would. And so for this reason it is dangerous to write the history of current events."[10] How Pius confronted these "dangers" in the *Commentaries*, and how they shaped the substance, structure, and interpretive framework of his text, are still other important questions to which students of his apology must attend.

For all these reasons, the *Commentaries* are an exceptionally complicated text both to study as an organic whole and to unravel as a work of apology. The myriad challenges of the work may help to explain why the pontiff's magnum opus, while still widely acknowledged as one of the most important texts of Renaissance Italy, and while frequently the subject of more circumscribed studies, has yet to receive the rigorous, comprehensive analysis that it so deserves.[11]

Within the last few decades, however, scholarship has opened a wide door to such an investigation. The Latin text of the *Commentaries*, once so difficult to access, exists now in four critical editions, two with accompanying translations.[12] There is also a wealth of new editions and translations of Pius II's other writings.[13] At the same time, historians have developed a fuller, more nuanced understanding of the events, aims, and tensions that defined Pius's papacy. Particularly valuable are the studies that explore his pontificate within the broader context of ecclesiastical and secular politics – a context that is central to the *Commentaries'* own portrayal of Pius's papacy – and that examine his relationship to the intricate diplomatic dynamics of the Italian peninsula.[14]

In turn, scholars have offered a variety of tools with which to confront the particular challenges posed by the text. Studies of humanist historiography, especially works of apologetic history, provide invaluable models for analysing Pius's own self-defence in the *Commentaries*.[15] So, in turn, does new research on Renaissance papal historiography, and on Nicholas V in particular,[16] and on humanism at the courts of Martin V and Eugenius IV.[17] Meanwhile, fresh studies of Pius's other historical writings help to illuminate his methodology, interpretive frameworks, and in particular, the political resonances of his work.[18] Finally, many of the studies devoted to individual themes, sections, and features of the *Commentaries* have begun to uncover the nature and construction of the work. Among other topics, these studies investigate the *Commentaries'* reception of certain ancient and contemporary authors,[19] its use of documentary sources,[20] its portrait of Pius,[21] its portrayal of important allies and opponents of the papacy,[22] and its sixteenth-century legacy.[23]

If a comprehensive analysis of the *Commentaries* is now more possible than ever before, it also seems more necessary. This need has grown first and foremost out of recent scholarly reassessments of Pius II and his pontificate. Over the course of the last century, Pius earned from many historians the label of a backwards-looking idealist. In an age that saw Europe fracturing both politically and spiritually, Pius persistently defended and promoted the waning universal powers of papacy and empire. After ascending the papal throne, moreover, he continued to embrace this world view. The centrepiece of his policy, a crusade against the Ottoman Turks, has until recently been read as a product of that world view and as a naive attempt to resuscitate what was a fundamentally medieval and long-moribund concept.[24] Thanks, in part, however, to new research on Pius II's pre-papal writings, on his pontificate more generally, and on his plans for a crusade specifically, these interpretations have been largely dismissed. Instead, scholars now maintain that Pius was profoundly aware of the disintegration of the old political and spiritual order – indeed, that from his own experience he had a better understanding than most of the centrifugal forces reshaping Europe. Rather than a symbol of his backwards-looking vision, they read his program for a crusade as the design of an astute and practised politician, and one fully engaged with the ecclesiastical and political challenges of his age.[25] In the wake of this revisionist scholarship, it seems more necessary than ever to explore the *Commentaries* – a work that not only offers Pius's own account of his papacy, but that also places at the forefront of that account his unwavering commitment to crusade.

It is, thus, as grateful beneficiary of this recent scholarship and in continuous dialogue with it that this book takes up a topic both urgently needed and ripe for study: the anatomy of the apology that is Pius II's *Commentaries*. It answers its first and most fundamental question – what purpose does this defence serve? – by reading and analysing the text in sustained conversation with the context of crisis in which it took shape. It understands that crisis to be both institutional and individual: it was not only the papal monarchy that needed defending but also the pontificate of Pope Pius II himself. It was, moreover, not just his actions as pope that made him vulnerable: over the course of his long pre-papal career Pius, then Aeneas, had done much, and especially with his pen, to exacerbate the crisis in which the papacy was embroiled. Reconstructing these different and interrelated vulnerabilities is, thus, a crucial preliminary step to understanding how the *Commentaries* function as a work of apology. That task is both substantial and complex. As this book will go on to argue, Pius responded in a detailed way in the *Commentaries* to the many threats facing both himself and the papacy. If we are to understand the subtleties and nuances of his defence, we must first become familiar with the specifics of the crisis that prompted it.

For this reason, the first half of this book is devoted to mapping out – and more fully than ever before – what exactly Pius and the papacy needed to defend themselves against. Chapter 1 illuminates the vulnerabilities of the institution of papal monarchy on the eve of Pius II's pontificate. It makes the case that when he took the papal throne, the authority, legitimacy, and relevance of the papacy remained under heavy assault. Chapters 2 and 3 consider Pius's own complex and changing relationship to this multi-level crisis. Their primary aim is to elucidate the various ways he contributed to it over the course of his three-decade career. The vulnerabilities and liabilities these three chapters point up then become crucial tools for the textual analysis unfolded in the subsequent three. Only by reading the *Commentaries* against this detailed map of crisis can we detect the text's broader apologetic rhythms and hear the defensive resonances of particular images, passages, and words.

There is still another reason why this book is structured as two parts. In assessing Pius II's own contributions to the crisis engulfing the fifteenth-century papacy, chapters 2 and 3 put forward a series of new interpretations of Pius's pontificate. They do so, in large part, by building on recent studies of Pius's six years on the papal throne and, first and foremost, on the archival research of Barbara Baldi.[26] Still more extensively, these two chapters revise long-standing perceptions of Aeneas and his views on papal authority in the years before he became pope. They argue that Aeneas was at odds with the Roman Church far longer than he is traditionally thought to have been; and that his conciliarist past was only one of several ways his pre-papal career threatened him as pope. These new arguments grow out of a fresh and rigorous study of hundreds of his letters and more than half a dozen texts that he wrote during this period. Developing and defending these important claims is difficult to do effectively in the middle of an analysis of the *Commentaries*. For this reason, too, then, these arguments are separated out from that analysis into discrete chapters. To help the reader integrate these sequenced interpretations of context and text, there are frequent references in chapters 4, 5, and 6 to the specific details of the arguments put forward in the preceding three.

My reading of the *Commentaries* is guided by other scholars' interpretations of the fifteenth-century papacy as well as by my own. In particular, it is informed by a new wave of studies that significantly reassesses the conciliar movement. Over the last two decades, historians have increasingly and convincingly rejected the traditional narrative of papal history that states that by the middle of the fifteenth century, the papacy had definitively triumphed over the conciliar threat.[27] New studies have emphasized instead the popes' ongoing vulnerability to the conciliar movement through the fifteenth century and beyond and, in so doing, have made a persuasive case for the fundamental instability of the "Restoration" papacy.[28] To understand how the *Commentaries* serve as an apology, thus, requires us to determine how and to what extent they respond to this significant conciliar threat. What makes this question especially germane to the study of this particular text is its author's own shifting relationship to the conciliar movement. For years, Pius, then Aeneas, had been one of the most prominent and vocal conciliarists of his generation. First introduced to conciliar theory in 1432 at the Council of Basel, he spent the next decade making a name for himself as diplomat, orator, and publicist in support of the conciliar cause. He was hardly the only conciliarist to abandon camp for the papalists, nor was he the most distinguished of these converts. None of them, however, had embraced the radicalism of the Basel council – or had promoted that radicalism in writing – in the way that he had. None, moreover, had gone on to become pope. For these reasons, conciliarism represented the most formidable threat Pius faced on the papal throne. With this in mind, this book pays particular attention to the conciliar dimension of the crisis of the fifteenth-century papacy; and it devotes an entire chapter to exploring how the *Commentaries* respond to that threat.

Scholarship of a different kind informs the second line of inquiry this book takes up: how does Pius construct his apology? Recent studies of his writings have demonstrated how he mined his sources selectively, eliminating some parts while amplifying others, and in a way that served specific political needs.[29] This book seeks to build on those findings by elucidating still further the methodology Pius employed when constructing his politically charged *Commentaries*. Like these other studies, it does so in part by considering how Pius used historical sources, and in particular, how he adopted and adapted his own earlier accounts of the events he discusses in the text. At the same time, it brings into focus other aspects of his methodology, and necessarily so: much of what Pius discusses in the *Commentaries* he experienced firsthand, and consequently, he did not need to rely on written accounts to discuss them. In these instances, this analysis will, when possible, compare Pius's account in the *Commentaries* with other sources documenting the same events. At the same time, this book aims to illuminate other dimensions of Pius's methodology. In particular, it seeks to identify the specific techniques or strategies he relied on the most when writing historical narrative.

It is in the context of this methodological investigation that this book engages current interpretations of the evolution of papal imagery in the fifteenth and sixteenth centuries. As noted earlier, those arguments identify in representations of papal authority the imprint of secular political culture and, in particular, the figure of the contemporary Italian *signore*. To what extent do the *Commentaries* participate in and contribute to those developments? This book will answer this question by considering how the image Pius constructs of papal authority relates both to the ideas and practices of secular rule and to literary and historical representations of contemporary secular rulers. At the same time as it maps out this relationship, it seeks to explain it. Prodi coordinates these shifts in papal imagery with concurrent changes in the temporal dimension of papal authority: it was during this period that the papacy was consolidating its power in the Papal States and transforming these territories into a principate. Working largely from studies about the sixteenth-century papacy, he explains that the new princely image of papal authority reflected the new reality of its temporal power.[30] This explanation cannot, however, account for any political imprint we might find in the representations of papal authority in the *Commentaries*; the text was written at a time when the popes' temporal authority was unstable and, indeed, when the institution as a whole was in crisis. Accordingly, one of the aims of this book is to consider other possible reasons why Pius might or might not have adopted the language of secular rule when constructing his vision of papal authority in the *Commentaries*. In particular, it will consider how, in making these choices, he was responding to the crisis of temporal and spiritual authority in which he and the papacy were immersed.

Following these two main lines of inquiry, then, this book puts forward a series of interrelated claims. The *Commentaries*, it argues, constitute a far more ambitious and aggressive work of defence than has yet been realized. The narrative Pius unfolds therein serves, for one, to shield the fifteenth-century papacy from the serious assaults it endured to its authority, legitimacy, and relevance. At the same time, it functions as a still more rigorous rehabilitation of Pius II's own pontificate, which had seen the crisis engulfing the papal monarchy worsen on its three main fronts. Crucial to these institutional and personal defences is the text's portrayal of Aeneas – that is, Pius before he took the papal throne. In the *Commentaries*, he is systematically stripped of the views and actions that proved so dangerous both to his reputation and record as pope and to the papacy more generally. Of all the threats facing Pius II and the institution of papal monarchy, the *Commentaries* offer their most sustained response to conciliarism. Chapter 4 presents a detailed analysis of the text's comprehensive and forceful assault against the papacy's formidable enemy. Chapter 5 looks instead at how the *Commentaries* defend against other forces weakening papal sovereignty in its spiritual and temporal realms. It argues that in the way he constructs his relationship with Europe's secular princes, Pius responds directly to the specific threats these rulers posed to his spiritual authority. At the same time, it shows how his account shores up the particular liabilities he faced as a temporal prince. Detailed, nuanced, and remarkably thorough, this multilayered apology dominates Pius's *Commentaries*, and from beginning to end. While it is pervasive, it is not always unified: at times, Pius's defence of his pontificate clashes with his defence of papal monarchy more generally; at other points, he shores up his temporal authority at the expense of his spiritual. Chapters 4 and 5 both point up and interpret this pattern of tensions and, in so doing, illuminate still further the text's complex apologetic dynamics.

How do the *Commentaries* construct this wide-ranging and complicated defence? They do so primarily, this book argues, by consistently concealing, erasing, and misrepresenting the weaknesses plaguing Pius II's papacy and the institution of papal monarchy. Chapters 4, 5, and 6 elucidate both where and how the text builds such a narrative. Together, they argue that while Pius's apologetic toolbox was well stocked, he tended to favour some tools more than others. As they unfold the layers of his apology, these chapters identify those tools; and in many cases, they also trace their presence in Pius's earlier writings. In so doing, they illuminate how, as a work of apology, the *Commentaries* are integrally linked to the broader corpus of Pius's writings.

Among the most important tools Pius used to build his defence, this book argues, were the images and ideals of secular politics. The language and culture of secular power are imprinted on fundamental aspects of Pius's self-portrait and in a way that significantly enhances the image of the popes as strong sovereigns in both their temporal and spiritual spheres. These parallels help Pius not only to project an image of strong authority: they also help him to legitimize his own and the popes' sovereign power and to make a case for the institution's continued relevance in the changing landscape of fifteenth-century Europe. Chapter 5 begins to make this argument by examining how the ideals of secular authority inform aspects of Pius II's spiritual leadership. Chapter 6 argues this claim far more extensively. It does so by comparing Pius's self-portrait in the *Commentaries* with representations of contemporary secular rulers and by illuminating the considerable common ground they share. Both chapters emphasize the apologetic benefits of constructing papal authority in the language of secular power. At the same time, they connect the princely features of this papal imagery to Pius's – and Aeneas's – own experiences in secular politics.

Together, these arguments allow us to bring into sharper focus both the historical and historiographical significance of Pius II's magnum opus. The *Commentaries*, this book argues, are not so much an account of what happened in Pius's papacy as they are his vision of what he had hoped his pontificate would achieve: a papal monarchy secure in its authority as both temporal and spiritual sovereign. In fulfilling this purpose, the *Commentaries* exemplify the very kind of history that Renaissance historians were long thought to have abandoned. The fact that such a text was written by one of the premiere historians of the fifteenth century suggests we should define Renaissance historiography still more as a fundamentally political act. If this analysis brings out the broader historiographical significance of the *Commentaries*, it also reveals the important position the work occupies in other dimensions of intellectual culture. As much as it is a work of political history, the *Commentaries* must be considered a vital contribution to the debate over ecclesiastical authority that dominated the fifteenth-century church. In particular, Pius's text represents a powerful weapon in the papacy's long and arduous struggle against conciliarism. Finally, this study identifies in the *Commentaries* a turning point in the evolution of papal imagery. By infusing his portrait of the papacy with distinctly secular ideals, Pius II helped to reconceptualize traditional representations of papal authority. His reasons for doing so serve to complicate current understandings of why this shift happened. If in the sixteenth century such imagery reflected the reality of the popes' secular rule, in the mid-fifteenth it shored up their weaknesses as both temporal and spiritual sovereigns.

The focus of this book and the claims it puts forward require some concluding remarks about the source at the centre of investigation. While it is unnecessary to review in detail the extensive scholarship on the manuscript tradition of the *Commentaries*, it is important to explain here the edition of the text adopted in this study and to consider issues of audience and composition that relate directly to its argument.[31] Of the three completed critical editions of the *Commentaries*, this book works from that of Luigi Totaro.[32] Totaro's edition is based on ms. Corsiniano 147 in the Biblioteca dell'Accademia dei Lincei, the manuscript generally considered by scholars to be the version to which Pius gave his final approval.[33] Cors. 147 includes all twelve complete books of the *Commentaries* but not the fragment of the thirteenth.[34] This splendidly illuminated parchment codex was copied for Pius by Giovanni Gobellino in elegant humanist hand in the spring of 1464 and was completed 12 June of that year – only six days before the pontiff left for Ancona to launch a crusade. The manuscript contains corrections in the hand of

Agostino Patrizi, Pius II's secretary, and Gobellino; notes by Francesco Todeschini Piccolomini (Pope Pius III, r. 1503), the pontiff's nephew and the manuscript's heir; and other notes dating to the sixteenth century, when Francesco Bandini Piccolomini, archbishop and relative of Pius, used the manuscript when preparing his printed and heavily censored edition of 1584. Also in this manuscript – and clearly meant by Pius as a complement to his own text – is a letter his secretary and confidant Jacopo Ammannati Piccolomini received from Giannantonio Campano, Pius's close adviser, court poet, and the man he had tapped to review and revise his work.[35] Campano's letter explicitly states that his intervention in Pius's text was minimal, thus offering further evidence that Cors. 147 represents the work of the original author rather than the revisions of another.

Cors. 147 is predated by Vaticano Reginense Latino 1995, a paper codex located in the Vatican Library and the working copy of the *Commentaries*.[36] While Reg. Lat. 1995 is written for the most part in the hand of papal secretary Agostino Patrizi, to whom Pius II dictated much of the work, the pontiff's own hand has been identified on numerous pages making corrections, additions, and penning passages of the original text.[37] Such markings are valuable evidence of the work's compositional techniques; but they also reveal that while Pius composed the *Commentaries* quickly (between the summer of 1462 and the spring of 1464), he revised it carefully, thoughtfully, and repeatedly.[38] Reg. Lat. 1995 includes the unfinished fragment of Book Thirteen, which presumably was interrupted by Pius's sudden death in August 1464.[39] It is clear from this continuation that he was planning to extend the *Commentaries*, but it is also clear from the finished nature of Cors. 147 that he considered the twelve previous books to be a distinct work, complete in itself. Although the few other differences between Cors. 147 and Reg. Lat. 1995 are overwhelmingly stylistic in nature and are considered by most scholars to be minor (it is presumed that these represent Campano's corrections), nevertheless Cors. 147 offers the most accurate image of how Pius II wanted to be remembered.[40]

The idea of the *Commentaries* as memory raises the important question of audience: for whom did Pius II leave this self-portrait? And did it, in fact, reach its intended readers? Pius's sudden death in Ancona only two months after Gobellino had completed his copy and the antagonism between Pius's followers and his successor, Paul II, have made it difficult to answer this question with certainty. The elegance of Cors. 147 has led one expert on Pius II to suggest that this manuscript might have been the *archetypus* from which other transcriptions were to be made.[41] If this was, in fact, Pius's intention, then it was never fulfilled. The radical change in circumstances at the papal court after Pius's death on 15 August 1464 made circulation of the text almost an impossibility. The manuscript tradition that has been established to date attests to this reality: other than Reg. Lat. 1995 and Cors. 147, there are no known fifteenth-century manuscripts of the text. Moreover, the vast majority of those dating to the sixteenth and seventeenth centuries descend from Reg. Lat. 1995, a pattern that suggests that Cors. 147 circulated for some time only in very restricted circles.[42]

While the *Commentaries* themselves may have been seen by only a few eyes in the fifteenth century, there is ample evidence that the image they contained continued to circulate. Ianziti has argued through a comparative analysis of Pius's text and Giovanni Simonetta's *De rebus gestis Francisci Sfortiae commentarii* that the Milanese court was familiar with at least parts of Pius's text, that it recognized it as a work of self-promotion, and that Pius's choice of genre directly influenced Simonetta's.[43] Moreover, recent scholarship on the letters, poems, and other writings composed by Pius's circle of humanists after his death (including Jacopo Ammannati Piccolomini, Giannantonio Campano, and Leodrisio Crivelli) has repeatedly suggested that their flattering portraits of the pontiff, shaped in response to attacks on his memory, originated in the *Commentaries*.[44] So, in turn, did the frescoes Francesco Todeschini Piccolomini (Pius III) commissioned for the Piccolomini library in the cathedral of Siena, where Pius's library was to be housed.[45] The *Commentaries*, it is important to note, were not meant as propaganda according to the usual understanding of that word, nor did they serve this purpose in the end. The term propaganda implies a level of publicity incongruous with the intellectual culture of this age. On the other hand, the text's apologetic style, the nature of Cors. 147, and the similarities between Pius II's self-portrait and the images promoted by his humanist followers together suggest that the *Commentaries* were not only meant to be a work of self-promotion with a controlled circulation, but that, at least to some extent, they succeeded in fulfilling this goal.

1 An Institution in Crisis: The Papal Monarchy on the Eve of Pius II's Pontificate

Christendom has no head whom all wish to obey. Neither the supreme pontiff nor the Emperor is given his due. There is no reverence, no obedience. Like fictional characters or like figures in a painting, so do we look upon the Pope and the Emperor.[1]

Aeneas Silvius Piccolomini, the future Pope Pius II, wrote these words to his friend, Leonardo Benvoglienti, in July 1454. Then imperial legate, Aeneas had attended shortly before the Diet of Regensburg, an assembly summoned by Emperor Frederick III to organize a crusade in the wake of Constantinople's stunning fall to the Ottoman Turks in May of the previous year. Aeneas was already preparing for another diet to be held in Frankfurt; and on the basis of the previous one, he confided to Benvoglienti that he was not optimistic about its outcome. But Aeneas does more than decry the failure and futility of the imperial diets: he identifies them as symptoms of a broader and deeper crisis, one that was transforming Western Christendom as radically as the Ottomans were transforming the East.

The aim of this chapter is to draw out of Aeneas's brief sketch one dimension of this crisis: the crisis that was affecting and unsettling the fifteenth-century papacy. Closely intertwined with developments in the Holy Roman Empire, the troubled history of the fifteenth-century papacy can be charted and explained in myriad ways. The narrative presented here takes as its cue Aeneas's own words. A pope no longer given "obedience" and "reverence" is one whose authority is no longer respected and whose legitimacy has been cast into doubt. A pope who seems more like a "figure in a painting" is one whose relevance, whose very reason for being is in question. Together, this language and this imagery offer an apt description of the institution that Aeneas inherited on 19 August 1458 when he was elected pope. The fifteenth-century papacy was, indeed, engulfed in a crisis of legitimacy, authority, and relevance. Complex in both its origins and its manifestations, that crisis can be attributed in large part to the presence and influence of new models of ecclesiastical authority that were competing directly with the pope's traditional claim to be sole sovereign of the universal church.[2] One of these competing models grew out of the multifaceted ecclesiastical movement called conciliarism. The other, which saw secular rulers assume authority claimed by the pope, gained traction as a result of political developments. On the eve of Pius II's pontificate, these competing visions of church government, one conciliar and one princely, were well established as both serious and successful rivals to papal sovereignty. They encroached significantly on the pope's jurisdiction and successfully resisted his attempts to reclaim it; and they found compelling ways both to protect and to legitimize their authority. To their many supporters, these competing and coexisting structures of ecclesiastical power seemed far better suited than a papal sovereign both to resolving the pressing problems of the contemporary church and to meeting the political needs of the consolidating states of Europe. In short, as the popes' traditional power had eroded, so had their very place and purpose in Western Christendom become increasingly unclear.

The crisis of the fifteenth-century papacy was still broader in scope: it embraced the pope's temporal sphere as well as the ecclesiastical. In the years before Pius II's pontificate, the papacy was in the difficult early stages of building its Italian lands into a territorial state. As temporal princes, the popes faced significant resistance – from fellow princes or would-be princes and from their own subjects. That resistance was so significant, in fact, that papal sovereignty over its territories was, in the late summer of 1458, more ambition than it was fact. What made that ambition still more difficult to achieve were the challenges the popes faced about the legitimacy of their authority, including questions about the value and viability of a pope who would also be prince. Thus, in the temporal as much as the ecclesiastical, the future of the papal monarchy was, in a word, uncertain.

This uncertainty, this book argues, was profoundly important to Pius II's *Commentaries*; it influenced both the conception and the composition of the work, and it shaped the images therein of papal monarchy and of Pius II's own pontificate. Its imprint, moreover, can be found on both the broad contours and the fine details of his text. For these reasons, the causes, nature, and consequences of this uncertainty demand our close attention.

The Challenge of Conciliarism

One of the primary causes of the papacy's uncertain future was the enduring power and influence of conciliarism.[3] More than a single, coherent theory, conciliarism was an ecclesiological movement that sought to loosen the very keystone of the medieval papal monarchy – the idea that the pope holds supreme jurisdictional authority in the church (*plenitudo potestatis*). The conciliarist reconceptualization of church governance had initially coalesced in the late fourteenth century in response to two major ecclesiastical crises. The first and more protracted was a church badly in need of reform. Demands for a sweeping *reformatio ecclesiae in capite et membris* (reform of the church in head and members) had begun in earnest in the second half of the thirteenth century, and they continued to intensify over time in response to a wide range of perceived abuses.[4] Harshest criticism was reserved for the material excesses and corruption of the Roman curia, especially during its lengthy residence in Avignon (1309–77). It was also directed at an increasingly centralized administration that was imposing steep fiscal burdens on provincial churches – and with growing efficiency – while dramatically restricting local control over appointments and judicial appeals.[5] At the same time, there was widespread concern that moral erosion, incompetence, and administrative abuse were disabling all levels of church leadership. The popes were routinely considered both the worst offenders and the root cause of these problems; and when they proved unwilling or unable to resolve this crisis, both church leaders and the Christian faithful alike began looking elsewhere for direction. The second and more acute crisis erupted in 1378, when rival claimants to the papal throne split the church into two obediences. Claiming their plenitude of power made them immune from judgment, and refusing to resign, these two papal opponents plunged Western Christendom into what came to be known as the Great Schism (1378–1417).[6] In the spiritual confusion and administrative chaos that followed, a consensus gradually emerged among prelates, theologians, canon lawyers, and secular rulers: in its current form, the papal monarchy had become unworkable.

It was from out of this impasse that the conciliar movement emerged. In its most basic form, conciliar doctrine locates ecclesiastical sovereignty not in the pope but instead in the church as a whole – the *congregatio fidelium*, or community of the faithful – and held that this community is represented in a general council of the church.[7] The extent to which the council was to exercise its sovereignty depended on the strand of conciliar theory. The majority of conciliarists advocated an intermittent and limited role for the council in church government: it represented the final authority only in certain ecclesiastical matters; and in situations where the pope was deemed detrimental to the *status ecclesiae* – by adhering to heresy, for example, or by causing schism or scandal – the council, as the pope's superior, could overrule, punish, or even depose him. Other conciliarists supported more permanent and wide-reaching functions for the council. The most radical formulations of the doctrine reassigned to the council the *plenitudo potestatis* or unlimited sovereignty traditionally claimed for the papacy, and it demoted the pope from absolute monarch to the council's executive servant.[8] Another line of thought joined conciliar theory to real power that the college of cardinals already enjoyed: it envisioned the church as an oligarchy in which the cardinalate, as representative of the *congregatio fidelium*, would share in and, in some cases, restrict papal authority.[9] Painstakingly developed by leading jurists and theologians, the arguments marshalled in defence of conciliar theory were formidable: they were grounded in canon and Roman law, in corporation theory, in the history of the church and biblical exegesis, and in ancient and medieval philosophy. Still more formidable were their larger implications, for the changes they sought called for nothing less than a fundamental restructuring of traditional church government.

By the reign of Pope Pius II, conciliar doctrine had proven itself a bold, widely accepted, and largely successful contender to papal absolutism. It had done so first and foremost at the Council of Constance (1414–18), where an international assembly of church fathers had asserted conciliar supremacy in dramatic fashion by deposing the rival claimants to the papal throne and electing a new pope, Martin V (1417–31).[10] By healing the schism and by initiating a program of reform, the council succeeded in doing in four years what the papacy had failed to do for decades.[11] Its actions were supported (and largely directed) by Europe's secular princes, and they met with the overwhelming approval of the Christian faithful. For many, the council's accomplishments alone did much to legitimize the core principle of conciliar doctrine – that the sovereign universal church as embodied in a general council can restrict the authority of the pope. But the fathers at Constance had sought a more formal, legal, and permanent foundation for the sovereignty that they claimed and that they sought to ascribe to future general councils. In April 1415, they promulgated the decree *Haec Sancta*, which declared that the council held its authority directly from Christ and that it and all general councils were superior to the pope in matters relating to unity, heresy, and reform. Two years later, they followed with *Frequens*, which provided that general councils were to be convened at regular and specified intervals.[12] Through these two decrees, the council fathers designed an apparatus in which they envisioned Pope Martin V and his successors in the capacity of constitutional not absolute monarchs.

Still more aggressive, more comprehensive, and more relentless in its assertions of ecclesiastical sovereignty was the council that assembled thirteen years later.[13] Backed by the decrees *Haec Sancta* and *Frequens* and assigned the task of reforming the church *in capite*, the Council of Basel (1431–49) had both the means and the motive to do serious damage to both the theory and the practice of papal sovereignty – something that the newly elected Pope Eugenius IV (1431–47) well understood. It also had ample opportunity and seized upon it almost immediately: when Eugenius abruptly dissolved the assembly four days after its first public session, the fathers boldly defied the claim of papal superiority that such a move implied. Invoking and reaffirming the Constance decrees, they refused to disband; and after a two-year stand-off, they succeeded in pressuring a weakened Eugenius to retract his dissolution. From thereon in, the council was to clash almost continuously with the pontiff, who after this initial defeat became as determined to reassert his authority as the newly emboldened council was to restrict it. Their conflict reached a turning point in 1437 as pope and council clashed over where to negotiate reunion with the Eastern Church. In September, after a pro-papal minority of the council fathers declared the assembly transferred to Italy, those remaining at Basel responded with their boldest attack on papal sovereignty to date: declaring *Haec Sancta* an article of the Catholic faith, they tried and deposed Eugenius as a heretic (June 1439) and five months later elected in his place Duke Amadeus of Savoy as Pope Felix V (1439–49).[14]

While these radical moves won little endorsement from Europe's secular rulers, the Basel assembly still continued to erode papal sovereignty, and for another ten long years.[15] It did so by issuing a fresh torrent of arguments in defence of both conciliar theory and the controversial decision to depose an unchallenged pope.[16] It also weakened the papacy through more indirect channels. While France and Germany officially adopted positions of neutrality in the conflict between Eugenius and the Basel fathers, both still enacted much of the assembly's recent reform legislation that stripped away papal revenues, judicial prerogatives, and control over provisions to benefices. King Charles VII of France adopted substantial parts of the Basel council's reform legislation in the Pragmatic Sanction of Bourges (7 July 1438), while Emperor Albert II, his successor, Frederick III, and the German princes did the same in the *Acceptatio* of Mainz (26 March 1439). These rulers also empowered conciliarists by endorsing, implicitly or explicitly, the principle of conciliar supremacy enshrined in *Haec Sancta* and *Frequens*, and by advocating that a "third council" be given the authority to resolve the new schism.[17] German princes continued to express their endorsement of these ideas in the proposals they put forward in 1446–47 to establish peace with Eugenius.[18] By April 1449, after Europe's secular rulers had overwhelmingly thrown their support to Eugenius, the council dissolved, Felix V resigned, and the papal monarchy was, in some sense, restored. But the concept of "restoration" must be used cautiously when describing this institution in the aftermath of these events. In reality, the Council of Basel left in its wake a papal monarchy severely bruised and battered by eighteen years of relentless assaults on the theory and practice of papal sovereignty, by a staggering loss of revenues, and by the humiliation of an entire decade without universal recognition as Western Christendom's legitimate pope.

The scarring experiences of Basel were, in fact, only part of the long shadow that conciliarism cast over the papal monarchy that Pius II inherited. The council may well have surrendered to Eugenius, but its demise represented no resounding defeat for the movement behind it – nor, for that matter, did it fully conclude the influence of that assembly itself. The conciliar model of church government continued to challenge papal absolutism in theory, to restrict papal authority in practice, to enjoy a sizeable and powerful following, and in the eyes of many, to offer the best remedy for the problems ailing the contemporary church. On the eve of Pius II's papacy, then, papal monarchy could claim only an incomplete victory over its conciliarist rival. The spectre of another Constance or Basel assembly was very real, and the future of papal absolutism remained unclear.

That uncertainty was readily apparent in the continuing resilience of conciliar doctrine. The Council of Basel had yielded no ideological ground to the papalists at the end of their struggle: the assembly ultimately dissolved because it had lost the support of the secular princes who, significantly, were drawn to Eugenius far more by his generous concessions and shrewd diplomacy than by papalist arguments for absolutism.[19] The complex theoretical underpinnings of conciliar doctrine, consequently, remained intact, as did the vast arsenal of weapons its advocates had employed against the defenders of papal monarchy. In the decade before Pius II's pontificate, conciliar apologists continued to draw these weapons by circulating tracts both old and new in defence of their ideas. In short, the council fathers may have adjourned, but in the world of ideas, the assaults on papal monarchy had not let up.

On this battlefield, the papacy's apologists could celebrate few tangible victories. To be sure, they continued an aggressive campaign in defence of papal absolutism by echoing and elaborating on the strategies employed during Eugenius's reign.[20] Under Nicholas V (1447–55), they also harnessed humanism to their cause.[21] But in the clash of legal arguments, biblical exegesis, philosophical explication, historical *exempla*, and humanist rhetoric, neither side could claim definitive ideological victory. For an institution desperate to re-establish its legitimacy as the sole repository of ecclesiastical sovereignty, the inability to halt this dispute constituted a serious threat.

Just how significant a threat becomes apparent when we survey the make-up of the conciliar movement when Pius II took the throne. Among Europe's secular rulers, King Charles VII of France still championed the idea of conciliar supremacy.[22] So, in turn, and in overwhelming numbers, did the prelates, monks, and university faculties within the kingdom and, indeed, in many states in northern Europe.[23] In Germany conciliarist sentiment remained particularly fierce and widespread, in large part because of the peace agreement forged with Eugenius IV's successor, Nicholas V. The Concordat of Vienna (February1448) was little more than a private pact among the emperor, his allies, and the pope, and it effectively protected most of the papal prerogatives that the German princes had soundly rejected nine years earlier in the *Acceptatio* of Mainz.[24] While the more moderate threads of conciliar doctrine prevailed in all these places, the radical conciliarism of Basel continued to find support in the influential law faculty in Paris and at the University of Vienna.[25] Of still greater concern to the post-Basel papacy was the strong support for the oligarchic strand of conciliar thought within the college of cardinals. On the eve of Pius II's election, this strand found powerful expression in the electoral capitulations which, in August 1458, all cardinals swore to uphold, if elected pope.[26] These capitulations required the pope not simply to consult with the college on significant matters of church government (e.g., organizing a crusade, initiating church reform, transferring the papal curia, distributing major benefices), but also to win its consent. The pope was also obliged to submit himself to an annual review in which the cardinals would determine if he had met his obligations.[27] Through this document, the cardinals effectively sought a direct share in church sovereignty and in a way that seriously challenged the papacy's renewed efforts to preserve that authority for itself alone.[28] Thus, in one form or another, conciliarism could count among its supporters some of the most influential clerics, learned theologians, and powerful rulers in Western Christendom, not to mention a seasoned corps of rhetoricians and publicists.

It could also count on a legacy of legal instruments through which conciliar supremacy effectively remained a reality. The *Compactata* or Prague Compacts (1436), which the Basel fathers in defiance of Eugenius had negotiated with the moderate Hussites, continued to remain in force in Bohemia. Among other things, this agreement sanctioned the distribution of Holy Communion in both species (*sub utraque specie*) – a practice that the papacy had expressly condemned.[29] In France, meanwhile, most of the reform legislation enacted at Basel had found legal sanction in the royal ordinance of the Pragmatic Sanction of Bourges (1438). Directed primarily at the head of the church rather than its members, these reforms stripped the pope of most of his traditional prerogatives in the French church and cut off his largest source of ecclesiastical revenue.[30] The papacy continued to challenge the legitimacy of these rulings, but with little effect. Nicholas V failed in his efforts to persuade France to revoke the Pragmatic Sanction, while his envoys' aggressive tactics in Bohemia ended up rallying rather than weakening support for the Prague Compacts.[31] As a result, the Council of Basel, dissolved though it was, continued to exercise its claims to ecclesiastical supremacy in matters of heresy and reform and at great cost to the papacy. At the same time, it made it impossible for the pope to exercise his claim to sovereignty over a universal church.

Still more damaging to both the authority and the legitimacy of papal primacy were the decrees *Haec Sancta* and *Frequens*. Though they did not reshape ecclesiastical government in the ways they had been designed to do, they became powerful weapons of a different sort in the hands of the pope's enemies. To advocates of conciliar doctrine, *Haec Sancta*, in particular, lent invaluable legitimacy to their cause. Pointing to the decree they could – and did repeatedly – argue that the concept of conciliar sovereignty was protected in the legal apparatus of the church itself.[32] They were also quick to point out that every pope since 1415 effectively owed his authority to the decree and so that for Martin V's successors to deny the legality of *Haec Sancta* was, in essence, to deny their own legitimacy.[33] But it was not just ardent conciliarists that this decree and the decree *Frequens* empowered. They offered recourse to anyone dissatisfied with a papal ruling by claiming a superior authority, either in session or soon to be so, to which an aggrieved party could issue an appeal. In effect, *Haec Sancta* and *Frequens* helped to legitimize the defiance of papal authority. At the same time, these decrees created a powerful tool with which secular and ecclesiastical leaders alike might pressure concessions from the pope.[34]

When Pius II reached the throne in 1458, the papacy had yet to find an effective means of neutralizing or countering these potent weapons. After years of refuting in vain the validity of *Haec Sancta* and *Frequens*, it shifted strategies in 1447–48 when forging peace with the Holy Roman Empire.[35] Given widespread German support for the conciliar movement, rejecting these decrees outright was no longer a viable option. Instead, Eugenius IV and then Nicholas V both chose to adopt an attitude of "studied ambiguity"[36] towards *Haec Sancta* and *Frequens*: in the terms of reconciliation with German princes and with the emperor, they spoke of the Council of Constance with reverence and acknowledged respect for the eminence of its decrees, while they carefully sidestepped any direct acknowledgment of conciliar supremacy.[37] This new strategy, which became the standard papal response to the decrees in northern Europe, laid the foundations for peace with Germany in the short term.[38] But it did nothing to reduce the threat *Haec Sancta* and *Frequens* posed to papal sovereignty. By equivocating on the significance of the decrees, the pontiffs still left the door wide open for people to invoke a future council as a sovereign body, as an imminent event, and as a court of appeal – and such appeals continued unabated through the reign of Pope Calixtus III (1455–58).[39] Paradoxically, then, the "restoration" popes found their authority repeatedly challenged and checked by decrees whose validity they had never officially sanctioned.

But their sovereignty was threatened still more by the unresolved and urgent problem of church reform and by prevailing views on how to address it. To many, including secular princes and leading clerics in the Holy Roman Empire, France, and Poland, the regular assembly of general councils remained the best strategy for resolving the ongoing crisis.[40] From the perspective of the papacy, this was a dangerous consensus. The memories of Basel were only too clear: any council, even one that willingly acknowledged its subordination to a papal sovereign, had the potential to slip from the pope's control. Reform, moreover, could be interpreted in various ways; and the popes were only too aware of the interpretation adopted by the Council of Basel: a systematic assault on papal prerogatives. Accordingly, the papacy sought to respond to calls for reform in ways that shielded it from this conciliar threat. Both Eugenius and Nicholas pledged to convene a new council, and soon, but these promises were vague and ultimately empty. Their words offered hope as a temporary means of alleviating concerns.[41] At the same time, the papacy began to pursue a program of reform over which it had complete control: Nicholas V employed loyal papal legates to implement reform in parts of Germany.[42] None of these strategies, however, succeeded in muting calls for a reforming council. When he failed to summon one, Nicholas only ended up fuelling further the already significant support for such an assembly. He also met resistance from papal allies in the empire, who advocated a new council, fully obedient to a sovereign pope, as the key to maintaining Germany's fragile peace with Rome.[43] The popes' ongoing failure to address reform *in capite* rallied additional support for a council, as did their sale of jubilee indulgences, collection of crusade tithes, and in Germany, control over benefices – acts that to many signalled papal commitment to abusing power rather than to correcting those abuses.[44] The stiff resistance met by papal legates dispatched to Germany to reform the church *in membris* testified to growing sentiment that the pope alone was neither a credible nor a legitimate leader of such a vital enterprise.[45] It is not surprising then that calls for a new council went up frequently in the decade before Pius II's pontificate. In the context of the current and urgent needs of the church, an absolute monarch was, to many, not simply inadequate: given both past and present examples, such a ruler seemed downright dangerous to the future well-being of the church.

In the lead-up to Pius II's papacy, these sentiments were particularly pronounced in Germany, where the conciliar movement was gaining new momentum. In response to Calixtus III's bull demanding that tithes be collected across Germany to fund his crusade, German princes and prelates organized in 1456–57 to appeal the papal tax to a future council and to resurrect the decrees of Basel enshrined in the *Acceptatio* of Mainz but left out of the Concordat of Vienna.[46] Almost a decade after its demise, the Council of Basel seemed on the brink of another victory in the form of a new piece of legislation: a Pragmatic Sanction of Germany.

This, then, was the legacy conciliarism left to the new heir to the papal throne: a weakened, unstable, and still vulnerable institution, and thus one whose future remained as unresolved as the threat of the conciliar movement itself. Could the papal monarchy survive the conciliar challenge? How could the pope reassert his sovereignty over a church that in large part still recognized the superiority of a general council? And how could he justify his claims to ecclesiastical supremacy given the strong foundations of conciliar doctrine in theory and law? Just as significant: could the pope convince the church that papal absolutism *should* survive, especially given the papacy's chronic failure to answer insistent calls for reform?

The Challenge of the Secular Princes

Complicating the papacy's response to these urgent and unsettling questions were the other highly successful contenders to ecclesiastical sovereignty: the secular princes of Europe. The same crises that had spawned the conciliar movement had, in turn, both prompted and permitted these rulers to extend their authority over their provincial churches and to the greatest extent since the Gregorian reform movement of the eleventh century.[47] In the councils themselves, moreover, they had found effective vehicles for accumulating this power.[48] But while Europe's princes had worked hand in hand with the conciliar movement, they had also benefited from working in opposition to it and at its expense, and especially in the context of the Basel assembly. They did so most explicitly when, in exchange for full obedience to the Roman Church, they negotiated generous concessions from Eugenius IV and Nicholas V – a move that deprived the Council of Basel of vital political support. But they did so first and foremost ten years earlier by first declaring neutrality in the context of the new schism between Eugenius and the Basel fathers and then reissuing much of Basel's reform legislation as their own decrees. Through the Pragmatic Sanction of Bourges and the *Acceptatio* of Mainz, French and German rulers gained great control over their own provincial churches.

But while their challenges to papal sovereignty took root in the crises of the church, they were also the product of more long-term developments in secular politics. Beginning in the second half of the twelfth century, a new system of states had been coalescing across Europe and effectively replacing the *respublica christiana* as the defining framework of the West. To some extent, these rulers challenged papal jurisdiction within their borders – jurisdiction that had grown substantially over the course of the fourteenth century – in order to protect and promote the spiritual welfare of their provincial churches.[49] Their primary aim, however, was political: to consolidate authority over their own territories, whether monarchies, principates, or regional states. By asserting control over ecclesiastical appointments, revenues, and courts, these rulers saw the means of extending and strengthening that power still further.[50]

Collectively, these princes were as responsible as their sometime conciliar ally for the uncertain future facing the papal monarchy – indeed, arguably, they were still more so. In their own territories, they had already assumed many of the papacy's traditional roles and responsibilities, and the justifications for their authority in many cases clashed with the popes' competing claims to supreme power. Not only did they resist the popes' reassertions of sovereignty, but they also sought to expand their ecclesiastical power still further, and some even vied to assume the pope's universal prerogatives. The ambitions and successes of these princes only further called into question the need for a papal monarch cast in a universalist and absolutist mould.

When Pius II came to the throne, the papacy's once-extensive powers over the universal church now lay largely in the hands of secular princes. These rulers prohibited papal taxation in their territories or collected those taxes themselves; they limited or banned judicial appeals to Rome; they curbed or outlawed annates; and they enjoyed substantial control over provisions to benefices and appointments. The ecclesiastical power of Europe's princes ranged widely: in England and France, for example, the kings ruled over what were effectively independent churches, while in Germany, the Concordat of Vienna left provincial churches largely subject to papal control.[51] Collectively, though, these rulers exercised considerable sovereignty over the churches in their own territories. This reorganization of ecclesiastical government threatened the future of the papal monarchy in more ways than one. The extension of princely control over their churches' resources had significantly curtailed revenues to the papal curia – so significantly, in fact, that its very survival was in jeopardy unless they were recouped or replaced.[52] But the new power structure also created problems for the pope's very identity. By assuming substantial control over papal revenues and prerogatives in their territories, these princes in large part stripped the pope of his purpose as monarch of a universal church. Effectively, the expansion of their power was rendering his traditional role increasingly obsolete.

Reclaiming that role, moreover, was likely to prove difficult, and in part the papacy was responsible for this predicament. In the preceding decades, Martin V, Eugenius IV, and Nicholas V had consistently fed these particularist interests and ambitions: they had made the deliberate choice of sharing their sovereignty with many European rulers in a series of concordats or ecclesiastical treaties and in more informal agreements.[53] Political pressures had prompted them to negotiate some of these arrangements, but in most cases, the catalyst was conciliarism and the threat of reform *in capite* that it carried with it.[54] By investing secular rulers with substantial jurisdiction over their local churches and by appeasing them with vague acknowledgments of conciliar authority, these popes aimed to undermine what they perceived as a far more dangerous enemy: the concept of conciliar supremacy. Their plan, which was only partially successful, secured from these rulers the formal recognition of the pope as supreme monarch of the universal church. At the same time, however, it worked to undermine the popes' continuing claims to sovereignty – and to complicate their task of reclaiming what they had conceded – for it legitimized in practice a competing form of ecclesiastical government.

Concordats and agreements were only some of the tools these princes had at their disposal to protect against reassertions of papal sovereignty and to leverage still more ecclesiastical authority. In the decade preceding Pius II's pontificate, they had made use of these many tools frequently in clashes with the papacy. Sometimes they invoked tradition and custom to defend their ecclesiastical privileges.[55] Other times, they brandished the threat of calling or appealing to a general council to win further concessions.[56] Still other times, they relied on allies within the college of cardinals or on sheer military force to prevent the pope from exercising his traditional prerogatives, or they attacked the pope's political weaknesses, threatening consequences for the vulnerable Papal States should he not comply with their demands.[57] The papacy had by no means lost all of these contests, but in many confrontations it had yielded to princely pressures. In the process, it became clear that the popes' own means of self-defence, which included the once-potent spiritual weapons of excommunication and interdict, were of limited value against rulers armed with deeper arsenals and a diminished respect for the spiritual and moral authority of the pope.[58] These limits made the prospect of the papal monarchy regaining and preserving its sovereignty over a universal church increasingly uncertain.

By the beginning of Pius II's pontificate, that uncertainty was nowhere more evident than in the papacy's recent attempts to organize a crusade against the Ottoman Turks. Over the course of the fifteenth century, the Ottoman Empire had been following an aggressive policy of westward expansion under the leadership first of Sultan Murad II (ruled 1421–51) and then his son, Mehmed II (ruled 1451–81).[59] By 1458, the Turks had extended their control over much of the Balkans, including most of Serbia and Salonika. With their conquest of Constantinople in May 1453, moreover, they also had taken command of the heart of Eastern Christendom, the capital of the Byzantine Empire, and one of the chief centres of Roman civilization. These conquests fuelled Western outrage against the Turks and concern for the security of Europe, and especially the vulnerable Adriatic coast and kingdoms of Central Europe. Ever since Pope Urban II (1088–99) had called the first one in 1098, the papacy had claimed for itself the prerogative to call for military expeditions against Muslim aggressors – better known as crusades. In the first half of the fifteenth century, however, weakened by schism and the Council of Constance, the popes had been forced to relinquish this right to the Holy Roman Empire.[60] Thus, when Nicholas V and then Calixtus III summoned princes to a crusade after the catastrophic fall of Constantinople, their appeals tested their ability to regain this lost sovereignty.

It was a test that both popes would fail. Preoccupied with the affairs of their own states, suspicious of papal intentions, and indignant at both the heavy financial burden of crusade indulgences and tithes and the jurisdictional interference they represented, rulers across Europe defied the popes' summons in various forms. The reaction of the German princes has already been noted: they threatened to appeal the papal ruling to a council and to draw up a German version of the French Pragmatic Sanction of Bourges. Resistance elsewhere was equally stiff. Appeals to a future council went up in France, too, and the king refused either to promulgate the crusade bull or to collect any tithes. Burgundy and Naples diverted promised monies and ships to other purposes, while the Republic of Venice boldly defied the papacy by negotiating a trade agreement with the Turks.[61] Between 1456 and 1458, a small papal flotilla managed to check the Turkish advance in the northern Aegean.[62] But the papacy's limited victories over the Ottoman Turks were offset by the humiliating defeats they suffered at the hands of Christian princes. In their resounding rejection of the popes as crusade leaders, these rulers did more than underscore the challenges facing an institution intent on reasserting its supremacy. They also seemed to confirm that in the Europe of their day, there was little need – indeed, little tolerance – for the pope in the traditional role of universal sovereign.

That same message was echoed loudly by the princes who themselves sought to assume the initiative to direct a crusade. In 1451, King Alfonso of Naples, seeking to strengthen his claim to the Neapolitan crown, announced that he was ready to summon a diet and assume command of a crusading army.[63] For similar reasons, the duke of Burgundy followed suit a few years later.[64] The three diets assembled by Emperor Frederick III (1452–93), in 1454 and 1455, ended up undercutting, not promoting papal authority: with neither the pope nor the emperor in attendance, these assemblies rapidly deteriorated into arenas for grievances against the Holy See.[65] None of these princes was either strong or committed enough to follow through on his crusading plans. But simply by contesting the papal program, they had done it significant damage. So, in turn, did the expansive crusade literature that circulated at princely courts. In Naples, the intellectual circle surrounding Alfonso made the king's crusade leadership a centrepiece of its celebrations.[66] Meanwhile, humanists in northern Italy and France promoted Charles VII in the role, as did prophecies that forecast his reconquest of Jerusalem and conversion of all Muslims to Christianity.[67]

Secular rulers contested more in the world of ideas than the popes' claims to crusade leadership. They also challenged papal leadership of church reform. The most popular German reform tract of the age, the *Reformatio Sigismundi* (c. 1438) endorsed a future German emperor, a priest-king, as leader of reform and did so, in part, by underscoring the impotence of the Holy See in promoting such initiatives.[68] Reforming princes also vied with reforming popes in contemporary apocalyptic prophecy. In the mid-1400s, popular prophecy that had originated more than two centuries earlier with Joachim of Fiore held that a pope, crowned by angels – a *pastor angelicus* – would appear in a time of tribulation to usher in a new spiritual age, launch a radical reform of the church, and initiate a succession of angel popes.[69] These prophecies were paired with others in which secular rulers shared or even usurped the pope's reforming role. According to some, a saintly French king and descendant of Pippin would be crowned emperor of east and west by an angel pope and then join with a succession of four angel popes in reforming and purifying the church.[70] From Germany came prophecies that identified in a German emperor, sometimes also known as the

Third Frederick, the sole leader of the church reform movement.[71] While the influence of these various apocalyptic prophecies is difficult to measure, the manuscript record suggests that these ideas were widely circulated in the fifteenth century, especially at princely courts, and that they were owned, annotated, and discussed by powerful prelates and political figures.[72] Their presence in these circles and conversations points to a new confidence in Europe's secular princes as legitimate ecclesiastical leaders. At the same time, it exposes attendant and deep-seated concerns about the viability of the church's traditional sovereign, the papal monarchy.

When Pius II ascended to that post in the summer of 1458, both broader trends and recent events made clear that secular rulers would continue to challenge or ignore his authority, legitimacy, and very necessity as sovereign of the church. The centrifugal forces reshaping Europe's political map were undeniable, and as these states continued to consolidate their power, they would both press for more ecclesiastical liberties and jealously guard those they had already obtained. At the same time, their own political borders rather than the spiritual community of Christendom promised to serve as the basis for their identity and allegiance, just as domestic interests seemed likely to trump those of traditional universal authorities of both pope and emperor. Indeed, the parallel crisis in the Holy Roman Empire – the crisis that Aeneas alludes to in the letter that opens this chapter – was one of the papacy's greatest concerns and chief vulnerabilities. For the post-Basel popes, a strong imperial power seemed invaluable to their efforts to reassert sovereignty against both their princely and conciliar competitors, not to mention the threat of invasion by the Turks. With authority and influence in both Bohemia and Hungary, the emperor could serve as a vital ally in the popes' ongoing attempts to suppress the Hussite heresy and, at the same time, he could help to secure one of the borders most vulnerable to Ottoman attack. As supreme commander of a powerful German military, he could help raise an army for the crusade; and by exercising his imperial authority in a different way, he could help to suppress some of the papacy's most aggressive and resilient conciliar foes. But like the popes Aeneas described in his letter of 1454, Frederick III was more "a figure in a painting" than a powerful emperor. Struggling to stabilize his own Austrian territories and to give real authority to his imperial title, he was unable to fulfil the emperor's traditional role of *defensor ecclesiae* and its particular fifteenth-century manifestation. Nor did he always choose to, especially when his own interests diverged from those of the papacy. Despite his disavowal of conciliarism, for example, Frederick III was still urging Nicholas V to summon a reform council in the early 1450s; and despite calling the three diets Aeneas attended in the mid-1450s, he showed only lukewarm support for their mission to organize a military response in support of a crusade.[73] In short, while Frederick III was a papal ally, he was a weak, inconsistent, and sometimes unwilling one. In this way, the parallel decline of empire and papacy were inextricably intertwined, and to the detriment, it seemed, of the increasingly defenceless popes.

None of these rulers, however, posed a more urgent or greater threat to papal sovereignty than the king of France. The most powerful of Europe's secular rulers, Charles VII (1422–61) effectively ruled over the Gallican church. The instrument on which he grounded that authority, the Pragmatic Sanction of Bourges, explicitly recognized the supreme authority of councils. At the same time, it further endangered papal sovereignty by offering other rulers both a powerful precedent and a useful model for forging their own ecclesiastical independence.[74] Charles VII expressed his power in titles that rivalled those of the pope: he styled himself *Rex Christianissimus*, and he embraced the quasi-sacerdotal status conferred on him by influential French prelates and theologians as "right arm of the church" and "first prelate of the realm."[75] Still loftier were the king's ecclesiastical ambitions, which, because of their scope, menaced the papacy far more than those of other princes. The French king did not simply aspire to retain and extend ecclesiastical sovereignty within his own kingdom: his aim was to assume control of the papacy itself.[76] Paired with these bold ecclesiastical designs were political ones that would help bring about these plans. Kings of France, the French monarchs also sought to win the imperial crown, thereby also assuming the role of *defensor ecclesiae*.[77] Charles was equally committed to pursuing France's interests on the Italian peninsula, by supporting, for one, Angevin claims to the papacy's vast and powerful neighbour to the south, the Kingdom of Naples.[78] In the months preceding Pius II's pontificate, French influence on the peninsula had grown measurably. In May 1458, at the request of the Genoese, French forces occupied the city and established it as a formal protectorate.[79] A month later, when King Alfonso of Naples died suddenly, the Duchy of Anjou stood poised to reassert its claim over the Neapolitan kingdom; and because of strong anti-Aragonese sentiment on the peninsula, they seemed unlikely to face dangerous resistance.[80] Less than a month after Alfonso's death had opened the door to French territorial ambitions, Calixtus's demise did the same for ecclesiastical ones. When the cardinals entered the conclave in early August 1458, there was no small chance that the one who would emerge as pope would be French.[81]

The unexpected election of Aeneas Silvius Piccolomini made a French conquest of the papacy more difficult, but it in no way diminished the broader threat, both real and potential, that France continued to pose to the papal monarchy more generally.[82] Nor did it remove the very difficult questions that the European princes collectively forced the newly elected pope to confront about the legitimacy, authority, relevance, and very identity of the papal monarchy. Was there still a place and a need in contemporary Europe for the pope as sovereign of a universal church? If so, how could he successfully assert, and reassert, that authority over his princely rivals, and how could he strengthen his weakened claim to that position? If not, should he – could he – recast his traditional role and, in so doing, make a case for his relevance in a changed and changing world?

The Challenges of Building a Territorial State

The answers to these urgent questions about the future of the papal monarchy hinged, in large part, on the pope's success as a temporal prince. The papacy claimed sovereignty over a wide band of territories in central Italy known collectively as the Papal States.[83] If it hoped to strengthen and secure its spiritual sovereignty, it was crucial that it build these lands into a strong territorial state. Such a consolidation of power was, first and foremost, a financial necessity: conciliar reform legislation and the concordats brokered between popes and princes had reduced the curia's spiritual revenues dramatically.[84] To replace such substantial losses, the papacy had no choice but to tighten fiscal control over its temporal holdings. A secure, sovereign state was also critical to the *libertas ecclesiae*: without it, the papal monarchy would remain dangerously vulnerable to its spiritual opponents north of the Alps, and in particular, to French ambitions to uproot the papacy only recently replanted on Italian soil.[85]

Building a strong territorial state was no easy task. The Papal States were made up of a political patchwork of communes, *signorie*, and feudal territories yoked to papal rule through a wide range of jurisdictional relationships.[86] Historically, this diverse collection of authorities had enjoyed considerable autonomy, and their independence had only become more entrenched during the Great Schism. The challenge of consolidating such territories into a unified sovereign state was further exacerbated by internal rivalries among feudal families, neighbouring *signori*, and urban factions; by the disruptions in policy and administration inherent in an elective monarchy; and by a long history of turbulent relations with the traditional seat of papal power, Rome. Papal sovereignty was also threatened by the military strength and expansionist ambitions of *condottieri*, both those who ruled in the capacity of apostolic vicars, like Sigismondo Malatesta and Federigo da Montefeltro, and those who sought to carve out independent states within papal territories. Among the latter, Jacopo Piccinino posed the greatest threat, for he commanded a powerful network of alliances whose aim was to subvert the dominant system of states on the peninsula.[87] Sharing their borders with the Papal States, these powers, in turn, posed a threat to the papacy, and not simply because they found its territories economically and strategically attractive: through their own political connections, interests, and needs, they risked drawing ultramontane influence deeper into Italian politics and closer to the Papal States.[88] It was for these reasons that building a strong territorial state hinged on another task as challenging as that of establishing internal stability and security, namely, taking command of the political dynamics of the Italian peninsula. Only by controlling diplomatic relations among the Italian states and by establishing a balance of power among them could the papacy hope to ensure that its interests would not be threatened by a system of hostile alliances or an invasion by a northern European power.[89]

On the eve of Pius II's election in August 1458, the papacy's transformation into a powerful principate was anything but a sure thing. The process of state building initiated four decades earlier by Martin V had been a slow and uneven one: the Papal States that Pius inherited were unstable, their resistance to papal sovereignty widespread, and their vulnerability to outside invasion very real. Nor had the popes achieved the crucial goal of commanding political relations in Italy – indeed, their position was quite the opposite. Overshadowed by Milan, bullied by Naples, and inadequately protected by the newly formed Italian League (1455), they were struggling for diplomatic influence and respect.[90] In short, the papacy as Pius II found it had yet to prove it could succeed as ruler of a strong territorial state. To many, moreover, it also had not proven that it was entitled to that role: the legitimacy of the popes' temporal power was under serious attack and, most significantly, by those who questioned the fundamental compatibility of their princely and pastoral duties. The strategy of strengthening spiritual sovereignty through temporal sovereignty, thus, itself seemed problematic – a dilemma that only further clouded the future of the papal monarchy at the dawn of Pius II's pontificate.

Precarious is the word that best describes the papacy's control of its temporal states in late August 1458. In a familiar pattern of progress and retreat, the considerable successes Nicholas V had achieved consolidating and stabilizing the Papal States had largely unravelled in the reign and under the policies of his successor, Calixtus III.[91] In the final weeks of Calixtus's pontificate, resentment against his overwhelmingly Catalan administration had erupted in open rebellion in Rome and other cities. The situation only worsened at his death, when the pontiff's nephew (one of Calixtus's many nepotistic appointments) refused to surrender a string of papal fortresses. Instability was endemic to almost every region of the papal territories, and for other reasons, too. The Agro Romano was engulfed in a fresh outbreak of war between leading baronial families, the Orsini and the Colonna. Jacopo Piccinino, meanwhile, had led his army into Umbria and occupied Assisi in August 1458. Further north in Romagna and the Marche, conditions were still more volatile. At the centre of the storm stood Sigismondo Malatesta, *signore* and papal vicar of Rimini.[92] Malatesta had been attacked the previous year by Alfonso of Naples for failing to fulfil his contract as the king's *condottiere*, and he remained a target of the king's son Ferrante and of fellow apostolic vicar Federigo da Montefeltro. Besieged by their forces, Malatesta had turned for support to the French and was encouraging their designs on the Neapolitan crown – designs that seemed still more attainable since Ferrante's hold on the kingdom was weak. Thus, far from presiding over a stable and secure principate, the papacy was clearly struggling to establish its authority as a temporal sovereign and in the face of virtually all the challenges with which it was confronted.

That struggle extended to its diplomatic aspirations on the Italian peninsula. The delicate balance of power that existed among the five major Italian states when Pius II became pope was the work not of the papacy but of Venice, Florence, and Milan. Indeed, the papacy had been thwarted in its own attempts at orchestrating peace on the peninsula.[93] To be sure, the popes held the titles of *custos*, *protector*, and *conservator* of the Italian League, the mutual defence alliance designed to preserve the balance of power, but it was not the position of dominance they had sought. The terms of the league not only placed the pope in a subordinate relationship militarily to other members of the alliance: they also included generous concessions to Alfonso of Naples, whose territorial ambitions in central Italy had long been a threat to the Papal States.[94] The years leading up to Pius II's pontificate had repeatedly confirmed the papacy's inferiority and vulnerability in this alliance. Leadership of the league was squarely in the hands of Francesco Sforza, the duke of Milan. In 1455, when Piccinino had first invaded the Papal States and the territory around Siena, it was Francesco Sforza who took charge of the military response; and it was Sforza again who took the lead in championing the league's implicit anti-French stance.[95] While the papacy lacked a de facto position of command in the league, it also lacked confidence in its allies' ability – even their willingness – to offer it effective protection, especially against Naples. Piccinino's invasion of Sienese territory and the Papal States had met with a slow response from Florence and Venice and had won the open support of the Neapolitan king. In the fall of 1457, moreover, when Alfonso had enlisted the *condottiere* to attack Malatesta's vicariate, the league had honoured its pledge not to interfere, despite knowing that both the king and Piccinino had designs on papal territory.[96] Hardly the position of leadership to which it aspired, the popes' role in the Italian League testified instead to its diplomatic impotence on the peninsula, its vulnerability in the face of its neighbours, and its consequent inability to protect its interests, spiritual as much as temporal.

The papacy's role in peninsular politics was still further diminished in the writings of contemporary humanists and, in particular, in their depictions of other Italian signori. In an effort to promote their own accomplishments and in many cases to defend the questionable legitimacy of their rule, these figures were hailed in prose and verse as the key to Italy's peace, stability, and security. Among those whom humanists anointed as the *defensor Italiae* in the years before Pius II were Francesco Sforza, Alfonso of Naples, Cosimo de' Medici, and even Sigismondo Malatesta.[97] The very figures who, in one form or another, were thwarting the popes' ambitions as temporal sovereigns were, thus, also weakening that role in historical memory. When humanists did afford the papacy a position of prominence on the Italian stage, moreover, it did not always stand out for the right reasons. In his famous attack on the Donation of Constantine, a document alleged to record the emperor's donation of the Western Roman Empire to Pope Sylvester I (314–35), Lorenzo Valla accused the pontiffs of the first half of the fifteenth century of bringing "ruin and devastation" to "all of Italy."[98] In reputation as well as reality, the popes were clearly falling far short of their aims to bring leadership and stability to the Italian peninsula.

Tarnished in turn – and in a similar way – was their reputation as princes of the Papal States. Among the foremost targets of attack was the papacy's approach to state building. Both Martin V and Eugenius IV had relied heavily on military force and violent generals to consolidate power in the Papal States.[99] Valla labelled the most notorious papal *condottiere*, Cardinal Giovanni Vitelleschi, "a depraved monster," but he saved his harshest words for the institution that had employed him.[100] Valla condemned the popes, and Eugenius IV in particular, as savage and barbarous warmongers who, in raping and pillaging their peoples, acted more like enemies and executioners than fathers and masters.[101] Criticisms of papal rule extended well beyond condemnations of violence, however, to broader denunciations of governance. Valla's pen, once again, was the source of particularly venomous attacks, but he was hardly alone either in launching accusations or in the particular censures he made. He and others decried papal rule as tyranny and slavery; they lamented in particular the fiscal burdens and foreign influence the popes had introduced into the Papal States; they condemned their extravagant expenditures (and especially Nicholas V's building projects); and they hailed those who resisted papal sovereignty as defenders of liberty and the public good.[102] Among other places, these images and ideas surfaced in humanist writings that detailed and celebrated some of the most significant rebellions in the Papal States since the process of state building had begun: Stefano Porcari's plot to assassinate Nicholas V and Braccio da Montone's battle to carve out an independent state in Umbria.

That these images of the popes and their rivals constituted a threat to the papacy is suggested by the writings of papal apologists. In expounding on the merits and achievements of papal government, and in denouncing the rebels and their attacks, the popes' supporters did more than defend an institution struggling to consolidate its temporal power. In many cases, they also addressed and revised disparaging representations of the pope as prince.[103] In a sense, then, the papacy Pius II inherited was working hard to establish its temporal authority on two fronts: as it fought to secure its sovereignty over the Papal States, it was also engaged in a battle for historical memory.

Still more dangerous to the papacy, more pervasive and more difficult to answer were the questions about the legitimacy of the pope's temporal authority. As were the criticisms of his approach to government, these attacks were clearly triggered by the popes' recent efforts to consolidate their state, but they were also fuelled by concurrent calls for church reform. The challenges to the pope's legitimacy as a temporal prince took many forms. Beginning in the fourteenth century and in the context of the conciliar movement, the Donation of Constantine, one of the foremost legal documents on which the papacy rested its claim to sovereignty in the Papal States, came under increasing scrutiny.[104] The following century, it was publicly denounced as a fake, first by Nicholas of Cusa and, more famously, by Valla.[105] But the attack on the Donation ranks as only one of the many levelled at the pope's claim to power in the Papal States.[106] Accusations of tyranny gave rise to still other arguments against the legitimacy of papal government – and in support of overthrowing it. By abusing their power, Valla contended, the recent popes had effectively forfeited their right to rule the Papal States: "Can we justify the principle of papal power, when we observe it to be the cause of so many crimes and so many evils of every kind?"[107] And while he fell short of calling for revolt, Valla openly voiced his approval of previous rebellions, including the Roman uprising against Eugenius IV in 1434.[108] This and other references to Rome fed, in turn, into arguments that drew on the long-standing current of Roman republicanism – one still latent in the city when Pius II took the throne. The pope, Valla maintained, cannot claim sovereignty over the Roman people, for they were "born to freedom" and thus were entitled both to choose and to reject their ruler.[109]

Of the many charges levelled at the pope's temporal claims, however, the one at once most common and most threatening to the papacy was basic incompatibility: the pope's responsibilities as prince, it was argued, stood in direct conflict with his mission as pastor. Papal authority in the temporal sphere had long been lamented as a "poison to the church," but in the context of the reform movements and the papacy's determined efforts to consolidate its state, these concerns had intensified.[110] As they worked to build their territories into a principate, the popes to many seemed committed to the very interests and priorities widely condemned in the clergy as both morally corrupting and spiritually distracting: ownership and management of property, a preoccupation with money and profit, a taste for pomp and circumstance, and entanglement in war against fellow Christians. Indeed, in combining spiritual and temporal rule, the popes seemed to spurn an idea that shaped the program of many reformers, and especially those in Germany: a good prince makes a bad bishop.[111] Only the most extreme critics called on the pope to step down from his princely throne and explicitly argued he was neither meant nor able to be a prince.[112] At the same time, however, it is hard to see how a papal prince could satisfy the demands of many moderate reformers. Both radical and mainstream visions of church reform took as their model the apostolic church – the *ecclesia primitiva* – and in particular, its tradition of a leadership committed to poverty.[113] As Pope Pius II took the throne, these ideals continued to find strong support and in places where hostility to papal authority was most pronounced.[114] The vision of poverty and purity that these reformers exalted did not simply oppose the pope's exercise of spiritual authority: it also did little to accommodate a pope who was also a temporal prince.

In this tension between the popes' spiritual and secular powers, between the changes demanded by reformers and the very different, temporal transformation of the papacy already underway, the popes of the fifteenth century faced a difficult and unsettling dilemma: the need to consolidate their temporal authority was at once a necessity for preserving their spiritual sovereignty and their potential undoing. By becoming princes of a territorial state, they risked discrediting themselves further as spiritual monarchs and eroding the already slim expectations that they could carry out church reform. Indeed the expansion of their role in temporal politics risked turning people still further towards those who claimed they could initiate that spiritual change: councils and secular rulers. The new model of authority to which the papacy had committed, thus, seemed seriously problematic. How or even if the popes could resolve these problems was far from clear on the eve of Pius II's pontificate.

For many reasons, therefore, both the viability and value of the pope's new temporal ambitions remained very much in question. Could the papacy achieve the domestic stability and the diplomatic pre-eminence necessary to secure a strong territorial state and, thereby, a stronger hold on its spiritual authority? How could it strengthen the case for its temporal rule – especially in a religious culture that identified the secular preoccupations of clergymen as the root of the church's woes? Could the pope, in fact, fulfil his responsibilities as prince without compromising those of pastor? In short, would a papal prince weaken the pope's spiritual authority more than he could strengthen it?

The context of uncertainty in which Pius II's pontificate began is an essential framework within which to understand his *Commentaries*. Indeed, as this book argues, Pius's text can and should be read in part as a sustained response to the daunting questions of authority, legitimacy, and relevance facing the papal monarchy. His answers were inevitably shaped by his own experience with these questions, and it was an experience that extended well beyond his years as pontiff. Indeed, in a career nearly three and a half decades in length (1431–1464), Aeneas was almost a perpetual eyewitness to the crisis engulfing the papacy. The decade he spent at the Council of Basel, for example, coincided with the council fathers' most radical attacks on papal sovereignty. The years he worked in the service of Emperor Frederick III (1442–55) saw the crucial reconciliation of Germany with Pope Eugenius IV and the Roman Church, the resurgence of Hussite power in Bohemia, and the forging of a papal-imperial alliance that included joint efforts to launch a crusade. In the three years before his papacy, Aeneas was in residence at a papal curia that was still more focused on fighting the Ottoman advance. It was also deeply embroiled in rebellions in the Papal States and pushing back against a dangerous resurgence of the conciliar movement in Germany. In short, over the course of his career, Aeneas had an almost continuous firsthand experience of the most pivotal events and developments in the crisis of the fifteenth-century papacy, and on all the fronts on which the popes were fighting.

Still more than his presence, it was the nature of his involvement in the crisis that put him at its epicentre. A survey of his curriculum vitae demonstrates his many roles of distinction and influence. In 1439, he was appointed papal secretary to Felix V – a post that was more than simply administrative: Aeneas functioned as the pope's chief publicist, and at a time when the Council of Basel was under fierce attack from Eugenius and his defenders. He gained more influence and a still higher profile in the crisis of the papacy after he transferred to the imperial court in January 1443. There, he was instrumental in implementing the emperor's various efforts to resolve the schism and most notably as chief agent in forging a reconciliation between the Holy Roman Empire and the Roman Church. He would go on to play a crucial role nurturing, protecting, preserving, and promoting the imperial-papal alliance deemed so essential to the papacy's ability to navigate and resolve the crisis. In his capacities as both papal legate and imperial ambassador, moreover, Aeneas would become deeply immersed in developments in Bohemia; and in the years when the Hussite threat grew particularly acute, he advised Frederick III, Nicholas V, and Calixtus III on policy. He also played a major role in coordinating first imperial and then papal efforts to launch a crusade against the Ottoman Turks – a role that involved him in peace negotiations both in Italy and in the empire. Aeneas served, in turn, on the front lines of the papacy's response to conciliar crises in the empire – in 1452, when Austria appealed to a general council, and the still more serious crisis of 1457 when the German princes prepared to issue their own Pragmatic Sanction. His subsequent six-year pontificate represented only the final stage of a career that saw him exercise considerable authority over the affairs of the church. Aeneas may not have been the most significant figure in the crisis of the fifteenth-century papacy, but it would be difficult to find anyone whose influence over that crisis was more sustained.

Nor are we likely to find anyone with a more complex relationship to this crisis. That complexity is perhaps best illustrated by Aeneas's about-face on the question of ecclesiastical sovereignty. But there is more to this complicated relationship than the fact that he spent time in both papal and conciliarist camps. Aeneas approached and experienced the church crisis from a wide range of vantage points. While they were not always in direct conflict with one another, these perspectives were nonetheless highly diverse, multifaceted, and often in flux. Aeneas viewed the church crisis through the eyes of a layman and a cleric, a deacon and a pope, a low-level administrator and a high-ranking adviser. He served the varied interests of two popes, an anti-pope, and an emperor, and in positions that sometimes overlapped: he was, for example, still technically in the employ of Felix V in his first years at the imperial court; and during the decade he worked for Frederick III he also held the positions of papal secretary and/or legate. These various posts and perspectives allowed Aeneas to experience the ecclesiastical crisis in different forms – as a complex and heated debate about ideas; as a dance of diplomacy; as a catalyst for moral reflection, political commentary, and historical writing; as an opportunity for professional advancement; and as a web of human relationships.

Even at a cursory level, knowing Aeneas's experience with the crisis facing the papacy prepares us in several ways to analyse the *Commentaries*. For one, it tells us that he wrote this text intimately familiar with the ideas, events, and people involved in that crisis and with a profound and highly nuanced understanding of the challenges facing the church. It also tells us that he already had considerable experience as an apologist when he wrote the *Commentaries*, and experience defending the interests of both the popes and their opponents. Perhaps most importantly, it underscores that, for Aeneas, the crisis of the institutional church was fundamentally and inextricably a personal experience. He had helped to shape its course, and, in turn, the crisis had shaped him – his career, his values and beliefs, and his reputation.

It is only by conducting a more thorough examination of Aeneas's experience of this crisis, however, that we can begin to grasp how the *Commentaries* function as a complex work of apology. That examination is the task of the following two chapters. The two central questions with which those chapters grapple are expressly designed to set up the analysis of the subsequent three chapters that analyse the *Commentaries* themselves. In its simplest form, the first question is as follows: how did Aeneas's involvement in the crisis of the fifteenth-century papacy represent a liability – both to him and to the papacy – when he was writing the *Commentaries*? In other words, how did it threaten his pontificate, his reputation, and the future of papal sovereignty in both theory and practice? The other question is more methodological in nature: what tools did he use – and what weapons did he draw – when writing about this crisis over the course of his career? Answering this second question will allow us to position the *Commentaries* in the longer trajectory of Aeneas's career as a humanist historian and in the broader currents of humanist historiography of his age.

2 The Conciliar Crisis in the Career of Aeneas Silvius Piccolomini and the Pontificate of Pius II

The waves of Basel are not yet calmed; the winds are struggling beneath the water and rushing through secret channels ... We have a truce, not a peace ... We wait for a new battlefield, where we will again struggle for supremacy.[1]

Aeneas's words of warning to Pope Nicholas V (1447–55) in the fall of 1448 clearly signal the gravity with which he viewed the conciliar threat. From his perspective, the papacy's struggle against the conciliar movement was nothing less than all-out war. Already a sixteen-year veteran of the conflict, Aeneas spoke with authority when he described the 1448 Concordat of Vienna as a "truce" and with accuracy when predicting that new battles lay on the horizon. He also drew on his considerable experience on the front lines when he went on to offer the pontiff strategies for engaging the enemy: "If there must be a battle, fight where neither the winds harm you, nor the sun shines in your eyes, nor the unevenness of the ground works against you."[2] Aeneas's recommendation to Nicholas, that he control the conditions under which he fought, was advice that he himself adopted ten years later when he initiated his own sweeping anti-conciliar offensive from the papal throne. He did so in part by spearheading a program of reform *in capite* – a move that sought to eliminate the primary impetus for summoning a new general council. He also sought to strip conciliarists of their claims to legitimacy by promulgating the bull *Execrabilis* (January 1460), which effectively pronounced the decrees *Haec Sancta* and *Frequens* null and void. At the same time, he worked to neutralize the instruments by which conciliarists of various ideological stripes were actively restricting papal sovereignty, or at least trying to do so: the electoral capitulations of the cardinals, the Bohemian Compacts, the Pragmatic Sanction of Bourges, and the practice of appealing papal judgments to a future council. In so doing, Pius II was offering concrete solutions to some of the most serious dilemmas facing the fifteenth-century papacy.

When he took up his pen to write the *Commentaries*, Pope Pius II remained deeply entrenched not only in these battles but also in a related one of self-defence. His actions on the battlefield had come to represent a serious liability – to his own reputation, to the viability of his pontificate, and to the future of papal sovereignty. Those actions dated in part to the period preceding his papacy and included the years he had worked as a conciliarist ally. Threatening papal authority at the time, Aeneas's deeds and, still more, his words now jeopardized Pope Pius as well as the sovereign authority he claimed to embody. At the same time, Pius needed to defend the campaign he had been waging against conciliarism from the papal throne. Despite his sustained efforts to reassert papal sovereignty, conciliarists continued to restrict it, and with growing determination and success. They were also enhancing their defences of conciliar supremacy and simultaneously gaining support for the idea that a new council was both urgent and necessary. Thus, rather than hailing a triumphant turning point for the papacy in its struggle against the council, Pius II's pontificate instead seemed to confirm the trends against which his predecessors had struggled: the continued strength of conciliarist models of church government and their defiant resistance to renewed expressions of papal authority.

With an eye to the subsequent analysis of the *Commentaries*, this chapter offers a full and fresh analysis of Aeneas's long and complicated involvement in this conciliar crisis, both before and after he became Pope Pius II. It begins from what is now a commonplace in scholarship: that Aeneas's long-standing allegiance to the conciliar movement became a difficult and embarrassing burden once he had joined the papalist camp, and even more after he became pope.[3] It also accepts as a basic premise more recent narratives that frame Pius II's pontificate not as a triumph over conciliarism but instead as part of the papacy's ongoing struggles against its conciliar foes.[4] Building on these foundations, the following pages offer several new arguments that come together in defence of an important claim: when Pius was writing the *Commentaries*, his involvement with the conciliar crisis gave him much more to be concerned about than what scholarship has so far suggested. This chapter builds this argument first by explaining how the pro-conciliar writings of Aeneas's early career offered conciliarists new and important ammunition in their assaults both on papal sovereignty and on Pius II himself. It goes on to argue – and in a significant break from traditional scholarship – that even the works he penned in the ten years after his papalist conversion threatened to undermine the battle he waged against conciliarism as pope. The final section reads Pius II's pontificate not simply as a protracted struggle against his conciliar enemies, but as a measurable setback in the broader war in which the papacy was engaged. Together, these arguments represent a vital step in the textual analysis at the heart of this book. Only by studying the *Commentaries* in this interpretive context will we be able to explore how and to what extent his text functions as an apology for the conciliar crises he faced as pope.

Aeneas's Conciliarist Legacy (1432–1445)

Nor was I a minor figure [at the Council of Basel], but exalted in spirit, proud of mind, and full of wind, I did battle in the front ranks ... Nor was the name of Aeneas of little consequence among the enemies of the Roman curia.[5]

In his long career on the front lines of the war between pope and council, the lowest point from the perspective of Pope Pius II must have been the almost decade and a half that he had fought in the conciliar camp. Aeneas did not rank among the leading conciliar thinkers, nor did he number among the most influential administrators at the Council of Basel. Nevertheless, and as he observes above with regret in a letter he wrote after abandoning the conciliar party, he did play a prominent role in the assault on papal sovereignty. He did so, moreover, from the moment he arrived at Basel in the spring of 1432. Aeneas's very reason for attending the council was to help defend Domenico Capranica's claim to a position in the college of cardinals in the face of opposition from Pope Eugenius IV. By approaching the Basel council as a court of appeal for papal judgments, Aeneas was effectively defending the doctrine of conciliar supremacy. Promoted to *abbreviator major* within a few years of his arrival, Aeneas became responsible for drafting the council's correspondence and documents in the period of its most heated clashes with Eugenius. He also participated directly in its most violent attacks on papal authority, albeit in what were essentially minor administrative roles. In the fall of 1439, he served as master of ceremonies in the conclave that elected Felix V (Duke Amadeus VIII of Savoy, the "anti-pope"), and he was among the ambassadors dispatched to deliver the election results to the council's new pope. Appointed shortly thereafter as secretary to Felix V (1439–49), his very job was to promote the interests of Eugenius's arch-enemy.[6]

Aeneas continued to advance the conciliar cause after his move to the imperial chancery in January 1443. He did so openly by promoting the emperor's plan to hold a third council to resolve the new schism, a solution Aeneas advocated until May 1445.[7] In more covert ways, he continued to serve the interests of the Basel council – and not surprisingly, given that he continued to hold his post in Felix's chancery until April 1444.[8] Aeneas's private letters from 1443 show him using his not inconsequential connections at the council to explore conditions under which Frederick III might be convinced to abandon neutrality and declare for Basel.[9] Aeneas's own faith in the Basel assembly was clearly slipping even as he made these overtures.[10] Nevertheless, in spite of these doubts, he remained in the conciliar camp. Such sustained allegiance to the conciliar cause inevitably became an awkward chapter in his career once he became pope.

As he was writing the *Commentaries*, however, it was not his actions as a conciliarist as much as the words he wrote in this capacity that caused him concern – and concern of considerable magnitude. In April 1463, Pius II issued a formal denunciation of his pro-conciliar writings in the context of a solemn papal bull, *In minoribus agentes*.[11] Several of Aeneas's writings from this period fall into this pro-conciliar category. The first, and the only one identified by name in the bull, is the *Libellus dialogorum de generalis concilii auctoritate et gestis Basileensium* (early November to early December 1440).[12] The text consists of a series of fourteen imaginary dialogues among four figures who had attended the council proceedings.[13] While the topics of discussion range from the core tenets of conciliar theory to the importance of rhetoric for diplomacy, the central issue of debate is Eugenius's recent transfer of the council to Ferrara – a move the text systematically attacks as illegitimate. In so doing, it aims to validate indirectly the controversial moves of the council fathers who stayed behind at Basel: the deposition of Eugenius IV and the election of Felix V. Aeneas takes up the defence of these last two acts still more explicitly and extensively in the *De gestis concilii Basiliensis commentariorum, libri II* (late 1439 to early 1440).[14] In its account of the debates that took place in April and May 1439, Book I defends the arguments the council fathers used to justify Eugenius's deposition, including the council's boldest claim to date: that *Haec Sancta* was an article of faith. The second book then offers a favourable account of the procedures the council fathers followed in their subsequent and equally radical move of electing a new pope. In August 1440, Aeneas continued this narrative in a brief epistolary account of Felix V's coronation.[15] Three years later, he addressed to imperial secretary Hartung von Kappel a treatise-like defence of conciliar authority as it had been conceived at Basel, stating that "the pope is inferior to the council in all matters."[16] Collectively, these texts did more than advocate for the conciliarist movement; they defended the most extreme form of that movement and the Basel fathers' most radical attacks on papal sovereignty.

In the 1463 bull that retracted these texts, *In minoribus*, Pius II begins to reveal why, almost two decades after he had renounced the conciliar doctrine, he continued to view his conciliarist writings with such concern. From what he says, they were still in wide circulation ("they fall into many hands and are read by the rabble"), and as a result, would have posed a threat to the war he was currently waging against a host of conciliar enemies.[17] He also feared his writings would continue to inflict danger beyond his own reign: "One must fear lest such things be used at some point against our successors."[18] He viewed the liability of these texts, thus, in both personal and institutional terms.

Exactly how did these writings threaten to diminish his authority and that of future popes? The precise nature of this threat is not explicitly discussed in the bull, nor has it been elucidated sufficiently in scholarship. To do so requires a much deeper analysis of Aeneas's writings than has been attempted to date.[19] The first section of this chapter proposes to undertake such an analysis for the most substantial of Aeneas's pro-conciliar texts: the *De gestis* and the *Libellus*. The source of the threat, it will argue, was not simply that these writings endorsed radical moves and theories at Basel: it was that they fashioned new and dangerous weapons in defence of those actions and ideas, and in a way that responded to recent papalist attacks on the Basel assembly. This novelty is not immediately apparent. Aeneas's writings rehearse the same arguments typically marshalled in defence of the general council's claim to ecclesiastical sovereignty and the Basel assembly's radical moves. Aeneas, however, does more here than simply present a catalogue of other people's ideas. He enhances those arguments by enlisting a different set of tools. Unlike his contemporary conciliarists, Aeneas wrote these defences as a humanist, choosing genres (dialogue) and disciplines (history) typical of the humanist repertoire and focusing in particular on his characters as orators.[20] In so doing, he trained his focus on the people involved in heated debates over ecclesiastical sovereignty as well as on their ideas. It is in how he sketches these interlocutors – their thoughts and actions, their characters, and their consciences – and in the authority he summons when doing so that Aeneas builds his defence.

In the period Aeneas was writing the *De gestis* and the *Libellus*, the papacy was engaged in a fierce campaign to de-legitimize the Council of Basel by attacking the council fathers themselves. Those who had voted to transfer the assembly to Avignon, to elevate conciliar supremacy to the status of dogma, and to depose Eugenius were – so papalists contended – an evil, uneducated, and self-seeking mob, bent on revolution and driven by ambition.[21] Delivered in a series of tracts, letters, orations, and papal bulls, these attacks represented more than simple character assassination. Scholars have long pointed to how, by casting the Basel fathers as a threat to secular as well as to ecclesiastical monarchy, these portraits aimed to draw princely support back to their fellow monarch, Pope Eugenius.[22] These portraits threatened the Basel fathers at still another level, and one that has yet to be fully explored and elucidated. Conciliarist claims to authority rested in part on a crucial premise, namely, that the general council was composed of men both wise and virtuous and, thus, capable of the good judgment necessary to govern the church.[23] It was this premise that allowed Basilian conciliarists to enlist the formidable authority of Aristotle in defence of their broad claims to sovereignty: "Where there are free men strong in talent and virtue," wrote conciliarist Juan of Segovia, citing Book III of the *Politics*, "it is better for the state to be ruled by many wise and virtuous men rather than by one man."[24] The arguments put forward by Pope Eugenius and his defenders struck hard at the premise that the Basel assembly was indeed made up of wise and virtuous men. Pointing to its novel structure (its broad membership, its organization by deputation, its extension of voting privileges to all ranks) and to its few remaining prelates, they repeatedly and explicitly condemned the Basel fathers for their very lack of wisdom and virtue. The council, they insisted, was dominated by uneducated, ignorant, and unskilled men, and their actions were driven by sheer wickedness.[25] As a result, the assembly at Basel was fundamentally incapable of exercising good judgment – and, thus, of fulfilling its own prerequisite for ecclesiastical rule.

Aeneas was well aware of the importance of this premise of conciliar theory and of its vulnerability. In the defence of conciliar doctrine he addressed to Hartung von Kappel in 1443, he begins by establishing the council's superior good judgment as one of the justifications for its claims to sovereignty: "In all matters we should prefer the opinion of the person who discerns better than anyone else and who possesses greater authority. You will find these two things in the general councils, not in Roman pontiffs."[26] In this text, and also in the *Libellus*, Aeneas simply follows the lead of his fellow conciliarists by accepting the council's skills of discernment as a point of fact.[27] In his *De gestis*, however, he actually builds a defence – and a sustained defence – of this premise. He does so by writing an eyewitness account that testifies to the Basel fathers' wisdom and virtue and to the resulting good judgment they showed in making their most controversial moves.

The narrative in Book One of the *De gestis* puts front and centre the defence of the council fathers' exceptional skills of discernment. It does so through its explicit and repeated references to the diligence, care, and length of time the fathers took in developing and debating the resolutions that condemned Pope Eugenius as a heretic ("no matter had ever been investigated at greater length or more carefully").[28] He hails in particular their embrace of Socratic methods as a means of ensuring their conclusions were sound.[29] The same sense of good judgment emerges from the specific arguments the fathers put forward in lengthy discussions of these proposals – discussions, Aeneas is quick to point out, that he himself attended.[30] Aeneas presents the arguments in favour of the resolutions as well reasoned, thorough, grounded in a nuanced and respectful reading of authoritative texts, and guided by an unwavering commitment to the good of the church.[31] They read, in short, as the work of men of excellent judgment – a point Aeneas further underscores by explicitly pointing to the virtues and wisdom of those putting forward these arguments.[32] The second part of Book One, in which the princely ambassadors attempt to stall the council's vote on these resolutions, furthers this argument in a different way. Forced to defend the legitimacy of their voting procedures, the council president, Louis d'Aleman, cardinal of Arles, expounds at length on the moral integrity, wisdom, and learning of the assembly's members and especially those of low rank.[33] Moreover, by likening them explicitly to martyrs, he not only brings into sharp relief their unwavering commitment to the *bonum ecclesiae*, but he also associates them with an idea at the heart of so many contemporary reform movements – that the key to restoring the church lay in the *ecclesia primitiva*.[34]

Book Two of the *De gestis* maintains this same emphasis on the Council of Basel as a body of skilled and responsible judges. Indeed, its very focus, the detailed account of the procedures to elect the new pope, serves to point up first and foremost the careful reasoning the fathers adopted when choosing the papal electors and the exemplary wisdom, learning, and virtue of those selected; of those electors he writes, "Wherever is there such a band of Fathers where such a splendour of knowledge, where the wisdom and the goodness that can be compared to the virtues of these Fathers?"[35] Their excellent judgment finds definitive confirmation in their choice of Duke Amadeus of Savoy, who is first introduced as "the wisest,"[36] and then presented at greater length as a man of superior wisdom, learning, and virtue.[37] As in Book One, Aeneas's presence at these events adds authority to his account. The sheer level of detail with which he is able to discuss the conclave, for example, serves to make it believable. Credibility, however, comes still more from the official role Aeneas played at this crucial event: as one of the clerks of ceremonies, it was his responsibility to ensure the integrity of the election. By his account, it was a task he fulfilled with great success.[38]

Aeneas continues to reinforce his portrayal of the council fathers' good judgment with a contrasting portrait of their opponents. That opposition consisted chiefly of princely ambassadors, many of them prelates; and it was led by two Neapolitan legates, the bishop of Palermo, Panormitanus (Niccolò de' Tudeschi), and protonotary, Ludovico Pontano.[39] Aeneas undermines the arguments these men adopt, first in opposition to the charges of heresy against Pope Eugenius and then to the formal passage of the resolutions, by exploring what drove their objections. In sharp contrast to the council fathers, Aeneas maintains, it was not good judgment that motivated them: it was princely intimidation, self-interest, and in particular, a fear of losing their rich benefices.[40] In the case of Pontano and Panormitanus, it was first and foremost a misguided sense of duty to their king, Alfonso of Naples. Aeneas dwells in particular on these two ambassadors and on their total lack of conviction in the position their prince forced them to take. Again and again, he goes behind their public proclamations to reveal their very different private stances, their resentment towards Alfonso, and their tormented consciences.[41] Aeneas builds this characterization with memorable and entertaining anecdotes. "It also became generally known," he reports, "that Panormitanus, when he came to his house retired to his bedroom, and after complaints to himself about his king for compelling him to fight against the truth and to endanger his reputation and his soul, in the midst of tears he fell asleep."[42] As he did with the council fathers, moreover, Aeneas adds to the authority of these portraits by explicitly identifying himself as an eyewitness to the events he records: "I often observed [Panormitanus] complaining in his library about his prince for following the advice of others."[43] By questioning the sincerity and integrity of those challenging Eugenius's deposition and by testifying to the authenticity of these characterizations, Aeneas enhanced his already favourable portrayal of the church fathers.

If the *De gestis* responded to papalist assaults on the Basel fathers themselves, the *Libellus* met attacks levelled at one of their most controversial moves: their decision to defy Pope Eugenius's September 1437 bull of dissolution and to maintain that their assembly, not the gathering in Ferrara-Florence, was the true general council. As Aeneas was writing the *Libellus* in the final months of 1440, Eugenius's envoys were travelling to princely courts and diets across Europe, making a case for the legitimacy of Eugenius's council in an effort to win the allegiance of these rulers.[44] Aeneas joins this heated and high-stakes debate by directing his opposing argument to the rector of the University of Cologne. The university was an institution whose positions on matters of ecclesiastical authority were widely respected and influential, and which in the fall of 1440 had not yet pronounced on the legitimacy of the assembly at Basel.[45] As in the *De gestis*, Aeneas's case rests on more than simply a reiteration of the Basel fathers' position. The key to his argument is the figure he casts as the papalist engaged in the debate, Nicholas of Cusa (Cusanus). A learned theologian, canon lawyer, and philosopher, Cusanus had supported the Council of Basel in its early clashes with Eugenius. By 1437, however, he had shifted his support and became one of the pope's most prominent and most committed defenders. In the spring of that year, Cusanus had played a central role at Basel in defending the legitimacy of the council's transfer to Italy. He was also one of the chief legates the pope had assigned to plead his case to the German princes in the aftermath of the new schism.[46] In casting Cusanus in the *Libellus* in the role of the papalist, then, Aeneas was taking aim at one of the papacy's most formidable weapons – and there is no question that he knew what he was doing: in the *De gestis*, he explicitly identifies Cusanus as "the Hercules of all the Eugenians."[47]

As in the *De gestis*, Aeneas relies here in the *Libellus* primarily on characterization to undermine the arguments in Eugenius's defence. His methods are similar but not identical to those employed in the *De gestis*. Aeneas does not question the motives that drove Cusanus to defend Eugenius, nor does he suggest the former conciliarist entered the debate a secret adherent to Basel's cause.[48] Instead Aeneas documents how, over the course of his lengthy discussion with one of Felix's secretaries, Stefano della Caccia, Cusanus concedes his points one after the other.[49] As might be expected, the Hercules of the Eugenians does not yield his ground easily. At one point, he likens himself to a gladiator who, struck down by a lance, fights on with a sword.[50] In the end, however, he admits total defeat, and not simply on the issue of the Basel assembly's legitimacy after Eugenius's bull of dissolution. In their wide-ranging discussion, Cusanus and della Caccia cover most of the key points of conflict between the Basel fathers and Pope Eugenius, including the fundamental question of who holds sovereign power in the church.[51] After excusing himself from their discussion to attend Vespers, Cusanus returns to announce his complete conversion to the "truth" of the conciliarist position – a conversion, he suggests, that might have been divinely motivated.[52] In short, more than on conciliarist arguments themselves, Aeneas relies on his portrayal of Cusanus in order to undermine the papalist cause. And he relies on Cusanus for something else, too. In contrast to the *De gestis*, the *Libellus* is not presented as an eyewitness account of real events. To be sure, Aeneas works hard to make the dialogue seem authentic – by casting real people as his interlocutors, and by writing himself into the text eavesdropping on the debate and offering commentary in a parallel conversation. It is not, however, the personal testimony of the author that gives the *Libellus* its authority. It is its central character – a fervent and deeply respected papalist who, guided by reason and perhaps revelation, embraces the conciliarist cause.

Aeneas, then, did not need to be a theologian or a canonist in order to contribute in a new and significant way to conciliar assaults on papal legitimacy and authority. Indeed, it was by relying on the very different skills of a humanist that he could both counter papalists' dangerous attacks on the council fathers' controversial moves and strengthen conciliarists' broader claims to ecclesiastical authority. And while he continued to turn to traditional authorities to defend the conciliarist cause, it was by establishing a new one – his own eyewitness experience – that he worked to justify the Basel assembly's most radical moves. The result were texts that had the potential to inflict serious damage on papal authority.

Just how serious can be grasped by the response of both the papalist and the conciliarist camps. Within months of its completion, the *Libellus* triggered a strong counterattack by Cusanus himself. Between February and April 1441, he penned his own dialogue, one that reached the opposite conclusion to Aeneas's about the legitimacy of the Basel council's transfer and that established Cusanus as a firm defender of Eugenius's sovereign power.[53] At the same time as they presented a danger to papalists, Aeneas's writings offered conciliarists a valuable resource. In 1443, the *Libellus* served as a central source for Johannes Keck's pro-conciliar *Tractatus de sacro Basiliensi concilio si in facto depositionis olim Eugenii potuit errare*. Keck's treatise represented an important contribution to the debate and enjoyed wide circulation among German religious orders where support for the Council of Basel was exceptionally strong.[54] As such, Aeneas's text continued to serve as an important weapon in the defence of the Basel assembly's legitimacy, even after he himself had officially adopted a neutral stance. His ability to fuel conciliar arguments is also suggested by aspects of the manuscript tradition of his conciliarist writings. A survey reveals the presence and circulation of his texts in important strongholds of conciliar support, including Basel, the University of Cracow in Poland, and German Benedictine communities.[55]

We can also pinpoint particular instances where Aeneas's conciliar writings actually did threaten papal authority. One of those moments was the summer of 1447, a critical one for the cementing of papal authority in Germany. While in July the emperor and two electors officially recognized Nicholas V as legitimate pope, four others, including the archbishop of Cologne, had yet to submit. Instead, they established an alliance with the king of France in an effort to negotiate terms of obedience they deemed more favourable to their own interests.[56] Among their stipulations was the demand that Nicholas profess the decree *Frequens* and other decrees on conciliar authority – terms not included in the imperial obedience. It was in this context that Aeneas set out on an embassy to Cologne, charged with the difficult task of convincing the city's archbishop to abandon this alliance and embrace instead the emperor's terms of obedience. His task, not surprisingly, was made more difficult by his own erstwhile endorsement of conciliarism and by the awkward fact that, seven years earlier, he had addressed his *Libellus* to the rector of the city's university. Aeneas acknowledges those difficulties explicitly in a series of letters dating to this period: he alludes to personal attacks he faced from lawyers and bishops who saw greed and raw ambition as the catalyst for his ideological shift.[57]

One of these letters suggests that Aeneas's credibility as a papalist was being undermined not just by his conciliarist past but by specific arguments in his pro-conciliar writings. The letter in question, now often referred to as the Letter of Retraction, was written during Aeneas's stay in Cologne and, not coincidentally, to the new rector of the city's university, Jordan Mallant.[58] The letter, which explains Aeneas's decision to abandon the party at Basel, works to dismantle key arguments he had made in his pro-conciliar writings that the Council of Basel was never legitimately transferred to Ferrara and that the deposition of Eugenius was legitimate. It also undermines another important and related argument that he had unfolded in the Basel fathers' defence. Their collective portrait in the Letter of Retraction is consistently painted in terms that upend their image in the *De gestis* as discerning judges. Aeneas repeatedly condemns the fathers' radical decisions as the product of dulled intellects, foolish advice, blind judgments, and irrationality bordering on madness.[59] He revises just as radically his earlier vision of the assembly's culture of rigorous debate: "There was no one heard among the Fathers who defended the law of the Apostolic See, who praised the Roman curia, or who praised Eugenius."[60] The portrait effectively retracts the portrait that for conciliarists had represented a valuable defence.

Aeneas's own self-portrait as a conciliarist should be read as an extension of this retraction. Scholarship on this letter has long noted that Aeneas blames his adherence to the Basel assembly on his youth, inexperience, and reliance on the example of others, and that in so doing, he was defending himself against those who labelled him a turncoat and a sell-out.[61] Aeneas's self-portrait does more, however, than repair his reputation: like his broader portrayal of the assembly, it serves to undercut his earlier defence of the Basel council as an assembly of wise judges. The explanations Aeneas gives for his own years as a conciliarist – he was young, inexperienced, and reliant on the opinions of others – all link his support of the Basel fathers to a lack of sound judgment. They do so, moreover, explicitly: throughout the letter, Aeneas consistently and repeatedly singles out his poor skills of discernment as the essential reason why he remained at Basel in its most radical years. Again and again he describes himself in terms that accentuate his weak judgment: he was, he writes, foolish, ignorant, stupid, and blind.[62] Above all, he concludes, he was uncritical: "I took to be truth anything that was said, and I wrote things I heard, not what I examined carefully," he laments. "I trusted those who spoke."[63] As in his earlier pro-conciliar writings, Aeneas calls here on the authority of personal experience to support his claim about the council. Here, however, he uses his experience to de-legitimize the Basel assembly, and to undercut the specific arguments he had once made in its defence. He does so, moreover, by acting as more than an eyewitness: by tying his advocacy of conciliarism to his own faulty judgment, Aeneas is, in effect, offering himself as evidence of his negative portrayal of the Basel assembly as decidedly undiscerning.

He does so again in his account of his conversion. What ultimately drove him to abandon the conciliarist camp, he explains, were his newly developed skills of discernment. It was his early years at the imperial court that fostered this development: there, he explains – and in direct contradiction to what he had written in the *De gestis* – he finally had the chance to hear the papalist as well as the conciliarist position.[64] "I applied my ears," he explains, "and strove to become more learned in the wisdom of great men who came [to the imperial court]."[65] Aeneas emphasizes that this time he did not simply accept what others told him: "I began to reflect on and examine what was being said"; "I scrutinized everything diligently."[66] Here, too, then, Aeneas summons the authority of his own experience to reinforce the claim he makes through his revised portrait of the Basel fathers, that is, support for the conciliar position is inherently incompatible with good judgment.

This was not the only instance in the Letter of Retraction where Aeneas turns to himself as an authority. Indeed, throughout the text, he retracts his earlier, pro-conciliar arguments chiefly on the basis of his own experience. He insists, for example, that Eugenius's deposition was illegitimate in part because he knew from his embassy to the pope in January 1447 that Eugenius did not hold the beliefs of which he was accused.[67] He goes on to defend the legitimacy of the council's transfer to Ferrara on the basis of his own personal understanding of how that decision was made,[68] and he cites official correspondence that he read while working in the imperial chancery as evidence that the assembly at Basel was not a true general council.[69] Here, too, then, Aeneas structures his self-defence in a way that effectively neutralizes a weapon he had entrusted to conciliarists – his authority as an eyewitness. The fact that he did so would seem to imply that he was concerned about more than simply rehabilitating his own reputation: he was also concerned about the power of his own arguments to damage papal authority.

Aeneas continued to reverse and, indeed, further develop this counterattack in a work of history that he wrote three years later, the *De rebus Basiliae gestis commentarius*.[70] While shorter in length than his earlier conciliar history, the *De gestis*, the *De rebus* is more chronologically expansive: it unfolds a long narrative that begins with the resolution of the Great Schism at the Council of Constance and concludes with the death of Antipope Felix V. The *De rebus* is a complex text, and as the next section of this chapter will demonstrate, it resonates in various ways with Aeneas's experience in the conciliar crisis. Placed side by side with the pro-conciliar *De gestis* and the *Libellus*, one of those resonances becomes very clear: the *De rebus* reverses the portrait of the Basel fathers as discerning judges.[71] Moreover, it does so in the context of discussing the very events that in the *De gestis* and the *Libellus* were made to exemplify the council's discernment. At the same time, the *De rebus* introduces a new element into this counter-attack by maligning the council fathers' motives. It was self-interest, Aeneas claims, that drove them to strip Eugenius of his prerogatives.[72] He goes on to note the arrogance and deviousness of the council fathers as a whole, while observing that their president, Louis d'Aleman, was filled with hatred for Eugenius.[73] Their lack of virtue, moreover, finds expression in one of the most memorable scenes of the entire text: Aeneas describes how Tommaso Parentucelli, then bishop of Bologna and soon-to-be Pope Nicholas V, decries the entire assembly as the "synagogue of Satan."[74]

The different aims of these works help to explain why they respond differently to Aeneas's pro-conciliar arguments. The Letter of Retraction is first and foremost a work of self-defence. Had he condemned the council fathers' motives, he would have risked tarnishing his own image. In contrast, by explaining his allegiance to Basel as blindness rather than malice, as misdirected but well-meaning religious zeal, Aeneas is able to preserve and possibly even strengthen his portrait as a man of great integrity. The work's audience also helps to explain this circumscribed attack on the council fathers. Aeneas writes the letter to the pro-conciliar University of Cologne, an institution that he risked offending, should his confession be read as an insult to their beliefs. In short, there were very good reasons why, in 1447, Aeneas was only retracting half of his argument. In the *De rebus*, in contrast, these reasons did not exist. Rather than to conciliarists, the text is addressed to Cardinal Juan de Carvajal, one of Eugenius's staunchest defenders. Moreover, it is written not as a personal confession but as a chronicle – and a chronicle in which Aeneas assigns himself a minor role until the narrative reaches 1446, when he emerges as a central figure in the empire's reconciliation with Pope Eugenius. In this context, he was in a position to put forward a fuller retraction of his pro-conciliar arguments.

Neither work, however, had overturned those arguments sufficiently in the eyes of Pope Pius II. The text of *In minoribus*, the bull he issued in 1463, indicates that those same pro-conciliar arguments were still plaguing him as he wrote the *Commentaries*. In addition to issuing a solemn rejection of the conciliarist writings of his youth, and to reiterating the standard biblical, theological, and philosophical defences of papal supremacy, the bull extends and amplifies the revisions in both his Letter of Retraction and his *De rebus* of his earlier and favourable portrait of the Basel fathers. As in the Letter of Retraction, Aeneas embeds his assault in a synopsis of his days at Basel and his subsequent alienation from the assembly. And again in keeping with this letter, his account underscores the irrationality of the council fathers' actions. Aeneas builds on this portrait of poor judgment substantially by casting the council fathers as calculating manipulators of the truth. He explains how the entire assembly was organized in a way that actively discouraged critical thinking. It was flooded with pro-conciliar lawyers and theologians whose reputation intimidated anyone from speaking against them. To suppress dissent, however, the fathers relied on more than these unanimous voices of authority. They also issued threats: "To mutter anything against the honour of the council was a crime of heresy," Aeneas reports, with the result that "everyone with one voice preferred the council to Eugenius."[75] Aeneas's emphasis on the council's oppressive intellectual atmosphere has the effect of lessening his own responsibility for embracing conciliarist views. While the bull continues to attribute his support for the Basel assembly to his own naiveté, it lays still more blame on the council fathers for essentially suppressing his ability to develop his critical sensibilities. "What were we to do?" he writes, underscoring his helplessness. "How could we not accept what we heard? It is a weak mind that does not take up the things it hears, that are forced upon it day after day … Thus we spoke what we heard."[76] In the process of accentuating his role as the council's victim, Aeneas also intensifies the counter-attack he had levelled against the Basel fathers in his Letter of Retraction and in the *De rebus*. *In minoribus* dramatically reverses the image of the assembly sketched in the *De gestis* – and, in a sense, dramatized in the *Libellus* – as a forum for enlightened Socratic debate. The lessons offered at this very different "school," as he characterizes it in the bull, were tantamount to brainwashing, psychological intimidation, and spiritual threats.

Aeneas also revises his earlier account of his conversion to the papalist position. Here, he does not simply note, as he does in the Letter of Retraction, his many unrestricted discussions and debates with "the wisest men" that opened his eyes to "the truth" about the Basel fathers. He also recounts at length a particular discussion he had with Cardinal

Giuliano Cesarini, the former president of the council who, along with Nicholas Cusanus, had swung to Eugenius in 1437. Aeneas had already singled out the cardinal earlier in his account for his exceptional skill at convincing the assembly of the Basel council's claims to authority.[77] Here, in this conversation, Aeneas has Cesarini himself first condemn these actions and beliefs as products of poor judgment. Then he explains how careful scrutiny of the council's position, along with divine revelation, prompted him to abandon the conciliar camp. "If you are wise, you will do the same,"[78] Cesarini warns in his final words, and in so doing underscores the lack of wisdom Aeneas would demonstrate by maintaining a conciliarist stance.[79]

Aeneas's decision to quote Cesarini at length in his bull of retraction can be explained only in part by the influence he claims the cardinal had on his own decision to abandon the Basel assembly. By having the former president of the council explicitly state that he exercised poor judgment during his tenure, Aeneas was adding further authority to his own disparaging portrait of the Basel fathers. He was doing so, moreover, in a way that countered the figure of Cusanus in his pro-conciliar *Libellus*. In that fictional dialogue, a distinguished papalist confesses to seeing "the truth" in the conciliarist position after a rigorous scrutiny of their arguments. In *In minoribus*, it is another distinguished papalist who, in a speech of equal drama, confesses to the very opposite.[80] Aeneas's papalist Cesarini does not, however, simply compete with his conciliarist Cusanus; he also, it seems, speaks with greater authority. Not only are Cesarini's words made out to be real – and witnessed by Aeneas himself – but they also gain authority from the solemn nature of the document within which they are couched.

In many ways, then, the 1463 bull *In minoribus* is a particularly important document to consider when analysing the *Commentaries* as a work of apology. The most basic reading reveals that when Aeneas wrote the text, he still understood his conciliarist past to be a dangerous enemy. Scrutinized more closely, and as the above analysis has argued, it demonstrates that Aeneas continued to see that threat in the particular arguments he had previously used to undercut papal authority. The bull's forceful counterarguments to the *Libellus* and the *De gestis* in particular are indicative of that concern; so is the considerable space he devotes to unfolding them – almost half of the entire bull. Perhaps the clearest indication, however, of how dangerous he considered them to be was that he chose to cast these counterarguments in the formidable instrument of a papal bull. At the same time, *In minoribus* alerts us to something else worth remembering when reading the *Commentaries*. It shows Aeneas developing new approaches not only when revising his own conciliarist past, but also when rebutting his earlier pro-conciliar arguments. It is worth keeping in mind these particular defensive strategies when analysing the more substantial work of apology he was writing at the same time.

Aeneas, Councils, and Tensions with the Papacy (1447–1455)

In minoribus represents in still other ways a crucial point of reference when examining the *Commentaries* as a work of apology. A close examination of the instructions contained in the bull demonstrates why. Pius exhorts his audience to renounce those writings of his that "struck by whatever means at the supreme authority of the Apostolic See or that added anything which the Roman Church does not embrace."[81] As mentioned earlier, he explicitly identifies the *Libellus* as one such text, but he also indicates these viewpoints are scattered through his letters and in "other little writings."[82] At the same time as he commands his audience to spurn these texts, he directs them to reject the man who wrote them. "Believe the old man more than the youth," he commands, "do not think more highly of the private man than the pope. Reject Aeneas; accept Pius."[83] Scholarship has traditionally understood in these statements Pius's attempts to divorce himself dramatically and definitively from the views he held before spring 1445, when he formally repented of his conciliar past at the papal court and abandoned his long-held conviction that the schism should be resolved by a so-called third council. Yet, interestingly, the language Aeneas uses in the bull to characterize himself conflicts with this chronology: Aeneas remained "Aeneas" and a private man, if not a youth, long after 1445 – indeed, he fit this description up until the moment of his election on 19 August 1458. The discrepancy between the literal words of the bull and the prevailing scholarly interpretation of them raises an important question: could the "little writings" Pius repudiates in *In minoribus* – ones that "struck by whatever means at the supreme authority of the Apostolic See" and that "added anything which the Roman Church does not embrace" – include works he penned after his formal disavowal of conciliarism? A close scrutiny of several writings supports this interpretation.

Such a claim does more than reinterpret the bull's dramatic exhortation to "reject Aeneas": it also revises – and in a significant way – traditional narratives of his career and thought. Typically, Aeneas's embassy to Eugenius IV in spring 1445 is seen as the final step in his slow process of conversion to the papalist camp.[84] It was at this point, scholars have concluded, that Aeneas became a champion of the papal party.[85] As evidence of his alliance with Eugenius they point to his honorary appointment as papal secretary in March 1446 and still more to the central role he played in re-establishing German obedience to the Roman pontiff. Aeneas's subsequent string of appointments as papal secretary and legate, as bishop of Trieste and then of Siena, suggests that like his predecessor, Nicholas V also enlisted Aeneas to serve the interests of the papacy. However, to read this curriculum vitae as evidence of Aeneas's complete elision with papal policy would be to gloss over important tensions and complexities in his relationship with the Roman curia.[86] It is also to ignore the fact that the term papalist accommodates a wide range of viewpoints.[87] According to its most basic definition, Aeneas was unquestionably a papalist by 1445: he had renounced the doctrine of conciliar supremacy and had condemned the Council of Basel's claims to legitimacy. There is also no question that he began at that point to defend papal sovereignty in various capacities against conciliar demands.[88] And yet, between 1445 and 1455, Aeneas also wrote several works that either struck at the authority of the Apostolic See or that were perceived in the papal curia as doing so – or that had the potential to be seen that way. As the following analysis of those works will illustrate, that opposition lay, in part, in Aeneas's stance on general councils and the role he envisioned they should play in a church where popes ruled supreme.

This analysis will also work to explain the reasons for Aeneas's divergence from papal policy on councils. In part, it was a product of his role at the imperial court. As secretary and ambassador for Holy Roman Emperor Frederick III – roles played simultaneously, it will be remembered, with papal ones – Aeneas consistently advocated policies that would bring stability to an empire divided politically and religiously and that would strengthen imperial authority in the face of German princes.[89] That stability, as discussed in chapter 1, hinged on a strong papacy, but not when papal strength came at the expense of imperial interests. Aeneas's attitude towards councils was also conditioned by his firm commitment to political pragmatism and nowhere more so than in the context of papal-imperial relations: the success of that alliance – and for the pope as much as for the emperor – hinged, Aeneas maintained, on a policy of mutual compromise and accommodation. It was this combination, then, of professional duty and personal philosophy that led Aeneas to pen several works that would become liabilities for him during his papacy: unquestioning in his support of papal sovereignty, Aeneas nonetheless envisioned a role for general councils that effectively compromised the extreme stances supported not just by Eugenius and Nicholas but by Pius II as well.

The distance between Aeneas "the papalist" and the papacy on the role of councils first emerges in an oration he delivered before Eugenius IV in January 1447.[90] Together with other imperial and princely legates, Aeneas had been sent to Rome in January of that year to present the terms by which they would agree to return to full obedience with Eugenius. Speaking on behalf of the various German delegations, Aeneas presented an oration that outlined and explained those conditions. Scholarship has traditionally presented Aeneas's embassy as the work of a papal ally as well as an imperial ambassador, and not without good reason. His commitment to establishing Germany's reunion with Pope Eugenius is unquestionable; and it had only been galvanized in March of the previous year when the imperial electors, united in outrage by Eugenius's sudden deposition of the archbishops of Trier and Cologne – the two electors most sympathetic to conciliarism – seemed increasingly likely to declare instead for the Basel assembly. Their collective antagonism towards Eugenius also represented a threat to the emperor: having all but declared his own allegiance to the pontiff, Frederick now faced dangerous isolation in his own empire.[91] The conditions Aeneas presented to Eugenius in 1447 grew directly out of this crisis, as much imperial as it was papal, and out of the efforts of imperial legates who, in consultation with their papal counterparts, spent the summer and fall of 1446 hammering out terms for obedience, known as the imperial compromise proposal, that they hoped would be acceptable to electors and pope alike. There was no mention in this imperial compromise proposal of the electors' recent and steep demands of a few months before that the pope profess the conciliar decrees *Haec Sancta* and *Frequens* word for word, and that he summon a new council to resolve the schism.[92] While the terms were much friendlier to papal authority, in the eyes of the curia, they were not friendly enough. As a result, when Aeneas first unfolded those terms in his oration before the pontiff, he was in some sense still delivering a threat to papal sovereignty.

The nature of that threat first becomes clear when comparing those terms with the instructions Eugenius issued in August 1446 to his legates in Germany.[93] The compromise proposal exceeded those parameters in its very first condition: the pope was to summon a council within eighteen months of Germany's declaring obedience to Eugenius.[94] The council's purpose was not, as the electors had once requested, to determine Eugenius's legitimacy, but its tasks were still weighty: to advance much-needed church reform and to develop in place of the *Acceptatio* of Mainz a permanent solution to the German grievances against the Roman Church and one that compensated the papacy for lost revenues.[95] In the written instructions to his legates, Pope Eugenius did not consent to calling a new general council, and his oral instructions seem to have been to offer only vague promises of such an assembly sometime in the future.[96] Furthermore, while he directed his legates to agree to negotiations over the *Acceptatio*, he indicated that those negotiations were to be conducted directly with German prelates and princes.[97] The compromise proposal also asked the pontiff to do more in his profession of conciliar authority than Eugenius had allowed. In a carefully worded statement, the pontiff had instructed his legates that he was prepared to "take up, embrace, and venerate the general councils of Constance and Basel from their beginning to their translation by us, but without prejudice to the rights, dignity, or pre-eminence of the holy Apostolic See."[98] Aeneas seems to respect this crucial qualification in how he characterizes Eugenius's authority.[99] Elsewhere, however, he is more ambiguous. He asks the pope to profess not just to the power and authority of general councils but also to their "pre-eminence" (*praeeminentia*) – a word Eugenius had not used to characterize conciliar authority, and for good reason: it was customary for the papacy to use this term when characterizing its sovereign power, and, in fact, Eugenius had used it in just this way in his own instructions.[100] The written version of this proposal diverges still more explicitly from Eugenius's instructions, for it asks the pontiff to profess specifically to the authority of councils as expressed in *Frequens* and other decrees of Constance and Basel.[101] Given how they overstepped Eugenius's orders, it is easy to see how the conditions Aeneas pronounced might be read as a threat to papal sovereignty.[102]

There is, moreover, ample evidence that the curia read them in just that way. In his eyewitness account of Aeneas's oration, the abbot of San Galgano condemned the terms of obedience offered by the German ambassadors as "exorbitant and hateful to the Holy Father and in general to the entire college of cardinals."[103] A more specific account of the curia's objections came from Aeneas himself. In the official report of his embassy later submitted to Frederick III, Aeneas enumerates the "difficulties and struggles" he faced in discussions with the cardinals whom the ailing pontiff had appointed to consider the German offer. That resistance, he reports, came in part to the demands regarding councils: "It seemed severe to the cardinals ... to call a council"; and he notes that "there was greater difficulty regarding the [pontiff's] profession [of authority of the councils]."[104]

It is Eugenius's own carefully hedged response that best illustrates the serious threat he heard in Aeneas's speech.[105] The pope did agree to summon a council, and he also agreed to profess to the authority and eminence – though not the pre-eminence – of councils as outlined in *Frequens*. But his acceptance took a form that effectively stripped his words of real significance. For one, he chose to issue these pledges as a papal brief, "Ad ea ex debito" – a private and confidential document with a far more restricted audience than that envisioned for publicly proclaimed bulls. The audience for this brief consisted only of the emperor and those princes to whom the pope had recently and strategically granted lucrative privileges, and it excluded those sympathetic to conciliar supremacy.[106] At the same time, he set conditions on his acceptance that made it unlikely that a new council would ever transpire – by making it contingent on consultation with Europe's princes (whose inevitable disagreement over the assembly's location would stall its summons), and by effectively depriving it of the very purposes for which it had been envisioned.[107] Eugenius's brief does not acknowledge, for example, that the council will or should have any role in promoting reform; and while he does agree it could negotiate the *Acceptatio*, his bull *Ad tranquillitatem* identifies an alternative vehicle for those negotiations – bilateral discussions between Germany's rulers and a papal legate.[108] Eugenius, however, undermines his promises most completely and most explicitly in still another document: the very day he issued this bull and brief, he secretly abjured any promises that compromised papal sovereignty, explaining that he did not intend in any way to take away from the privileges or authority of the Apostolic See.[109] Together, these public, private, and secret responses to the imperial compromise agreement bring into still sharper focus the atmosphere Aeneas encountered in the papal curia: they reveal a pontiff deeply alarmed by the prospect of a new council and by the power it might wield.

It was these fears, then, that Aeneas was feeding when he articulated and advocated the 1447 proposal and that made his oration, its deference to papal sovereignty notwithstanding, a tangible threat to a sovereign pope. In a curia scarred by the actions of Basel and deeply wary of conciliar authority in any form, Aeneas's words simply did not go far enough in shielding papal sovereignty from the conciliar spectre. Why a papal ally would support such a proposal makes sense when we remember that, as imperial ambassador, Aeneas's primary responsibility was to serve the interests of the emperor.[110] To be sure, imperial and papal interests aligned insofar as both Frederick and Eugenius sought reunion, but those interests were not identical.[111] For Frederick, the larger goal was to protect his authority in the face of serious challenges from his imperial electors; for Eugenius, it was to protect papal sovereignty at all costs, and especially against the conciliar threat. In order to fulfil the former, Aeneas was asking for concessions that effectively hindered the latter.

If the substance of Aeneas's oration was threatening to Eugenius IV in 1447, it also would have been a concern to Pius II fifteen years later when he was writing the *Commentaries*. That threat is easily obscured by the outcome of the 1447 negotiations: the imperial ambassadors, Aeneas included, accepted how Eugenius modified their proposal and, in so doing, themselves helped to neutralize the threat it posed to the pontiff.[112] Nevertheless, Aeneas's association with the original proposal endured. Almost immediately after he delivered the address, it began to circulate: "Many afterwards sought copies of [Aeneas's] oration," he reports to Frederick, "not so much for its eloquence as for its content."[113] That content pitted Aeneas not simply against the conciliar policies of Eugenius. The positions he advocated therein – the recognition of general councils as valuable tools for reform, the concept of councils as holding "pre-eminent" power and authority – sat uncomfortably at best with his own policies as pope. With this in mind, it seems reasonable to think that when Pius II wished in his 1463 bull *In minoribus* that some of his earlier writings had "languished in obscurity," he counted this oration among such texts.

The pontiff would have found still greater cause for concern in the account he penned three years later about how this controversial 1447 proposal had been negotiated. The account appears in his 1450 history of the Council of Basel, the *De rebus*, a text traditionally classified as papalist in its perspective.[114] As discussed in the previous section of this chapter, there is no question that the text is in many ways pro-papal. It offers a sustained criticism of the Basel council and its actions and in ways that overturn the arguments made in Aeneas's staunchly proconciliar writings. It is also clear that Aeneas casts himself here as a crucial defender of the papal cause: he appears in this account as the indispensable architect of the negotiations that brought Germany back to Roman obedience.[115] Nevertheless, Aeneas's account draws attention to the tensions involved in those negotiations as well as the triumphs they eventually yielded. Still more importantly, it highlights the central role he played in creating those tensions. In the *De rebus*, Aeneas is not simply the spokesman for the proposal that met resistance in the papal curia: he appears as its chief author, and one committed to defending its merits in the face of its critics. Compared with the oration, then, the *De rebus* links Aeneas still more closely to a policy that, from the perspective of the papal curia, threatened to weaken papal sovereignty.

Aeneas highlights that threat in the *De rebus* by recounting a clash he had with papal legates at the Diet of Frankfurt after presenting them with the imperial compromise proposal in early October 1446.[116] As it would at the papal court a few months later, this conflict arose in part out of what the proposal said about conciliar authority. Aeneas zeroes in on the objections of one of the papal legates, the bishop of Bologna, who, because of his late arrival at the diet, had not been consulted during the proposal's drafting process. The bishop claimed, or so Aeneas reports, that had he been present for that process, he would never have agreed to those matters concerning *Frequens* – namely, the demand that the pope profess to conciliar authority as expressed in that specific decree.[117] The legate's objections come as no surprise given, as discussed above, his instructions did not permit him to accept such terms. Aeneas, moreover, makes them ideological as well by explicitly grouping the bishop with the cardinals who "did not want under any circumstances to acknowledge the authority of councils as articulated in the decrees of Constance."[118] In so doing, Aeneas positions himself not just against one legate but against an influential faction at the papal court.

Aeneas emphasizes this opposition through a sustained rebuttal to the bishop's objections. That rebuttal first emerges indirectly in his description of the circumstances from which the proposal arose. Eugenius's position, he reports grimly, was desperate at the Diet of Frankfurt. After a frustrating reception at the papal court in July and failed negotiations with both imperial and papal legates, the German electors were preparing to send a new embassy to Eugenius with a series of steep and specific demands. Unless the pope met the conditions they sought to impose on him – something, Aeneas writes, the pontiff would never do – the electors would then and there declare their obedience to the Council of Basel and to its pope, Felix V.[119] Finding compromise, it seemed, was the only hope – a point Aeneas drives home very clearly by forecasting the results of a more inflexible approach. "If [the bishop of Bologna] had objected about the authority of the council," he observes, "everything likely would have been thrown into disorder."[120] Aeneas goes on to report that the compromise he went on to forge eventually won the approval of all the papal legates, and their endorsement becomes part of Aeneas's defence.[121] He offers further justification for the proposal's demands in his account of their reception at the papal court. His 1447 oration summarizing the terms of obedience was well received by the pope, he writes, and while he acknowledges difficulties in the subsequent negotiations with the cardinals, he passes over them swiftly, stressing instead the successful outcome: "at last all things were obtained that had been sought" and "the obedience of the German nation was restored."[122] Aeneas's account leaves a very strong impression that the key to achieving that obedience lay in his insistence on taking the path of compromise.[123]

Why would Aeneas have deliberately drawn attention to this disagreement with papal legates over the decree *Frequens*? And why build such an extensive defence of his own position? The context for the *De rebus* helps to explain why. When Aeneas wrote it, the man sitting on the papal throne, Nicholas V, was the papal legate whom Aeneas describes balking at his demands regarding *Frequens*. Just as significant is the person to whom the *De rebus* is addressed, Cardinal Juan de Carvajal. Carvajal was another papal legate at the Frankfurt diet and, according to the *De rebus*, the one who contested Aeneas's proposal the most.[124] Already a powerful figure in the papal curia at the time of those negotiations, his influence only grew after the election of Nicholas in 1448. He was also Aeneas's chief intermediary with the new pope.[125] In short, at the time Aeneas wrote the *De rebus*, the men largely responsible for papal policy were the very ones who appear in the *De rebus* as resistant to his philosophy of pragmatism and compromise.

Whether or not the account in the *De rebus* is accurate, it is clear that this clash of diplomatic philosophies was, to Aeneas, both very real and very troublesome – and it had been for some time. In late 1443, in response to Carvajal's attempts to win Frederick to the papal party, Aeneas wrote in frustration about the refusal of both Basilians and Eugenians to resolve the schism through compromise: "You and your party want union, but on your terms – namely, that your pope stays and the church is unified. The other party wants the same thing but according to different terms. Nobody spurns peace, nobody spurns union, but nobody will accept a peace that takes away from him. Everyone wants to win; nobody bends. Oh men of stiff necks!"[126] Aeneas underscores yet again the importance of compromise and mutual accommodation in a letter he addressed to Carvajal on the heels of Nicholas's election. He does so this time when reminding how Nicholas V should deal with a particularly lucrative benefice: "I ask, I pray, I beg that you permit nothing to be done without letters from the king. Do not offend the prince … If you wish to be received well at Gers and our Vienna, take care lest something should happen against us in Rome, and that all we ask for be done."[127] Against the backdrop of these letters and of the tensions they reveal, the episode in the *De rebus* reads, thus, as more than just an account of a specific event: it served as a valuable justification for Aeneas's approach to papal-imperial relations. Not only does it draw a sharp contrast between the philosophies of compromise and intransigence that shaped and complicated those relations, but it also builds a case for the superiority of the former. At the same time, it reminds Carvajal and Nicholas that they had at one point embraced this approach, and with excellent results. Given its audience's tendency to adopt an opposing philosophy, the *De rebus* would have served as a useful tool in his dealings with the curia. It would have been particularly useful at the time he was writing the *De rebus*, precisely when Aeneas was working to negotiate the specifics of Frederick's imperial coronation at the papal court. Under these circumstances, making a case for compromise and accommodation was particularly urgent.[128]

What had been useful in 1450 to Aeneas, imperial legate, became a serious liability to him as pope. Aeneas may have cast himself as the shield and saviour of the papacy in the *De rebus* – by claiming to craft terms of German obedience that removed all that for the pope was "hard, harsh, and horrible to hear."[129] From his vantage point on the papal throne, however, Aeneas would not have seen his portrait in this text as heroic, nor could he have agreed with this positive assessment of the proposal he penned. Not only does the *De rebus* show him facing down a papal legate – and one who went on to become pope – but it champions a willingness to compromise on conciliar matters that was directly at odds with the attitude he adopted as pontiff. Ultimately, what made the *De rebus* so problematic to Pius II is that the rigid attitude he adopted was the same one he, when Aeneas, had attributed in the text to his opponent, the papal legate. In essence, then, in explicitly opposing himself to the bishop of Bologna, Aeneas was also implicitly undermining the position on conciliar authority held by Pius II.

The *De rebus* is not the only text in which Aeneas advocates a position at odds with both Nicholas V's and his own stance on councils and conciliar authority. Around the time (1450) he was composing his history of the Council of Basel, he also penned an oration respectfully requesting on behalf of Frederick III that the pontiff convene a new council in Germany.[130] The goals of such an assembly overlapped in some ways with those outlined in his 1447 oration, but they differed in others: "Many Christian princes are at war; we must seek peace. The morals of the clergy and the people are in decline; we must search out more sober behaviour. Many bring harm to a church oppressed; we must restore its liberty."[131] Frederick's request, Aeneas makes very clear, in no way signalled a newfound sympathy for conciliarist ideas at the imperial court. "It is true that your authority over these matters is sufficient," he is quick to emphasize, and he is at pains to reassure that the council he requests would not usurp that authority.[132] Aeneas also makes his petition without reference to the papal brief, reissued by Nicholas in 1448, that promised a new council within eighteen months of Germany's declaration of obedience. It is pragmatism, not legalism, Aeneas explains, that drives his request: "These matters ... cannot be resolved easily without convening prelates," and he both introduces and concludes by describing the emperor's request as "useful."[133]

Useful for whom? There is no question that Aeneas saw it as a means of stabilizing and strengthening the Holy Roman Empire. His oration acknowledges the considerable pressure within Germany for a new council, while it hints indirectly at another pressure: competition from arch-rival Charles VII, who was at the same moment petitioning the pope to hold a council in his kingdom.[134] Just as important was the role the council could play in fostering peace. Aeneas's letters from this period reveal his growing despair over the sharp divisions, violence and war consuming the kingdoms of Europe and destroying the empire in particular. At the same time, one of these letters reveals his deep frustration with both pope and emperor for not doing enough to restore unity and peace. Moreover, it shows him explicitly critical of papal legate Carvajal, who left Germany after a failed mission to negotiate peace in Hungary.[135] In its role as peacemaker, then, the council was particularly important because it could help to remedy what Aeneas saw as a desperate situation within the empire. As he had in the *De rebus*, Aeneas frames his petition explicitly in terms of the benefits it would bring to the papacy. "You will call a general council," he explains to Pope Nicholas, "if you want to bring peace to Christians, cultivate temperance and good morals, if you want to win back freedom of the Church, if you want to preserve the union that has been brought forth."[136]

Aeneas's perspective was not shared, however, by the man on the papal throne – or, for that matter, by the one who would sit there eight years later. From their vantage point, the drawbacks of calling a council far outweighed the benefits. After his election, Nicholas V had remained a staunch defender of papal sovereignty against the slightest hint of conciliar threat. While promising to call a council after the Jubilee, he took care not to follow through on his pledge. At the same time, he appointed papal legates to tackle the tasks commonly envisioned for such an assembly – church reform and peace negotiations. Indeed, the fact that Aeneas spoke of a council fulfilling these very responsibilities would have been particularly unsettling for Nicholas. Aeneas and Frederick may not themselves have been conciliarists, but they shared too much in common with conciliarist positions for a pope like Nicholas V. What made this oration a problem for Aeneas after 19 August 1458 is that he himself had become a pope like Nicholas. As Pope Pius II, he shared the same wariness of councils, and he was just as careful to guard church reform and peacemaking as exclusively papal prerogatives. As such, Aeneas's petition to Nicholas for a new council would have been a source of considerable embarrassment to Pius, but it was also something much more. To his opponents in Germany, France, and beyond, who throughout his papacy demanded a council for church reform, this oration offered particularly potent ammunition.[137]

It was an oration Aeneas delivered five years later, however, and in front of Nicholas V's successor that left Pius the most vulnerable of all. In the fall of 1455, Aeneas was sent as imperial envoy on an embassy to the newly elected Calixtus III. Aeneas delivered two orations in the early months of his Roman sojourn: the first was a formal profession of the emperor's obedience;[138] the second concerned the question of how the Hussites could be reunited with the Roman Church.[139] The impetus for the oration, Aeneas explains, was to inform the pope of the discussions he had had with George Podiebrad earlier in the year during the Bohemian governor's visit to the imperial court at Wiener Neustadt.[140] In the course of the discussions, Podiebrad had proposed terms by which the Bohemians were willing to return to Roman obedience. Aeneas's aim in his oration, or so he claims, is simply to lay out the arguments in favour of and against that proposal and to explore possible alternative paths to reunion. Nevertheless, his self-portrait as objective reporter, and one unqualified to weigh in on such a debate, is implausible. The arguments he presents make a powerful case for making concessions to the Bohemians, first and foremost by confirming the Prague Compacts: not only do the benefits – both to the papacy and to the empire – far outweigh the drawbacks, but according to Aeneas there are no other viable alternatives to achieving peace. As such, Aeneas's long speech reads as an endorsement of conciliar authority as preserved and protected in the Prague Compacts – authority that the papacy had consistently and adamantly refused to recognize since they had been negotiated by the Council of Basel in 1436.

Just how much at odds Aeneas's position was in the eyes of the papacy becomes clear from his correspondence. In the years before he delivered this oration, Aeneas's many efforts to reunite the Hussites with the Roman Church had consistently received a cool reception from the papal curia. Those efforts began in an unofficial capacity in July 1451 when, on an imperial embassy to Benešov, he had an impromptu discussion with Podiebrad, then only an influential Hussite baron, about ecclesiastical matters. In a lengthy letter addressed to Cardinal Carvajal, Aeneas reports that Podiebrad, of whom he had a very high opinion, was open to negotiation on all points that divided the moderate Hussite and Roman churches except the Compacts.[141] Aeneas does not explicitly recommend that the papacy yield on the Compacts; his aim in writing the letter, he stresses, is simply to pass along information that Nicholas V might find useful in advance of an upcoming embassy to Bohemia.[142] And yet by emphasizing both Podiebrad's intransigence on this issue and the crucial role he would inevitably play in any peace agreement, Aeneas was implying that compromise on the Bohemian Compacts was the papacy's only choice.[143] In offering this advice, Aeneas was directing Nicholas V towards a policy very different from the one the pontiff had been pursuing. A few years earlier, the papal legate to Bohemia had adamantly refused to recognize the validity of the Compacts and spoke out against the distribution of Holy Communion in two species (*sub utraque specie*) that it enshrined. That legate was none other than Juan de Carvajal, the recipient of Aeneas's letter.[144] Given the disastrous failure of his Bohemian embassy, Aeneas might have hoped to find Carvajal receptive to the contents of his letter; and given his authority in the papal curia over Bohemian matters, he was certainly the one to consult on a possible change of policy.

There was, however, no such change during Nicholas's pontificate, despite the fact that Aeneas was appointed papal nuncio and legate to Bohemia less than a year after penning his letter to Carvajal.[145] Indeed, based on his correspondence during this period, the appointment seems to have brought Aeneas nothing but frustration. In September 1452, Nicholas rebuffed Aeneas's recommendation to rethink the curia's approach to achieving peace in the wake of the dramatic extension of Hussite control over Bohemia.[146] The pontiff also ignored his legate's requests to hold discussions with Podiebrad, who now ruled as Bohemia's governor.[147] Indeed, from what he writes, Aeneas struggled to get Nicholas to attend to any of his Bohemian concerns.[148] In an effort to change this pattern, Aeneas resolved to go to Rome in early 1454 and discuss matters face to face with the pontiff – a plan that, in the end, he was unable to carry out.[149] Just what Aeneas would have advised the pontiff about the Compacts is unclear; his letters never explicitly state his position. What they do make clear, however, is that Aeneas realized that in the face of Hussite strength, the papacy was not in a position to dictate the terms of reunion, and that on this point of strategy he and the curia remained far apart. To a large extent that gap can be explained by the fact that Aeneas viewed Bohemian affairs from the vantage point of the imperial court. There is no question that, from there, he saw peace with the Hussite Church as essential to the strength of both papacy and empire. However, what had him pressing for that peace with such urgency in the early 1450s was the serious danger he saw Hussitism posing to the latter. That sense of urgency grows measurably as he writes of the transfer to Prague of the young king of Hungary and Bohemia, Ladislaus (1440–57), posthumous son of Emperor Albert II and ward of Frederick III. Ladislaus, Aeneas had learned, was being isolated from all Catholic influence, and the Bohemians were making concerted efforts to convert the young king to utraquism.[150] Such a conversion would have split religiously an empire already deeply fractured politically and chronically ravaged by war. Committed to promoting a strong, peaceful, and unified empire, and to drawing on Frederick's alliance with the papacy to do so, Aeneas saw papal negotiations with Podiebrad as crucial. The view from the papal throne, however, was very different. Such negotiations threatened to undermine papal authority on an issue that Nicholas had already proven reluctant to compromise on, namely, conciliar authority. By choosing instead to sponsor the violently anti-Hussite preaching of Capistrano, the pontiff demonstrated how different his priorities and his policy were from those of his legate.

When Aeneas finally did reach Rome in autumn 1455 and delivered his oration on the Bohemian Compacts, he was clearly taking a risk. While he did not have to face Nicholas V, he did have to make his case to a curia that had been consistently unsympathetic to compromise on the Compacts and to a pope whose own position on the matter was an unknown. The results were initially successful; and in the years following the oration, Calixtus and Podiebrad appeared to be working towards a peace based on the acceptance of the Compacts.[151] Nevertheless, in the spring of 1458, when the papacy suddenly found itself with the authority to sanction Podiebrad's coronation as king, it shifted its position abruptly: under careful instruction from Carvajal, the bishops would only agree to crown the king-elect if he first renounced Hussitism and swore full obedience to the Roman Church.[152] Aeneas once again found himself at odds with papal policy, and not just Calixtus III's: a few months later, when he himself took the papal throne, he chose to pursue the very same uncompromising position towards Podiebrad that Calixtus had recently adopted. Aeneas's oration in favour of the papacy's acceptance of the Compacts soon became a dangerous one for Pius II. Not only does his speech take a radically different position towards the Compacts than the one Pius took up, but it argues adamantly against the very paths the pontiff ended up following in an effort to reunite Bohemia with the Roman Church. As such, his oration was not simply an embarrassment: it was a dangerous weapon that could be used to undermine his own authority as pope and that of future pontiffs, too.

When Pius II began writing his *Commentaries* in 1462, there was, thus, another Aeneas besides the conciliarist one whom he had reason to fear. It was a pro-papal Aeneas, to be sure, but it was one whose views on general councils and on the Bohemian legacy of the Basel assembly set him both apart from and against a papal curia that perceived a council in any form as a dangerous threat. Together, Aeneas's orations to Eugenius, Nicholas, and Calixtus, and his *De rebus*, reveal this important and overlooked dimension of his pre-papal past. At the same time, they complicate our understanding of one of the most important documents of his papacy, the bull *In minoribus*, and arguably, that bull's most important line: "Reject Aeneas, accept Pius." Still more importantly for this book, these texts will help us to understand the significance of the *Commentaries* as an apology.

Cardinal Aeneas, Pope Pius, and the Battle against Conciliarism

By 1457, Aeneas had clearly retreated from his recent positions on the value of councils that had created tensions with the papacy. Now a cardinal, and ensconced in the papal curia, Aeneas was defending papal policy he had pushed up against in his writings. Rather than advocating for a new council, he was speaking out against one and in a way that overturned his earlier arguments. The pope was under no obligation to honour the synodal decree *Frequens* – or, for that matter, any human law, he insisted. Indeed, the pontiffs had been wise not to do so in recent years.[153] The Basel assembly had proven how easily general councils can be hijacked by private interests, and besides, there were no compelling matters of public interest that warranted a new assembly. "For general councils are not summoned unless something exceptionally unusual happened in the universal Church, unless there is complaint, or upheaval or trouble" – a dubious statement given the ongoing calls for reform and the wars continuing to plague Europe.[154] To be sure, Aeneas conceded, collecting an army to meet the Turkish threat was a serious concern – but not one that could likely be handled effectively by a council, "where there are as many opinions as heads."[155] Aeneas had also retreated from the philosophy of compromise that he had once insisted the papacy ought to embrace in its relationship with the Holy Roman Empire. In a letter he wrote on behalf of Calixtus III, his interpretation of the Concordat of Vienna (1448) casts papal obligations in a very different light: "Although the authority of the Apostolic See is entirely unrestricted and did not have to be confined by the bonds of pacts, nonetheless out of pure generosity, and out of our zeal for peace, and out of the love we have for you and your nation, we wanted there to be a place for the concordat."[156] The papacy, in other words, does not bargain; it grants concessions that, at will, it can take away.

Even though he now served as spokesman for papal policy against conciliar interests, Aeneas's involvement with conciliar matters during his cardinalate still would have been a source of deep concern for him when he wrote the *Commentaries*. The concern lay not in what he wrote as cardinal but in what he did – and in what someone else had written about him. Aeneas's difficulties can be traced to renewed anti-papal opposition that began to coalesce in Germany in early 1456 and that was still gaining momentum a year later. Part conciliar in nature, that crisis saw a block of German princes and several electors accuse Calixtus of violating the decrees of Basel and Constance. In a move that implied their acceptance of the doctrine of conciliar supremacy, they threatened, among other things, to appeal his new crusade tax to a future council.[157] It was Aeneas who spearheaded the curia's response to this dangerous revolt. Through much of 1457, he was directing letters to friends and allies well placed in German courts and carefully managing the moves of the papal legate on the ground in Germany.[158] He also penned several responses to the accusations launched against the pope, including the substantial tract *Germania* (1457–58) from which his above comments on a new council are drawn.[159] Aeneas's efforts, aided by the sudden death of the king of Hungary and Bohemia, Ladislaus Posthumous, were successful in quelling the princes' rebellion. It was not, however, his response to the crisis that would have troubled him as pope: it was his role in precipitating it – or, more precisely, the role attributed to him. The accusations came from the pen of Martin Mair, who served as chancellor to the archbishop of Mainz – the man leading the anti-papal assault. In a letter he wrote to Aeneas in 1457, Mair held Aeneas up as a symbol of the Roman Church's exploitation of the Germans.[160] The cardinal held the right of reservation to benefices in three German dioceses – an authority Mair condemned as unprecedented, egregiously abusive and typical of the Roman Church's insatiable greed. In short, Aeneas may have suppressed the conciliar uprising, but on some level he had also been the impetus for it. In so doing, he had earned for himself a reputation as traitor and enemy of the Germans.[161]

For the author of the *Commentaries*, this reputation was a liability on several levels. For one, it threatened to erase the very different role he had perceived himself as fulfilling in Germany and the very different image he sought to cultivate as cardinal. In several letters he wrote upon his elevation to the cardinalate, Aeneas explicitly defines himself as advocate of imperial and German interests in the Roman curia and as a German cardinal.[162] He defends that image still more vigorously in a series of letters to Mair, and most extensively in the *Germania*, which he addressed to the chancellor.[163] When he took up his pen to write the *Commentaries*, Aeneas would have wanted to preserve this reputation, and for more than personal reasons. The image of Cardinal Aeneas leeching German wealth to Rome had the potential both to upset Rome's fragile relations with Germany during his own pontificate and to precipitate problems for his successors.

While the events in Germany left Aeneas vulnerable, they also complicated the task of apology he faced as Pius II when writing the *Commentaries*. As the above analysis has demonstrated, Pope Pius II was threatened by his conciliarist past and by the papacy's perception that, in his role at the imperial court, he had been too sympathetic to the empire's interest in a council. At the same time, however, he was endangered by opposing accusations from Germany – that he had been too sympathetic to papal interests on conciliar matters, and at Germany's expense. How could he defend himself from one of these threats without making himself more vulnerable on the other? How, in other words, could he mitigate his past as a threat to papal sovereignty and, at the same time, strengthen his reputation as defender of those who continued to challenge it?

This dilemma was hardly the only challenge facing the author of the *Commentaries* as he weighed the results of the battles he had been waging from the Roman curia. From the beginning of his pontificate in August 1458, Pius had launched a series of offensives against his conciliar enemies using strategies more direct, comprehensive, and aggressive than those of his immediate predecessors. Now, four years into his reign, the pope committed to staunching the conciliar threat was facing a resurgent enemy and a defensive battle on several fronts. Pius II's war against conciliarism should by no means be understood as a resounding defeat. The greatest threat he faced over the course of his reign, the assembly of a new and antagonistic council, in the end never materialized. Pius, however, was writing the *Commentaries* without the benefit of hindsight; and for most of his papacy, the threat of a new council remained very real. Moreover, there was already ample evidence – and from conciliar camps, forceful arguments – that he had weakened papal authority in the face of the conciliar challenge. Pius II's attacks not only failed to disable the enemy; they actually seemed to have strengthened it – by further entrenching conciliar authority, by enhancing its legitimacy, and by reaffirming for many the necessity of conciliar supremacy. When he began writing the *Commentaries* in 1462, in poor health and preparing to embark on a crusade from which he was unlikely to return, Pius II recognized the consequences he was facing: he risked being remembered as a pope who had not only failed to quell the conciliar movement, but who had also aggravated the threat it posed, both to himself and to his successors.

Pius II's difficult struggle against the conciliar threat is evident in his failed effort to reform the church *in capite*. Weeks after his election, he had appointed a reform commission to tackle what remained the central focus of anti-papal criticism – a corrupt, worldly, and grasping Roman curia. The commission worked fast. Within less than a year, two of its members, Nicholas of Cusa and Domenico de' Domenichi had prepared substantial reform programs.[164] It took five years, however, for Pius to begin to act on their recommendations, and at that point, it was too late. The pontiff only drafted his reform bull, *Pastor aeternus*, in the final weeks of his pontificate – a bull he never had a chance either to revise or to promulgate.[165] His failure to see his plan through not only failed to undermine urgent demand for a council: it also served to deepen widespread scepticism that the papacy could bring about meaningful reform.

It was more than a failed program of reform that seemed to validate these perceptions. Throughout his papacy, Pius II's policies as both pope and prince earned him the reputation of someone who fostered rather than corrected abuses. By exacting heavy annates, by demanding a levy of crusade tithes, by appointing numerous family members to positions in both ecclesiastical and state administration, and by committing himself to costly wars in Italy, he seemed to many to fit the very definition of a pope who was himself in need of reform.[166] Pius II's enemies seized on his long and costly Neapolitan war as a particularly egregious example of abuse, accusing the pontiff of channelling crusade tithes to fight Christians. Together, Pius's actions and the accusations launched against him did more than sully his reputation. In October 1460, he learned that Charles VII of France was threatening to appeal to a council on the basis of the pope's alleged mismanagement of crusade funds.[167] A few months later, German princes met papal demands for crusade tithes with a still greater threat: they proposed to convene a council to deal with a variety of grievances.[168] In short, not only did Pius II not reclaim church reform as a papal prerogative, but he also gave significant momentum to the concept of the council as a vehicle for that crucial activity. Indeed, at one point, he even gave such a vision his own endorsement. In April 1461, in an attempt to break apart a dangerous anti-papal faction of the German princes, Pius pledged that, under certain conditions, he himself would convene a council to address issues of reform.[169]

Pope Pius II also had limited success facing down a very different but equally formidable conciliar threat: the oligarchic strand of conciliar thought underpinning the constitutional ambitions of the college of cardinals.[170] From the beginning of his pontificate, he adopted various means to limit the influence of the cardinals and, in particular, the powers of consultation and consent they demanded in their electoral capitulations of August 1458.[171] Immediately after his election, he radically restructured the curial administration in a way that significantly reduced the college's ability to shape papal policy.[172] From that point onward, Pius was to depend almost exclusively on a small circle of hand-picked advisers known as the *Pieschi*, which included a few cardinals and his personal secretaries Jacopo Ammannati Piccolomini and Goro Lolli. He also repeatedly and boldly disregarded the specific restrictions on his conduct prescribed in the electoral capitulations and from the very moment he swore to uphold them.[173]

Nevertheless, while his strategies may have cut off existing channels of cardinals' authority, they did not prevent the college from opening up new ones – and in a way that both challenged and damaged the sovereign authority claimed by the pope. It would seem, in fact, that Pius II's uncompromising defence of his *plenitudo potestatis* only further galvanized the college in its efforts to check papal absolutism. The cardinals both clashed and competed with Pius most effectively in the context of his crusade efforts and, in particular, at the assembly he designed to coordinate that campaign: the Congress of Mantua. For the eight months the curia was there in residence (June 1459 to January 1460), many in the college, and the Francophile faction in particular, circulated harsh criticisms of Pius's planned campaign.[174] Among other things, they condemned the proposed expedition as childish and unrealistic; they dismissed his leadership as incompetent; and they pronounced his scheme a grave danger to the *status ecclesiae*.[175] At the same time, they sought to expand their own power at the congress by opening independent lines of communication with Venice and France through letters and personal embassies.[176] The cardinals' schemes seriously disrupted Pius's efforts to win support for his crusade; and when events seemed to validate their criticisms, Pius's public image suffered significant damage.[177] At the same time, they exposed the ineffectiveness and injustice of the pope's assault on the capitulations. Pius may have ignored the capitulation that gave the college a role in organizing a crusade. Nevertheless, by voicing and publicizing their opinions subversively, they still found ways to shape those plans in fundamental ways. What is more, they made a compelling case for their right to do so. In advising the pontiff about the dangers of uprooting the curia from Rome, and in warning him of the potentially dangerous consequence of a poorly attended congress, the cardinals came across as wise councillors indeed – ones to whom the pontiff would have done well to listen.[178] In short, in trying to strip them of their power, Pius inadvertently seemed to have strengthened it.

The cardinals' interference in his crusade was only one example of the resilience of the oligarchic strand of conciliar thought during Pius II's pontificate. Indeed, throughout his papacy, many in the college worked systematically to thwart the pontiff's efforts to rule autocratically.[179] In addition to ad hoc and subversive resistance, they also sought to find more permanent and legitimate means of curbing absolute rule and carving out for themselves a share of ecclesiastical sovereignty. In his *Reformatio generalis*, Nicholas of Cusa reiterated the cardinals' essential role in governance by noting that they formed with the pope "a daily, comprehensive council of the church."[180] His reform of the curia also prescribed that the pope subject himself to the evaluation of visitors – a prescription that recalled the demand in the electoral capitulations that the pope submit himself to an annual assessment at the hands of the cardinals.[181] Not surprisingly, these points were not among those Pius II folded into his own reform bull. He was not, however, always as successful in suppressing other challenges from the cardinals. So damaging, in fact, and so relentless were the cardinals' attacks on Pius's mismanagement of the crusade that his defenders found themselves engaged almost constantly in repairing the damage and repairing his reputation.[182] They were still deeply embroiled in those apologetic battles as Pius was writing his *Commentaries*.

Pius also struggled against another dangerous conciliar threat in the Pragmatic Sanction of Bourges (1438), the French royal ordinance that upheld the sovereignty of general councils. That danger seemed to subside momentarily in November 1461 when Louis XI (1461–83) announced that he had abrogated the Pragmatic. He did so, moreover, unconditionally; it was only after making the withdrawal official that he put to Pius a series of political and ecclesiastical requests. What might seem a clear victory for Pius and the papal monarchy proved, in fact, to be the very opposite. Louis's primary request was that the pontiff recognize Duke Réné of Anjou as legitimate heir to the Neapolitan throne instead of King Ferrante. (Pius's recognition was crucial: as pope, he held the Kingdom of Naples as a fiefdom.) From Pius's vantage point, Louis's request seemed more dangerous than the Pragmatic itself. With an Angevin king on the Neapolitan throne, the French would have been in an excellent position to realize their larger ambitions of controlling the papacy. Pius recognized that threat well. As chapter 3 will explain, it had already driven him to take up arms against the Angevins when they had invaded Naples the previous year. When Louis XI learned that Pius would not meet his demands, he did not immediately withdraw his abrogation. But by the end of 1463, he had effectively reinstated the Pragmatic in a series of decrees.[183]

Pius must have anticipated a much easier contest when he looked to eliminate another dangerous instrument of conciliar authority: the Bohemian Compacts. When George Podiebrad had accepted the

Bohemian crown just months before the start of Pius's own reign, he had sworn a solemn oath that he would restore Bohemia to full unity with the Roman Church.[184] The dissolution of the Compacts was, thus, in theory, simply a matter of holding the king to his word.[185] It was not, however, loyalty to the Roman Church that guided Podiebrad's policy or, for that matter, that motivated the oath. His principal concerns were to stabilize the volatile relations between Bohemia's Hussite majority and powerful Catholic minority, and to strengthen his own position as Bohemia's king. In his effort to achieve the latter, he undermined Pius's authority in Germany by joining the powerful faction of princes coalescing around an anti-papal and anti-imperial agenda.[186] His attempts to achieve the former resulted in still greater damage to papal sovereignty. When Podiebrad's embassy arrived in Rome in March 1462, purportedly to present Bohemia's obedience to Pius, the envoys instead offered only the obedience of the king himself. Rather than abrogating the Compacts, as he had pledged to do, Podiebrad now asked that they instead be confirmed. In the face of the king's unexpected recalcitrance, Pope Pius attempted to achieve through coercion what he had expected to do through cooperation: he nullified the Bohemian Compacts.[187]

Rather than strengthening his authority as universal sovereign, Pius's act served ultimately to weaken it, and in several ways. The king's immediate reaction to the pontiff's demands was a source of public embarrassment to the papacy: he threw into prison the papal legate sent to explain Pius's decision. What he did afterwards created far more lasting damage. Podiebrad became a confirmed enemy of the Roman Church and a staunch protector of the Hussite Church. His support helped to ensure that the Compacts remained in force in his kingdom through Pius's reign and beyond. The pope's strategy had, in other words, completely backfired: rather than uprooting a dangerous remnant of the Basel council's legacy, he had instead helped to root it still more firmly in the ground.

Of all the weapons Pius II employed against conciliarism, the one that seemed the boldest and, in its scope, the most ambitious was the bull *Execrabilis*.[188] Drawn up on 18 January 1460, before he departed Mantua, *Execrabilis* prohibited appeals to a future general council from the judgment of the pope on pain of excommunication and lèse-majesté. The bull did much more than attempt to eliminate a practice that had plagued the papacy for years and that had become a familiar recourse to those objecting to crusade tithes.[189] By denying such appeals, Pius was effectively invalidating the claim of *Haec Sancta* that councils were the supreme authority in the church on matters of faith, heresy, and reform, and thereby stripped conciliar theory of one of its critical legitimizing tools.[190] By choosing to draw up such a bull, Pius broke sharply from the approach the papacy had consistently adopted on the Constance legislation since 1447 and one that Pius had himself supported since that time: rather than launching a direct assault on *Haec Sancta* and risking a rebellion, papalist strategy was to remain deliberately ambiguous about the decree's validity.[191]

If, however, the existence of *Execrabilis* was a bold departure from papal precedent, its application was anything but. Drawn up in secrecy, the bull was not even promulgated for another eleven months and was never included in the papal chancery registers. Moreover, the few extant copies indicate that its circulation remained heavily restricted.[192] Perhaps most telling is the fact that despite numerous appeals to future councils, Pope Pius II only drew this weapon twice and with considerable caution.[193] He directed it first at a young Duke Sigismund of Tyrol, familiar to Pius during his years at the imperial court and more recently as a fierce opponent of the Roman Church in his territories. On 13 August 1460, after Pius had excommunicated the duke for imprisoning the bishop of Brixen, Cardinal Nicholas of Cusa, over a jurisdictional dispute, Sigismund appealed his sentence to a future council.[194] It was not until early November, and after the threat of crusade tithes had united German princes in a pro-conciliar coalition, that Pius issued *Execrabilis* publicly for the first time and used it as justification for branding Sigismund and his supporters heretics.[195]

The only other figure to be sanctioned for raising an appeal was Diether von Isenberg, elected to the powerful archbishopric of Mainz on the eve of Pius's own election as pope.[196] Censured by the pontiff for failing to pay his annates on time, Diether appealed his sentence to a future council in February 1461 shortly after assuming leadership of the anti-papal movement. As in the case of Sigismund, Pius did not issue *Execrabilis* immediately: this time he waited a full six months. It was only after he had stripped Diether of his princely allies and settled on the prelate's replacement that he felt confident about drawing it again.[197] Pius's cautious and sparse use of the bull is a strong indication that the weapon he had fashioned looked far more formidable than it actually was.

Just how little power it carried can best be seen from the events that followed its promulgation. The appeals to a future council continued unabated, from Diether, Sigismund, and their allies, including many powerful German princes.[198] While Diether eventually withdrew his appeals and surrendered to the Holy See, it was not *Execrabilis* that cowed him. Instead it was the army of his papally appointed replacement, Adolph of Nassau, who after fighting a bitter war with Diether through the summer of 1462, dealt him a sound defeat that October. Even at his formal submission to the papacy a year later, *Execrabilis* appears to have played no role. There is no evidence that Diether had to acknowledge papal supremacy in order to receive absolution, as the bull stipulated he should.[199] The fate of Sigismund offers further evidence of the impotence of *Execrabilis*. Unable to bring the duke to heel with ecclesiastical weapons, Pius reluctantly agreed to negotiate a peace with the help of Venetian arbiters. The settlement, concluded after the pope's death, did not require the duke to confess to heresy, the very crime for which *Execrabilis* had condemned him.[200] Pius's use of the bull, thus, as much as his cautious approach to employing it, exposed the pope's powerlessness in the face of appeals to future councils. At the same time, it reinforced how helpless he was to strike down the dangerous decree that gave them authority, *Haec Sancta*.

Execrabilis did not just fail to strip conciliar theory of its legal sanction: it actually ended up galvanizing the movement that theory underpinned.[201] It did so, first and foremost, by precipitating a fresh flood of pro-conciliar writings – the largest and fiercest since the 1448 Concordat of Vienna – and precisely at the time when princes' resentments against papal authority in Germany were already on the rise. While this campaign had begun as soon as Pius had excommunicated Sigismund in August 1460, the introduction of *Execrabilis* three months later served to intensify it significantly. Crucial to these relentless assaults was a humanist and lawyer whom Pius had met and admired in his years at Basel: Gregor Heimburg. A tireless publicist for both the anti-papal and the anti-imperial factions of the German princes, Heimburg penned numerous pro-conciliar tracts in defence of Sigismund and Diether and on his own behalf, too. These included his *Appellatio* of January 1461, considered the harshest attack on papal sovereignty before Martin Luther.[202] Directed to both princes and prelates, many of these texts were translated into German; and on the basis of their manuscript copies, they enjoyed a wide circulation.[203]

The arguments put forward in these tracts were threatening on many levels to papal sovereignty and to Pius II specifically. For one, they communicated to a powerful audience, and one already unfavourably disposed towards the papacy, a sharply argued case for the legitimacy of conciliar supremacy. They made that case in part by reiterating the validity of *Haec Sancta* and *Frequens* – the very decrees *Execrabilis* had sought to invalidate.[204] However, these texts did more than confirm the legitimacy of conciliar theory: they also argued that implementing that theory was now more than ever an urgent necessity. The best argument for conciliar supremacy, they argued, was none other than Pius himself. Tracts and pamphlets painted him as a dangerous tyrant, bent on enslaving Germany to his own unbridled *libido*. As evidence of this tyranny, they pointed first and foremost to his repeated contempt for the law – contempt of which *Execrabilis* was only a particularly egregious example. Such attacks did more than assault Pius II's own rule: they also undercut papalists' ongoing efforts to promote the pope as ruler *supra legem*. Pius did more than expose the dangers of a monarch unchecked by positive law: his actions represented an assault on the laws of nature and of God himself.[205] Heimburg frames these accusations in a way that injures Pius's reputation as a humanist as well as indicting his rule as pope. The pontiff's devotion to the Muses is made out to be fundamentally incompatible with respect for the law: indeed, he employs his skills as a rhetorician to conceal his illegal acts.[206] The only means to stop this tyrant-pope, Heimburg maintains, is a general council.[207] "The Council is the fortress of your liberties, the cornerstone of your dignity," he writes to princes and prelates in his 1461 *Appellatio*. "Should the Pope succeed in wresting this stronghold from you, you will find yourselves left without shield or spear and constrained to buy your lives at a heavy price, in the tribute which under the mask of the Turkish war, is levied only to be spent for shameful and criminal purposes."[208] Spurred on by *Execrabilis*, Heimburg underscored for the princes the literal cost they would shoulder by enduring such tyranny. In so doing, he gave conciliar doctrine fresh appeal to princes, and in a way that threatened to do serious damage to Pius's plans for a crusade.

The princes did not, in the end, act on Heimburg's suggestions, but *Execrabilis* went on to weaken papal authority in still other ways. In April 1461, as this pro-conciliar polemic spread and after Heimburg, Diether, and Sigismund had united with the German princes in calling for a council, Pope Pius II dispatched nuncios to Germany to make two substantial concessions: they announced that Pius was amenable to holding a council and that he would levy crusade tithes only with the princes' consent.[209] Just how much *Execrabilis* contributed to this turn of events is unclear, but there is no question that the ferocious outcry against it significantly weakened Pius's position. The result was that the bull ended up accomplishing the very opposite of what it had intended. Designed to suppress appeals to a future council, *Execrabilis* ended up encouraging the use of this weapon. Conceived in part as a means of thwarting resistance to crusade tithes, the bull ultimately led the papacy to consent to such resistance by the German princes. Finally, instead of shielding Pius from the threat of a future council, it resulted in his proposing such an assembly himself.

In the months Pius began composing his *Commentaries*, the war between pope and council continued to rage on all fronts. In Germany, fresh anti-papal tracts were circulating, and more widely than before, thanks largely to the introduction of the printing press.[210] Both Diether and Sigismund continued to win princely support for their appeals to a future council; and in June 1462, the former archbishop of Mainz added military victory to his verbal assaults, crushing in battle the troops of his replacement, Adolph of Nassau. From Bohemia, Pius awaited word through the summer of Podiebrad's pledge to enforce Pius's ruling on the Bohemian Compacts. In August, he learned instead that the king had imprisoned the papal legate. Besieged on all sides, Pius must have felt particularly acute the need to strengthen his defences against his conciliar enemies.

Judging from the chorus of apologies that went up from Pius's allies, that need remained pressing as he wrote. In October 1462, Diether's assaults prompted the strongest verbal response yet from papal publicists: the *Defensorium obedientiae apostolicae* written by German theologian Gabriel Biel. A systematic retaliation against Diether's March 1462 manifesto, the text also mounted a rigorous defence of one of Gregor Heimburg's favourite targets: the pope's position *supra legem* and Pius's alleged abuse of that authority.[211] While Biel was writing in Germany, at the papal curia Teodoro Laelio was penning a tract arguing the cardinals' rightful subordination to the pope.[212] A few months later, Pius himself launched an assault on yet another conciliar menace: himself, or more accurately, his former views on papal sovereignty and the role of general councils. *In minoribus*, the notorious bull of retraction, is perhaps the most powerful evidence that Pius II saw himself writing the *Commentaries* under the threat of conciliarist siege. Just how this text responds to that siege is the topic of chapter 4. The next chapter turns instead to the two other major fronts on which Pius was fighting as he wrote his *Commentaries*. Conciliarism may have been Pius's most formidable enemy, but it was hardly his only one.

3 Papal Sovereignty and the Challenge of Princes: The Experience of Aeneas and Pius

News of this great calamity will prove more damaging to you than to anyone else. For all Latin writers who shall relate the deeds of popes, when they come to your time, will say … beautiful and seemly things of your name, but what they shall add at the end will ruin everything: "but in his time the royal city of Constantinople was captured and sacked by the Turks"… No blame can be attributed to you, and yet, posterity, in its ignorance, will blame you when they learn that Constantinople fell during your reign.[1]

Aeneas Silvius Piccolomini wrote these words to Pope Nicholas V on 12 July 1453 – the very day, or so he tells us, that he learned of Constantinople's spectacular fall to the Ottoman Turks. Aeneas speaks at length in this letter of the devastation suffered by the city's inhabitants, its churches, and its rich cultural legacy. In the passage quoted above, however, he focuses on the damage this event would inflict in the future, and on a very different victim: the pope. The fall of Constantinople came at a time when Nicholas V was attempting to organize a military expedition to prevent just such a catastrophe. In the wake of the Ottoman victory, Aeneas warned, the pope's failed crusade would blacken his otherwise praiseworthy record of accomplishments. In making this prediction to Nicholas, Aeneas tells us something important about himself. For one, he reveals how much stock he put in historical memory and in posthumous reputation. He also demonstrates a profound awareness of the vulnerability of the historical record – how it could be easily misunderstood, misrepresented, and distorted, and how damaging the consequences could be.

A few years later, when Aeneas (now Pius II) was writing the record of his own papacy, the words he had written to Nicholas must have resonated powerfully. Pius's papacy saw no event as catastrophic as the one that took place in May 1453, but his own curriculum vitae – and his own record on his crusade – were just as vulnerable to attack as Nicholas's, if not more. The previous chapter has argued as much by illuminating how Pius's and Aeneas's extensive involvement with the conciliar crisis posed a serious threat to his reputation and policies as a pope and to the very future of papal sovereignty. This chapter illuminates other significant liabilities Pius II faced by analysing his involvement with the two other wars that the fifteenth-century papacy was waging. In one of those wars, the popes were fighting the secular rulers. In the other, they fought as secular rulers themselves.

When he took the papal throne in August 1458, Pius committed himself fully to battle on both fronts. He pushed back with determination against Europe's secular rulers, who continued to compromise the pope's claims to ecclesiastical sovereignty and to challenge his relevance and legitimacy as a universal monarch. To do so, he focused first and foremost on taking charge of the crusade, and to a far greater extent than his immediate predecessors. By controlling the expedition at all stages, Pius could both reassert his authority over secular rulers and strengthen his claims to spiritual sovereignty. At the same time, he could make a case for his own and the papacy's relevance in a world that increasingly questioned the need for a sovereign pope.[2] Pius II was no less determined to assert his authority as a sovereign temporal prince. Within his own territories, he sought to subdue those contesting or disrupting papal rule. To consolidate his authority still further, he fought to make himself head of the Italian League in practice as well as in name.[3]

Pius II wrote the *Commentaries* in the heat of these battles and well aware that he had lost considerable ground. As the second part of this chapter will argue, the crusade was proving a resounding failure as a vehicle for re-establishing the authority, legitimacy, and relevance of the papal monarchy. Indeed, as the analysis below maintains, the pontiff's crusade efforts actually accomplished the opposite of what they were intended to do: they served to weaken these dimensions of papal sovereignty. Deeply humiliating for Pius himself, the pope's crusading failures offered, in turn, powerful testimony of just how powerless the papacy was in the face of Europe's princes. They also served to undercut the papacy's claim to spiritual sovereignty more generally and to jeopardize still further its claim to relevance in fifteenth-century Europe.

Pius's crusade record was not the only liability he faced as a pope bent on subordinating secular powers to papal rule. This chapter will begin by illuminating how, long before he took the papal throne, and in a very different context, Aeneas had defended – and defended in writing – the superiority of princes in ecclesiastical affairs. These views have rarely been explored in scholarship; and in contrast to his conciliar affiliation, they have never been identified as a serious threat to him as pope. Even after abandoning these views, his pre-papal career left him vulnerable as pope, though in a different way: during his tenure at the imperial court, Pius, then Aeneas, had struggled to convince Europe's princes to obey the calls to crusade issued by both pope and Holy Roman emperor. Indeed, on some level, even his own election as pope exposed the weakness of papal authority in the face of secular power. In the context of unfolding these arguments, this chapter will look, in turn, at how Aeneas sought to shore up these weaknesses in his pre-papal career. As we will see in chapter 5, some of the defensive tools he shapes here are redeployed on a grand scale in the context of the *Commentaries*.

Pius II also found himself on the defensive as a temporal prince when he was writing the *Commentaries*. As the second half of this chapter will argue, these vulnerabilities, once again, can be traced in part to his views on papal authority in the early part of his career – and to his penchant for putting them to paper. But overwhelmingly, it was what happened during his six years on the papal throne that created liabilities for the pope. Pius II's papacy is often characterized by scholarship as a period of progress in the papacy's efforts to consolidate its authority over the Papal States.[4] The argument put forward in the third part of this chapter is that many of these successes were not yet visible to Pius as he was writing the *Commentaries*. Nor could they fully mitigate what were significant liabilities in his record as prince. Over the course of his papacy, Pius II had struggled both to assert his authority and to establish his legitimacy – as ruler of the Papal States, as aspiring leader of the Italian League, and as a papal prince. These struggles not only hurt Pius's own legacy: they also threatened to weaken the future of papal monarchy.

A Dangerous Past: Aeneas, Secular Rulers, and Papal Sovereignty (1443–1458)

The position Aeneas took on church sovereignty during the early 1440s is typically characterized as conciliarist, but this is, in fact, only a partial reflection of his stance. Shortly after his transfer to the imperial court at the beginning of 1443, Aeneas was also advocating a significant role for secular rulers in resolving the schism between Pope Eugenius IV and the Council of Basel. Aeneas's stance is in no way comparable to his long tenure in the conciliarist camp. He served only briefly as an advocate of the princes, and there are only a few of his writings that reflect these views. Nonetheless, even this fleeting allegiance to princely ambitions in the ecclesiastical realm would have been a concern and an embarrassment to Pope Pius – especially since he had given these short-lived ideas the permanence of the written word.

Aeneas's views first appear in a work he composed for Frederick III between February and March 1443: a dialogue with five interlocutors, aptly named *Pentalogus*.[5] Framed as a spontaneous discussion that transpired at the imperial court, the text recounts how Aeneas, Frederick, and three other of the emperor's closest advisers debate, among other things, how best to restore unity to the church. The Aeneas in the dialogue begins the discussion by actively discouraging the emperor from throwing his obedience to Pope Eugenius. He explains that by acknowledging him as the true pope, Frederick would seem to be accusing Germany of being in error when it declared itself neutral in the dispute. He adds that such a move might also make Germany look indecisive.[6]

Alone, these passages from the *Pentalogus* would have been embarrassing enough to Pope Pius, but what follows would have been far more troubling. The Aeneas in the dialogue is convinced that the best way to resolve the schism – indeed, the only viable way – is to entrust this decision to a new general council, and a council in which secular rulers are to play a significant role. One of the other interlocutors, Silvester Pflieger, the bishop of Chiemsee, begins by explaining that this council should be preceded by a diet of princes, which, under the direction of the emperor, would consult about the dangers facing the church.[7] On the basis of these discussions, both sides in the dispute (Eugenians and those supporting Felix V and the Basel council), would be summoned. It was no obstacle, Pflieger maintains, if not everyone came. In consultation with the prelates who were present and the princes' ambassadors, the emperor could designate that very assembly a council and empower it to resolve the schism.[8] In this scenario, Pflieger assigns secular rulers a crucial role at various stages of the process: their ambassadors begin by coming together in a joint assembly to discuss matters of the church; the conclusions they reach then form the basis of summoning others to the assembly; those ambassadors then continue to participate in that assembly; and that assembly is then designated a "council" by Frederick III and given the authority to resolve the schism. While Pflieger's plan does not place the resolution of the schism exclusively in the hands of secular rulers, it nonetheless assigns those rulers a vital role in restoring unity to the church.

As a participant in this discussion, Aeneas's contribution is to build a case for an important aspect of Pflieger's plan: the emperor's right to call a council. He unfolds his argument as a response to another speaker, imperial chancellor Kaspar Schlick, who raises serious questions about the emperor's authority in this area.[9] Aeneas draws on a variety of evidence in defence of his position: the Bible, historical precedent, the emperor's responsibility as *protector ecclesiae*, and necessity.[10] He also builds his case by watering down the traditional understanding of what a council is: "For what else is it to call a council than to call together prelates? Who wants to prevent the emperor from summoning prelates to a certain location?"[11] Aeneas is careful to circumscribe the role he sees the emperor playing in the council he summons: Frederick is not actually judging ecclesiastical matters; rather, he is assembling others to do that important work. He also offers an alternative solution that reduces the emperor's role still further: rather than by Frederick, the council could be summoned instead by prelates.[12] Neither of these qualifications, however, changes the fact that in the *Pentalogus* Aeneas writes a work that assigns the emperor a position of sovereignty in the church – a position that was diametrically opposed to the one he defended as Pope Pius II.

Nine months later, Aeneas was at work defending still another plan to resolve the schism and one that substantially expanded the role that secular rulers were to play. In a letter to Pflieger dated 21 December 1443, Aeneas recalls a conversation they had had on an earlier occasion – a conversation that echoes but also modifies the one recorded in the *Pentalogus*. "I remember," Aeneas writes, "when ... we were talking about this very matter [ending the schism] ... your excellency said these words: if I were in the Emperor's position, I would ask all princes to send ambassadors who had full power [*plenitudo potestatis*] to resolve matters of the church. For what princes do, the clergy and the people follow."[13] The position Aeneas assigns Pflieger here is not the same one he assigned him in the *Pentalogus*. There, the princely ambassadors were to work in unison with prelates, and in the context of a council, to bring unity to the church. Here, in contrast, Aeneas suggests that the clergy are not part of this decision-making process – a point he seems to confirm when dismissing potential objections to this plan from Eugenius or the Basel assembly: "Whether they like it or not, princes can assemble and declare themselves for one side or another [Eugenius or the Council of Basel]."[14] It is a position that, interestingly, goes against what he had written in the *Pentalogus*, where he determined that it would be dangerous for secular rulers to resolve the schism on their own.[15] Aeneas's letter also diverges from the *Pentalogus* on another crucial point. It no longer matters to him whether the schism is resolved by a council. The assembly he proposes here is not, he acknowledges, a council.[16] "So be it, and what is that to us? … What matters is that this schism be removed from our midst; whoever can do this can call themselves whatever they want."[17] Here Aeneas clearly and defiantly shifts the responsibility for resolving the schism to the princes, and in a way that is downright dismissive of ecclesiastical authority.

Aeneas advocates this position still more strongly seven days later in a letter to Kaspar Schlick, another interlocutor in the *Pentalogus*, and the one who had opposed the idea that the emperor could call a general council. Noting that the king of France had already signalled his support for the plan proposed in his letter to Pflieger, Aeneas writes:

> Neither pope nor council can block this [solution to the schism], as if without them this could not happen. For secular princes are allowed to assemble even when the clergy is unwilling to, and there, notwithstanding, unity could take place. For the pope whom all princes obey is the undoubted pope … Everyone is of this opinion, that if our princes worshipped idols, we also would do so; and that we would deny not only the pope but even Christ at the urging of secular powers."[18]

Here, Aeneas's plan for resolving the schism is the same one he pitches to Pflieger, but the terms in which he presents it are far more blunt. They betray in Aeneas the same disregard for papal authority – indeed for ecclesiastical authority at all – that he went on to battle so hard against as pope.

Like the other solution to the schism under discussion at the imperial court, the idea of a "third council," the strategy Aeneas discusses in his letters to Pflieger and Schlick was eventually abandoned; indeed, aside from its alleged endorsement by Charles VII, it is not clear whether it got much traction at all, at either the imperial or other princely courts.[19] But for the person who promoted it so ardently, it remained a permanent part of his professional record, a presence in his written correspondence, and a dangerous liability when he became pope. Pius II must have wanted to reject this Aeneas as much as he did the conciliarist one: not only does that man boldly defend the princes' authority to choose a pope, but in so doing, he also explicitly advocates a plan endorsed by none other than his arch-enemy, the king of France.

And reject that Aeneas is just what he did in 1450, when he wrote his second history of the Council of Basel, his *De rebus*. He begins to distance himself from his earlier position when reporting that, in 1436, the duke of Milan had political motives for supporting the council's transfer to Avignon. Aeneas registers his disapproval of the duke's actions immediately and, indeed, draws from them a general statement that turns on its head the stance he took in 1443: "But we did not have a venal soul. We thought synodal business should be transacted not at the pleasure of princes but by the command of God."[20] He continues this retraction still more explicitly when his narrative reaches the very period when he is pitching his plan to the emperor. According to the *De rebus*, the only strategy for resolving the schism emerging from the imperial court was the proposal for a third council. The idea that Aeneas broached to Pflieger and Schlick, that an assembly of princes bring unity to the church, is made here to be the brainchild of the French and, more specifically, of France's king. "The king of France wrote that the word 'council' should be left out, and that it would be good to convene the princes to review and compose the affairs of the church. No one could doubt that the church was to be found where the princes were, and no one could prohibit their gathering."[21] Here, Aeneas is putting in the mouth of the French king the very words that he wrote to Pflieger and Schlick, but this time he is not endorsing them. Not only does the text's disparaging portrait of the king reflect this, but so does the authorial intrusion that follows up this quotation: "Nor is it reasonable that, where there are many princes, things can be well disposed."[22]

Even though the *De rebus* retreats decisively from Aeneas's position of 1443, the work still represented a liability to Pius as pope, and not just because of what it says about councils. Chapter 2 has explained how, when reporting the 1446 peace negotiations between imperial and papal legates, the *De rebus* presents Aeneas's views on councils in terms that conflicted with those of the papacy. That very same section of the text shows him taking another position at odds with the papal curia. The imperial compromise proposal that Aeneas identifies here as his own work asks that the pope recognize the Basel decrees incorporated into the *Acceptatio* of Mainz – decrees that curtailed papal control over ecclesiastical appointments and revenues in Germany, while opening the door for the princes to assume more power in these areas.[23] The papacy's resistance to this condition of the proposal is evident in the very same documents that register its resistance to the proposal's demands about councils.[24] For Pope Pius, the most troublesome record of that resistance appears in his own *De rebus*. Chapter 2 has already noted how, in Aeneas's work, one of the papal legates negotiating the peace in 1446 balked at the conciliar elements of Aeneas's imperial compromise (that legate was the bishop of Bologna, Tommaso Parentucelli, who became Pope Nicholas V). Another of those envoys, Juan de Carvajal, is described as still more opposed to the proposal, and specifically on the basis of what it gave to the princes. According to the *De rebus*, when Aeneas turned his proposal over to the legate, Carvajal "bristled" and replied, "Nothing will happen ... even today we are at the starting blocks."[25] Aeneas makes clear that Carvajal's objections echo those of a sizeable contingent in the curia who set themselves squarely against surrendering papal authority over local churches.[26] He makes equally clear his own exasperation in the face of the legate's opposition: "But Aeneas, indignant, replied, 'Nobody can satisfy you!'"[27]

The Aeneas who makes these remarks and, indeed, who composed the imperial compromise, was not promoting princely authority in the church as a general principle. He seems instead to have simply been doing what a good imperial legate should have been doing, namely, acting in the best interests of the empire. Aeneas recognized that unless the pope compromised with the German princes, he risked creating another and equally damaging schism, between an emperor loyal to Eugenius and the German electoral princes who would throw their support instead to the pope's rival, Felix V. That attitude of compromise, as chapter 2 has demonstrated, was one that Aeneas continued to impress upon Carvajal in the context of his correspondence; and he clearly still considered it fundamental to the papal-imperial alliance that he was fostering when he wrote the *De rebus* in 1450. But what Aeneas advocated as an imperial legate was not at all what he supported as pope. In the *De rebus*, Aeneas was on record enabling the papacy's two chief rivals for ecclesiastical authority, the councils and the princes – rivals that he in his own pontificate had pledged to subdue. For still another reason, then, it seems reasonable to think that in his 1463 bull *In minoribus*, Aeneas included the *De rebus* among his writings that should be forgotten.

For similar reasons, Aeneas would have taken the same atttitude to the oration he delivered at the papal court in early 1447. It was here that he outlined to Pope Eugenius and other members of the curia the demands of the imperial compromise proposal. In addition to advocating a new council (and one that would take on the task of church reform) and calling on the pontiff to recognize the "pre-eminence" of general councils, Aeneas presents the German princes' request that the pope recognize as valid the Basel decrees in the *Acceptatio* of Mainz.[28] Labelling this request as "modest," Aeneas plays down the fact that he was asking the pope to concede substantial authority over the German church. But from the perspective of Pius II, this was anything but a modest proposal. Viewed from the papal throne, it was an unwanted reminder of his dangerous past defending the ecclesiastical prerogatives of princes.

For Pius, the dangers of his involvement with Germany's princes did not simply stem from defending their ecclesiastical prerogatives. It also came ten years later when he was protecting those same prerogatives for the Roman Church. Aeneas in 1456–57 was a member of the college of cardinals and one who exercised control over a series of lucrative benefices in the empire. As such, he represented precisely what the princes had tried and failed to cast off in the imperial compromise proposal: the subordination of the church in Germany to the Roman Church.[29] Chapter 2 has already discussed how, in the context of resisting the crusade tithes recently imposed by Calixtus III, the German princes made Aeneas a target of attack. Indeed, as a living example of what they perceived as Roman oppression, he was, in some sense, the very impetus for their rebellion. That rebellion had ambitious goals. The princes proposed not just to appeal Calixtus's crusade tax to a future council, but they also began to draw up their own version of France's Pragmatic Sanction – a document that they hoped would achieve at last what the imperial compromise had not.[30] In these circumstances, Aeneas did more to weaken the papacy than simply inflame conciliarist sentiment. At the same time, he was galvanizing the other major competitor for papal sovereignty: the princes.

Responding to these attacks in his *Germania* (1457–58), Aeneas develops an argument that, in the context of analysing the *Commentaries*, is worth keeping in mind. The German princes' proposed pragmatic sanction, he argues, is an egregious act of ingratitude: Germany has received an inestimable number of benefits from the Apostolic See.[31] Aeneas makes no attempt to go through all of these gifts, but he does single out the ones he considers most significant. One is, of course, Christianity, and with it, the chance for salvation. The other is political in nature: according to Aeneas, it was the popes who transferred to Germany the Roman Empire and with it, a pre-eminence unmatched in Europe.[32] The German princes of his own day, Aeneas bemoans, show no respect for this imperial authority; and their states have suffered significantly as a result.[33] But if they were to show due respect for this papal gift of empire, he writes, and if, at the same time they were, among other things, to give their obedience to the pope, they would become still more powerful rulers: "If you do this, there is no doubt that, recuperating your old name, you will deliver laws to many great peoples."[34] Aeneas here is defending papal sovereignty by connecting it both to Germany's past political successes and to its future political growth – and it is growth defined in terms of Germany's princes as much as their emperor. Just how obedience to the papacy could translate into political benefits Aeneas does not explain. What he does do, however, is suggest that in their capacity as sovereigns, the popes have a role to play in the politics of fifteenth-century Europe and an important contribution to make. As we will see in chapter 5, it is an idea that Pope Pius II takes up and expands upon still further in the *Commentaries*.

The events of 1456–57 were not the only occasion in which Aeneas found himself defending papal authority against secular rulers. Between 1454 and 1455, Emperor Frederick III convened a series of diets at Regensburg (April 1454), Frankfurt (September 1454), and Wiener Neustadt (February 1455) in order to organize a military response to the recent collapse of Constantinople. Aeneas attended all of these diets in the capacity of imperial legate, and as chief spokesman for the emperor who, much to his legate's frustration, attended none of these assemblies in person. Working alongside the papal legate, Aeneas exhorted the princes and ambassadors (those who had bothered to come) to organize and mobilize their troops. However, while a few princes gave what seemed like promising responses, most were unwilling to make any firm commitment to military action.[35] In a letter to Carvajal dated October 1454, Aeneas describes his frustration and disappointment at the princes' inaction. He also, interestingly, concludes that rhetoric was an insufficient tool for accomplishing his task: "I think that even if Cicero or Demosthenes were to make a case [for the crusade], they would not be able to move these hard hearts."[36]

To Aeneas, the princes' resistance to the crusade was as much a papal defeat as an imperial one, and this despite the strained relations between empire and papacy at the time.[37] In his oration at the Diet of Frankfurt, Aeneas makes note of Nicholas V's spiritual contributions to the crusade,[38] while his November letter to Carvajal reports that in the same assembly princes were attacking the pope as well as the emperor.[39] It was also in the context of these diets that Aeneas wrote to Benvoglienti that neither pope nor emperor was being given his due – the letter that begins chapter 1 of this book.[40] Aeneas's words here are significant. In recognizing the diets as a failure for the pope as much as for the emperor, he signals how he might have viewed from the papal throne his own involvement with these assemblies. To Pope Pius, his failure to rally the princes to the idea of crusade did not just expose the fragility of imperial rule: it also put on view how compromised papal authority was in the face of secular powers. Thus, more than simply a low point in his career at the imperial court, his struggles in these diets must also have seemed a liability for his own papacy – especially since one of his chief aims as pope was to take charge of a crusade.

It is in the context of these failed crusade efforts that Aeneas began to develop in his writings another view of princes that, like the one he presents in the *Germania*, will resurface in the *Commentaries* as an important apologetic tool. Even before the three imperial diets had convened, Aeneas looked disfavourably on the princes' indifference to papal and imperial appeals to organize a crusade. In another letter to Benvoglienti, this one dated 25 September 1453, he accuses Europe's princes of putting their private interests above public ones when they adopt such an attitude.[41] It was an interpretation that he would put forward again in the context of his correspondence[42] and also in other texts that date to this period, most notably, his dialogue *Dialogus de somnio quodam* (1453–57?)[43] and the *Historia de dieti Ratisponensi* (1454).[44] What Aeneas means by "private" in these writings is of considerable significance. On the one hand, it refers to personal self-interest, stemming primarily from undisciplined passions and from avarice in particular. Following Cicero, he identifies "avaritia" as the worst possible characteristic of a prince.[45] For Aeneas, however, private interests meant something else, too. In his *Historia de dieti Ratisponensi*, his eyewitness account of the Regensburg diet, the prince who attends to his "private interests" is not someone who is neglecting the affairs of his state: rather, he is someone who is attending to them diligently. The contrast Aeneas is drawing here is beween the political interests of a prince and the interests of a higher authority whom that prince is bound to obey. These definitions of public and private emerge in the *Historia* when Aeneas is explaining how the duke of Burgundy made the decision to attend the diet. When the duke received the emperor's invitation to the assembly, Aeneas reports, he was immersed in a war, defending Flanders against a recent English invasion. "He wondered if he should stay in order to protect his fatherland [*patria*]," Aeneas continues, "but he esteemed the emperor's orders more than the demands of his subjects; he put more important affairs ahead of minor ones and public ahead of private."[46] The duke's decision to put holy war above his own political one is clearly a move of which Aeneas approves: Burgundy is the hero of the *Historia* and the mirror image of Frederick III who, choosing to stay back in Austria to attend to business there, appears in the text as no better than the other princes.[47]

Aeneas's ideas of what constitutes "public" and "private" make sense in both the intellectual and political contexts in which he was working. They align, for one, with the vision of empire he put forward in his treatise on imperial authority, *De ortu et auctoritate imperii Romani* (1446). In this text, he makes a case for why princely interests should be subordinated to imperial authority, and he defines public good exclusively in terms of what benefits the empire.[48] But Aeneas's views on public and private interests also fit with the particular historical context in which he found himself in the early 1450s as one of the chief advocates of the crusade. By describing princes' interests of state as "private," he was using damning language to conceal what, from the princes' own standpoint, constituted legitimate reasons for not obeying calls to crusade. Effectively, he was delegitimizing their resistance to pope and emperor. At the same time, Aeneas was concealing from view what was, from his own perspective in the 1450s, a dangerous truth: that one of the princes' main motives for ignoring calls for a crusade was their deep contempt for papal and imperial authority.

In 1458, while Aeneas was equipping himself with this powerful arsenal of verbal weapons, secular rulers continued to challenge papal sovereignty, and in a way that affected him more directly than ever before. Dispatches of Milanese and Neapolitan ambassadors make clear that Aeneas's election to the papal throne was largely engineered by Duke Francesco Sforza and King Ferrante of Naples.[49] Driven by fear that a French or Francophile pope would be the cardinals' choice, the two princes promoted as their candidate Domenico Capranica, the cardinal in whose service Aeneas had travelled to Basel twenty-six years before. When Capranica died suddenly on the eve of the election, Sforza and Ferrante scrambled to find someone else in the college to oppose the favourites of France, Guillaume d'Estouteville and pro-French Giovanni Castiglioni.[50] Several candidates emerged, but in the end they settled on Aeneas; and their ambassadors proceeded to make their case to the colleges of cardinals.[51]

Given that one of the aims of Pius II's papacy was to reclaim a position of authority over secular powers, the circumstances of his election would have been particularly humiliating to him. What made them even more difficult to swallow was what he had written fifteen years before. In both the *Pentalogus* and his correspondence, Pius was on record arguing that secular powers be given the authority to resolve the schism and thereby determine who was the legitimate pope. Now pope himself, Pius was living out an idea that he had long since abjured: he was himself the product of a conclave that, while not entirely orchestrated by secular authorities, had been shaped nonetheless by their influence. In the battle over ecclesiastical sovereignty, Pope Pius II thus suffered a loss to Europe's princes even before his papacy even began and, in so doing, created another liability both for his own reputation and for the papal monarchy.

Pius II, Secular Rulers, and the Failed Crusade (1458–1464)

It wasn't long before the newly elected pope began preparing his most ambitious counter-attack against Europe's secular powers and their challenges to papal sovereignty. Within the first few weeks of his election, Pius began actively planning an expedition against the Turks, and although his attention was at times diverted from this venture, the significance of his initiative never changed.[52] Pius undertook to organize a crusade for many reasons, but there is no question that he envisioned such a venture in part as a means of re-establishing papal sovereignty over those contesting it so fiercely.[53] Directing a crusade would enable him, for one, to reassert his authority over secular rulers in a direct and powerful way – by taxing their territories, controlling their armies, winning their obedience, and in some cases, reclaiming control over churches in their states. By taking charge of an expedition in defence of the Christian faith, he could also help to rehabilitate the papacy's compromised claims to spiritual sovereignty. At the same time, he would be dismissing pressing questions about the relevance of the pope as a spiritual sovereign. In the face of the Ottomans' rapid advance, a crusader pope would not simply be relevant to fifteenth-century Europe: he would be indispensable. Finally, by reclaiming crusade leadership as a papal prerogative, Pius could prevent secular rulers from making it their own, and Pius was well aware that over the last several years they had been trying to do just that. Of particular concern to the pontiff were the crusading ambitions of the French kings, who saw leading such an expedition as a way to fulfil their own aspirations to control both papacy and empire.[54] Preventing the French from capturing this role was, for Pius, almost as important as gaining it for himself.

The crusade that Pius II had envisioned was not the one that unfolded – indeed, it ended up accomplishing the opposite of what he had intended. Rather than an occasion for reasserting his authority over Europe's secular powers, Pius's crusade quickly transformed into an opportunity for them to express their resistance to that authority, and in a very public and sustained way. That resistance took many forms. It manifested itself first in how they responded when the pope convened a congress of princes in the northern Italian city of Mantua to make plans for the expedition.[55] Despite being summoned to this assembly well in advance, most of the princes and their envoys arrived months after its scheduled opening in June 1459, if they came at all, and departed before it concluded.[56] Not even Emperor Frederick III, whom Pius envisioned as the central partner in his campaign, made an appearance, and the delegation he sent was so powerless that Pius promptly demanded a new one be dispatched.[57] Most of the princes who did appear actively and successfully resisted the pope's efforts to secure their financial and military contributions to his campaign. Sceptical about the viability of his plans and protective of the interests of their states, they considered it good judgment to hold back definitive expressions of support.[58] Florence and Venice refused to sign the document that granted Pius the power not only to collect tithes in their territories but also to reassert sovereignty over their churches.[59] The German envoys insisted on bringing Pius's requests before a diet to be convened in Nuremberg, a prospect that must have alarmed Pius given the direction taken by such assemblies in the past. France, indignant that Pius had recognized the Aragonese and not the Angevin claimant to the crown of Naples, was entirely unresponsive to the pope's requests.[60] In short, the Congress of Mantua was hardly the triumphant reassertion of papal authority that Pius had intended it to be. On the contrary, the assembly allowed Europe's princes to loosen themselves still further from the hold of their spiritual sovereign.

As he attempted to move forward with his expedition, Pius continued to meet with the princes' fierce and frequent resistance. Almost without exception, secular rulers balked at the crusade tithes the pontiff sought to impose on their states, and even those who had pledged financial support at Mantua backed down from their promises to do so.[61] In Germany, resistance to crusade tithes was so strong that, out of fear of inciting further rebellion, Pius promised that none would be collected without the princes' prior approval. Money was not the only thing these rulers refused to give the pope. Aware that the success of his expedition hinged on first creating conditions of peace in Europe, Pius had been working feverishly since announcing the crusade to forge truces and create peace among those at war.[62] No sooner had the Congress of Mantua concluded in January 1460 than the few fragile peace agreements he had succeeded in forging fell apart. In the ensuing weeks and months, Pius looked on helplessly as the princes of Europe descended into battle against one another. Even he became embroiled in a costly war on the Italian peninsula, defending King Ferrante of Naples from both internal rebellion and French invasion.[63] This instability offered still more evidence that, in the years following the congress, Pius was proving no more effective in turning secular rulers to his will than he had at Mantua. Rather than a means of reasserting authority over Europe's princes, his crusade continued to expose how very little authority he really had.

In October 1463, when Pius II announced the crusading forces would depart under his leadership in June the following year, it was not because he had succeeded at last in bending European rulers to his sovereign authority. Rather than commanding a pan-European expedition, he was joining an alliance of a few rulers who had come together of their own accord. The duke of Burgundy's participation came on the basis of terms he himself had set – that he would undertake the mission provided that another prince of equal stature joined. In the case of Venice and Hungary, moreover, it was the victories of Mehmed II, not Pius II, that made them declare war.[64] When Burgundy then withdrew from the expedition in the spring of 1464, and when the duke of Milan declined Pius's request to serve as the crusade captain, it became still clearer that the pope's crusade was in no way the product of his sovereign authority.

It is against this backdrop that we can understand the last steps Pius took in his crusade. In the summer of 1463, frail and unwell, he made the difficult journey north to Ancona, where the crusading fleet was to gather. His deteriorating health made it unlikely that he would be able to fulfil his plan of joining the expedition; indeed, when he died on 15 August, few of the ships had even arrived in port.[65] But simply by coming to Ancona Pius was making a powerful statement that he was still in charge of the crusade. The reality, of course, was very different. As this chapter has argued, from beginning to end, the narrative of Pius's attempted crusade told the story of secular rulers' increasing independence from papal authority. Such a narrative was a dangerous liability for a pope who had focused so much of his pontificate on reversing this very trend. It also threatened to cause serious long-term damage to the papal monarchy as it sought to protect its ecclesiastical sovereignty.

Pius was no more successful in making the crusade an occasion for reinforcing his claims to spiritual sovereignty. The pontiff may have presented his Turkish expedition as a courageous defence of the Christian religion, but Europe's rulers saw it in very different terms. For many, the crusade was simply Pius's excuse to fleece them of their wealth and a prime example of why the church needed reform first and foremost at its head. In Germany, in particular, the financial demands of the crusade bred fresh criticisms of a grasping Roman Church, while voices from France reinforced the same impression of unethical leadership: the pope, so the rumours went, was funnelling crusade tithes into the wars he was waging against fellow Christians.[66] Thus, instead of underscoring his moral integrity, Pius's crusade efforts actually ended up damaging his reputation. In so doing, the pontiff left the papacy's claims to spiritual sovereignty even more compromised than when he had started.

At the same time, Pius's crusade efforts served to undermine the papacy's efforts to defend the relevance of its sovereign power in fifteenth-century Europe. For Pius II, claiming leadership of the crusade was one way to accomplish that goal. But he could only succeed if others considered him up to the task; and it soon became clear that many were sceptical of his capabilities as well as his intentions. Their doubts stemmed in part from the particular kind of leadership role Pius envisioned for himself in the crusade. In contrast to the popes who preceded him, Pius planned to take control of all stages of the crusade, including the military dimension of the campaign.[67] It was an area in which he had little expertise, and his inexperience soon raised serious questions from the princes about the viability of his plans. These questions and concerns continued to surface through the final months of crusade preparations, as the pontiff struggled to collect sufficient revenues to fund the expedition and to organize his troops in time for the scheduled date of departure.[68] Pius's difficulties in these areas proved costly, and to more than the expedition itself. They offered concrete evidence that it was a risky venture to entrust crusade leadership to a pope.

If Pius's crusade compromised the papacy by raising these concerns, it also did so by spawning a wave of competing expeditions. Only a few months after he had concluded the Congress of Mantua, Pius learned that French envoys were in talks with Venice about organizing such a venture.[69] A year later, Poland and Bohemia began organizing a League of Princes whose leadership was to be entrusted to France and whose immediate order of business was to take up arms against the Turks.[70] In May 1462, Pius learned that French plans to organize a crusade were proceeding in earnest: Louis XI was planning to convene a diet to discuss organizing his campaign. A few months later the Bohemian king, George Podiebrad, began soliciting princely support for his League of Princes and the crusade he hoped it would undertake.[71] None of these plans ever came to fruition, but the repercussions for Pius and the papacy were significant nonetheless. Rather than thwarting French crusading ambitions, Pius had instead helped to enflame them, and in so doing, endanger papal sovereignty still further. At the same time, he was raising anew the question that had plagued his predecessors: if secular rulers were themselves able to organize and lead a crusade, what need was there for the pope?

When Pius II began writing the *Commentaries* in spring 1462, he would have been well aware of the liabilities that his crusade plans had created both for himself and for the papacy more generally. As a vehicle for reasserting the authority, legitimacy, and relevance of papal monarchy, his planned expedition had failed and failed repeatedly – and on a very public stage. Indeed, because Europe's secular rulers had rejected his demands so soundly, had challenged his spiritual integrity so sharply, and had dismissed so completely his claims to crusade leadership, the pope had actually weakened the authority, legitimacy, and relevance of papal sovereignty. Judging from the letter he wrote to Nicholas V in 1453, Pius would have recognized the long-term consequences of his crusade efforts. He also would have known how he could begin to shore up these liabilities: he needed to take control of his own historical record. Doing so was the best way to ensure that the narrative of his crusade did not do for him what the fall of Constantinople had done to Nicholas, that is, "ruin everything."

Further Liabilities: Pius as Prince

While Pius II could not declare victory over Europe's princes at the end of his pontificate, he was able to celebrate some significant victories as a prince himself. By the end of 1463, he had succeeded in consolidating his authority over a good part of the Papal States. He did so by finally subduing the dangerously rebellious Sigismondo Malatesta and by stripping him of most of the territories he ruled as papal vicar; by neutralizing the equally threatening Jacopo Piccinino, Malatesta's fellow *condottiere* and occasional ally; by beating back the Angevins and their allies in the protracted war over the Neapolitan crown; and, with the help of his nephews, by strengthening his authority significantly in the Romagna, the Agro Romano, and the neighbouring Kingdom of Naples.[72]

But when Pius, the prince, took a longer look at his curriculum vitae – at his pre-papal career as well as his entire pontificate – he would have found good reason to be on the defensive. At different points in his pre-papal career, Aeneas had taken positions that clashed directly with his later views on the pope's temporal rule. Of greater concern was what happened during his papacy. In the course of his pontificate, his decisions and actions had sparked intense rebellion against his authority, seriously aggravated existing instability in the Papal States, and stirred up questions about the legitimacy of the pope's temporal power. Still greater were his weaknesses on the diplomatic front. Pius had failed, and failed repeatedly, to gain leadership of the Italian League and, in so doing, had weakened the papacy's position in what was already a delicate alliance. Just as troubling, his pontificate had exposed serious tensions and incompatibilities in his dual role of papal prince – a role that was vital for the papacy's future survival.

Pius's liabilities on this front, as on all the others, can be traced to a period long before he ever imagined he would be pope. From his vantage point on the papal throne, the greatest danger of his earlier career lay in his *Pentalogus* (1443). As seen in the previous section, Aeneas's stance in this text was a serious embarrassment for a pope bent on re-establishing spiritual sovereignty over Europe's secular rulers. It was equally problematic for a pope whose aim was to consolidate his power in the Papal States and to take the reins of the Italian League. Those liabilities emerge in particular in the second half of the *Pentalogus*, when the conversation shifts from resolving the schism to the prospect of Frederick's imperial coronation. Aeneas takes the occasion to present the emperor with an ambitious political program and one opposite to Pius's own interests as pope. Aeneas counsels Frederick not simply to travel to Italy for the coronation: he should go there with the intent to conquer it, with the help of Duke Filippo Maria Visconti of Milan and King Alfonso of Naples.[73] Aeneas, in short, envisioned the emperor in the role that, in more circumscribed terms, Pius reserved for himself as pope: the fulcrum of a system of Italian alliances and the dominant political force on the peninsula. But the *Pentalogus* is still more dismissive of the pope's temporal authority. Just before shifting from council to coronation, the discussion turns to the Donation of Constantine.[74] Here, it is Kaspar Schlick who speaks what, from Pope Pius's perspective, were particularly dangerous words. Condemning the document as a fake and irrelevant to papal claims to temporal power, Schlick characterizes the popes as usurpers of imperial lands. The imagery he uses to do so is vivid: the pope is like a pregnant dog who, after birthing and raising her puppies in her master's home, tries to evict him.[75] In short, the *Pentalogus* assigns a role to Frederick that not only ignores the papacy's diplomatic aspirations: it also robs them of the principate altogether.

After 1446, now reconciled with Eugenius IV and committed to a papal-imperial alliance, Aeneas had developed a very different position on the pope's temporal authority from the ones he had recorded in 1443. In his treatise on imperial authority, the *De ortu et auctoritate imperii Romani* (1446), Aeneas explicitly acknowledges the pope's right to rule the Papal States.[76] In the *Dialogus de Somnio Quodam* (1453–57) he offers a robust defence of that claim to temporal power,[77] and in the *Germania* (1457–58), which he wrote as cardinal from the papal curia, the popes of the *Pentalogus* have been turned on their heads: rather than stealing territory from the emperor, they are the ones who gave Germany the empire in the first place.[78] Viewed together, these texts show Aeneas distancing himself further and further from the views he put forward in 1443. It is reasonable to think that when he ascended the papal throne in 1458 he would want – and need – to do so even more.

This shift in Aeneas's views makes it all the more interesting to discover a position he takes in a text written on the eve of his papacy, the *De Europa* (1458).[79] As has been noted in recent scholarship, the *De Europa* offers an overwhelmingly flattering portrait of the popes as both spiritual and temporal rulers. But it also develops an even more glowing one of Alfonso of Naples – the king who, as chapter 1 explained, had long been a menace to the papacy and on several levels. Since his conquest of Naples in 1442, Alfonso had clashed with Eugenius IV, Nicholas V, and Calixtus III over ecclesiastical privileges; he had proven a serious obstacle to the crusading plans of the latter two, and he had consistently represented a dangerous threat to the stability and integrity of the Papal States.[80] The *De Europa* alludes to some of these tensions, but its emphasis is on a very different kind of dynamic between the king and the papacy: mutual respect and cooperation.[81] Indeed, hardly a threat to papal territory, Alfonso is shown again and again defending and protecting the Papal States.[82] To some extent, this rosy picture of royal-papal relations benefited the papacy: Alfonso had come out the winner in some of these conflicts, and thus by concealing them, Aeneas was also masking the papacy's weaknesses. But if the portrait of Alfonso helps to hide some of the papacy's vulnerabilities, it exposes others, and first and foremost on the diplomatic front. The *De Europa* hails Alfonso as "magister italicae pacis," a claim it amply substantiates with examples of his peacemaking prowess.[83] In making this designation, Aeneas demonstrates that even as late as 1458, he was promoting ideas at odds with the Roman curia. The portrait of Alfonso as peacemaker would certainly not have been well received by Pope Calixtus III, who knew Alfonso as a dangerous warmonger, and who saw him turning the Italian League to his own purposes. Moreover, it also would not have been welcome to Pope Pius II who, determined to gain leadership of that league, sought the title *magister italicae pacis* for himself.

Shortly after he ascended the papal throne, Pius seemed poised to do just that and in a way that promised to eliminate the greatest weaknesses in the Papal States. The reason was Ferrante of Naples. The young king had succeeded his father Alfonso only weeks before the conclave that had elected Pius, and he had yet to win the recognition of his papal overlord as legitimate king. The precariousness of his position was further underscored by internal rebellions that had erupted shortly after his succession. In Ferrante's vulnerabilities Pius found an excellent opportunity to strengthen his own position as prince. He did so by making his support for the king's claim to the throne conditional on several factors. Among other things, Ferrante was to ensure that Jacopo Piccinino, who was currently in his pay, withdrew from papal territory (the *condottiere* at the time was occupying the strategic town of Assisi). The pope also demanded full powers of arbitration in the disagreement that Ferrante had inherited from his father that pitted the king, papal vicar Federigo da Montefeltro, and Piccinino against another papal vicar, Sigismondo Malatesta.[84] The terms of the king's investiture would go a long way towards combatting the chief sources of instability in the Papal States: a powerful military captain ambitious to carve out his own independent state; internal division between *signori* in the Marche and Romagna; and an untrustworthy papal vicar, who was very friendly with the French. The agreement would also significantly strengthen Pius's vulnerability in the Italian League by making an ally out of the member who had traditionally been the most threatening to the papacy; and it would give him a voice of authority in the context of this alliance. Finally, and most importantly, by setting aside Angevin claims to the Neapolitan throne, Pius's agreement with Ferrante was thwarting French ambitions to expand into southern Italy. In so doing, the pontiff was not simply shielding papal territories from French encroachment: he was also protecting the entire peninsula from a similar threat.

Pius's plans unravelled quickly and dramatically, however – so much so, in fact, that the situation in the Papal States soon grew markedly worse and stayed that way for some time. Rather than peace and stability, it was war, rebellion, and serious French threat that defined most of his papacy – and all on a far grander scale than in the reigns of his immediate predecessors. At one point or another during his pontificate, all the weak points of the Papal States grew weaker, and in part because of his efforts as a peacemaker. Indignant at the settlement Pius had mediated between them in August 1459, Piccinino violated the terms almost immediately and in so doing threw the northern region of the Marche into upheaval. He stepped up his attack on Malatesta's lands, prompting the latter to turn again to the French for support. By early 1460, the situation had worsened significantly: both had allied with the Angevins and with one another, and Piccinino was moving his troops southward to join the forces fighting against Ferrante. Pius's pontificate, thus, did not simply see a sharp resurgence of hostile forces within the Papal States: it also witnessed their convergence.[85]

It did so, moreover, on a scale unprecedented in the fifteenth century. In the summer of 1460 Piccinino turned south, joining forces with a series of other insurgents – baronial families in the Agro Romano (the Savelli, d'Anguillara, and Colonna) and Roman rebels led by Tiburzio di Maso. Aided both by the French and by Pius's long absence from the city, these varied groups combined to create months of violent upheaval in and around Rome.[86] Because of where it was taking place, this insurgence was both particularly dangerous and particularly humiliating for Pius. Having long since adjourned the Congress of Mantua (the final session had been in January 1460), the pontiff was not able to return to the city until October – and when he did, he came under armed guard.[87]

Along with instability, the surge of rebellions raised fresh questions about the legitimacy of Pius's rule in the Papal States, and nowhere more so than in Rome. Here, where republican sentiment ran deep and where the history of anti-papal uprising was long, the pontiff endured one of the fiercest revolts of his pontificate. The make-up of the rebellion was as troubling to Pius as its intensity: the handful of rebels who initiated the upheaval were reported to be widely if secretly supported by the Roman citizenry, including its ruling factions. Such widespread and sustained resistance to papal government served for Pius as an unwanted reminder that his claims to temporal power were no more secure than his spiritual ones.[88]

While the pontiff had subdued the rebellion by late 1460, he did not regain significant control of the region until the following spring, by which time the situation to the north was rapidly deteriorating. A year before, Malatesta had violated the peace agreement of 1459 by occupying territories that had reverted to direct papal control. Subduing the rebellious vicar proved difficult. In July 1461, papal forces suffered a devastating loss to Malatesta and his powerful army. Struggling to contain him militarily, Pius had issued against him sentences of excommunication. The fact that the pope had to do so repeatedly suggests that his spiritual weapons were no stronger than those used on the battlefield.[89]

The interconnected war in the Regno exposed still further weaknesses in Pius's authority as prince. Fighting alongside his allies, Ferrante and Sforza, papal troops were unorganized, their *condottieri* poorly controlled, and their supplies inadequate. Their poor performance, moreover, seemed largely to blame for some of the weakest moments in the allied campaign. It is no surprise, then, that as a military strategist, Pius won little respect from his chief ally, Francesco Sforza, who was, in contrast to the pope, a distinguished *condottiere*. The two clashed repeatedly over central points of strategy and over the idea of forging a peace treaty with the French. The war also exposed the financial fragility of the Papal States. Shouldering the long war, Pius effectively drained the papal treasury and stopped a series of other projects in their tracks.[90] At the same time, the war with Naples drained the pope of something equally precious: his credibility as *magister italicae pacis*.

Much to Pius's frustration, that title was no more applicable to his role in the Italian League. From the very start of his papacy to the end, the pontiff failed in his efforts to gain leadership of the alliance – indeed, at times he struggled simply to win the respect owed him as one of its members. That impotence was clearly on display whenever he called upon the league to come to his defence (in theory, the very reason for its existence). In 1459, when Ferrante balked at Pius's command to drive Piccinino from papal territory, the league offered the pontiff no support; and when he appealed shortly thereafter to Florence and Venice to take up arms in defence of Ferrante, they refused, declaring themselves neutral in the conflict.[91] Aeneas was successful in forging a crucial axis of alliance with league members Milan and Naples, but even these princes were ultimately more committed to protecting their own interests than to serving the defensive mandates of the league. Ferrante refused to comply with Pius's demands about Piccinino, for example, out of concern the *condottiere* would join forces with the French.[92] Still more dangerous were Pius's differences with Sforza. The Milanese duke was without question Pius's most reliable and strongest ally, but his own political ambitions left him far more sympathetic to the French than Pius liked. For still other reasons, Pius viewed his alliance with Sforza as a mixed blessing. The duke was not simply Pius's ally: in many ways he was the means to achieving the pope's goals. It was Sforza who helped defend the Papal States while Pius was away in Mantua; and it was Sforza who played a key role in stabilizing Bologna, one of the most important and most unstable cities in papal territory. It was Sforza's troops again who protected Pius when he returned to the city in October 1462, and Sforza who played an important part in forging several of the pope's peace agreements. In short, Pius was not just indebted to Sforza: like his predecessors, he was also overshadowed by the powerful Milanese duke.[93] More than simply an ally, Sforza was to the pope also a dangerous competitor.

Pius II's diplomatic impotence in Italy is also revealed in the fact that league members, either individually or in unison, actively worked against papal interests. They did so by covertly funding Pius's enemies (including Piccinino) and by maintaining good relations with the French.[94] Particularly troublesome for the pontiff was their involvement – or, from Pius's perspective, their interference – in his dealings with Sigismondo Malatesta. In the summer of 1462, as the pope stepped up his campaign against the *signore*, the Italian League put heavy pressure on the pontiff to pull back – a position they took in defence of their own political interests. Then in 1463, Venice accepted from Pandolfo Malatesta, Sigismondo's brother, the vicariate of Cervia – effectively annexing territory under the pope's jurisdiction. In October of that year, as Pius was setting terms of peace for the now-defeated vicar, league members again stepped in to plead for leniency. This time the pope conceded. Intending to strip Malatesta of all his possessions, Pius bent to the league's demands and gave him Rimini.[95]

The pope's concession to Malatesta was in many ways symbolic of the relationship he had with the Italian League throughout his papacy. Pius remained from beginning to end a subordinate member of the alliance – sometimes ignored, sometimes bullied, and little respected. On one level, his position was little different from that of his predecessors, Calixtus III and Nicholas V. But given that Pius depended on the league's support far more than his predecessors had, his struggles and his failures were that much greater.

It was not just Pius, the prince, who had reason to be concerned by this record in temporal politics. It was also Pius the spiritual sovereign. One of the central challenges facing the fifteenth-century papacy was the growing importance of the pope's role as secular ruler. Were those responsibilities compatible with or detrimental to those the pope assumed as a spiritual monarch? Pius II's pontificate could certainly be seen as evidence of the inherent incompatibilities of these two dimensions of his power. His decision to enter the Neapolitan war effectively brought his crusade preparations to a halt, and the money he continued to invest in those military campaigns left little for his war against the Turks. It was not, however, just that Pius the prince could be seen as incompatible with Pius the pope: he *was* seen that way, and portrayed in just those terms by none other than the kings of France. In October 1460, a few months after Pius had entered Ferrante's war, the papal court received confirmation that the French were planning to appeal to a council on the grounds that Pius was neglecting the crusade. In February of the following year, news came that the king himself was at work organizing that council. The threats and accusations continued in subsequent months and years. In May 1462, Louis XI said that he would hold a crusade diet in the face of Pius II's incompetence. In July 1463, after Bosnia falls to the Turks, the French circulated rumours and sent letters to both Pius and the cardinals that accused the pontiff of pursuing "his desires."[96] Stung by the pope's decision to invest Ferrante with the Neapolitan crown, France fought back hard against the pope and with words as much as with swords. In so doing, it effectively made of Pius II the very symbol of why a pope could not at the same time be a prince.

Pius's Neapolitan policy compromised more than his image as a papal prince. It also threatened his spiritual sovereignty in real terms. As the previous paragraph has demonstrated, the French kings menaced Pius with something far more dangerous than damaging rumours: they threatened to call or at least to appeal to a council. Again and again they drew this weapon – in November 1458, October 1460, February 1461, and May 1464. They also did so more indirectly in November 1461, when they withdrew the Pragmatic Sanction of Bourges, only to request shortly thereafter that Pius withdraw support from Ferrante.[97] On all these occasions, the French kings acted on their conciliarist views because of the pope's policy on Naples. The motives of that policy were, of course, as much spiritual as they were temporal: a French king in the Regno would likely result in French domination of the papacy as well as of the Papal States. Nevertheless, it was in his capacity as a secular ruler – prince of those Papal States and member of the Italian League – that Pius II adopted the Neapolitan policy that he did. In other words, it was Pius the temporal prince who was jeopardizing the sovereign authority of Pius, the pope.

That Pius recognized the repercussions of this dilemma is clear from his reaction to France's conciliar threats. In early 1461, Pius turned his attention and troops from the war in the Regno to the rebellions in the Papal States. In 1462, when conciliarist pressure from the French was again particularly intense, Pius approached the Angevins about forging a truce in the Neapolitan war, and he continued to pursue plans for such a settlement well into 1463.[98] Pius was willing to make such a radical shift in his temporal policy because he recognized the dangers that policy posed. In supporting Ferrante, Pius had struck a serious blow to his efforts to suppress conciliar forces and to his integrity as sovereign of the church. At the same time, his policy had weakened him severely in the face of his most dangerous enemy.

In the late spring and early summer of 1462, when Pius first turned his attention to the *Commentaries*, the Papal States may have been more stable and secure than they had been earlier in his papacy, but they could still not be said to be comfortably under the pontiff's control. In the Agro Romano, Everso d'Anguillara had escaped Pius's violent suppression of other rebellious barons; and while for the moment he respected the peace, Pius continued to view him as a significant danger to papal authority.[99] The situation in Rome was similarly delicate.

Pius's decision to hold the Corpus Christi festival in Viterbo in June 1462 is one indication of how uneasy he felt in his seat of power at the very time he began writing the *Commentaries*.[100] And almost a year and half later, as he prepared to depart for the crusade, he made security in the city one of his highest priorities.[101] Moreover, while Pius and his allies seemed to be gaining the upper hand against Malatesta and the Angevins in the late spring of 1462, the real turning points of the war did not come until mid-August.[102] Perhaps more importantly, however, was that with victory came a new set of problems. In the Marche, the defeat of Malatesta did not lead to restored stability. In Senigallia, Pius's nephew Antonio Piccolomini, the new papal vicar, clashed bitterly with the local oligarchs; nor was this was the only vicariate where papal rule came under attack.[103]

At the same time, Pius was profoundly aware of his weakness in relation to Italian powers. Dispatches from the Milanese ambassador to the papal court show that in spring 1462, Pius was well aware of how little he and his policies were esteemed by Venice and Florence. He also expressed concerns that Francesco Sforza was becoming a friend of the French.[104] As he continued to write the *Commentaries*, Pius's weak standing in the League of Italian States was confirmed again and again by the indifference his alleged allies showed to his crusade. Even Sforza proved a disappointment: he declined the pontiff's repeated pleas to lead the expedition. Just as troubling was the duke's new relationship with France. In December 1463, he effectively became a vassal of Louis XI by accepting Genoa and Savona as royal fiefs. Long covetous of French power in the former city, Sforza had pledged in exchange to safeguard French interests in Liguria, Savoy, and his own territories. And while he promised to fulfil these conditions only when they did not violate the provisions of the Italian League, his words rang hollow: the two agreements were, in truth, fundamentally incompatible.[105]

These, then, were the conditions under which Pius II composed his *Commentaries*. To be sure, when he began writing in the late spring of 1462, he was at a more decisive turning point in several of these battles than he was in his war against conciliarism. Nevertheless, the bulk of the work he penned in the context of continued and shifting threats to the Papal States, and with a growing awareness of his dwindling influence and prestige among Italian powers. In this context, the pontiff could not but have felt a profound need to repair his public image. Such an apology must have seemed increasingly necessary after the middle of 1463, as Pius's alliances began to unravel, as European support for the crusade continued to shrink, and as conditions in the Marche grew more unsettled.

Self-defence must also have seemed particularly urgent in the late spring of 1462 when he first took up his pen. As Pius began to envision a real crusade against the Turks, he was faced with another reality: by crossing the Adriatic to confront this threat himself, he opened the doors of the Papal States to the dangers of internal rebellion and external invasion. Both history and his own experience had taught him that if it was dangerous for the pope to be in Rome, it was also dangerous for him to be away from it.[106] And sailing across the sea, Pius would be in no position to hurry back to the city as he had done before both to quell insurrection and to contest the memory of his weak rule. As he looked ahead to his departure from Ancona, Pope Pius II must have perceived already at this moment the need to protect both his authority and the image of his authority from what would have seemed the inevitability of future assaults.

4 Pius II and the Triumph over Conciliarism: A New Reading of the *Commentaries*

I know that you have heard many things about me that are neither good nor worthy of relating. But those who have told you about me have not lied. While I was at Basel I spoke, I wrote, and I did many things against you. I do not deny it. But my intention was not so much to hurt you as it was to benefit God's church. For when I attacked you, I thought I was serving God ... Now I am here before you, and because I sinned in ignorance, I ask that you pardon me.[1]

The humble words that Aeneas Silvius Piccolomini spoke at the feet of Pope Eugenius IV in early 1445 make a fitting beginning to this analysis of the *Commentaries*. One of the best-known episodes of the entire work, Aeneas's confession of his conciliar errors captures the position of acute vulnerability from which he wrote the text. That vulnerability was, in part, deeply personal. Over the course of his professional career, Aeneas had significantly aggravated the conciliar threat facing the papacy – or at least, so the papacy had perceived. He did so first very consciously and deliberately as a prominent member of the Council of Basel and, in particular, as a publicist who introduced powerful new weapons into the assembly's anti-papal assaults. As imperial secretary, legate, and adviser, he continued to take positions on conciliar authority and on the role of general councils that were perceived in the curia as hostile to papal sovereignty. Once he himself joined the curia, first as cardinal and then as pope, he strengthened the conciliar movement in ways that were inadvertent but no less significant. He provoked two of the papacy's most dangerous conciliar enemies, the college of cardinals and Germany's princes, to launch fresh attacks on papal authority. His actions, moreover, ended up further reinforcing the already formidable legal and theoretical foundations of conciliar doctrine, and they offered those with conciliar sympathies new justification for embracing a council as a vehicle for reform. As a result, the vulnerability Pius II faced when writing the *Commentaries* was institutional as much as it was personal. In the face of conciliarism's unflagging strength, the very future of papal sovereignty hung in the balance.

The *Commentaries*, this chapter argues, offer a sustained, powerful, and aggressive response to these powerful conciliarist forces. They do so by effectively stripping the conciliar movement of its legitimacy, authority, and relevance. They also cleanse Pius himself of what had for him become incriminating conciliar affiliations, and at the same time, they purge his pontificate of its legacy of failed struggles against a host of conciliar challenges. In short, in the *Commentaries*, Pius forges a potent weapon in his and the papacy's long and arduous struggle against its conciliar foes.

This chapter does more than simply document what the *Commentaries* do to the conciliar threats facing Pius II. It also sets out to investigate *how* they do it – in other words, it aims to elucidate and to explain Pius's methodology as a historian. From this analysis, several important claims will emerge. The first is that Pius's counter-attack on conciliarism is one of significant proportions: it is extensive, multidimensional, complicated, and imprinted on the entire text. It includes some of the same apologetic techniques present in Aeneas's other writings on conciliar matters, but it does not simply adopt those techniques wholesale. The *Commentaries*, this chapter argues, represent a distinct and significant step in the evolution of their author's assault on conciliarism as it is charted in chapter 2. In the *Commentaries*, Pius launches his boldest and most aggressive attack yet on both his own conciliar past and on the broader conciliar crisis engulfing the Western Church. The result is a work of history that significantly misrepresents one of the central struggles of the fifteenth-century papacy and Pope Pius II's relationship to it. These methodological shifts and the significant distortions that they create grew out of the particular circumstances in which the *Commentaries* were composed. Those same circumstances appear to explain still another dimension of Pius's apology that emerges from this chapter, namely, the fortifications Pius builds in his defence are not consistently strong.

The Crisis That Never Happened: Conciliarism in Book One of the *Commentaries*

In the letter he wrote to Nicholas V in 1448, Aeneas spoke bluntly of the inevitable struggles he saw ahead for the new pope.[2] Those struggles, he maintained, were a direct consequence of the conciliar conflicts that had shaken the church over the past decade and a half. "The waves of Basel are not yet calmed," he wrote, with reference to the council that had assailed papal authority so relentlessly almost from its opening session in December 1431.[3] Aeneas proceeds in this letter to survey the legacy of unresolved conflicts and tensions that the council had left in its wake, and in so doing, brings into sharper focus the daunting challenges facing a papacy keen to reassert its claims of ecclesiastical sovereignty in Western Christendom.

The author of this letter, however, does not sound like the same person who wrote Book One of the *Commentaries*. According to the latter, there was no need to sound any warning about the ongoing threat of conciliarism. Indeed, not only were the waves of Basel calm in 1448: there had hardly been any waves at all. The *Commentaries*, and Book One in particular, illustrate what for Pius was a new historiographical approach to combatting conciliarism. In contrast to his other anti-conciliar writings, which worked to invalidate conciliarists' ideas and actions, the *Commentaries* prefer simply to wipe the conciliar threat from the historical record. In so doing, they hide from view a troubled era of papal history and at the same time obscure serious questions about papal authority, legitimacy, and relevance that this era left as its legacy.

The account of the Council of Basel in Book One of the *Commentaries* exemplifies this apologetic approach.[4] During the eighteen years it was in session, the Basel assembly offered undeniable evidence not just of the challenges conciliarism posed to papal sovereignty but also of the ability of the conciliar movement to assault that authority with considerable success. In Pius's account in Book One, the most extensive discussion of the Basel council in the entire *Commentaries*, there is no evidence of these successes nor, indeed, of the ambitions that prompted them. In short, Pius reports the Council of Basel in a way that effectively eviscerates its threat to papal sovereignty.

Pius is able to leave this innocuous impression of the council first and foremost by offering a very selective narrative of the assembly's events. Missing from his account are almost all the major attacks the council fathers launched against papal authority and their major victories. There is no reference, for example, to the fact that the council had challenged and challenged successfully the sovereignty of Pope Eugenius IV by remaining in session after Eugenius dissolved it in December 1431. Nor does he make reference to significant events in the subsequent four years: how the council threatened Eugenius with suspension; how it negotiated the Compacts with the Hussites; how it legislated a series of reforms that stripped the papacy of significant judicial and fiscal prerogatives and drastically curtailed its control over benefices; and how it succeeded in exacting from Eugenius a humble retraction of his earlier decree of dissolution. Also missing from Book One's account is the crucial period when the council fathers' assaults reached their height. There is no report of the explosive clashes in May 1437 between Eugenians and conciliarists over where to relocate the assembly or of the refusal of most fathers to obey Eugenius's bull, issued five months later, that declared the council reconvened at Ferrara. In fact, there is no evidence that this competing council ever assembled. Pius's account also leaves out the Basel fathers' decision the following January (1438) to suspend Eugenius and their momentous declaration almost a year and a half later (May 1439) that the decree *Haec Sancta* was an article of the Catholic faith. Aeneas does acknowledge their deposition of Eugenius a month later.[5] But by isolating this event from its historical context and by confining his report to a single sentence, Aeneas effectively prevents readers from understanding either the causes or the significance of this event.

Indeed, based on what he does write about the council, it is possible to come away with a serious misunderstanding of just what this deposition implied. According to Book One, the council and Eugenius clashed over only two issues before the latter's deposition. The first is framed as a personal disagreement with Eugenius rather than as an attack on papal supremacy: the Basel fathers recognized Pope Martin V's *in pectore* appointment of Domenico Capranica as cardinal – an appointment that Eugenius had refused to acknowledge when he became pope.[6] The second conflict has the appearance of a minor, even petty, squabble. The *Commentaries* report that Eugenius and the council fathers had a protracted dispute over how to draw up a set of documents – indulgences that would be used to help pay for Greek envoys to attend the council. The two parties were in agreement on the indulgences themselves, the *Commentaries* stress, thereby minimizing still further the significance of the dispute.[7] What they do not mention is that this disagreement was the overture to the far more serious stand-off between pope and council over where to transfer the assembly – a stand-off that led directly to the council's decision to depose the pope. As a result, Book One makes it is easy to conclude that Eugenius's deposition was more the result of a personal vendetta or a minor dispute spun out of control than it was the climax of a fierce and high-stakes battle over ecclesiastical sovereignty.

What obscures the magnitude of this conciliar assault all the more is the absence in Book One of any reference to *Haec Sancta* and *Frequens* – the decrees issued by the Council of Constance that gave conciliar supremacy a powerful legal foundation. From their initial defiance of Pope Eugenius in 1431, the council fathers at Basel had justified their resistance to papal commands by renewing these decrees. It was this act, they believed, that gave them the authority to legislate on matters of unity, heresy, and reform; and it was their subsequent elevation of *Haec Sancta* to an article of the Catholic faith that convinced them they could legitimately depose Eugenius. In its one-sentence account of the deposition, Book One of the *Commentaries* simply notes that the council fathers deposed Eugenius "with their decrees."[8] This vague statement conceals from view not just the legal basis of the council's actions, but also the broader attack on papal sovereignty that these decrees represented.

If the *Commentaries* obscure this threat by erasing from the narrative conciliarist triumphs and weapons, they also do so by redirecting attention to a very different kind of drama. Again and again, Aeneas deflects attention away from what were the council's most serious assaults on papal sovereignty by recounting remarkable events in his own life. Instead of the bold reaffirmations of *Haec Sancta* and *Frequens* in the wake of Eugenius's first bull of dissolution (December 1431), Pius offers a rivetting and now famous account of his harrowing journey to Basel.[9] Equally dramatic and entertaining tales of his embassy to Scotland in 1435 and 1436 help to obscure the fact that, back at Basel, the council fathers were simultaneously issuing a raft of anti-papal legislation.[10] The subsequent and decisive conflict over relocating the council for negotiations with the Greeks vanishes in the *Commentaries* into a speech competition in which Aeneas puts on a memorable display of oratorical genius.[11] What was a turning point in the council's relationship with the papacy becomes instead a turning point in Aeneas's own career: it was after he delivered this oration, Book One reports, that he took on roles of importance and prominence at the council.[12] The *Commentaries* offer similar distractions for the momentous events of fall 1437 and 1439. Instead of reporting Eugenius's dissolution of the Basel council and its transfer to Ferrara, they offer details of a serious stomach illness that gripped Aeneas for two and a half months and ravaged him so badly that he reportedly had to get up ninety times in a single night.[13] And while Pius does acknowledge the council's most severe attacks on papal sovereignty – the deposition of Eugenius IV and election of Felix V – he reduces them to background for tales of personal triumph and tragedy. About the conclave, we are told that despite lacking the technical qualifications, Aeneas was given a prestigious ceremonial role during the proceedings. Eugenius's deposition is given still more cursory treatment. The single, matter-of-fact sentence that acknowledges this momentous event is dwarfed by a lengthy and graphic account of the famine and plague that struck Germany in the summer of 1439. Through the tragic stories of Aeneas's friends cut down by the disease, to the vivid details of his own furious and ultimately successful struggle against it (his treatment, it is reported, involved a mysterious powder and compresses of horseradish and clay) Aeneas succeeds in making this pathological crisis far more memorable than the one that was simultaneously striking the papacy.[14]

To be sure, given that the *Commentaries* are primarily a discussion of the author's own life and career, it makes sense that Book One unfolds a personal narrative. But at the same time, the text purports to be something more than a *res gestae* of Aeneas and Pius: the text is entitled *Commentaries on Memorable Things that Happened in [Pius's] Lifetime*. Presented at the expense of these other notable events, Aeneas's life story effectively becomes a shield for a badly battered papacy. Book One, in other words, does not simply leave the impression that this was a memorable period in Aeneas's life. It leaves the impression that there were no other memorable things happening outside of it.

The *Commentaries* do much more than neutralize the dangers the Basel fathers posed to papal sovereignty. They also obscure another equally serious threat facing the fifteenth-century papacy: the conciliar sympathies of Europe's rulers and, in particular, their support for Basel's claims to authority and its anti-papal legislation. There is, for example, no reference in Book One to France's Pragmatic Sanction (1438), which adopted much of Basel's reform legislation and the principle of conciliar supremacy. Similarly, there is no reference to the *Acceptatio* of Mainz (1439), which embraced similar decrees; and while Germany's neutrality is mentioned in passing, the meaning of this term is never explained.[15] The *Commentaries* do acknowledge the emperor's proposal of a "third council" to resolve the schism between Eugenius and the Basel fathers. But there is no sense here that in supporting this solution Emperor Frederick III was advocating a position perceived by the papacy as fundamentally threatening to its sovereignty. Instead, the *Commentaries* focus on the logistical inconvenience that such an assembly would pose to Eugenius, because the proposed location of the council was so far from Rome.[16] What obscures the danger of a third council still more is the account in the *Commentaries* of the embassy that delivers this proposal to the pope, an embassy that Aeneas himself headed up. There is no mention in the text that the embassy's aim was to win Eugenius's approval of this plan – or that the pope categorically rejected the proposal. Instead, the *Commentaries* train their focus on the imperial envoy's personal reconciliation with Eugenius, the life-threatening illness he suffers on the heels of this event, and the extraordinary medical attention he received at the command of Eugenius and his cardinals alike.[17] Germany's strained relationship with the papacy over conciliar matters, thus, disappears from view behind another dramatic episode in Aeneas's own life – and an episode that, at a moment of serious division between empire and papacy, usefully underscores harmonious relations between the two.

The conciliar divide between Germany and the pope is closed still more dramatically in the account of a crucial development that took place in March 1446. It was at this point that the German electoral princes articulated a series of conditions under which they would abandon neutrality and declare their full obedience to Eugenius: the pope was to acknowledge word for word the decrees of conciliar supremacy enacted at Constance and renewed at Basel; he was to confirm the reform decrees taken up in the *Acceptatio*; and he was to hold a council in May of the following year.[18] Pius's account glosses over the conciliarist elements of these demands. It does so first in explaining what precipitated the electors' proposal in the first place. Having obscured up to this point why there was any need for a reconciliation between pope and Germany, the *Commentaries* attribute the strained relations to Eugenius's deposition of the archbishops of Trier and Mainz in January 1446.[19] In so doing, they paper over the fact that this move merely compounded long-standing divisions between Germany and Rome over conciliar authority. It wasn't just the conciliar causes for the rupture that are obfuscated. According to Pius's account, the princes' proposal asked simply that the pope recognize "the authority of Councils, as it had been declared at Constance"[20] – a demand whose threat to the papacy is obscured by the vague language in which it is expressed and, still more, by the fact that Book One makes it impossible to understand what it really means: that the pope acknowledge the legitimacy of *Haec Sancta*. Pius leaves out completely the demand for a new council; and instead of reporting that the princes wanted Eugenius to observe the decrees taken up in the *Acceptatio*, he simply says they asked Eugenius to relieve "the burden of the nation."[21] Not only does he dilute the princes' conciliarist demands by distorting their content, but he also does so by reducing their significance. At the core of the princes' proposal stood the demands that Eugenius recognize the authority of general councils, observe the reforms ratified at Basel, and summon a new council in the immediate future. The *Commentaries*, in contrast, make their central concern the reinstatement of the two archbishops – a condition to which, in reality, they gave hardly any attention.[22] The effect of Pius's misrepresentation is significant: it masks dramatically the strong support that both conciliarism and the Basel assembly's reforms enjoyed among Germany's rulers on the eve of their reconciliation with Eugenius.

It should come as no surprise, then, that in a subsequent chapter of Book One, Pius strips down in a similar way the revised version of the princes' proposal drawn up several months later and endorsed by Frederick III. As described in chapter 2, this proposal, known as the imperial compromise, altered the conditions laid out in the princes' proposal to make it more acceptable to Eugenius. Despite these changes, its stance on conciliar matters was still perceived by the curia as not going far enough. In the *Commentaries*, however, this rift between Germany and the papacy is nowhere to be seen. Missing from the imperial compromise described in the *Commentaries* are the very pro-conciliar elements that Eugenius and the cardinals found so objectionable: that the pontiff profess specifically to the decree *Frequens*, that he recognize the pre-eminent authority of general councils, that he summon a council within eighteen months, and that this assembly be responsible for initiating a program of ecclesiastical reform and for giving permanent expression to the Basel decrees adopted in the *Acceptatio*. The imperial compromise does, according to Pius's account, ask the pope that "the authority of general councils not be trampled,"[23] but from the papacy's perspective this was not a dangerous concession to make. On the contrary, the vague language in which this condition was couched was precisely the rhetoric that Eugenius was advocating for and that he eventually adopted in his own brief that laid out the terms of peace with Germany. Effectively, the *Commentaries* present the German princes and the emperor asking only for what Eugenius was willing to concede; and it is for this reason that Pius can write, plausibly, that the imperial compromise eliminated "all the poison that Eugenius abhorred."[24] Nor is this the only place in this account that Pius misrepresents German demands as being compatible with papal interests. According to the *Commentaries,* all aspects of the imperial compromise proposal were embraced immediately and unconditionally by pope and cardinals alike – a reception that flies in the face of the official report Aeneas wrote for the emperor about these same events. There is no mention of the tense negotiations that followed the proposal's presentation at the papal curia or that Eugenius revised its demands significantly before he agreed to accept them (and even then, his acceptance was heavily qualified). By continuing to collapse the significant differences between the two parties, the *Commentaries* make it impossible to discern how the imperial compromise represented, in the eyes of the papacy, a serious threat to papal sovereignty.

Nor does this account acknowledge that this threat continued long after 1447. There is no evidence in Book One that Germany's peace with Eugenius was fragile and in jeopardy from its very establishment. Pius does not report, for example, that four electors immediately balked at the revised terms of reconciliation won by Eugenius and attempted to forge peace independently with the papacy on the basis of their original conciliarist demands. Once again, the *Commentaries* drown out these disagreements in an account of Aeneas's own accomplishments: they underscore how well he was treated by the leader of this electoral faction, the archbishop of Cologne, when he was dispatched there as imperial legate to encourage the archbishop's approval of the existing peace agreement. The *Commentaries* also, significantly, make no mention of the Concordat of Vienna (1448), the subsequent peace settlement that further stoked papal resentment in Germany during the reigns of Nicholas V and Calixtus III. Nor is there any evidence that in 1452 Frederick III was still urging Nicholas to hold a council or that five years later the German princes had banded together to protest papal crusading tithes and had threatened to appeal their grievance to a future council. The *Commentaries* do not erase all evidence of Germany's resentment towards the papacy and its efforts to win more control over the German church. However, these references are fleeting, and more importantly, they fail to acknowledge the conciliarist elements of these complaints and ambitions – the ongoing demand, for example, that the papacy summon a new council to initiate reform.[25] In short, Book One offers no evidence that the papacy faced any conciliar threat in Germany on the eve of Pius II's papacy – indeed, it implies that there had never been such a threat at all.

With its well-placed omissions, distractions, and distortions, Book One of the *Commentaries* succeeds in achieving a formidable goal: it effectively hides from view the very existence of the conciliar crisis that engulfed the papacy from the inception of the Basel Council to the start of Pius's own pontificate. It does so, moreover, at a level that is unprecedented in Pius's other anti-conciliar writings. In his 1447 Letter of Retraction, in his *De rebus* (1450), and in his 1463 bull *In minoribus*, Aeneas/Pius made no attempt to conceal from view the battles waged between conciliarists and the papacy or, for that matter, from openly acknowledging that the Basel fathers were launching serious attacks on papal sovereignty – and with potent weapons.[26] Moreover, while the anti-conciliar arguments in those works are furthered by Aeneas's dramatic and suspenseful narrative, these features are not as prominent as they are in Book One of the *Commentaries*, nor do they serve the same end. In his Letter of Retraction, the *De rebus*, and *In minoribus*, they are one of the ways Aeneas openly discredits conciliarists' arguments, actions, and legal instruments. In Book One of the *Commentaries*, in contrast, they help to obscure the very existence of this conciliarist assault.

What might have prompted these shifts in methodology? The different approach Pius takes in this first book of the *Commentaries* definitely offered advantages to someone who, from his vantage point on the papal throne, was more aware than ever both of the papacy's vulnerabilities and of his own duty, as pope, to shore them up. By sparing the institution these relentless assaults, papal sovereignty appears all the more stable, papal claims to authority all the more legitimate, and the future strength and success of papal primacy more certain. But there were still other, more personal advantages to silencing this conciliar threat. By hiding Basel's serious assaults on papal sovereignty and, in particular, by concealing that Germany was a conciliar tinderbox in the late 1440s and 1450s, Pius weakens dramatically the conciliar threat that he himself would face in his own pontificate. The narrative in Book One effectively neutralizes what were the most dangerous aspects of that threat: the widespread support for the doctrine of conciliar supremacy; the broad and growing consensus that a council should lead ecclesiastical reform; and the firm conviction that *Haec Sancta* and *Frequens* were legitimate. By concealing this reality, Pius is able to minimize the conciliar challenges he faced as pope even before he begins to recount them in the *Commentaries*. Isolated from what was actually widespread, powerful, and determined support of the conciliar movement, those challenges can easily be portrayed as small-scale, short-lived rebellions. In short, the narrative in Book One does not just strengthen the image of the papacy as sovereign authority in the church: it is also the first step to building a defence of Pius's own pontificate as an example of the strength and resilience of papal sovereignty.

Papal Ally and Friend to German Princes: Aeneas in Book One of the *Commentaries*

In still other ways, the silences, distractions, and distortions in Book One offered Pope Pius II a valuable form of self-defence. For one, they helped to protect him from one of the greatest personal liabilities he faced as pope: the legacy of his pro-conciliar writings. As chapter 2 has argued, Aeneas's pro-conciliar writings introduced a series of new arguments in defence of Basilian conciliarism, and despite several attempts to overturn these arguments, Aeneas was unable to prevent their circulation and their potential use by conciliarists. Now himself pope, they represented weapons both to attack his reputation and to undermine the anti-conciliarist policy of his pontificate. In Book One of the *Commentaries*, Pius neutralizes the threat of these writings by simply ignoring the events they justify and the people they defend. There is no record, for example, of the council fathers' arguments for deposing Pope Eugenius – arguments that the *De gestis* work hard to defend. The *Commentaries* only tell us that this deposition happened. The events and ideas at the heart of the *Libellus* are, similarly, nowhere to be seen in Book One. The chief aim of the dialogue was to contest the legitimacy of Eugenius's transfer of the Basel council to Ferrara. In the account in the *Commentaries*, there is no reference to the fact that the council had been transferred there at all.

In taking this approach, Pius was again breaking from what he had done in his other anti-conciliar writings. As chapter 2 has demonstrated, Pius confronted his earlier, pro-conciliar arguments head on in his Letter of Retraction, in the *De rebus*, and in *In minoribus* by systematically reversing his flattering characterization of the council fathers as wise and virtuous judges. Pius doesn't entirely abandon this strategy in Book One. There are a few points when he does explicitly characterize the Basel fathers as irrational and unprincipled. In the wake of the council's dispute with Eugenius over indulgences, for example, we learn that Tommaso Parentucelli, the future Nicholas V, condemns anyone supporting the council as "out of his mind" and that the council was a "synagogue of Satan."[27] The fathers' reaction to this criticism only seems to confirm this withering assessment: rather than defending themselves with words, they seize the bishop and throw him in jail.[28] Later in the book, and as he had done in his earlier writings, Pius attributes his own abandonment of the conciliarist cause to his growing skills of discernment: it was only after a period of long and considered reflection, he reports, that he perceived the error of his ways.[29] But this portrait of conciliarists as foolish, mad, and even unvirtuous – so pervasive in Aeneas's Letter of Retraction, his *De rebus*, and his *In minoribus* – is otherwise muted in Book One of the *Commentaries*. Overwhelmingly, rather than reinterpreting the narrative of his pro-conciliar writings, the *Commentaries* opt for the more indirect assault of historical silence.

This approach makes sense when read in the context of *In minoribus*, the momentous bull that Pius issued as he was writing the *Commentaries*. As chapter 2 has demonstrated, the bull shows Pius developing new approaches to combatting what he perceived as the dangerous resilience of his conciliar writings. One of those approaches consisted of developing the most extreme reversal yet of his earlier pro-conciliar portrait of the Basel assembly: the undiscerning council fathers transform here into sinister and calculating manipulators of truth. The second and ultimately central strategy he develops is equally radical: Pius commands his audience simply to ignore his writings altogether – or more accurately, to treat his writings as if they had never existed. Pius is doing something similar to this second approach by leaving out of the *Commentaries* the events to which these writings relate. In both instances he is suppressing information as a way to defuse what were seriously dangerous texts. What Pius does in the *Commentaries* actually serves to complement what he attempts in his bull. While *In minoribus* commands its audience to ignore those writings, the *Commentaries* effectively force them to do so by emptying the *De gestis* and the *Libellus* of both purpose and meaning.

Pius's silences and distortions about the Council of Basel also helped the pope to defend another related vulnerability. Pius had not just written works in defence of the council: he had spent ten years of his career there, much of the time occupying prominent roles. A curriculum vitae of this nature presented the pontiff with a particular apologetic challenge: while single moments of his career might easily be omitted from an account of his life, it was much harder to ignore an entire decade.

Pius's selective narrative of the Council of Basel serves to resolve this dilemma. By obscuring from view the council's attacks on papal sovereignty, he was able to acknowledge a stretch of his past that would otherwise prove compromising to his reputation as pope and, in particular, to the anti-conciliar policies of his papacy. The well-placed silences even allow him to admit openly to having supported "the cause of Basel"[30] – for in the *Commentaries*, that cause is effectively concealed from view.[31]

Pius similarly benefits from – indeed, builds on – Book One's suggestion that the Basel fathers' conflict with Pope Eugenius was more personal than ideological in nature. From the moment of his arrival at Basel, the *Commentaries* cast Aeneas explicitly not as an enemy of papal authority, but rather as an enemy of Eugenius specifically and exclusively. As the one who defended Capranica's claim to a cardinal hat, Aeneas is shown taking a position that opposed Eugenius's ruling but respected that of his immediate predecessor, Pope Martin V.[32] In the following chapter, the divide between Eugenius and Aeneas is again explained in purely personal terms: he fears he has earned the pope's enmity because of his association with the bishop of Novara, whom Eugenius had recently accused of serious misconduct.[33] Their strained relationship is again defined in purely personal terms on the eve of Aeneas's reconciliation with the pope in 1445. There, Aeneas's relatives urge him not to carry out his embassy to Rome on behalf of Frederick III because they consider Aeneas to be "hostile to Eugenius."[34]

It is in the account of what happened when he arrived in Rome, however, that we can see how personalizing his conflict with Eugenius represented such a powerful apologetic tool. In the scene quoted at the beginning of this chapter, Aeneas is repenting at Eugenius's feet of what he did at Basel and asking for the pope's forgiveness. Scholarly discussion of this important passage in Book One is substantial; but until now, it has gone unnoticed that in, describing his years at Basel, Aeneas explicitly and repeatedly frames his actions as an attack on Eugenius and Eugenius alone: "While I was at Basel I spoke, I wrote, and I did many things against *you*. I do not deny it. But my intention was not so much to hurt *you* as it was to benefit God's church. For when I pursued *you*, I thought I was serving God"[35] (emphasis added). The pontiff, in turn, is reported as acknowledging in his absolution the fundamentally personal nature of Aeneas's assaults: "'We know,' he said, 'that you sinned gravely against *us*'"[36] (emphasis added). It is worth noting that here, too, the *Commentaries* break with some of Aeneas's (and Pius's) other discussions of his involvement with conciliarism. The Letter of

Retraction, the *De rebus*, and the bull *In minoribus* all explicitly identify his actions at Basel as attacks on papal sovereignty and defences of conciliar authority specifically.[37] By recasting these elements of his self-portrait in the *Commentaries*, Pius II is able to minimize still further an awkward and damaging chapter in his life.

This crucial episode in Book One does more than simply obscure from view Aeneas's past attacks on papal sovereignty. It also deflects attention away from another liability: Aeneas's ongoing divide with the papal curia over the role of general councils. The very purpose of Aeneas's audience with Eugenius was to deliver Frederick's request that Eugenius accept the proposal that a "third council" resolve the schism – a position that he himself personally endorsed. That position was fundamentally inimical to the papacy, precisely because it was perceived by the curia as too sympathetic to conciliar views. But this rift is hidden from view in Book One, and not simply because there are only vague references to the business he was sent to transact.[38] Because the narrative of Aeneas's embassy centres on the drama of his personal confession at the feet of Eugenius, the *Commentaries* portray it as a moment when tensions were resolved and when Pius gave his full obedience to the papacy.

That same impression is furthered by two events that, according to the *Commentaries*, happened immediately thereafter. No sooner had Aeneas made peace with Eugenius than he fell gravely ill. Book One reports the extraordinary measures taken by the papal curia to ensure that he received the best care. Bishop of Bologna Tommaso Parentucelli helps him to pay for a doctor; papal legate Juan de Carvajal comes to visit him every day; and Pope Eugenius personally sends him a trusted doctor.[39] By drawing attention to this extraordinary treatment, the *Commentaries* usefully emphasize the deep respect with which Aeneas is held in the papal curia at a time when between them there was a considerable divide. Just as significant, the text identifies as his most devoted supporters the very people with whom he was still particularly at odds on conciliar matters: Eugenius IV, Juan de Carvajal, and Tommaso Parentucelli.

Pius continues in the same chapter to elaborate on his relationship with Parentucelli and, once again, in a way that serves a very specific apologetic need. As chapter 2 has demonstrated, Aeneas and the bishop of Bologna did not see eye to eye on conciliar issues. The tensions grew in 1446 in the context of negotiating the imperial compromise, and they continued once Parentucelli was elected to the papal throne as Nicholas

V. This strained relationship, which is clearly imprinted on several of Aeneas's writings dating from the 1440s and 1450s, represented a significant liability for Aeneas once he succeeded Nicholas. It did in large part because, as pope, Aeneas held many of the same positions that Nicholas had. As we will see, the *Commentaries* offer a very different narrative of this relationship and that narrative begins during the account of his embassy to Rome in 1445. The *Commentaries* do acknowledge that there were tensions between Aeneas and Parentucelli, but they attribute them to a simple misunderstanding on Parentucelli's part: the bishop of Bologna was under the false impression that Aeneas was still allied with the Council of Basel.[40] That misunderstanding, Book One reports, was cleared up shortly after Aeneas recovered from his illness, and "all rust of dissension was wiped away and their friendship was renewed stronger than before."[41] The *Commentaries* are clearly at pains to emphasize the bond between the two: in the space of a few lines, they mention their strong friendship three separate times, and they also point out that Aeneas was now "even more committed to making himself useful to Tommaso in all matters of necessity."[42] In short, the *Commentaries* imply that the divisions between the two had been inconsequential, that they were resolved even before Germany had begun peace negotiations with the papacy, and that they were replaced by a deep mutual commitment to serve one another. This rosy picture of steadfast friendship served a valuable apologetic need for Pope Pius II. Through it, the *Commentaries* were revising Aeneas's earlier writings that documented a very different kind of relationship and one that, for him, now carried potentially dangerous consequences.

This is not the only way that Book One obscures Aeneas's divisions with the papacy over conciliar issues. Just as crucial to his self-defence is the account of Germany's reconciliation with the papacy. The previous section of this chapter has emphasized how, by drastically editing the demands of the German electoral princes, Aeneas made Germany and the papacy essentially in agreement on the role of councils going into their negotiations. This way of presenting the situation significantly affected the role that Aeneas played in that negotiation process. As chapter 2 has discussed, Aeneas's writings record that that role had not only been significant, but that it later became a significant liability to him as pope: they identify him as the architect of the imperial compromise proposal that made demands about councils and conciliar authority that the curia had balked at; they include the oration that he personally delivered to the pope, outlining these demands; and they openly advocate a policy of compromise in reconciliation, in the face of challenges from none other than the bishop of Bologna, Tommaso Parentucelli. By stripping the 1446 imperial compromise of its most dangerous conciliar demands, the *Commentaries* are obscuring not just Germany's sharp divide with the papacy on these issues: they are also suppressing Aeneas's. At the same time, they completely transform the nature of his role in brokering the peace agreement. Because the two sides are shown beginning their rapprochement already very close to one another, there is no need for either one of them to make any significant concessions in order to reach peace. In such a context there is no need for Aeneas to advocate a policy of compromise. Thus, by misrepresenting the demands of the imperial compromise, Book One effectively buries the political philosophy that was such a liability to Pius as pope. It accomplishes the same thing by leaving something else out of its account. Missing from the *Commentaries* is the episode in the *De rebus* in which Aeneas describes himself at odds with Parentucelli over the princes' demand that the pope acknowledge the decree *Frequens*.[43] Instead, the Aeneas of the *Commentaries* seems to be fulfilling what he pledged to do only a few pages before: become "even more committed to making himself useful to Tommaso in all matters of necessity."[44]

In its subsequent description of Aeneas's relationship with Parentucelli, Book One continues to reinforce this same impression: once the latter was elected pope, the two worked in harmony with one another and never broke on matters involving general councils. The *Commentaries* do this in part through the familiar technique of selective omission. While they mention that Aeneas delivered a speech before Nicholas V in 1451, they make no reference to his recommendation that the pope summon another council – a recommendation, as chapter 2 has pointed out, that went against the interests of both Nicholas V and Pius II. Instead, by simply saying that he spoke against the idea of a council being held in France, they seem to imply that he did not support a new council at all.[45] The *Commentaries* offer a more blatant misrepresentation of Aeneas's position on Bohemia. While Book One ultimately speaks very little about his relationship with Nicholas V on Bohemian matters, what it does say obscures something that had become a dangerous liability to him as pope: the fact that Aeneas advocated that the papacy negotiate with Podiebrad about the Bohemian Compacts. As discussed in chapter 2, his position grew in part out of his very first encounter with George Podiebrad in 1451, when he came to the conclusion that Podiebrad's commitment to the Compacts was unwavering. Again, the *Commentaries* tell a very different story. They report that Aeneas came away from that meeting with Podiebrad convinced that "the man was more taken by his desire to rule than he was fooled by the error of heresy."[46] This presentation – or more accurately, misrepresentation – of Aeneas's position is crucial for understanding what follows: an Aeneas convinced that Podiebrad's commitment to Hussitism was not genuine would have no reason to advocate that the papacy bargain with the governor on the Compacts. And it is this Aeneas who appears in the *Commentaries*. There is no evidence, for example, of how he cultivated friendly relations with Podiebrad during Nicholas V's papacy. On the contrary, by mentioning that Podiebrad was saddened by Pius's election as pope, the work creates the very opposite impression of their relationship.[47] In the context of this narrative, it is easy for the *Commentaries* to pass over in silence what was the culmination of Aeneas's own Bohemian policy: the oration he delivered to Nicholas's successor, Calixtus III, which called for the papacy to embrace the Compacts. As a result, the text is able to eliminate from view what, for Pius II, was one of the most dangerous and embarrassing elements of his past: a profoundly compelling defence of the very position that as pope he adamantly opposed.

At the same time as the *Commentaries* shore up one of Pius's vulnerabilities by emphasizing his smooth relations with the papal curia, they remedy another by demonstrating his strong relationship with Germany's princes. Chapter 2 explained how, as a cardinal, Aeneas had been branded a traitor to German interests and condemned as a symbol as well as a supporter of a ravenous Roman Church. It was a reputation that had helped to rekindle anti-papal sentiment in Germany and the threat by some princes to appeal their concerns to a future council. As pope, Pius would have been particularly eager to conceal this reputation, given its potential to enflame his volatile relationship with Germany during his pontificate – and Book One does just that. It does so most blatantly by underscoring the German princes' very positive response to his appointment to the college of cardinals. "All the German princes sent Aeneas letters of congratulations," the *Commentaries* report, "as if in him Germany itself had been honoured."[48] By placing words of praise in the mouths of those who had criticized him, the *Commentaries* cast Aeneas's turbulent relationship with Germany during his cardinal years in a usefully positive light. They do so still more by claiming that the princes were correct in their assessment. "Nor were they mistaken," Book One continues, "because Aeneas was always a champion and defender of Germans, not only during his cardinalate, but also during his papacy."[49] These words are then immediately backed up by the account of Aeneas intervening in two episcopal elections, one in Kulm and the other in Regensburg, to the great benefit of the German church.[50] His loyalty to Germany is underscored still more in the account a few pages later of the papal conclave. There, the cardinal of Rouen discourages others from voting for Aeneas with the suggestion that, if elected pope, Aeneas would transfer the papacy to Germany.[51]

A still more powerful shield for Pius's difficult relationship with Germany was the account in the *Commentaries* of Aeneas's role in crafting the imperial compromise proposal. We have already seen how the *Commentaries* report, and inaccurately, that the terms of reconciliation he drew up in this proposal did not ask the papacy to make any concessions to its stand on conciliar matters. The *Commentaries* also state (and also inaccurately) that Aeneas was not asking the princes to make any compromise either. On the contrary, they report that Aeneas's aim was not simply to preserve the princes' original demands but to amplify them – including their request that "the authority of general councils not be trampled."[52] The decision to include here in the *Commentaries* such a bold statement of Aeneas's support for Germany's conciliar interests can best be understood in the context in which he was writing the text. In the 1460s, conciliar sentiment in Germany was growing and had intensified significantly after he had drawn the decree *Execrabilis* against Diether of Mainz, Sigismund of Austria, and, indirectly, Gregor Heimburg. In the face of this backlash, Pius had worked to dissipate these tensions by floating the possibility of summoning a new council and by essentially shelving *Execrabilis*. It is in this context that Pius's statement in the *Commentaries* makes sense. By presenting the pontiff as a staunch defender of Germany's conciliar interests, Pius is, in still another way, working to calm "the waves of Basel."

At what cost, however? What did such a statement do to the simultaneous portrait in the *Commentaries* of Pius as unwavering ally of the papal curia? A statement this bold would seem to undermine it – indeed, it seems to go against a prevailing pattern in the *Commentaries*, one that systematically suppresses Aeneas's defence of conciliarist principles at all stages of his career. But the claim in the *Commentaries* that Aeneas supported the "authority of councils" is not as dangerous to this portrait as it might first appear to be. To understand why requires imagining the work's potential audience. Those familiar with the nuances of papal rhetoric would recognize in this statement the same deliberate ambiguity that the papal curia itself employed when talking about conciliar authority: while the words might be read as an acknowledgment of conciliar supremacy, they could just as easily be taken to mean the opposite. But even those who were not fluent in the language of papal diplomacy would be hard-pressed to see this statement as a challenge to papal sovereignty – or they would be, at least, within the broader context of Book One. The very first part of this chapter explains why: it is impossible to read Book One of the *Commentaries* and come away with any real sense of how the "authority of general councils" represented a threat to papal sovereignty. The *Commentaries*, thus, could safely state that Aeneas amplified the authority of councils for the same reason they could talk safely about his ten years at the Council of Basel: they prevent the reader from understanding the full significance of what is being said. Nonetheless, given that in the rest of Book One, Aeneas never shows himself promoting conciliar authority, this statement, at the very least, risks causing confusion and creating tensions in his portrait. The very fact that Pius chose to take that risk is very revealing: it tells us just how deeply concerned he was about the conciliarist crisis in Germany and the extent to which he envisioned Book One as a defence against that threat.

The tensions found in this line of Book One are not the only ones to appear in Aeneas's discussion of conciliarism. A still more significant one emerges for readers who move onto Book Six. There, they encounter a picture of the Council of Basel very different from the one they have already seen in the *Commentaries*.[53] In sharp contrast to the first book, Book Six openly acknowledges that the Council of Basel was mired in a heated struggle with Pope Eugenius for ecclesiastical supremacy and that it had launched a series of direct assaults on papal authority.[54] In this context, Pius even makes reference to the decrees *Haec Sancta* and *Frequens*, though in keeping with the approach he takes in Book One, he obscures more than he illuminates about these decrees, and in so doing, minimizes their importance.[55] It is also here that for the first time in the *Commentaries* Pius offers explicit criticism of the Council of Basel's actions. The scathing portrait he presents breaks sharply from that in Book One, but it is a familiar one to its author: In keeping with his Letter of Retraction, his *De rebus*, and his *In minoribus*, it directly upends the image of the council fathers in his earlier pro-conciliar writings. The *Commentaries* explain how the council members, drawn against tradition from all ecclesiastical ranks, were driven first and foremost by an unbridled lust for liberty that typifies the mob mentality.[56] If not from an instinctive urge to assault authority, they acted out of greed, ambition, and a deep hatred for the pope. It is on the basis of this portrait that Pius concludes that all the laws that the Basel council enacted were "devoid of what is just and right" and thus inherently illegitimate.[57]

This portrayal of the Council of Basel makes good apologetic sense at this particular juncture of the *Commentaries*. It appears at the beginning of Aeneas's discussion of the Pragmatic Sanction of Bourges (1438), the decree issued by the king of France, which essentially co-opted a host of the Basel assembly's most radical anti-papal legislation. This powerful remnant of conciliar authority was, both for Pius and the papacy more generally, a dangerous point of weakness and one Pius was anxious to shore up. Book Six's damning portrait of the council fathers, essentially the authors of the contents of the Pragmatic Sanction, helped him to do just that. But what was a fitting defence in the context of Book Six becomes problematic in the larger context of the *Commentaries* as a whole. The aggressive Council of Basel in Book Six sits, at best, uncomfortably beside the neutral sketch in Book One. At worst, it threatens to undermine that book's apologetic value. These tensions and contradictions echo those illuminated in Aeneas's account of the imperial compromise proposal. They also indicate a pattern that, as we will see, is a defining feature of the work: while the *Commentaries* build well-crafted defences against individual threats, they do not create an apology that functions consistently as a coherent whole.[58]

Papal Triumph over Conciliarism: The Pontificate of Pius II in the *Commentaries*

The triumphant account of Pius's battle with the Pragmatic Sanction of Bourges represents only part of the defence in the *Commentaries* against the conciliar struggles marking Pius II's pontificate and threatening thereby both his own reputation and the future stability of papal sovereignty. Just as in their narrative of his pre-papal years, the account in the *Commentaries* of Pius's papacy constructs an apology that is both wide reaching and sharply focused. It does so in part by building on the important groundwork laid in Book One that in the years leading up to his pontificate, conciliarism presented no grave threat to the papacy. At the same time, Pius continues to reuse, reshape, and redirect a host of defensive tools that he had employed in his other writings on conciliar matters. Given the reality of his struggles against conciliar forces, the result of this substantial counter-attack is striking: beginning with the account of the conclave in August 1458, the *Commentaries* transform

Pius's pontificate into a compelling example of the vigour of papal sovereignty. The conciliar challenges he faces – or rather, the ones that he even acknowledges – appear weak and are easily defeated by a pope presented as both confident and capable in his rule. The story of Pius II's papacy, thus, reads as a crucial chapter in the broader narrative in the *Commentaries* celebrating the legitimacy, authority, and relevance of papal supremacy in the fifteenth-century church.

Reform of the Church

One of the greatest vulnerabilities Pius faced as he was writing the *Commentaries* was his record on ecclesiastical reform. As chapter 2 has explained, the pontiff had done little to recapture the prerogative for such reform from conciliarists who, on the basis of both *Haec Sancta* and the papacy's perceived indifference to reform, maintained that a general council was the legitimate and necessary vehicle for enacting substantive change in the church. Pius had done more than his recent predecessors to confront the problems riddling the church *in capite*; but because his reform bull was never promulgated, he, too, risked becoming a symbol of papal inertia and being branded a failed reformer. In fact, to many of his contemporaries, even the latter title was too generous: the pontiff was repeatedly criticized for pursuing policies seen as the impetus not the solution for reform. Together, Pius's actions and inaction seem only to have strengthened the case that a council should rightfully be given this responsibility.

The *Commentaries* offer a powerful counterargument to the reality of Pius's struggle to initiate meaningful reform in the church. Instead of the pope who lost ground to conciliar competition, he appears as the one who claimed this responsibility as his own and who did so decisively. From the beginning of the *Commentaries* to the end, Pius is depicted as a committed, capable, and immensely successful reformer – and one who, significantly, faced no meaningful challenge from a general council.

Well before he ascends the papal throne, Pius II emerges in the *Commentaries* as someone with the potential to be an outstanding reformer. Book One recounts several superhuman feats of piety and sexual continence he performed during his sojourn in England and Scotland in the mid-1430s. We learn here that, in gratitude to God for surviving the sea voyage, Aeneas walked ten miles barefoot to a church in Whitekirk, and that he resisted the offers of no less than a hundred young beautiful Scottish women to spend the night with him.[59] These features distinguish Aeneas immediately and sharply from the spiritual indifference and moral corruption identified as the core of ecclesiastical abuse. So does the total disinterest he shows in climbing the ecclesiastical hierarchy, his abundant humility when appointed bishop and cardinal, and his immunity to the trappings of life in the papal curia.[60] In short, Aeneas emerges as the model prelate, and one whose values had already withstood exceptional temptation by the time he entered the conclave in August 1458. Indeed, that election serves to throw those values into still sharper relief: in his religious zeal, his chastity, his indifference to ambition, and his embrace of poverty, Aeneas seems the mirror image of the man who appears destined for the papal throne: Guillaume d'Estouteville. The cardinal of Rouen is not only enslaved to simony and lust, the *Commentaries* tell us. He also mocks the idea dear to reform movements of the fifteenth century when he dismisses Pius's candidacy by saying, "How can a poor pope help a poor church?"[61]

The account in the *Commentaries* of the papal conclave defends Pius's image as a reformer in still other ways. More than simply the model prelate, Aeneas emerges here as the one who will put the curia on the road to reform. The cardinal of Rouen, the *Commentaries* make clear, is on the brink of winning enough votes to make him pope. They also make clear that he has no intention of abandoning his corrupt ways should he reach the papal throne.[62] It is against this formidable threat, we are told, that Aeneas rises up, denouncing three cardinals whose votes Rouen has already bought, and exhorting them to retract their decision.[63] Still more significantly, he succeeds: moved by Aeneas's words – as well as, we are told, by the hand of God – these cardinals abandon Rouen and join together in supporting Aeneas as pope, well aware from their conversations with him that he champions integrity, poverty, and humility.[64] In the heroic act of steering the conclave away from the horrific act of electing Rouen, the *Commentaries* show Aeneas enacting curial reform, and a momentous one at that: he is doing nothing less than rescuing the papacy and the church it governed from what seemed an inevitable slide into a pit of sin and corruption. Moreover, the fact that he is the one chosen as pope instead of Rouen suggests that this is only the first of many acts of reform he will perform. Indeed, the details of Pius's election – his courage in facing down an intimidating spectre of corruption, his success in the face of impossible odds – seem to herald the dawn of a new era in which the curia will be purified – and at the hands not of a council, but of a pope.

According to what follows in the *Commentaries*, Pius does exactly that. They draw attention immediately to his efforts and successes at correcting one of the most notorious abuses: financial corruption. Immediately after his election, Book Two reports, Pope Pius II embarked on a comprehensive restructuring of the curia that was expressly designed to root out practices of bribery and simony endemic in the system of papal petitions.[65] In the new and streamlined structure, only men of spotless character have the authority to present petitions to the pope, and as a result, this practice of submitting such requests was made both more efficient and "free of corruption."[66] In this and other chapters, Pius reports how he corrected a series of other financial abuses: he jails a corrupt member of the college of auditors, returns vast sums of tribute money to the Papal States, and pays back to two Florentine banking houses a vast sum that he determined had been falsely extracted from them in the form of fines.[67] By reporting his concerted efforts to rectify these injustices, the *Commentaries* work to cast doubt on the charge that Pius had himself aggravated financial abuse in the curia during his pontificate. At the same time, they establish him firmly as a pope who makes ecclesiastical reform a top priority.

That commitment is further evident in how Pius is shown tackling an overlapping problem within the curial administration and another in which he himself had been implicated: corruption in the college of cardinals. According to the *Commentaries*, reorganizing the system of petitions, one the cardinals traditionally controlled, was just one way he moved to cleanse the college of abuse.[68] The most significant way he reformed the college, however, the *Commentaries* tell us, came through two waves of new appointments in April 1460 and December 1461. Speaking to the existing crop of cardinals at the first appointment, Pius makes clear how, by supplementing their numbers, he aims to strengthen the college as a whole. After bluntly condemning his audience for embracing values fundamentally at odds with their position, he asks them to put forward names of men who exemplify the very opposite ideals: sobriety, dignity, temperance, learning, and sanctity.[69] Though ultimately relying little on their advice, Pius succeeds, the *Commentaries* report, in accomplishing this goal. The six cardinals he appoints in 1460, for example, are characterized as being of the highest integrity; others in the second round are also identified as outstanding in both character and intellect.[70] Pius's reform of the college does not end there. The *Commentaries* suggest that the six members added in 1460 also helped to ensure a strong pool of candidates in the future. By naming only worthy people to the college, we learn, Pius encouraged others to commit themselves still more fully to a life of virtue in the hope of receiving a similar honour.[71] Moreover, there is evidence that even the less virtuous cardinals have, under Pius, experienced reform. During the solemn ceremonial procession in which the relic of Saint Andrew's head is carried through the city, the *Commentaries* pause to describe the cardinals: "On the faces of all were expressions of dignity, piety and devotion, nor were any of their gestures indecorous. So humble was the procession of cardinals that the hearts of those in the crowds were moved to piety."[72] While not on the scale of what he accomplished in the 1458 conclave, Pius seems here, too, to have won a remarkable victory for the cause of reform: the once vice-ridden cardinals are here described not simply as embodying the ideals of the college, they are even inspiring piety in the laity. In so doing, the *Commentaries* show Pius transforming the college of cardinals into just what critics of the curia were calling them to be – genuine spiritual leaders.

In still more fundamental ways, the *Commentaries* frame Pius's papacy as fulfilling contemporary visions of church reform. The ideal of poverty that Pius had invoked in the conclave becomes a defining feature of his papacy and a basis for ecclesiastical renewal. It is, moreover, an ideal explicitly connected to the one invoked so often by the reform movements of the fifteenth century: the return to the Apostolic Church. Explaining his decision to appoint as cardinal the general of the Augustinian order, Alessandro of Sassoferrato – a move that baffles the college – the *Commentaries* observe: "But Pius held that virtue should be rewarded even in a poor man, for he knew that the first princes of the Church had been humble and poor by earthly standards. He searched even monasteries for noble souls; nor did he condemn poverty in one made illustrious by his ability and skill."[73]

Pius does not name any other monks as cardinals, but it is clear from what he does and says that he considers Alessandro a symbol of the church at its best and a church that he seeks to restore. The other churchmen he holds up as models, Antoninus of Florence and San Bernardino of Siena, are also ones who championed the idea that through poverty the church will be enriched; and it is these ideals that the *Commentaries* explicitly underscore when extolling their praises.[74] They also report that when Pius instructs the new cardinals on how to execute their duties, he urges them to follow the lead of these holy men by making it their own priority to tend to the poor.[75] Pius himself, as the *Commentaries* repeatedly remind us, embraces a life of simplicity and modesty that contrasts sharply with the luxury he explicitly condemned in the curia of his day.[76] Pius ate moderately and drank less, we learn; when he travelled he preferred to lodge in humble cottages and monasteries of highest repute; and instead of sumptuous halls, he regularly held court in the natural majesty of the Tuscan countryside or the Agro Romano.[77] By thus emphasizing poverty as both his personal philosophy and the foundation for a renewed church, the *Commentaries* connect Pius II to ideals of considerable value for someone whose record on reform was seen as weak – so weak, in fact, that a council was considered necessary to assume those responsibilities. Such a council, the *Commentaries* imply, would be obsolete: the Pope Pius they describe is one who both understands and undertakes the very path of reform that so many in his age were charting.

Invoking the image of the early church helps Pius to shore up his image as reformer in still other ways. The pontiff's reputation on reform had been marred by accusations that he was using crusading tithes to fund his wars in Italy. His posture as a crusader pope was, thus, made out to be just that – a distracting façade for a warmonger, bent on stripping fellow Christians of their rightful possessions. Book Twelve of the *Commentaries* works to erode that image. There, in the context of explaining his plans to join the crusade himself, Pius explains that his decision grew out of a firm conviction: if he was to restore the moral authority of the church, he had to return to the values of the early Christians – abstinence, chastity, zeal for the faith, and martyrdom.[78] By framing his crusade as part of his broader vision of renewing the Apostolic Church, the *Commentaries* offer a sharp retaliation to those who used his approach to crusade as justification to appeal for a council for reform. On the contrary, the *Commentaries* seem to suggest that rather than justifying calls for a reform council, Pius's handling of the crusade offered evidence of why such a council was entirely unnecessary. The crusade was itself proof of Pius the reformer in action.

While Pius shields his weaknesses as a reformer through his own self-portrait in the *Commentaries*, he also does so through the portrayal of his competition. As he does in the face of so many other conciliar threats, Pius simply erases that competition from the historical record. The only place in the text where a general council is explicitly connected with ecclesiastical reform is Book Six. Here, in the context of his brief account of the Basel assembly, Pius refers to that council's decree (*Haec Sancta*, though Pius leaves it unnamed) that established conciliar supremacy in matters of reform. This decree is then explicitly and forcefully dismissed; and in the subsequent account of the Basel fathers' vicious assault on papal prerogatives, their claim to reform is still more thoroughly undermined.[79] The *Commentaries* identify the real opponent to Pius's reform program not in the council but in his papal predecessor. It was Calixtus III, Book One maintains, who had created some of the worst abuses in the curia that Pius had to correct: for one, he appointed a series of self-serving and incompetent men to the college of cardinals, among them, his own relatives.[80] The *Commentaries* do not shy away from openly criticizing Calixtus for his actions: "Nor did Calixtus escape infamy because he preferred the ties of flesh to the good of the church."[81] Doing so has the effect of enhancing Pius's own self-portrait, for Calixtus's mistakes allow Pius to present himself still more effectively as a capable and effective reformer.

If the portrayal of Calixtus helps Pius to build his own self-defence, it does not do much to advance the broader idea, also under attack, that ecclesiastical reform should, on principle, be under the purview of the pope. Indeed, the precedent of Calixtus III, as it is reported in the *Commentaries*, seems to call that argument into serious question. Why, then, would Pius have made such a comparison with his papal predecessor? Its presence may help to bring into sharper focus Pius's priorities when writing the *Commentaries*, for the sharp criticisms of Calixtus seem to suggest that Pius was more concerned with defending himself and his own pontificate than he was with the concept of papal sovereignty itself. That hypothesis finds corroboration in the fact that, by drawing attention to Calixtus's errors, the *Commentaries* are also able to combat another conciliar force threatening Pius during his pontificate, namely, the college of cardinals.

The College of Cardinals

As chapter 2 has outlined, the cardinals posed a dangerous threat to Pius because they subscribed to a fundamentally different understanding of papal sovereignty than he did, and one that was directly threatening to him: they envisioned themselves as co-sovereigns of the church. What made this vision an immediate threat to Pius was the form that it took. The cardinals had translated it into a series of specific rules that Pius had pledged, albeit it in qualified form, to follow upon his election. The guiding principle of the capitulations, the idea that the pope must consult and win the consent of the cardinals on all significant matters of business, also appeared in the program for curial reform that Cardinal

Nicholas of Cusa had developed at the pope's request. Pius II's repeated attempts to thwart the cardinals' strategies for realizing this vision – by qualifying his acceptance of the capitulations, by violating several of them almost immediately, by passing over Cusanus's recommendations in his own reform bull, and by sharply curbing the power that the cardinals already did exercise – had done little to suppress their resolve. On the contrary, the college became the pontiff's inveterate foe, relentlessly crying foul at his attempts to rule on his own. Doing so did not enable the cardinals to become the co-sovereigns that they had envisioned. Nevertheless, they were able to exercise considerable influence over papal policy, and the crusade in particular, and they did so in a way that did long-standing damage to both the pope's authority and his reputation. At the same time, the cardinals also strengthened the case for their claims to authority – or, more accurately, Pius did: by rejecting what turned out to be their very sage advice on how to manage the crusade, the pontiff inadvertently seemed to legitimize the cardinals' claims that their vision of shared sovereignty was best for the church.

The portrayal in the *Commentaries* of the college of cardinals offers a sustained and aggressive response to the daunting threat posed, in both theory and practice, by these would-be oligarchs. This response takes various forms. On the one hand, the *Commentaries* defend against this conciliar threat in the same way they do other ones: silence is a crucial weapon. Still more, however, they adopt and adapt apologetic approaches familiar from his earlier anti-conciliar writings. In so doing, they leave the strong, though not unqualified, impression that Pius was able to dominate comfortably an enemy that, in fact, he had struggled continuously to contain.

One of the central ways the *Commentaries* build this defence against the cardinals is through their discussion of the electoral capitulations, the centrepiece of the cardinals' program for oligarchic power. To those unfamiliar with the capitulations, this apologetic move may be difficult to detect. Pius acknowledges openly that he swore twice, and without qualification, to uphold the capitulations – first along with all the other cardinals as they entered the conclave, and then immediately after he was elected.[82] He also makes a point of underlining how respectful he is of them. Recounting Pius's second attempt to expand the college, the *Commentaries* record how Cardinal Cusanus accuses the pontiff of violating the capitulation that established the procedure for choosing new cardinals. Pius vigorously denies this charge and, at the same time, declares his commitment not to violate any of them: "Far be it from us to violate our oath. There is nothing that we dread more than that."[83] Pius's words should not, however, be read as a humble capitulation to the cardinals' own capitulations. The reason why is that with the exception of what they say about the election of cardinals, the *Commentaries* make no reference to what the capitulations actually contain. This silence is significant. Without any knowledge of the capitulations' demands, it is impossible to see that Pius did, in fact, violate several others – a fact that might seem to give the cardinals reasonable cause for indignation. Still more importantly, by leaving out the contents of the capitulations, the *Commentaries* effectively obscure from view the formidable threat that they represented. With the extensive control they gave the college over various areas of jurisdiction, the capitulations make very clear how severely the cardinals were seeking to restrict papal absolutism. With the extent of these ambitions obscured, the *Commentaries* are able to present any conflicts that Pius had with cardinals, whether collectively or individually, as far more innocuous than they really were. They also, as we will see, are free to attribute to the cardinals motives far less honourable and less rational than the ones that, in fact, underpinned their oligarchic aims.

The *Commentaries* work to minimize the significance of the capitulations in still other ways: they first introduce them almost dismissively as "certain capitulations";[84] and by noting that they were drawn up during the conclave itself, they make them seem like an ad hoc document rather than the reflection of a carefully developed vision of government.[85] Still more significant, when the *Commentaries* record the newly minted Pope Pius swearing to uphold the capitulations, they do so in the very same sentence that describes the cardinals kissing the pontiff's feet, hands, and face in reverence.[86] The most memorable detail from this passage is, thus, not Pius's recognition of the capitulations but the powerful image that shows the cardinals humbling themselves before the pontiff – performing the very opposite relationship mapped out in that document. In short, the *Commentaries* are doing with the capitulations the very thing they did in Book One with the Council of Basel and using similar techniques: they make the papacy seem stronger by hiding from view what was a very serious conciliar threat.

That threat is still further minimized in a heated conversation that reportedly took place between Pius and Cardinal Nicholas of Cusa. As chapter 2 explained, the cardinal's vision of oligarchic power also found written expression in the reform program Cusanus had authored. It is with this in mind that we should study in more detail this episode of the *Commentaries*.[87] The confrontation between pope and cardinal begins when, on the eve of Pius's second expansion of the college of cardinals, Cusanus openly states his disapproval of Pius's plan. After making the accusation previously noted that Pius was in violation of the electoral capitulations, the cardinal launches into a tirade about the immorality of the curia and complains that his views on reform were being dismissed: "Whenever I say something in consistory about reform, I'm laughed at."[88] These few lines, the only ones in the *Commentaries* that connect Cusanus to ecclesiastical reform, obscure the real threat his reform program contained. Not only does Pius pass over what Nicholas writes there about the cardinals serving as the pope's constant counsellors, but also he emphasizes instead his antagonistic relationship with the college: Cusanus is shown explicitly criticizing the cardinals ("neither you nor the cardinals care about the Church"), and the cardinals in turn are shown opposing, indeed, ridiculing him for these complaints.[89] This depiction hides from view how Cusanus, the reformer, actually served as a valuable ally for the cardinals in their pursuit of shared sovereignty. Indeed, rather than a spokesman for the college, Cusanus here is presented as an isolated voice, defending his own personal and unpopular views.

That position of isolation is important given how Pius responds to Cusanus's outburst. He reprimands him sharply for daring to suggest that the pope is obliged to take his advice – on reform or anything else for that matter. The pope then proceeds to lecture him bluntly about how cardinals are by definition inferior to popes:

> A cardinal should offer advice about what he thinks would benefit the interests of the Church; if his advice is taken, he should thank God that he gave good advice; if it is rejected, he should blame his own ignorance, not his prince's … The ship of St Peter is entrusted to us, not to you. Your responsibility is to give good advice; but nothing requires us to follow that advice unless it seems excellent. Remember that you are a cardinal, not the pope.[90]

Anyone familiar with Pius's battle with the cardinals will recognize that in these words he is rejecting vociferously the central principles underpinning both the electoral capitulations and Cusanus's reform plan. However, because they are directed to Cusanus alone, they do not read as a defensive attack against a cardinalate united in its ideal of shared sovereignty. Instead they appear as a rebuke of an individual, and one who hardly seems threatening to the pope. Cusanus appears in this episode as little more than a petulant child: he concludes his protest by declaring that he is going to run away from the curia, and then he promptly bursts into tears.

If Cusanus appears as puerile in this episode, he is also, significantly, repentant. As Pius is lecturing him in response, the *Commentaries* report, the cardinal continues to sob uncontrollably. His tears, moreover, are explicitly identified with his newfound sense of humility and profound awareness that he has committed a grave transgression. We learn that he resolves to take a "gentler" approach to giving advice – a decision that, according to the *Commentaries*, implies that Cusanus learned something useful from his papal admonishment. Pius then reinforces this victory with a powerful image: the *Commentaries* report that when Cusanus took leave of the pope, he walked past the other cardinals so distraught that he could not say a word.[91]

The impression left by this scene is that Cusanus, the reformer, posed no significant threat to Pius as sovereign. The *Commentaries* create that impression by using tools familiar from Pius's apologetic repertoire – detailed character sketches and a narrative as entertaining as it is dramatic. They also recycle another valuable tool: the figure of Cusanus himself. Here, however, he appears in a very different role than the one he had been given in the *Libellus*, the pro-conciliar dialogue Aeneas had written almost two decades earlier. In this text, Cusanus is shown defending the papalist position so unsuccessfully that he eventually concedes to his conciliarist opponent. In the *Commentaries*, in contrast, Cusanus again goes down in defeat, but this time, he concedes to the papalist – indeed, to the pope himself. The Cusanus of the *Commentaries* has also evolved into much more of a caricature of himself. An earnest, sophisticated thinker in the *Libellus*, he is reduced here to a rebellious boy, silenced and humiliated by what amounts to the stern scolding of a father figure. This very different portrait, nonetheless, blends well into the *Commentaries*, where Pius shapes an apology that appears bolder, more aggressive, and more extreme in its distortions than his earlier writings on conciliar affairs.

Cusanus's surrender forms part of still another front on which Pius does battle with the cardinals. The pontiff's unwavering defence of absolutism in the face of the cardinals had apparently emboldened the college to further rebellion. The episode with Cusanus described above, however, suggests the very opposite: here Pius's reassertion of papal absolutism in the face of the defiant Cusanus effectively drains the cardinal entirely of his rebellious tendencies. This is, in fact, only one such example. In a string of chapters at the beginning of Book Two, the *Commentaries* enforce the same idea: that in reasserting his exclusive claim to sovereignty, Pius succeeded in dissipating rather than enflaming the resistance of his cardinals. These chapters report four separate confrontations that Pius had with three different cardinals – James of Portugal, Pietro Barbo, and Cusanus again – whom he learns had either overridden papal authority or were attempting to do so.[92] Either in the course of listening to Pius's rebuke or in reflecting on it immediately afterwards, these cardinals are reminded of the pope's position of superiority in relation to the college. Barbo, for example, hears from Pius that his power is "subject to God alone and holy scriptures," and he comes to the conclusion on his own that the cardinals, like the moon, get their light from the papacy.[93] It is, moreover, with these principles explicitly in mind that they repent of their actions. The *Commentaries* report, for example, how the cardinal of San Eustachio "wept bitterly" and "sought mercy for his sin" after "repeating to himself the words of the pontiff."[94] The impression left by these episodes is clear: far from steeling the cardinals for a fight, Pius's efforts to reinforce his sovereignty helped to convince them they should surrender to his will.

While the *Commentaries* emphasize Pius's victory over the cardinals, they underline just as emphatically that the college could claim none of significance for itself. They note, for example, that despite their concerted and united efforts to block the pope's appointment of new cardinals, Pius prevailed in his aims – and twice.[95] Since limiting new appointments was a crucial way the cardinals could preserve their autonomy, mentioning these victories was a particularly useful way to counter the reality of the cardinals' erosion of papal sovereignty. Still more useful was Pius's pronouncement after the second round of appointments in December 1461 that, because his twelve appointees now made up almost half the college, "there was no doubt from that point forward that he would lead the college according to his own will."[96] The statement masks the very different reality that for two and a half more years the college would continue on many levels to represent Pius's most dangerous opponent.

The only apparent defeat the pontiff suffered, according to this account, was in yielding to the cardinals' relentless demand that he give a red hat to his nephew, Francesco Todeschini Piccolomini.[97] In reality, however, this was anything but a defeat for Pius: nepotism was one of the things the capitulations were dead set against.[98] By reporting that it was the cardinals who insisted on Francesco's appointment, the *Commentaries* do the same thing in words as with the earlier image of the cardinals kissing the pontiff's feet: they conceal the threat they posed to papal sovereignty by having them do the very thing they were fighting against.

The *Commentaries* find different ways to conceal what was a far greater vulnerability for Pius. In their battle with the pontiff, the cardinals had inflicted significant damage on Pius's plans for a crusade and on his reputation as leader of this military venture. It is no surprise that the *Commentaries* devote particular attention to obscuring their success here in contesting his authority. The serious blows the cardinals dealt to Pius are dismissed in the *Commentaries* as insignificant: the pope is entirely unmoved by the rumours that detract from his handling of the Congress of Mantua, while his plans to put together a princely coalition appear completely unaffected by attempts by the cardinal of Aquilea, Ludovico Trevisan, to foster an opposing alliance between Venice and France.[99] Pius also specifically discredits the cardinals involved in these schemes through succinct ad hominem attacks (the cardinal of Santa Anastasia, Jacopo Tebaldi, is described as being, among other things, "small of stature, but smaller in mind").[100] It is worth noting, too, that the *Commentaries* go on at length about how poorly the cardinals had counselled Pius on plans for the Congress of Mantua. Their suggestion that he summon the princes to Rome instead is condemned as bad diplomacy, unreasonable, and a reflection of their own laziness. Their advice that he obtain confirmation of the princes' attendance before committing to the long journey north is dismissed as a costly waste of time, and the concern that his reputation will suffer when they do not show up is mocked as illogical.[101] In addition to diminishing their counsel through commentary, Pius weakens it by leaving out the very useful warning they had given him: that departing Rome for a long stretch would make the city dangerously vulnerable to upheaval. Such a systematic response to their criticisms suggests that Pius was genuinely concerned about the damage they might do. At the same time, they suggest his determination to fight back.[102]

The portrayal here in the *Commentaries* of the cardinals as poor papal advisers is, in fact, part of broad and important patterns in both the *Commentaries* and Pius's other anti-conciliar writings. The first of these patterns emerges when we survey as a whole the cardinals' many appearances in the *Commentaries*. Whether acting alone or as a college, the cardinals are repeatedly shown in the act of making decisions and giving advice – and doing an overwhelmingly bad job of it. They are cast in this role from their very first appearance. When we first meet them in Book One, they are recommending to Pope Calixtus III that he appoint to the college a series of candidates fundamentally unqualified for the job, and they show equally poor judgment when advising him on episcopal appointments in Germany.[103] It is in the account of Pius's pontificate, however, that their bad judgment is put most fully on display. The *Commentaries* document a broad range of the cardinals' judgmental blunders. Some are of minor significance: two of them defy papal command by releasing a convicted criminal from jail, while another encourages the pontiff to lend money to a suspicious stranger.[104] Most examples of the cardinals' poor judgment involve matters of considerable significance: in addition to misdirecting Pius on the Congress of Mantua, they are shown giving him bad advice on governing the Papal States, on navigating delicate relations with the French king and other matters of diplomacy, on ensuring his own personal safety, and on making additions to the college.[105] Such a pervasive and consistent portrayal of poor judgment makes for a very powerful weapon with which to retaliate against the threat the cardinals posed as would-be oligarchs: by stripping them so completely of good judgment, the *Commentaries* expose the cardinals as fundamentally unable to exercise the authority they claimed as the pope's fellow sovereigns.

It is in the context of this pattern that we should revisit one of the best-known episodes in the *Commentaries*, the conclave of 1458.[106] This scene, key to the text on so many levels, represents the most egregious example in the entire text of the cardinals' bad judgment. Here, in the context of making their most important decision, the selection of a pope, their judgment is downright appalling: they are on the brink of electing as head of the church the very epitome of moral corruption. More than just as bad judges, however, the account of the conclave exposes the cardinals as bad counsellors: the centrepiece of this episode is Aeneas's conversation with three cardinals, each of whom tries to persuade him to follow their lead and vote for the cardinal of Rouen.[107] Thus, in their very first opportunity to advise the soon-to-be pope, the cardinals make a dismal showing. The *Commentaries* underscore their incompetence by including Pius's long and fiery responses to their suggestions. Those responses are replete with powerful imagery: he likens the cardinals to gluttonous flies, condemns them for selling Christ's tunic without Christ, and accuses them of inviting the Devil to sit on Peter's throne.[108]

The most famous of these images, that the cardinals hatched their plot in the latrines, is thus only one of a series that helps to make their poor judgment so memorable.[109] Just as important and equally entertaining is the catalogue of bad choices the cardinals make even after many in the college had decided to vote for Aeneas. At the final vote, we learn that when Pius's arch-rival, the cardinal of Rouen, deliberately under-counts the votes Pius gets, only Pius has the courage to call him out on it.[110] Then, just when Pius is about to be elected, several cardinals try to slip out to the latrine to stall the process, and when at last one has the courage to cast the deciding vote, two others tackle him and try to drag him out of the chamber before he can speak.[111] On its own, the account of the conclave offers a stinging indictment of the cardinals as counsellors and co-governors. As part of the broader portrayal of poor judgment, it becomes a dire and accurate warning of how this particular crop of cardinals will perform as papal advisers.

A still closer look at the cardinals' poor judgment in the *Commentaries* reveals the other broad pattern into which they fit. In sketching their portraits, Pius drew heavily on tools he used in his Letter of Retraction (1447), his *De rebus* (1450), and his bull *In minoribus* (1463) to describe a very different conciliar enemy: the fathers at the Council of Basel. Like those portraits, the cardinals in the *Commentaries* are explicitly and repeatedly described as foolish, unlearned, ignorant, and stupid,[112] and also like the council, the cardinals are at times so irrational that they seem to have lost their minds.[113] Finally, both collectively and individually, they are shown to be driven by dishonourable motives – in this case, anger, greed, and especially arrogance.[114] In developing the last of these features, the *Commentaries* expand on and darken the portrait of the council fathers in the three aforementioned works. In the *De rebus* and to some extent in his bull *In minoribus*, Pius disparages the character of those in the council along with their intellectual faculties, but not to the extent that he does the cardinals in the *Commentaries*.[115] In this last work, moral failings are actually cited as the main reason why the cardinals cannot do their job of advising. "You live in such a way," Pius tells the college when proposing to add new members, "that you seem not to have been chosen to govern, but to have been called to enjoy pleasures."[116] In this way, then, Pius is adapting more than simply adopting the portraits developed in these other texts. And he does so in still other ways, too. In characterizing the cardinals as undiscerning judges, Pius is not reversing an earlier, opposing argument as he was doing in the Letter of Retraction, the *De rebus*, and *In minoribus*; never in his writings had he promoted the authority of cardinals as co-governors of the church. Thus, in presenting the cardinals in the *Commentaries*, Pius is doing more than just reshaping existing weapons in his arsenal: he is also redeploying them on a related but ultimately different mission.

That mission, it should be emphasized, has a very specific target. While the portrait of the cardinals in the *Commentaries* is overwhelmingly negative, there are some important exceptions and some important shifts over time, too. Cardinal Juan de Carvajal, for example, is never described as showing poor judgment – a useful portrayal, given that Pius's past disagreements with Carvajal were, like those with Nicholas V, ones he would have done well to conceal. Nor, with one exception, does he ever single out for condemnation the twelve cardinals he names to the college. Moreover, after the second election, the point at which he says he now dominated the college, the *Commentaries* document significantly fewer instances of the cardinals mishandling their jobs as advisers, either individually or collectively. The shift makes good sense, given how the *Commentaries* characterize both Pius's aims and achievements in selecting new members. When explaining his reasons for naming new ones to the college in 1460, he observes, "We are looking for those cardinals who can advise us and the church"[117] – a task, he explains pointedly, he must take up because in its current form, the college is not serving as good counsellors. The ones he does appoint, the *Commentaries* go on to note, are overwhelmingly well suited to the task.[118] Thus, the disparaging portrait of the cardinals in the *Commentaries* does not represent a wholesale attack on the college, nor is it a rejection of the basic idea that cardinals should serve as the pope's counsellors. Rather, it functions as a pointed defence against the particular crop of cardinals who, in both their actions and in their own interpretation of what it means to counsel the pope, undermined his rule as sole and successful sovereign.

There is no question that such a narrative was a very valuable one for Pius II to put forward under the circumstances, but it was not one without its glitches. It is undermined by the portrait Pius paints of one of his own appointments to the college: the cardinal of Arras, Jean Jouffroy. The *Commentaries* make very clear that Pius does not give Jouffroy a red hat because he considers him well qualified for the job: his appointment is the price the pope must pay for the king of France to revoke the Pragmatic Sanction of Bourges.[119] Jouffroy's presence in the college, Pius explains, is the lesser of the two evils. While the *Commentaries* emphasize this point, they also dwell at length on the evil the cardinal represents. The detailed portrait of the cardinal in the final chapter of Book Twelve is one of the longest in the entire *Commentaries*; and, thanks to its signature anecdotes, it is also one of the most unforgettable (the cardinal is memorably described as pelting his servants with buns and punching out acolytes after saying Mass).[120] Such a portrait fits smoothly into another important dimension of Pius's apology: its sweeping attack on all things French.[121] But the reported magnitude of Arras's wickedness, along with the particular details of his portrait, sit uneasily with the simultaneous claim in the *Commentaries* that by the end of 1461, the college was serving only the will of the pope. In addition to underscoring his debauched character, the *Commentaries* paint Arras doing serious damage to papal policy: among other things, they accuse him of exposing the secret business of the consistory, of distorting crucial correspondence with the king of France, and of attempting to sabotage relations with Roman barons.[122] So many and so serious are these transgressions that the long excursus in Book Twelve leaves the distinct impression that, single-handedly, Arras was as dangerous to Pius as the entire crop of cardinals he had sought to silence with his new appointments. These tensions seem to confirm only further the pattern seen elsewhere in the *Commentaries*, namely, in his efforts to pull through one thread of his apology, Pius once again ends up loosening another.

Execrabilis

Perhaps because there was so much at stake, the *Commentaries* offer a more protective shield against the failure of *Execrabilis*, Pope Pius II's most ambitious attack of all against conciliarism. As chapter 2 discussed, the bull drafted in 1460 did not simply suppress appeals from pope to council: it also undermined *Haec Sancta*, the decree that had lent legitimacy to those appeals. Like so many other spiritual weapons the pope deployed in the fifteenth century, *Execrabilis* proved from its inception resoundingly impotent. Because it represented a lethal strike against a well-supported movement, Pope Pius was even reluctant to acknowledge its existence for fear that doing so would initiate a damaging backlash. Moreover, the handful of times he did use it, precisely that happened. The three people targeted by *Execrabilis* – archbishop Diether of Mainz, duke Sigismund of Austria, and Gregor Heimburg – made themselves into rallying points for the conciliar movement in Germany, cementing princes into a dangerous anti-papal coalition and spawning a wave of writings that targeted both papal supremacy and Pius himself. In the *Commentaries*, however, there is no sense of the weakness of *Execrabilis* or that it precipitated for the papacy a crisis of considerable magnitude. Indeed, it does not appear to have created any kind of crisis at all.

In contrast to what it really was, *Execrabilis* appears in the *Commentaries* as a powerful spiritual weapon. Pius creates this impression simply by openly acknowledging that this bull was drafted at the end of the Congress of Mantua.[123] If concealing the bull showed just how weak a weapon it really was in the face of conciliar claims to supremacy, its very public announcement in the *Commentaries* seems to communicate the very opposite. What creates this impression first and foremost is the fact that up to this point in the text, the conciliar movement has been made out to be essentially innocuous: missing is any sense of how widespread the support was for conciliar supremacy or any explicit reference to the legitimizing decree *Haec Sancta*. There is, in short, nothing to suggest the reality that *Execrabilis* could –indeed, almost certainly would – meet with serious resistance. The *Commentaries* continue to promote an impression of the strength of *Execrabilis* when discussing what happened when Pius drew this weapon. In reality, the bull did not succeed in intimidating either the three men it targeted or any of their supporters; indeed, long after its promulgation, Diether, Sigismund, and Heimburg continued to appeal their case to a future council and to rally people of influence to their cause. According to the *Commentaries*, however, the bull had a very different effect. Pius reports that in the spring of 1461 "few ... dared support [Diether's] appeal, fearing the censure of the Mantuan decree [*Execrabilis*]."[124] It was particularly useful in this instance for the *Commentaries* to exaggerate the bull's power of intimidation: the real reason why the princes withdrew from Diether at this point was because Pius had withdrawn his demand that they support his crusade tithes.

Based on what the *Commentaries* tell us, these princes had good reason to fear. In Pius's account, Diether, Heimburg, and Sigismund are stripped of the most important weapons they used to retaliate against Pius's bull. In describing their response to the pontiff, the *Commentaries* never once mention what was one of their most powerful arguments: they appealed to the higher authority of a general council on the basis of *Haec Sancta*. By passing over this decree in silence, Pius both disarms his conciliar opponents and at the same time delegitimizes the decree itself.

In still other ways, Pius strengthens *Execrabilis* by weakening the weapons of his enemies. His opponents not only lack *Haec Sancta*, but they also lack reason, learning, and honourable cause. As he does with the cardinals, Pius sketches Diether, Sigismund, and Heimburg as extensions and intensifications of the portraits of the Basel fathers in his other writings. They are foolish, ignorant, mad, and depraved. Once again, he enforces these unsavoury impressions with memorable details. Gregor Heimburg, the *Commentaries* note on two separate occasions, came to be known as "Errorius" on account of the many errors he made.[125] Diether is made out to be still worse – a veritable madman who rather than arguing "vomit[s] forth all his poison" against the pope.[126] It is Sigismund of Austria, however, a man described as a prisoner of his passions, who is described most colourfully: the *Commentaries* report that he was obsessed with getting his hands on a legendary Austrian sword that reportedly had been used to sever two heads in a single blow![127] These uniformly and strikingly pejorative portraits serve, like those of the cardinals, a very different purpose from the ones of the Basel fathers on which they are based: together, they effectively mask the fact that marshalled against *Execrabilis* stood a host of legal instruments, substantial arguments, and powerful publicists.

While Pius obscures the strength of his opponents' position, he also hides the weakness of his own position. He does so in part by transferring these deficiencies to his enemy. As chapter 2 laid out, the writings of Heimburg, Diether, and Sigismund of Austria painted a damaging picture of Pius as a tyrant who had no regard for law, whether positive, natural, or divine. But in the *Commentaries*, it is Diether, not Pius, who fits this description. The archbishop is condemned as "despising divine and human laws," for profaning the divine offices; and when Pius deposes him, the *Commentaries* report how the city rejoices and the priests proclaim that "the day had arrived in which they at last threw off cruel tyranny."[128] Pius, in contrast, is presented as meticulous in his respect for the law.[129] Perhaps the greatest weakness the *Commentaries* obscure is the utter failure of *Execrabilis* to bring Diether to heel. Chapter 2 pointed out that when Diether eventually submitted to the papacy, he was not made to acknowledge papal supremacy as *Execrabilis* stipulated that he should. The account in the *Commentaries*, however, presents a very different interpretation.[130] The short chapter on Diether's surrender is inserted into a series of triumphs that Pius catalogues in the final, climactic section of Book Twelve. As he reports what happened, moreover, Pius focuses his attention on Diether's humble submission to papal authority, first by noting how he prostrated himself in obedience to the man whom Pius had designated as his replacement in the archbishopric of Mainz, and then by recounting how he knelt before the apostolic legate for pardon.[131] In noting simply that Diether "was absolved," the *Commentaries* obscure the fact that the rebellious archbishop was never actually made to renounce his allegiance to conciliar theory. Once again Pius's compelling imagery of ceremony hides from view that *Execrabilis* had proven to be an imperfect tool in the pontiff's war against conciliarism. His defeat of Diether instead reads as an untrammelled triumph.

This claim represents a defence for Pius on more than one level. Of the many aspects of these events that the *Commentaries* conceal from view, the most significant is the fact that Pius's conflict over *Execrabilis* involved more than three individuals. In reality, Diether, Sigismund, and Heimburg tapped into and fanned the flames of conciliar sentiment in Germany, and they did so at a high cost to Pius. Significantly, the *Commentaries* make no mention of the fact that Diether served as leader of a powerful anti-papal faction of German princes; that it was under his leadership that these princes had sought to shape their own version of the Pragmatic Sanction of Bourges; and that when he and Sigismund enlisted the services of the talented publicist, Gregor Heimburg, their personal conflicts with the pope became a rallying cry for conciliarists across Germany. Instead, Diether comes across as a petty, disgruntled, and largely isolated individual. Once again, it is the backdrop of Book One that makes this image of isolation plausible: there, the papacy's relationship with Germany is presented as strong, and conciliar sentiment of any kind is virtually non-existent.

It is what the *Commentaries* record after Book One, however, that obscures this powerful alliance most fully. In discussing Diether's relationship with these princes, the *Commentaries* train their focus on what happened at the Diet of Mainz in April 1461.[132] Of all the assemblies over which Diether had presided, this was the one in which his efforts to organize the princes against the papacy met with the least success.[133] Pius emphasizes Diether's failure, and at the same time, does something more. According to the *Commentaries*, the speech that Diether addressed to the assembly summarized many of the grievances that Germans had voiced about the Roman Church: their suspicion of the crusade as a money-making venture, their complaint that the papal appetite for German money was both insatiable and unjust, and their conviction that obedience to the pope was tantamount to slavery.[134] Pius weakens these criticisms not only by putting them in the mouth of Diether, but also by reporting the response of the papal legate in attendance, Rudolph of Worms. Far longer, far more eloquent, and far more persuasive than Diether's, Rudolph's words – so the *Commentaries* report – easily convince the princes in attendance to abandon Diether's cause.[135] Pius's account leaves the very misleading impression that Diether's criticisms of the papacy no longer represented a concern either for Germany or for the pope, an impression that was hardly an accurate portrayal. By making Diether the primary mouthpiece of German anti-papalism, and a fundamentally ineffective one at that, the *Commentaries* are able to hide from view the seriously strained relations between Germany and Rome and, in particular, the widespread support for conciliarism across the Holy Roman Empire. In the absence of such threats, Pius II's authority seems in the *Commentaries* far stronger and far more stable than in fact it really was.

The Pragmatic Sanction of Bourges and the Compacts

In a similar way the *Commentaries* diminish the conciliar threats Pope Pius II faced in two other parts of Western Christendom: France and Bohemia. The Pragmatic Sanction of Bourges and the Bohemian Compacts were two unwelcome reminders for both Pius and the papacy of the enduring authority of the Council of Basel. Pius had tried to abrogate both, but had failed in his attempts, and in so doing only confirmed the resilience of conciliarism and Basel's legal legacy. The *Commentaries*, however, paint a very different picture of these events. By delegitimizing the Pragmatic Sanction and the Bohemian Compacts and by masking their resilience to papal attack, Pius conceals both the danger and the stigma that these two instruments represented to papal sovereignty.

In contrast to his more oblique attack on *Haec Sancta*, Pius confronts the Pragmatic Sanction and the Compacts head on in the *Commentaries*. As already discussed, he declares the Pragmatic Sanction invalid by tracing its origins to the allegedly illegitimate pronouncements of the Council of Basel. His attack on the Bohemian Compacts is still more extensive. Pius begins by attacking the spiritual core of the Compacts, Holy Communion *sub utraque specie*, by noting that it was the invention of an ignorant and anti-clerical grammar teacher; by associating it with the Devil; and by characterizing it as an error noxious to the spiritual health of Bohemia.[136] Still more attention is focused on emptying the Compacts of their legal value. According to Pius, to the envoy he sends to the Bohemian king, and to the clergy there still loyal to Rome, the Compacts are illegitimate for a host of different reasons. They argue that the agreement had long ago expired, that it had been voided by the Bohemians' failure to honour it, and that it had never been recognized by Rome in the first place.[137] These arguments were not new: they were the ones papalists typically marshalled when contesting the legitimacy of this instrument. But the *Commentaries* draw a new, still more potent weapon: they deny the Compacts even the sanction of the Council of Basel. Pius reports that when the papal envoy to Bohemia, Fantino della Valle, was leaving to return to Rome, something "miraculous" happened: the envoy was handed a suitcase containing numerous bulls and other instruments from the Basel and Constance assemblies. All of them condemned communion *sub utraque specie*.[138] Through this remarkable and uncorroborated account, Pius launches the same kind of attack on the Compacts that he had against Diether of Mainz, albeit more boldly and more directly. The *Commentaries* had deprived the archbishop of the legal basis for appealing to a future council by failing to acknowledge his use of *Haec Sancta*. Pius does the same thing here to the Bohemians: by claiming that the Basel assembly itself did not recognize the practice that represented the very heart of the Compacts, he is essentially saying that this agreement, as the Bohemians understood it, had never even existed. In effect, the *Commentaries* do what Pius was not able to do in his pontificate: abolish the Compacts once and for all.

In still other ways, the *Commentaries* present Pius's failed struggle against the Pragmatic Sanction and the Bohemian Compacts as tales of success. Chapter 2 has explained how, less than two years after abrogating the Pragmatic Sanction (November 1461), Louis XI had effectively reinstated it as a series of royal decrees. In the process he had reasserted with conviction French respect for conciliar authority. In the *Commentaries*, however, it is France's obedience to the pope that stands in the foreground. Recounting his audience with the royal legates who brought the news of the Pragmatic Sanction's withdrawal, Pius draws attention once again to the ceremonial performance of papal sovereignty: he notes how the French envoys kissed the pope's feet, how he addressed them from his throne, and how all listened to his words with rapt attention.[139] By then detailing the festivities that took place across Rome in celebration of the Pragmatic Sanction's withdrawal, Pius helps to make his temporary victory the most memorable moment of what was really a much longer and ultimately unsuccessful war to defeat conciliar forces in France.[140]

Images of celebration are not the only way the *Commentaries* mute Louis XI's eventual, and for the pontiff embarrassing, about-face. Folded into this same passage are remarks that seem to foreshadow Louis's change of heart and in a way that softens the blow to Pius's reputation. The king's retraction, he reports, seemed "all the more praiseworthy and admirable for being so unexpected. For there was nobody who considered that after twenty-four years the long-standing disease of the Pragmatic could be taken away. Everyone thought it was enough that the Apostolic See did not aggravate the problem."[141] Louis's decision to reinstate the Pragmatic Sanction cannot, Pius seems to suggest here, be counted as a defeat for the papacy since its withdrawal had never seemed an attainable goal in the first place. In the way he goes on to characterize Louis's about-face, Pius continues to minimize the king's defiant rejection of papal authority. "Louis ... seemed to withdraw a little bit from his faithful devotion to the pope," he begins the chapter that relates what was, in fact, a radical change in the king's position;[142] and he goes on to reinterpret the three decrees reinstating the Pragmatic Sanction as anything but a sign of his own weak authority. Instead, they evince in the king a weak and corrupted faith: "Louis seemed not so much religious for having abolished the Pragmatic Sanction as he did sacrilegious for having published these decrees."[143]

Pius's equally unsuccessful battle against the Bohemian Compacts unfolds in a similar way in the *Commentaries*.[144] In August 1462, when Pius had sent his envoy, Fantino della Valle, to the Bohemian king to explain the decision to declare the Compacts null and void, the mission proved to be a disaster. Not only had Podiebrad refused to comply with the pope's ruling, but he had also added insult to injury by throwing Fantino in prison. The *Commentaries* present these events in a far more positive light: drawing on the same parallels he had once used to characterize the fathers at Basel, Pius presents Fantino's persecution as a story of triumphant martyrdom. When, after hearing out the envoy's message, Podiebrad threatens him with punishment, Fantino exclaims, "You can take away my body, King, but you cannot take my soul. If I lose my earthly life, I will gain a heavenly one, dying for truth; I wish that you would do me such an honour!"[145] Later, the Bohemian clergy faithful to Rome make a similar pledge of self-sacrifice in the face of the king's threats: "[The Apostolic See] is the doorway to heaven. We would prefer to die than oppose it."[146] The effect of Pius's narrative is to shift the focus away from the failure of Fantino's mission and to rewrite it as a victory of a different kind: in the *Commentaries*, the Roman Church conquers Podiebrad not by winning his obedience but by boldly defending the true faith against an intractable heretic. For Pius, this is a familiar storyline: it bears striking similarities to the one he had developed in the *De gestis* when defending the Basel fathers' decision to depose a pope whom they deemed heretical. The closing passage of Pius's account of Fantino's embassy further confirms this interpretive framework. The reception Fantino receives upon his return to Rome makes his mission seem an unmitigated success: he is showered with great honours and awarded a bishopric; and no mention is made of how the king had received Fantino's news. It is here, moreover, where Pius makes his ambassador out explicitly to be a spiritual hero, noting that he been subjected to "a martyrdom for truth."[147]

The account of Fantino's triumphant return to Rome is a fitting ending to this analysis. Like Fantino the martyr, Pius emerges in the *Commentaries* as triumphant in his battles against his conciliarist foe. This narrative of triumph might be read as an incomplete representation of what happened during his papacy; given the evidence presented here, however, and in chapters 1 and 2, it could instead by characterized as misrepresentation. Indeed, by reading the *Commentaries* against a detailed backdrop of the conciliar crisis, this chapter has illuminated just how carefully and how systematically this text distorts the historical record. The fact that Pope Pius II would take the time to develop such a thorough and severe assault is unequivocal evidence of the dire threat he believed conciliarism posed, in various forms, to him and to the papacy. The results of his efforts demonstrate something equally significant. In the relentless war the papacy waged against conciliarism, humanism and, more specifically, humanist historiography proved to be a potent weapon.

5 The Triumph over the Princes and the Triumph of a Prince

I shall listen to you whenever and however long you like. But know that we will have the last word. Do not be surprised if you who came here to strike are struck in return. The Apostolic See does not yield to anyone, not even the greatest of kings.[1]

This bold and confident pronouncement of papal superiority offers a glimpse of still another way in which the *Commentaries* serve as a work of apology. According to his account in Book Three, Pius II addressed these remarks to a distinguished French embassy that was protesting his decision to invest Ferrante with the Kingdom of Naples. In his response to their protests, Pius acknowledges indirectly two defining features of his pontificate that are outlined in chapter 3: one, that he faced challenges to his authority from the secular powers of Europe; and two, that he faced challenges not just from princes, but also as a prince himself. But Pius's words do more than signal what he needed to defend himself against: they also tell us something about how he built that defence. The *Commentaries*, this chapter argues, present a portrait of Pius as an uncompromised and uncompromising sovereign. In both his temporal and spiritual realms, he dominates the same princes who, in reality, had consistently weakened his authority. At the same time as he diminishes the authority of these princes, he underscores the strength of his own princely authority against the host of opponents he faced. In short, the words Pius pronounced to the French envoys serve in the *Commentaries* as the common refrain of Pius the pope and Pius the prince: "The Apostolic See does not yield to anyone, not even the greatest of kings."

Pius, of course, does not always speak these words literally to his opponents, and one of the aims of this chapter is to elucidate the different forms this triumph of sovereignty takes. In the process of doing so, it will present several important claims about the nature, scope, and significance of his apology. For one, it identifies in Pius's account of his crusade, long considered a centrepiece of the text, a crucial building block for his apology. This chapter also demonstrates how the *Commentaries* continue to construct a defence of Pius by concealing his past as Aeneas. At the same time, it illuminates the remarkable scope of the text's apologetic design. More than simply a defence of his own authority, legitimacy, and relevance as both pope and prince, the *Commentaries* make a case for why papal sovereignty should endure in the reigns of his successors. Unfolding these layers of defence will, in turn, allow us to see the considerable common ground in the methods Pius employs as an apologetic historian: the tools he uses to defend against secular rulers, *condottieri*, Roman rebels, and sharp-tongued humanists are the same as those he takes up against his conciliar foes. We will also find evidence of another pattern that emerged from the analysis in chapter 4: at times, the defences Pius builds in one part of the book undermine those he constructs in another. The final pages of the chapter will take up an argument that will be addressed still more fully in the sixth and final one. In constructing Pius's portrait and, indeed, central elements of it, the *Commentaries* draw on the language, ideals, and values of contemporary secular politics.

Papal Advocate: A Revisionist History of Aeneas's Pre-papal Career

Pius's early involvement with the conciliar crisis was hardly the only liability he faced when he looked back on his pre-papal career. As chapter 3 explained, he had actively defended in writing the other competitor for papal sovereignty, the secular princes, and most notably in the context of Germany's reconciliation with the Roman Church in 1446–47. His later career created liabilities of a different kind. At the crusading diets of 1454–55, Aeneas's struggle to win princely support for the crusade served as an embarrassing reminder for the papacy of what little power popes (as well as the emperors) wielded over secular rulers. A year later, as a cardinal at the papal court, Aeneas exposed papal weaknesses in a different way: because of the authority he now exercised over the German church, Aeneas became for Germany's princes a symbol of papal oppression and a catalyst for their renewed efforts to win ecclesiastical independence. Ironically, even his own election as pope proved to be a liability to him since Italy's rulers had helped to orchestrate its outcome. In short, both intentionally and unintentionally, Aeneas had at several points in his career enabled Europe's princes to push back against papal sovereignty.

The *Commentaries* present this period in Aeneas's career as being far more innocuous to the papacy than it really was. Indeed, according to this account, Pius did much to strengthen and protect the authority of his immediate papal predecessors. The *Commentaries* create these impressions in familiar ways. In some cases, they simply erase from the historical record what had, for Pius, become particularly dangerous liabilities. At the same time, they shape Pius's skills as an orator into powerful and effective tools for promoting papal authority. The Aeneas of the *Commentaries* is, thus, transformed into an asset both for Pope Pius and for the institution of papal monarchy.

In the account of his years at the imperial court, the *Commentaries* hide any evidence that Aeneas promoted princely interests at the expense of papal sovereignty. While we learn that his influence at court grew quickly and that he was soon welcomed into the circle of Emperor Frederick III's closest advisers, we hear nothing of the advice he gave the emperor that, for Pius, would have proven so damaging: that an assembly of princes be summoned to put an end to the schism.[2] In a different way, the *Commentaries* conceal the liabilities Pius faced from his role in reconciling the German princes to Pope Eugenius in 1447. Among the demands Aeneas had included when drawing up the terms of peace (the imperial compromise proposal) was that the pope recognize the reform decrees of Basel – decrees that would significantly extend the German princes' control over their church.[3] The *Commentaries* frame this demand in very different terms and ones far more friendly to the papacy. Rather than asking the pontiff to observe these decrees, Aeneas here simply asks Eugenius in vague terms "that [Germany] be provided for."[4] According to the *Commentaries*, Aeneas's request is embraced by both cardinals and pope alike – still further evidence that his defence of the princes posed no threat to papal interests.[5] On the contrary, by bringing the princes back into the fold of the Roman Church, Aeneas is shown helping the pope to achieve one of his most crucial goals.

Aeneas appears still more the papacy's advocate – and a supremely successful one, too – in the context of the imperial diets of 1454–55.[6] Rather than failed attempts to rally Europe's princes to crusade, these assemblies appear in the *Commentaries* as overwhelming successes, and all because of Aeneas the orator. In direct contrast to his letter of 1454, which bemoaned princes' immunity to persuasive rhetoric, Aeneas in the *Commentaries* wins even the most recalcitrant rulers to his cause through his long and moving orations.[7] The fact that no expedition resulted from these oratorical triumphs was no fault of Aeneas's, we are told. What stopped the crusade, Pius explains, was instead the untimely death of Pope Nicholas V and a decision by God: "Divine Mercy did not want the Turkish empire to be destroyed at that moment. It was kept in place a little longer to correct our sins."[8] Pius's account of these diets does more than paper over his own early struggles to turn Europe's princes to crusade. It also helps him to defend his own claim to crusade leadership as pope. According to the *Commentaries*, not only had Aeneas earned considerable experience orchestrating an expedition against the Turks, but he had also been immensely successful doing so. The implication is that in leading a crusade from the papal throne, Pius would simply be completing a job that was already, and quite rightfully, his.

The Aeneas of the *Commentaries* again helps to protect papal interests shortly after the last of these diets. This time, he does so in the context of princely resistance to more than just the crusade. The archbishop of Trier, we learn, is appealing to his fellow German princes to demand new concessions from the newly elected pope, Calixtus III, before they offer him their obedience. The description of this new anti-papal uprising recalls in part the one of 1456–57, in which Aeneas became a target of attack. But in the *Commentaries*, this event is pushed back in time to a period before he was cardinal and thus, before he himself had become a target of the princes' attack. The chronological shift helps to relieve Aeneas of some of the responsibility for anti-papal sentiment in Germany; so does the *Commentaries'* account of how he responded to the archbishop's plan. Aeneas speaks out passionately against it and extols the benefits of obedience to the pope. His words, we are told, had a powerful effect: the plan for independence is abandoned and the princes agree to offer Calixtus their unconditional obedience.[9] The *Commentaries* thus present Aeneas doing the very opposite of what he had done unintentionally as a cardinal: rather than inciting the princes against the pope, he bends them to the papacy's will. In so doing, Pius does more than simply shore up his own portrait as pope. He also masks serious tensions between Germany and the papacy in the years preceding his own ascension to the papal throne.

The *Commentaries'* account of how he reached that throne serve to underscore still further the lack of power Europe's princes wielded over the papacy and over his own pontificate in particular. There is no evidence here of Milanese and Neapolitan ambassadors orchestrating the outcome of the conclave. Instead, we learn that Ferrante of Naples and Francesco Sforza were informed of the election after the fact; and we also learn that the Milanese duke had expected a different outcome.[10] The *Commentaries* do assign two other rulers a role in the election: both Frederick III and Alfonso of Naples predict that Pius will be made pope.[11] But as prophets, these kings exercise no direct control over the conclave. The person who does, the *Commentaries* report, and without the direction of any secular ruler, is Pius himself. Here, it is Pius, particularly Pius the orator who convinces the cardinals to abandon the French candidate to the throne.[12] Against the backdrop of the real election, the *Commentaries'* account of the conclave takes on new meaning: it is Pius's first victory as pope in what would be a long and contentious war against Europe's princes.

Authority, Legitimacy, and Relevance Regained: The Crusade in the *Commentaries*

Pius waged that war most fully in the context of his crusade, and he did so with little success. Chapter 3 has argued that in his efforts to lead an expedition against the Turks, Pius II suffered a devastating loss in his battle to re-establish papal authority, legitimacy, and relevance. Indeed, the crusade ended up by accomplishing the very opposite of what it was intended to do: rather than rebuilding Pius's position of authority over Europe's princes, it ended up undercutting that authority significantly. At the same time, Pius's struggles raised serious questions about the pope's claim to spiritual sovereignty and cast into further doubt the very need for his leadership in the context of the crusade.

The *Commentaries* unfold a very different story. Front and centre in their narrative is Pius's success at exerting his authority over the princes in the context of the expedition against the Turks. They do so in part by relying on tools employed elsewhere in the text when sketching Pius II's conciliarist battles: they sometimes erase from the historical record events, ideas, and individuals who challenged his authority; they hide princely insubordination behind accounts of ceremony that instead imply the very opposite attitude to papal power; and they fashion oratory into a powerful tool for asserting his authority. Moreover, by drawing on criticisms of secular rule that he had developed in earlier writings, Pius constructs an account that also defends his claim to spiritual sovereignty and underscores his indispensability as a crusade leader. In so doing, he accomplishes in the *Commentaries* what he failed to do in his own pontificate: through his crusade, he presents himself successfully re-establishing papal sovereignty over the secular powers of Europe.

The account of the Congress of Mantua is a good starting point for studying this defence. The assembly is given extensive treatment in the *Commentaries*: all of Book Three is given over to describing the proceedings while much of Book Two discusses Pius's preparations for the event and his journey to Mantua.[13] Given that Europe's princes proved overwhelmingly unresponsive to the pope's proposed expedition, the weight given to the congress might seem at first to undercut the apologetic aim of the *Commentaries*. But in Pius's account of events, there is little to suggest that the assembly was either an embarrassment or a disappointment for the pope. On the contrary, the Congress of Mantua becomes a powerful display of both Pius's authority over Europe's princes and the legitimacy of this sovereignty.

The *Commentaries* achieve this effect in large part through the imagery of ceremony. Their description of Pius's solemn entry into the city in May 1459 is a case in point. The arrival had, in reality, exposed the weakness of his authority: hardly any of the princes or their embassies had been on hand to meet him. The *Commentaries* transform this display of disrespect into something very different. They draw attention to the crowds of visitors filling the streets when he arrived while passing over the identities of those who were or were not there. The only people he singles out are ones who made for an illustrious presence: the *signore* of Mantua and the wife and family of the duke of Milan. Pius pauses to describe the solemnity and splendour of the procession that accompanies his entrance, carefully noting the presence of princely legates, though neither their origins nor their number. The little esteem the princes showed him is further obscured by his own majestic presence in the procession (he is carried on a seat, high above the others, and wears atop his head a bejewelled mitre), by the lavish decorations that adorn the buildings he passes, and by the cries of approval he hears from the crowd: "Long live Pope Pius!"[14]

As the narrative of the congress unfolds, Pius continues to employ images of ceremony in a way that conceals the little power he actually wielded over the princes. He makes a point of highlighting the majesty, splendour, and influence of those who arrive on time for the assembly, or those who throw their support behind the pope's venture. Pius lingers over Duke Francesco Sforza's magnificent entry in the city;[15] and when the legates from Florence, Lucca, and Siena make their entrance, he notes that theirs were distinguished retinues.[16] The magnificent accoutrements and superior credentials of these embassies suggest that these rulers hold the pontiff in considerable esteem. Their respect for papal authority is reinforced still further by references to the ritual whereby leaders of state or their representatives would kiss the pontiff's feet. That Pius wanted this particular gesture to highlight obedience to his sovereign power seems confirmed by the crowd's reported reaction when Francesco Sforza knelt before him: "'the majesty and authority of the pope must indeed be high and illustrious if such a prince comes to kiss his feet.'"[17] Even when this ritual is not being performed, Pius maintains a position of physical superiority in relation to the princes. Again and again, the *Commentaries* report how he receives embassies and delivers orations while seated on his throne.[18]

Oratory as well as ceremony serves to conceal the weakness of Pius's authority at the congress. The *Commentaries* report Pius delivering three orations to the general assembly, all of which had a profound effect on their audience.[19] The first two, we learn, left those in attendance spellbound, while the third inspired all who had pledged support for the crusade to confirm their promises.[20] Pius's meetings with individual princes and their ambassadors are similarly effective: they show the pontiff using rhetoric to subdue and silence some and to win the trust and admiration of others.[21] The *Commentaries* dwell in particular on a series of audiences Pius had with the French legates regarding the question of the Kingdom of Naples. In reporting these encounters, Pius focuses on the ambassadors' frustration in the face of Pius's steadfast defence of Ferrante, their struggles to overturn his arguments, and their humble admission of defeat.[22] With words as his weapons, the *Commentaries* seem to suggest, Pius proves invincible to even his strongest opponents. As he does elsewhere in the text, he conveys this message in brief but vivid images: the legates, after losing their argument, prostrate themselves at Pius's feet. They also do what Pius's enemies do elsewhere in the *Commentaries*: they explicitly confess to a position opposite to the one they really hold. Likening himself to a man just exorcised of a demon, a member of the delegation cries, "The same thing has happened to us: after seeing and hearing Pope Pius, all of our madness has disappeared."[23]

Interestingly, despite making princely deference to papal authority a dominant theme in his account of the congress, Pius does not hide the fact that some princes did not comply with his commands. Indeed, at several points, that insubordination is given a place of prominence: the very first words of Pius's opening oration, for example, note how many people have yet to show up.[24] At other points, too, he notes those who fail to come to the congress, who send unworthy embassies, or who, while in attendance, demonstrate little support and enthusiasm for his expedition.[25] The emphasis seems, at first, puzzling and at odds with other aspects of his account. Why would Pius choose to draw attention to the princes who paid him little heed? Why not simply do what he had done in the case of the Council of Basel – erase these liabilities outright from the historical record?

Rather than detracting from Pius's self-portrait of papal strength, these references actually serve to enhance it, and significantly. The *Commentaries* do not simply acknowledge this insubordinate behaviour: they explain it, and the motives they deduce are damning. Those absent, tardy, or uncommitted to his crusade, we are told, are driven by avarice, self-interest, a misplaced concern for their state, and depraved indifference to the Christian religion. "The Christian people care less for their religion than we thought," Pius observes in his opening oration, and he goes on to offer an explanation for their behaviour: "We are ashamed by the great negligence of Christians. Some indulge their desires, others are detained by avarice."[26] Pius saves his harshest attacks for the Venetians and the French, the most recalcitrant of those attending the assembly. The former, he declares, "no longer care about religion";[27] while the latter he mocks as hypocrites: "You call your king the most Christian, but he cares nothing about helping the Christian religion in peril."[28]

Pius's sketches of these figures will be familiar to anyone who knows his earlier writings on the crusade. He is using the same language and making the same accusations that he had when he first observed princely indifference to the papal and imperial crusade initiatives in the 1450s. As they did in that context, these comments serve an important apologetic purpose in the *Commentaries*. Pius's damning portrait of the princes' motives is crucial to the image of strong papal authority he constructs throughout his account of the congress. By masking the princes' deep scepticism about his expedition and their questions about his integrity, Pius effectively hides from view just how little authority he actually wielded over Europe's secular rulers. At the same time, by attributing to these rulers motives of avarice and self-interest, he effectively robs their objections to his crusade of any legitimacy. The implications are significant: by delegitimizing the position of the princes, the *Commentaries* help to legitimize Pius's own position as leader of the crusade.

That legitimacy is underscored still further in the pontiff's own self-portrait at the congress. In contrast to these negligent princes, Pius ascribes to himself only the purest of motives. Again and again, he explicitly defines his crusade as a mission to rescue the Christian faith – and so, significantly, do many of the princes, too.[29] Dramatic imagery reinforces this idea still further: the *Commentaries* note that Pius closed the assembly kneeling in fervent prayer, singing hymns and weeping for the cause of his campaign.[30] The text pairs the pontiff's noble intentions with genuine commitment. By underscoring the challenges he endured on the journey to Mantua, his account of the congress conveys his unflinching determination to carry out this mission.[31]

He appears equally capable as commander of the crusading army. The *Commentaries* report a long discussion Pius has with ambassadors from Burgundy in which he lays out his plans for the expedition. Even the legates who were "the most experienced in military matters" were deeply impressed by his words.[32] A few pages later, Pius again demonstrates his superior grasp of crusade logistics in a private council with Italian rulers and their ambassadors, many of whom were also seasoned generals.[33] According to his account, Pius began the assembly soliciting opinions on a series of issues – whether to conduct the war by land or by sea, how many troops would be needed, and how best to support the Hungarians. It soon becomes clear, however, that Pius needed no one's advice on these matters. Dominating the discussion, the pope demonstrates his sophisticated understanding of the Ottoman army, troop numbers, the role of cavalry, and battlefield topography. "If you have thought of better plans, bring them forward," Pius concludes, speaking to those assembled. But no one does. "The Pope's opinion," the *Commentaries* tell us, "pleased everyone."[34] Given the extraordinary military role Pius had assigned himself in the crusade, and given the questions raised about both his intentions and his capabilities as crusade leader, these features of his self-portrait hold significant apologetic value. Through them, the *Commentaries* make a compelling case for why he could and should lead this expedition.

Just as important is the related idea the *Commentaries* put forward: that no one else was capable of taking his place. That impression is created in part by the sharp contrasts the *Commentaries* draw between the unreservedly selfless pope and the obsessively self-interested princes. It is further underscored by several delegations that come to Mantua from the East; all of them appeal to the pope – and to him alone – as the only hope for protection from the Turkish threat.[35] Perhaps most important is that even the princes acknowledge Pius's exclusive claim to crusade leadership. In Book Two, as Pius is making public for the first time his plans to hold the Congress of Mantua, the royal ambassadors and others assembled to listen "praised ... his courage and purpose and exalted him to the skies as the only one who cared about saving the faith."[36] One of Pius's reasons for leading the crusade was to re-establish the papacy's relevance as a universal sovereign authority. Not only do the *Commentaries* claim that he has found that relevance by leading the crusade, but in a move Pius repeats elsewhere in the text, they put that claim in the mouths of the very people who, in reality, denied it.

On many levels, the narrative of the Congress of Mantua serves as a microcosm of the approach the *Commentaries* take to defending the authority, legitimacy, and relevance of Pius's crusade leadership. Ceremony and speech continue to serve as occasions for accentuating both his authority and the sincerity of his aims. The elaborate events organized to celebrate the arrival of a precious relic from the East, the head of Saint Andrew, is a case in point. It was carried in solemn procession through the city in spring 1462 and on to St Peter's for Mass. The *Commentaries* draw attention not just to Pius's spiritual fervour on this occasion, but also to his superior authority, especially in relation to Europe's princes. Carried aloft on a gilded seat, Pope Pius is shielded by a canopy held by royal legates; and one cardinal informs Pius that, as they are to St Peter, "Christian kings, princes and peoples are subject to you, they obey you, they follow your orders like the orders of God."[37] Elsewhere, it is Pius's own words that enforce this image of power and spiritual integrity. The *Commentaries* report that when the pontiff announces his plan to join the crusader ships, he likens himself to both Moses and the martyrs of the early Church.[38] Pius's orations reiterate, in turn, his competence in military matters, while the legitimacy of his leadership continues to be endorsed by the princes themselves. "You are the father of religion and the master of the faith," proclaims the Queen of Cyprus, who has come to Rome to solicit Pius's aid. "It is right for you more than for anyone else to see that the Christian religion does not come to harm."[39]

The *Commentaries* are able sustain this impression that Pius alone could lead the crusade by their unflattering portrayal of Europe's princes. Again and again, the pontiff decries their resistance to his expedition as a symptom of spiritual lethargy and avarice. "Because all princes are extremely avaricious ... they judge us according to their own inclinations," Pius explains to the cardinals while reporting the meagre support Europe's rulers have offered for his expedition. "Nothing is more difficult than extorting gold from an avaricious man." [40] The *Commentaries* further legitimize Pius's right to lead the crusade by eliminating any reference to the various competing expeditions that were being organized by princes across Europe.[41] Instead, they draw attention to the past incompetence of those rulers when leading similar campaigns.[42]

The pervasiveness of this image of Europe's princes has a profound impact in the *Commentaries* on the narrative of Pius II's crusade. Their avarice and spiritual indifference allow Pius to replace what would have been a very damaging portrayal of the papacy with another that was far more to his benefit. Instead of the tale of the declining authority of the papal monarchy, the story of Pius's crusade narrates the tragic erosion of Europe's spiritual fibre, or more specifically, the fibre of its secular rulers. The moral of such a tale is clear: the defence of Christianity rests – and should rest – solely on the shoulders of Pius II. It is a conclusion that confirms both the legitimacy and relevance of his sovereign rule as pope.

Spiritual Leaders and Temporal Diplomats: The Indispensable Papacy

Pius's crusade narrative has important implications for the broader battle that both he and the papacy more generally were waging against Europe's secular princes. As chapter 1 has explained, and as Pius himself knew only too well, crusade leadership was only one of the many battlegrounds on which popes and princes fought for ecclesiastical sovereignty. They wrestled with one another for control over ecclesiastical appointments, taxes, property, justice; and as ecclesiastical reform continued to languish, this too, became a contested prerogative. In all these areas, secular rulers had gained significant ground and were poised to gain still more, especially given the impotence of the popes to fight back. It is in this context that the *Commentaries* offer both Pius and the papacy a powerful weapon. This portrayal of Europe's princes calls into serious question their ability to exercise ecclesiastical authority. How can they do so when they show such total indifference to Christian values, indeed, to the very existence of the religion? In short, the accusations of incapability that undercut secular rulers' right to crusade leadership also effectively undermine their broader ambitions to claim leadership in ecclesiastical affairs more generally.

What the *Commentaries* imply through this sweeping portrayal of princes they argue explicitly in the case of France. Charles VII's adoption of the Pragmatic Sanction of Bourges (1438) becomes a vivid example of what happens when a prince takes charge of his church. According to the *Commentaries*, the Pragmatic Sanction caused nothing short of the spiritual disintegration of the French kingdom. The ranks of the French clergy swelled with corrupt, ignorant, and "monstrous" men, while worthy prelates were imprisoned and their property transferred to laymen. Crimes against the Church and heresy, in particular, went unpunished. Not even the sacraments were respected.[43] The *Commentaries* make very clear to whom they assign the blame for this disaster: Pius concludes by observing that "the Pragmatic caused many similar examples of foolish behaviour which were either ordered or permitted by the ungrateful king."[44]

Based on the nature of these rulers' portraits, the *Commentaries* do not seem to be criticizing only those princes who ruled during Pius's reign. On the contrary, the text leaves the distinct impression that the degenerate nature Pius ascribes to these rulers is typical of men in their position. This broad pattern is somewhat obscured by the portrait of a handful of rulers whose vice and religious depravity are unusually pronounced. Sigismondo Malatesta and Everso d'Anguillara, for example, are deemed more than just spiritually lethargic: they are unchristian, anti-Christian, and even pagan.[45] But alongside the monstrous portraits of these princes are the portrayals of many other rulers who exhibit the same characteristics in a more moderate form. Indeed, throughout the *Commentaries*, Pius indicts secular powers repeatedly on the same charges of moral corruption and religious indifference. His criticisms, moreover, are not restricted to a particular type of political regime: he targets republican governments, principates, duchies, and kingdoms alike. He also weaves through the text general statements about these kinds of government and about secular rule more generally that together confirm the pervasiveness – indeed, the seeming inevitability of their avaricious and ultimately anti-Christian behaviour.[46]

The implications of this sweeping indictment are significant. If Europe's princes are and will almost inevitably prove to be incapable of offering sound spiritual leadership, the papacy becomes an unquestionable necessity. In effect, by dismissing as invalid secular rulers' claims to ecclesiastical power, the *Commentaries* restore the legitimacy and relevance of papal sovereignty in the spiritual landscape of fifteenth-century Europe. In so doing, Pius offers a powerful response to one of the most pressing dilemmas facing the fifteenth-century papacy.

Just how effective a resolution, however, does he offer? While the *Commentaries* expose a chronic vacuum of spiritual leadership in republics and principates, they are less effective at demonstrating that this vacuum can always be filled effectively by a pope. Pius's own self-portrait, to be sure, projects an image of exceptional competence in ecclesiastical governance; and given the integrity of the cardinals he appoints to the college, there is good reason to believe that such leadership will continue in the future. But the *Commentaries* also leave evidence of a pope who, at best, showed questionable judgment in the role of spiritual sovereign and to the detriment of the church: Calixtus III. As chapter 4 has shown, there were advantages for Pius to include these unflattering references to his predecessor: they helped to enhance his own self-portrait in the face of conciliarist challenge. In responding to that crisis and the one here, Pius appears to have made a telling choice: he preferred to construct a defence of himself rather than of the institution as a whole. In so doing, he offers further evidence that the *Commentaries*, while on some level a defence of the theory of papal sovereignty, are more consistently and more effectively a defence of one pope's own claim to and practice of that authority.

Even as the *Commentaries* make the case for Pius's sovereign rule over ecclesiastical affairs, they carve out another vital role for the pontiff in the temporal realm. That realm, as Pius describes it, is ravaged by chronic war. The *Commentaries* document a seemingly endless sequence of confrontations among temporal rulers during Pius's lifetime.[47] This portrayal of contemporary Europe is one that surfaces often in his pre-papal writings and in particular in his correspondence. It also is one that corroborates the theory he laid out in his *De ortu et auctoritate imperii Romani*, the treatise on imperial power he wrote for Frederick III in 1446. In the absence of a strong and unifying imperial authority, Pius explains there, autonomous states will inevitably face off with one another in chronic and destructive war.[48] Indeed, Pius echoes this same idea explicitly in the *Commentaries* when he writes, "There is no charity among Christian princes, nor are family bonds ever strong enough to extinguish jealousy."[49]

It is in this context of seemingly endless warfare that the *Commentaries* present Pius playing the crucial role of peacemaker.[50] Throughout his pontificate, both the pontiff himself and his legates are shown arbitrating disagreements between states, forging peace treaties and truces, and preventing wars from breaking out or raging.[51] Their skills rest, significantly, on their rhetorical training: we are told, for example, that it was the persuasive words of the papal envoys that convinced the German princes, poised for battle in the summer of 1459, to put down their weapons and come to an agreement.[52] The impression the *Commentaries* creates is that Pius and his corps of skilled, humanistically trained diplomats are essential to the peace and prosperity of an emerging system of European states.

In making this case, Pius once again draws and builds on an argument he had begun to develop in a work penned before he took the papal throne. The text in question is the *Germania*, a work Aeneas wrote on the eve of his papacy. As chapter 3 explained, Aeneas responds in this work to accusations that the Roman Church was draining Germany of its wealth and prosperity. In its defence, he points out the benefits, both religious and political, that popes past bestowed on the Germans; and at the same time, he predicts that obedience to papal authority will help ensure Germany's future political prosperity. Pius does not explain in the *Germania* just how the pope will enhance Germany's political strength, but in the *Commentaries* he does – at least in terms of his own experience. It is by obeying not so much Pius the spiritual sovereign as Pius the peacemaker, the *Commentaries* contend, that Germany's and, indeed, all of Europe's princes can put an end to their chronic and violent disputes and bring prosperity to their states.

The *Commentaries* defend Pius's right to this position in part by emphasizing his exceptional qualifications for the job. Pius came to the papal throne, we learn, after years of diplomatic training and experience, and mostly in secular politics. In Book One, he emerges again and again as a successful mediator among warring rulers and uneasy neighbours, both in Italy and across Europe. The *Commentaries* note, for example, that Aeneas began his diplomatic career by participating in high-level peace talks between the kings of England and France.[53] They report how later, as imperial ambassador, he convinced the city of Trieste to swear loyalty to the Holy Roman emperor, settled border disputes twice between the empire and Venice, oversaw difficult peace agreements among the German princes, and struck a peace accord between the emperor and Hungary.[54] Thus, long before he reached the papal throne, Aeneas emerges from the *Commentaries* as a seasoned diplomat with a long list of successes to his name. Adding to his legitimacy is the explicit sanction he receives from secular rulers themselves. The *Commentaries* report numerous instances of princes at war seeking out Pius as their arbiter.[55] Indeed, just as he seems the only one capable of leading the crusade, so does he appear the only one capable of bringing peace: in the eyes of the Germans, "if the pope did not save them [from war], there was no one else who could extinguish this fire."[56]

But if Pius defends his own right to serve in this position, he is also quick to point out that he is not the first pope to do so. Over the course of the *Commentaries*, he points to pontiffs of the past who served in similar capacities. These papal precedents emerge most often in the long historical interludes he weaves into the account of his own pontificate. In his summary of the histories of Venice and France, for example, Pius takes note of how popes played crucial roles bringing peace to these states.[57] By framing peacemaking as a traditional papal responsibility, Pius implies that he was not inventing a new role for the papacy by taking these duties upon himself. Instead, he was simply giving new emphasis to an already existing dimension of papal authority. At the same time, he seems to imply that future popes, in turn, are justified in following in his footsteps – provided, Aeneas would no doubt add, that they were capable of executing such duties. Given how he portrays secular rulers in this text – aggressive, avaricious, and often downright savage – Pius indicates that there will always be a need for someone to fulfil the role of peacemaker.[58] By then identifying not just himself as pope but many of his predecessors fulfilling that role successfully, the *Commentaries* effectively stake out for the papacy an indispensable role in the turbulent politics of fifteenth-century Europe.

The Authority of Pius the Prince

While Pius II faced threats in the strength of Europe's temporal rulers, he also faced one in the weakness of his own rule as prince. As chapter 3 has demonstrated, Pius struggled through much of his pontificate to assert his authority as a temporal sovereign over a host of rebels within his territories. Indeed, the scope, location, and intensity of these rebellions gave Pius's papacy an unwanted distinction: it was one of the most turbulent periods of papal rule in more than half a century. His diplomatic accomplishments did little to improve this shaky record. Hardly the commander he sought to be of the League of Italian States, Pius found his alleged allies on the peninsula largely indifferent to his initiatives and often destructive to his own interests. More than simply a personal humiliation, his performance represented a threat to the papal monarchy, whose very survival depended on such diplomatic pre-eminence.

The *Commentaries,* in contrast, present Pius II as a prince secure both in his control of the Papal States and his command of the Italian League. The account of his papacy makes the case that while his sovereign rule was at times contested, it was never seriously threatened; and that his state, as a result, enjoyed enviable stability under his reign. Pius's command of the Italian League is equally strong and secure, despite the resistance he faced from league members. The *Commentaries* build this defence by drawing on a now familiar repertoire of apologetic techniques. Moments of particular weakness drop out of the historical record or are obscured behind ceremony and ritual that project an opposing image of papal strength. Pius further strengthens his own authority by diminishing the power of his enemies and by using language and imagery that make those weaknesses memorable. He also invigorates weapons of rule that, in reality, had proven of little use against his enemies. The result is an image of a skilled and successful sovereign, well-equipped to exercise that authority over his state.

As they do for his other liabilities, the *Commentaries* adopt ceremony as a powerful shield behind which to conceal the pope's weak princely authority. The text pays particular attention to the rituals through which Pius celebrated his victory over those contesting his authority in the Papal States. Pius lingers, for example, over his triumphant entry into Rome after the uprisings of 1460, the parade of prisoners of war through the city's streets, and the joyous welcome he receives from the once rebellious town of Tivoli.[59] He also dwells on the ceremonies of surrender and humble submission of some of his most threatening enemies. As he does elsewhere in the text, Pius paints these episodes with vivid and arresting images. Roman baron Jacopo Savelli is shown kneeling at the pontiff's feet, making tearful pleas of mercy; while Sigismondo Malatesta makes a public confession of his numerous crimes at the feet of a papal legate.[60] The *Commentaries* report an even more dramatic ceremony that Pius held on the occasion of excommunicating Malatesta in March 1462. According to Pius's account, the rebellious vicar was publicly burned in effigy, bearing a sign that read, "I am Sigismondo Malatesta, son of Pandolfo, king of traitors, hated by God and men, condemned to pyre by a decree of the Holy Senate."[61] Pius's fiery triumph over Malatesta conceals a very different reality: Pius lit the fire long before he had subdued the papal vicar on the battlefield. Thus, the *Commentaries* use ceremony not only to give emphasis to Pius's real princely triumphs; they also use it to multiply those victories.

While Pius defeats some rebels in the *Commentaries* through well-placed images of ceremony, he defeats others with the weapon of his words. Throughout the text, Pius is shown confronting and confounding his enemies directly with a commanding performance of speech. When, for example, Sigismondo Malatesta protests the terms of the peace agreement, Pius silences him with rebukes; and when Piccinino sends him threatening letters, Pius pronounces himself immune to such attacks.[62] Whether they are long orations or short quips, these weapons are fundamentally humanistic: Pius speaks as a skilled rhetorician and one well-versed in history, both ancient and recent. The presence of these verbal victories throughout the text does more than simply diminish the threat Pius faced from what were very formidable enemies. They also create the impression that the war of words he was fighting was as significant as the one being fought on the ground. That Pius consistently emerges as the winner of these confrontations has significant implications for his overall image as a prince: not only is he a strong ruler, but he also is equipped with weapons that make him almost unassailable.

If Pius strengthens his position against these rebels by how he characterizes his weapons, he also does so through the portraits he paints of his most dangerous enemies. Jacopo Piccinino is a case in point. In the *Commentaries*, this highly skilled and successful condottiere is stripped of his military prowess. It was not by might that Piccinino won Assisi, we are told in Book Two. It was the hefty bribe he gave the town's castellan. Moreover, the towns that subsequently surrendered to him did so not because of his powers of intimidation but, rather, because of the fond memories they had of his father.[63] Not even Piccinino's allies held him in much esteem as a soldier. Roman baron Everso d'Anguillara reportedly declared that "if Piccinino let himself be chased out of Assisi … he would deserve to be called a little whore."[64] Everso's stinging and memorable insult is later reinforced by the equally memorable comment Pius makes after Piccinino had successfully slipped past papal forces into the Regno. Insisting that his success was in no way due to his own merits, he observes, "Piccinino's admirers say that his expertise lies not in battle but in retreat. And we agree that he is better at fleeing than at fighting."[65] In constructing this vivid portrait of Piccinino as a cowardly, disrespected, and ultimately ineffective warrior, Pius diminishes what represented, in reality, a serious threat to the stability of his territories and the integrity of his sovereign rule. In so doing, he was adopting the same approach he used when describing those contesting his spiritual authority, namely, conciliarists and the secular princes; by weakening his opponents, he makes his own authority, and that of the papacy more generally, look that much stronger.

The *Commentaries* add to that strength by claiming for Pius the military might that he had robbed of his enemies. In reality, military matters had proven to be one of the weakest areas of Pius II's rule, but that weakness is nowhere in this account of his papacy. Again and again, Pius emerges here as a capable and successful commander, and one who took charge directly of the wars he and his allies were fighting. Pius never once appears on the battlefield; indeed, he states explicitly that a sword does not belong in the hand of a priest.[66] Instead, he relies on other techniques to illustrate his indispensable military leadership and his direct role in a series of important victories. Throughout the text, Pius presents himself as the central strategist in the wars against the French and Sigismondo Malatesta. He documents his direct involvement in important decisions about troop movements and command;[67] and when conferring with his allies, he notes the many times that his opinion prevails over that of these experienced warriors.[68] His talents as a strategist emerge in his accounts of other military ventures as well. When, for example, the papal retinue returns to Rome after the Congress of Mantua, it is Pius himself, the *Commentaries* report, who helps to orchestrate the capture of Tiburzio and his companions.[69] The pontiff also claims direct responsibility for thwarting Piccinino's carefully planned attack on the city and for rescuing Viterbo from the clutches of Everso d'Anguillara.[70] Based on what the *Commentaries* tell us, moreover, there is every reason to think that Pius will extinguish any future rebellions with ease. In describing the pope's tours through papal territories, the *Commentaries* pause to mention the ample fortifications of the many towns he visits; and because he offers only brief sketches of these settlements, the references to military might stand out all the more.[71] With the images of these strong walls and citadels, Pius constructs an image of his princely authority that seems equally impervious to attack.

It is, however, as much the absence of military might as it is its presence that announces the uncompromised authority of Pius the prince. Almost without exception, the Pius in the *Commentaries* encounters only peace and serenity in the course of his extensive travels through the Papal States and his sojourns in the Agro Romano.[72] Rarely is there mention of an armed guard accompanying him – in fact, he is often described walking through the countryside all alone or in the company of a few cardinals.[73] The greatest threat to his own safety comes, significantly, not from his enemies but from his admirers: at public festivals and ceremonies, we learn that Pius was routinely mobbed by adoring crowds and that he twice narrowly escaped with his life as excited admirers fought with swords to have his horse.[74] The ease with which he moves about the Papal States makes a powerful statement about his authority as prince; it implies not only that his territories are stable, but also that his control over them is secure.

The *Commentaries* extend this picture of Pius's authoritative command to the diplomatic role he played on the Italian peninsula. This claim may, at first, seem difficult to defend. Pius does not hide in his account the fact that Venice and Florence refused to support his crusade efforts as he had hoped they would, or that they lent him no support in the Neapolitan war. He also openly acknowledges that Venice poached the vicariate of Cervia from the Papal States, and that both Venetian and Florentine ambassadors pressured him to soften his punishment of Sigismondo Malatesta.[75] Yet, a closer examination of this and other evidence reveals that the Pius in the *Commentaries* does, in fact, assume a position of leadership in the Italian League and exercise authority in various forms over his alleged allies.

The *Commentaries* attest to Pius's diplomatic leadership even before he becomes pope and in a way that overturns his own earlier designation of Alfonso of Naples in this same role in his *De Europa*. In 1456, we are told, Aeneas travelled to Naples to forge a peace agreement between the king and the Sienese government. At the time, Alfonso was enlisting Piccinino to invade Sienese territories, and his assaults had taken a devastating toll on both the land and its inhabitants. Hardly the prince of peace he is made out to be in *De Europa*, Alfonso appears here as an aggressive warmonger, and even more so when he is first approached by Sienese envoys. In response to their request for peace, the king adamantly refuses to put down arms and proclaims the Sienese entirely unworthy of any mercy. But when Aeneas belatedly joins the embassy, Alfonso is described as experiencing a dramatic change of heart. "'Now,'" he said, 'I am ready to talk of peace now that a mediator whom I like has arrived.' And immediately negotiations began."[76] In this short scene, infused with all the drama typical of his apologetic vignettes, Pius effectively strips Alfonso of the mantle of Italy's peacemaker that he had given him a few years earlier and promptly takes it for himself. According to the *Commentaries*, if Alfonso was at all inclined towards peace, it was only because Aeneas had inspired him to be.

The *Commentaries* continue to construct a much fuller picture of Pius's position of dominance among other Italian powers in his account of the Congress of Mantua. Pius reports on the private assembly he held there with Italy's princes and their ambassadors to discuss their contributions to the crusade. The long and impressive list of those in attendance suggests that Pius had garnered the respect of the league members. So, in turn, does these participants' unconditional acceptance of his sole leadership of the campaign.[77] Moreover, as he reports the unfolding debate, the pontiff dominates the discussion. He appears to understand the psychology of the Italian infantry better than the veteran condottiere, Sigismondo Malatesta; he corrects the Venetians on the number of troops and ships necessary to wage a successful battle against the Turks; and he indirectly criticizes Sforza's leadership capacity in a polemic against mercenary armies.[78] Indeed, of all the leaders in attendance, Pius emerges as the one most familiar with military tactics and equipment, with the battleground geography on land and on sea, and with the political history of his opponents. Based on his knowledge of military matters and his superior strategy, Pius emerges as far and away the superior member of the League of Italian States.

It is not, however, just what he knows that makes him seem the leader of this defensive alliance: it is also what he does, or rather, how the *Commentaries* characterize those actions. Again and again, Pius emerges in this text as the *defensor Italiae* – the defender of Italy. His role in the Neapolitan war is cast explicitly in these terms. It was not so much Ferrante he was defending from the French, Pius explains in a conversation with Florentine ruler Cosimo de' Medici, as it was "Italian liberty." Citing the Francophile leanings of many Italian powers, Pius predicts that with the conquest of Naples, the French will soon control the entire peninsula. "By protecting Ferrante," the *Commentaries* conclude, "Pius was protecting Italy."[79] This equation is made elsewhere in the text, too. Upon hearing news of an Angevin victory, Pius allegedly exclaimed, "Oh, *genus Italicum* … I will help you as much as I am able, lest you suffer such cruel masters."[80] Pius's campaign against Sigismondo Malatesta is cast in similar terms. Far more than a menace to the Papal States, the rebellious *signore* is presented here as "poison of Italy";[81] and when a long list of his crimes is pronounced in a public consistory, Pius is urged to "liberate Italy from a hideous and abominable monster."[82] The *Commentaries* even claim that Pius defended Italy when he was elected pope – or more accurately, when he convinced the college of cardinals not to vote for the French candidate. Pius fashions his self-portrait as *defensor Italiae* by explicitly equating Italy with the papacy – "And what is our Italy without the pope?" – and by emphasizing both the inevitable permanence of a French papacy should d'Estouteville be elected, and the conquest of Italy by France.[83] By casting his opponents here and elsewhere as enemies of Italy, the *Commentaries* present Pius fulfilling the league's essential purpose as a coalition for mutual defence and, in so doing, taking a position of command.

Not even the transgressions of league members Venice and Florence undercut this authority, or so the *Commentaries* maintain. In the context of acknowledging their resistance, Pius casts his leadership in a different way: he is the league's moral authority, condemning the republics for dishonouring their solemn pledge to defend, protect and respect their allies. He does so first when reporting how Venice and Florence remained neutral in the Neapolitan war.[84] Still more extensive is his attack on Venice after the republic's annexation of Cervia: "Is this how you keep your word?" Pius accuses the Venetian ambassador. "[Even] Piccinino ... would have feared shame, public opinion, the reputation of being a traitor. But none of these things moves Venetians. The Republic is a soulless being, it does not feel shame, it does not blush, it does not grow pale, it does not hesitate."[85] What is more, that moral authority is acknowledged by the very people Pius is condemning. The *Commentaries* report Cosimo de' Medici's very improbable reaction after Pius criticized his stance towards Ferrante: "Cosimo praised the pope's position and admitted that it was true that popular governments do nothing honourable unless they are constrained by utility or fear."[86] Venice is shown making a similar admission. In his audience with the Venetian ambassador, Pius decries the republic's purchase of Cervia as a theft "worthy of barbarians" – and the envoy concurs: "When the Venetian ambassador had heard these words," the *Commentaries* report, "he grew terrified ... He said he hoped the Venetian senate, which had committed an injury in this instance, would compensate the Church in the future."[87] In the context of these scenes, Pius is not just fulfilling his titles as the league's *custos* and *protector*: he has the league's sanction in doing so. Here the *Commentaries* are adopting the same apologetic approach that they use to undercut the pope's spiritual opponents. Like the cardinals who kiss Pius's feet, or the princes who hail him as Christianity's sole defender, the members of the Italian League are presented doing the very opposite of what they actually believed.

The *Commentaries* draw still other familiar weapons in the context of this defence. They simply erase from their account moments of particular weakness in the face of the Italian League. There is, for example, no evidence in Pius's account of how league members left Piccinino to occupy Assisi long after the pope had ordered his withdrawal. Instead, Pius transforms this tale of abandonment into an example of his trust in God.[88] The *Commentaries* also fashion Pius's oratorical prowess into a powerful weapon against the challenges from the league. When Venetian and Florentine ambassadors plead leniency for Sigismondo Malatesta, Pius defends his position with passion and at length. Hardly intimidated by their requests, the pope holds his ground and intimidates them. His verbal victories leave the distinct impression of a pope who commands and controls the league.[89]

That impression is further confirmed in how the *Commentaries* depict Pius's relationship with Francesco Sforza, at once his chief ally and chief rival. According to Pius's account, the Milanese duke never seriously threatened the pope's dominant position in the league. He creates this impression in part by simply omitting the myriad ways Sforza came to the pope's assistance. There is no mention, for example, of the Milanese troops that protected Pius when he entered Rome in October 1460; nor is there evidence of the crucial role Sforza played in restoring Sienese nobles in civic government or forging the peace negotiations on the peninsula. Instead, the *Commentaries* credit Pius and Pius alone with these accomplishments.[90] Pius is also shown dominating Sforza more directly, and in both temporal and spiritual affairs. He corrects him on crusade logistics and wins arguments about battlefield strategy; and when the Duke threatens to pull his troops from the Neapolitan war unless Pius appoints his candidate bishop of Pavia, the pope stands firm and wins his apology.[91] Pius even emerges superior when Sforza declines his request to lead the crusader army into battle. "His soul, bound to present delights, spurns those of the future," Pius writes, masking his humiliation with moral victory.[92] Finally, it is also worth noting that of all the rulers and legates who make an appearance at the Congress of Mantua, it is the Milanese duke whom the *Commentaries* identify humbly kissing the pope's feet.[93] By consistently subordinating Sforza to Pius, the *Commentaries* help to make a powerful case for the pope's pre-eminence in the Italian League: here, the ruler recognized widely as Italy's diplomatic leader is decidedly secondary to the pope.

The Legitimacy of Pius the Prince and Pius the Papal Prince

Pius II's weakness as a secular prince also grew out of questions about the legitimacy of his authority, and on more than one level. Much to his embarrassment, those questions were ones that he himself had once voiced as the author of the *Pentalogus*. The most serious ones, however, emerged during his six years on the papal throne. The breadth and intensity of rebellion during his reign seemed to challenge his very right to rule as well as his ability to do so. This was nowhere more true than in Rome, where the citizens had long chafed at the idea of a papal overlord. The challenges to his legitimacy were more complicated still. As pope, Pius needed to demonstrate that his temporal responsibilities did not interfere with his ecclesiastical ones. It was a task that he struggled to fulfil. Pius's commitment to the costly Neapolitan war pulled him away from organizing the crusade that he himself was promoting as the defence of religion. In so doing, he opened himself up for attacks of his spiritual negligence – attacks that were steadily launched from the French throne. He also, in the process, incited France to retaliate against his spiritual sovereignty, making the spectre of a new council a very real prospect. Not simply a threat to Pius himself, these struggles were a danger to the fifteenth-century papal monarchy, whose very existence seemed to hinge on the viability of a papal prince.

The *Commentaries* strike back powerfully against these expressions and impressions of illegitimacy. As commander of the Papal States, Pius emerges from the text as a beloved and rightful ruler – and first and foremost in Rome. He seems equally adept at preventing his temporal duties from compromising his spiritual ones. Indeed, the *Commentaries* go so far as to argue that Pius the prince helped to make Pius a more successful pope. Those who read the *Commentaries* in their entirety will find this argument is made more effectively in some places than in others. There are several places in the text where this harmonious portrait of papal prince falls apart, and at the expense of the pope. The result is a somewhat uneven portrait of the pope as papal prince, and still more evidence of how the *Commentaries*, as a work of apology, represents a fractured text.

The *Commentaries* first shore up Pius's liabilities as a legitimate prince through their portrait of Aeneas at the imperial court. There is no mention in the text of the *Pentalogus*, and no hint that, in advising the emperor on political matters, Aeneas had ever challenged the integrity of the Papal States or the pope's claims to rule it. On the contrary, instead of the one who defended Frederick III's rightful claim to this territory, Aeneas is shown explicitly dismissing the idea that the emperor entertained such views. The context of these comments is the account in the *Commentaries* of Frederick's journey to Rome in 1452, where he received the imperial crown. The emperor's descent into Italy, we learn, raised concerns throughout the peninsula and, in particular, at the papal court, that he had ambitions of conquest. In a conversation with Nicholas V, Aeneas adamantly defends Frederick's motives and reassures the pontiff of the emperor's unwavering friendship.[94] Given that Aeneas had himself encouraged Frederick to use his coronation as a pretext for conquest, the words of the imperial legate have a double meaning. The Aeneas in the *Commentaries* seems to be reassuring the pontiff as much about his own views on empire and papacy as much as he is about Frederick's.

The legitimacy of Pius's rule in the Papal States is defended most powerfully in the *Commentaries* in the depiction of Pius's relationship with Rome and the Romans. Here, where both traditionally and recently, the legitimacy of papal authority had been called into question, Pius is embraced as an ideal ruler, and one who is indispensable to the safety and well-being of the citizens. The *Commentaries* communicate this idea in part through what they leave out. Absent from Pius's account are any references to tensions between Pius and the Roman people. The uprising of 1460 is pinned exclusively on Tiburzio di Maso, his brother, and a band of unruly young thugs who together terrorize the city. Rather than culprits, the *popolo* of Rome are, thus, made out to be the pitiable victims of this uprising. But even before they suffer the tyranny of Tiburzio, the *Romani* of the *Commentaries* express their unwavering devotion to their papal prince – and, in keeping with Pius's style, in memorably dramatic ways. When they first get word of his plans to travel to Mantua, the *Commentaries* report, women and children pour into the streets weeping, while men gather in droves, pleading for Pius to stay.[95] Not only do they embrace papal rule, Pius seems to imply, but they are utterly lost without it. The description of the pope's return to the city reinforces that impression still further, and this time through images of an extraordinary procession: the *Commentaries* report that the first evening Pius spent back in Rome, the "entire population" came to his residence with torches, and filing into a circular procession around his house, they rejoiced and wished him happiness and a long life.[96]

The jubilant reactions of the Romans are both explained and justified in the *Commentaries* in the response Pius offers to their ambassadors when they greet him outside the city.[97] There, he expounds on the many benefits the *Romani* enjoy under his rule. On the surface, Pius's words do not seem defensive: the envoys he is addressing are eager for his return, and their respect for his authority is clear. The language he uses, however, tells a different story. Pius's words here engage directly with criticisms hurled at his papal predecessors by Lorenzo Valla and others and reflected criticisms that continued to fuel republican sentiment during his own reign. Those accusations labelled the popes as greedy tyrants who robbed Rome of its liberty and ruthlessly enslaved its people to fulfil their own desires. Pius's words paint the very opposite portrait of papal rule. Here, the pope does not drain the Romans of their riches: he gives them those riches, by freeing them from tax burdens and by placing no restrictions on their prosperous economy.[98] When the Romans "serve" their ruler they are, thus, really ruling themselves: "You are truly wise and prudent men, who serve your master faithfully, although your servitude is the equivalent of ruling."[99] "Where will you find a city more free than Rome?" Pius exclaims, countering long-standing accusations that the popes had robbed Romans of their *libertas*.[100] In making these remarks, Pius was doing more than defending his own right to rule the city. He was also defending that claim for the papacy of the past and the papacy of the future.

The *Commentaries* offer more than the Romans as evidence of the legitimacy of papal rule. The text reports that several towns make pleas for Pius to intervene in their internal upheavals. Others specifically request that he govern them in the place of local lords.[101] The implications of these reports are clear. If Pius deserves to rule because he can do the job well, he also deserves to because his subjects recognize, sanction, and even thirst for his authority. That thirst comes, the *Commentaries* imply, because they do not find others up to the task. Pius underscores that point repeatedly in the portraits he paints of the signori and condottieri who contested papal rule: it is they, not the pope, who are the real tyrants of the Papal States. Once again Pius communicates that message through vivid details he sketches into their portraits. The Roman baron Everso d'Anguillara, we are told, "could kill a man as easily as he could a sheep."[102] Braccio da Montone, the nemesis of Pope Martin V, "enjoyed hurling miserable victims off the tops of towers."[103] Sigismondo Malatesta slept with the mothers of his godchildren and killed their husbands, and Jacopo Savelli decapitated his enemies and then chopped them into pieces.[104] This vivid catalogue of tyrants, past and present, constitutes more than just a violent assault on the popes' most dangerous enemies. It is also a tool with which Pius defends the justice, indeed, the necessity of his rule in the Papal States.

There is still another, very different argument that the *Commentaries* put forward in defence of both Pius II and the papacy. Here, it is not the papacy's right to temporal rule that Pius is defending specifically. Instead it is a much broader claim to ecclesiastical rule: priests make excellent princes – better ones, in fact, than do laymen. Pius weaves this argument directly into the narrative of his papacy, and he does so at various points in the text. The ideas first surface in a letter he reports writing to Paolo Fregoso, the archbishop of Genoa and the city's newly minted doge. Musing about Genoa's sudden shift to ecclesiastical rule, Pius suggests that "perhaps the Genoese having recognized that lay regimes were unjust and believing that from them derived so much upheaval" wanted to see if they were ruled with greater justice and mercy by a priest.[105] And from what Pius goes on to write, it is clear that he believes they would be: "The norms of [temporal] rule are not the same for a priest as they are for a layman," he explains. "An ecclesiastical government ought to be paternal and full of mercy, not tyrannical."[106] The distinction, according to Pius, was not owing to the fact that all priests are inherently more virtuous than laymen; rather, it was because their subjects hold them to a higher standard: "People tolerate things in a secular ruler that they abhor in an ecclesiastical one. What are considered to be insignificant and minor crimes in a layman are judged to be the greatest and most serious in a cleric."[107] While Pius's words offer specific advice to Fregoso about how to wield his new authority, they also promote the pontiff's more general and clearly appealing vision of ecclesiastical government: a clerical prince is more likely to be just and attentive to the public good, for if he is not, he will swiftly be removed from power.

Pius develops these ideas further in an exchange he reports having in September 1463 with the Florentine ambassador Ottone Niccolini. The purpose of Niccolini's embassy is to persuade Pius to decline Venetian support for the crusade.[108] Pius rejects Niccolini's argument outright and, in the course of his response, repeats his general claim that laymen operate according to a different set of standards when they govern – standards, he argues, that lead to endemic injustice. "Secular princes and rulers of cities are not concerned with the way they maintain their power, so long as they maintain it. And for this reason they repeatedly violate the law of men and oppose honorable customs."[109] Pius's principal aim in making these remarks is to show one reason why, as defender of the faith, he was obliged to back Venice in the crusade: if he did not, he was sure to endure harsh criticism, and the papacy was likely to suffer serious consequences.[110] What emerges indirectly from his words is a strong indictment of lay government and a claim still more explicit than he had made to Fregoso. Clerics are more likely than laymen to rule justly, Pius maintains. And they will do so not because of their inherently superior characters, but because the public will not tolerate their unethical behaviour.

Pius is most explicit about the influence of the pope's spiritual office on his temporal government when describing a dispute with the people of L'Aquila. When the citizens of the town had harboured Piccinino's troops in their territories, Pius had punished their treachery with a fine and, as guarantee for their payment, had confiscated their flocks of sheep. When the Aquilani protested, the papal auditors were summoned to review the case. Their investigation upheld the pope's penalty as just, but Pius decided nonetheless to return the sheep. "Our *clementia* will be greater than your treachery," he reports explaining to the town's ambassadors.[111] Then, in a sweeping statement, he declares ecclesiastical rule to be superior to lay rule on principle: "Learn from this how different ecclesiastical governments are from secular ones. Nobody who offended any other king in the way you have offended the Church would get from him the mercy that you have received from us today."[112] Pius goes on to recount that everyone who heard his decision "admired the pope's *liberalitas*: for on that day he gave to the Aquilani more than one hundred thousand sheep."[113]

Pius's words here and elsewhere in the *Commentaries* clearly distinguish the clerical prince from the lay prince, but they also align the two closely together. The features Pius claims as superior in an ecclesiastical government, and in his own in particular, are the very ones that were idealized in contemporary views of temporal rulers: justice, mercy, and *liberalitas*.[114] Thus, by singling out these ideals, Pius casts the direct rule of papal government very much in the mould of secular lay governments. Indeed, by claiming that ecclesiastical princes were more just, more merciful, and more *liberalis* than secular ones, Pius was in a sense vying to beat these lay rulers at their own game.

The *Commentaries*'s defence of the pope's temporal authority picks up on an important strand of thought that Pius had begun to develop years earlier in his *Dialogus de somnio quodam*. To some extent, the arguments put forward in this work and in the *Commentaries* overlap. In the *Dialogus,* for example, Pius maintains that while God wants all people to be without fault or blemish, He wants priests to be even more pure – a moral purity he defines as pre-eminence in wisdom and knowledge, courage, humility, kindness, mercy, justice, chastity, and zeal.[115] Pius's argument here is that if the clergy act in the way God desires, they will make excellent princes; and because, Pius claims, more is expected of them than of laymen in the same position, it follows that clerics will also make *better* princes. The *Commentaries,* in effect, play a variation on this theme. Here, too, ecclesiastical princes are supposed to be more morally upright than their lay counterparts, but it is not God who makes these demands. Instead, it is the clerics' own subjects – or more specifically, their higher expectations of him – that promise to make him a better ruler than a layman.

If a papal prince brought benefits to those subject to his temporal rule, what did this configuration of power mean for those whom he ruled as pope? Pius takes up this question, too, in his account, and in so doing, confronts one of the most serious threats to his papacy: the impression that, by choosing to enter the Neapolitan war, Pius II had seriously compromised his spiritual responsibilities, and first and foremost the crusade. The *Commentaries* defend Pius against this charge in part by directing our attention away from this decision and towards a different one he had made about the Congress of Mantua. In choosing to leave Rome to preside over the congress, Pius tells us, he correctly put the welfare of the church ahead of the interests of his state. Pius does not simply state this interpretation in the *Commentaries*: he repeats it again and again.[116] At the same time, he implies that his decision grew out of a broader philosophy of governance that recognizes his primary duties as spiritual. "If we go [to Mantua], the Church's temporal kingdom will waver," Pius explains to those pressing him to stay in Rome. "But it has often been lost and recovered. If we abandon our spiritual kingdom, it is unclear if we will ever get it back. Let us allow transient things to slip away and hold on to more lasting things."[117] With this blunt statement, Pius directly challenges the damning accusations of his spiritual neglect. His words sketch a very different portrait of someone committed in both theory and practice to being a pope before being a prince.

Pius further conceals his vulnerability by turning the accusations he faced against others. The *Commentaries* report that in a private consistory with his cardinals in March 1462, the pontiff blamed the crusade's long delay solely on the negligence of Europe's princes.[118] The war with Ferrante, which he had been fighting for almost two years at that point, is never acknowledged as a contributing factor – indeed, it is not mentioned at all. Elsewhere, Pius lays the blame for the stalled expedition squarely on the shoulders of the French, and in so doing, offers a familiar self-defence: as he did to his conciliarist opponents Diether of Mainz, Gregor Heimburg, and Sigismund of Austria, Pius defends himself by attributing to his critics the very same crimes they had pinned on him. Rumours from the French royal court had claimed that Pius was funding his war on the peninsula with tithes collected for the crusade. The *Commentaries* retaliate in kind: they condemn the French for using ships outfitted for the crusade to launch an attack on Naples.[119] Pius then goes on to claim explicitly that the French had "impeded the expedition against the Turks" with their relentless assault of the Regno.[120] The slow progress of Pius's crusade, thus, appears in the *Commentaries* to be a consequence not of Pius's Neapolitan policy, but of France's.

It is only in the final pages of the *Commentaries*, and when his wars on the peninsula had drawn to an end, that Pius begins to explore the links between his planned campaign against the Turks and the war he fought instead against the French. In the long public oration that represents the climax of the entire text, Pius acknowledges the accusation, that in defending Ferrante, he had neglected the crusade.[121] He then goes on to refute this claim vociferously, first by insisting on the justice of his temporal policy and then by explaining its relationship to the crusade. "We were fighting for Christ when we defended Ferrante," Pius explains, "We brought war against the Turks when we struck the lands of Sigismondo."[122] With these words, Pius effectively closes the divide between what were two divergent policies, and he does so in a familiar way: it is the same approach he takes in Book One when he narrows the gap between the German princes and Eugenius IV as they negotiate their reconciliation. In both cases, Pius presents what were, in reality, inherently conflicting positions as fundamentally compatible. In both cases, too, the result has considerable apologetic value: his words serve to conceal a major liability to both his own spiritual authority and that of the papacy more generally.

But the *Commentaries* go still further in refuting the charge that Pius the prince undermined the crusade plans of Pius the pope. They do so by making the very opposite case: it was Pius the prince who made those plans go forward. In Book Seven, Pius recounts how a certain

Giovanni da Castro arrived at the papal court in May 1462 with the announcement that he had discovered a rich strain of alum in papal territories, just outside Civitavecchia.[123] An essential ingredient in cloth making, one of Italy's major industries, alum was imported into the peninsula from the East at great expense. The discovery of the mineral on Italian soil meant a dramatic transformation of the industry, a near Italian monopoly on the alum market, and a significant increase in the flow of money into the papal coffers. In the *Commentaries*, however, the significance of this discovery is identified in purely religious terms. "Today, I bring you victory over the Turk," proclaimed da Castro, or so Pius tells us, as he stood before the pontiff with the news of his find.[124] The rest of da Castro's account continues to frame the alum specifically in terms of conquering the Muslim enemy. He notes the "double damage" the discovery does by pointing out that up until now the Turks had been the primary suppliers of alum to Italian markets: "Now you [Pius] can prepare the war against the Turks. This mineral will give you the means to war, that is money, and take it away from the Turks."[125] At the conclusion of the chapter, Pius makes it clear that he agrees with da Castro's understanding of the alum's significance, explaining that if administered properly, it "will help Roman pontiffs in no small manner to bear the burdens of the Christian religion."[126] The impression this chapter leaves is that Pius's temporal power was more than simply an asset to his papacy: it was the key to his crusade's success. Such a complementary relationship functioned as a valuable apologetic tool. It served to undermine contemporary criticisms of the pope's temporal power as a direct threat to his spiritual mission.

But do the *Commentaries* defend against these charges consistently? While Pius's war in defence of Ferrante does little spiritual damage in the *Commentaries*, there are other occasions where his twin roles of pope and prince do seem to conflict. The description of Pius's return to Rome in October 1460 is a case in point.[127] According to his account, entering the city was like entering a battlefield. Piccinino and his allies were on the brink of launching an invasion, while in Rome itself, Tiburzio's band of thugs was still at large. Many in the papal retinue recognized these dangers, the *Commentaries* report, and discouraged Pius from entering the city. The pope, however, dismisses their warnings, weighing the risks of attack with the knowledge of an experienced general and demonstrating the courage of a great warrior prince: "But if by some hidden design of God it is decreed that we fall into enemy hands, or if we are killed by an impious blade, we will not refuse to die for Rome and in

Rome. It is glorious to accept death for the Patrimony of blessed Peter, and it is shameful to avoid it."[128] Pius's self-portrait as a brave general serves to strengthen his position as ruler of the Papal States, but it detracts from his image as pope. A pledge of self-sacrifice for the sake of one's *regnum* sits easily on the lips of a fifteenth-century prince, but for a pope, who, at the same time was hailing self-sacrifice for a divine, not an earthly kingdom, as the highest achievement, it seems oddly out of place. Pius's sense of temporal duty stands here in an uneasy relationship with his spiritual responsibilities. Here, too, is more evidence of dissonance within Pius's apology and, it seems, an indication of his priorities in constructing this defence. At this moment in the text, at least, he chose to defend Pius the prince instead of Pius the pope.

This passage deserves our attention for still another reason: it raises an important question about the nature of the image Pius projects of himself in this work. The account in the *Commentaries* of Pius's courageous entry into Rome depicts him embracing what was an ideal of princely power: dying for the sake of one's *regnum* or *patria*. In this case, aligning himself with an ideal of secular rule seems to hamper more than help his authority as a papal prince. Does the Pius of the *Commentaries* adopt other ideals of a secular ruler and, if so, what are the consequences of doing so? The next chapter will take this question up in earnest, but evidence already presented in this one allows us at this point to begin shaping an answer. Several dimensions of Pius's portrait discussed in the preceding pages align him closely with secular political rulers. In all cases, those parallels serve to defend not detract from his image as a strong sovereign. As already noted, Pius characterizes his rule in the Papal States in terms that temporal princes considered to be ideals: *liberalitas*, mercy, and justice. In so doing, he helps to defend the legitimacy of his rule as prince. Elsewhere, both the ideals and practices of temporal authority serve to strengthen his portrait as a spiritual sovereign. The image of Pius as crusade leader is a case in point. On the one hand, the *Commentaries* construct this portrait by drawing on traditional religious imagery, including martyrs and biblical figures. They also do so by assigning Pius the role that popes traditionally played in the context of a crusade: he exhorts the rulers of Europe to embrace the expedition as a defence of the Christian faith. But there is another crucial dimension to Pius's crusade leadership in the *Commentaries*, and one integral to representations of secular rulers, that is, military command. It is this dimension, so unfamiliar to traditional papal imagery of the crusade, that is given particular prominence in the *Commentaries* and that casts Pius in the mould of a prince. Here, too, infusing his self-portrait with secular political values was a distinct advantage: it helped to shore up one of his greatest vulnerabilities – his weakness in military affairs, and in so doing, it reinforced both his authority and legitimacy as leader of the crusade.

The same pattern can be seen in Pius II's self-portrait as arbiter of Europe. The role itself is not what aligns him with secular rulers: what does so is the kind of training that allowed him to fulfil that role. We learn from the *Commentaries* that Pius's diplomatic experience came first and foremost from his years of service at the imperial court, and that it was an education in humanist rhetoric that equipped him and his legates with the tools for success. Humanist education was, of course, not the exclusive preserve of secular governments; but in many of his writings, Pius explicitly defined and valued it – and oratory specifically – as crucial to the success of temporal rulers. "How can provinces be pacified and friendships between states be forged or renewed unless there is eloquence?" he wrote in 1444 in an impassioned letter to a fellow humanist who had been criticized for defending the value of poetry. "Kings are reconciled with one another through letters, towns [use them] to strike treaties ... orations guide government, lead peoples, recommend laws. But who does these things well, unless he is steeped in the disciplines of poetry and oratory?"[129] Pius, then Aeneas, addresses similar arguments to Emperor Frederick III in his *Pentalogus* (1443), again singling out the importance of good oratorical skills; and to the young heir to the Hungarian and Bohemian thrones, Ladislaus Posthumous, in his treatise *De liberorum educatione* (1450).[130] Pius's consistent defence of humanist education as a vital tool of secular politics is essential for understanding the significance of his self-portrait in the *Commentaries* as a peacemaker. Indeed, it has implications for his image throughout the text as an exceptional rhetorician. It suggests that he himself would have recognized in his self-portait the presence of an ideal of secular leadership.

The next chapter continues to explore how Pope Pius II's self-portrait in the *Commentaries* was shaped and strengthened by images and ideas of secular politics. At the same time, it builds in still other ways on the arguments presented here. Those arguments have demonstrated how the central themes and features of Pius's narrative – among them, his fervent efforts to launch a crusade, the Neapolitan war, and the spiritual apathy of secular rulers – represent significant elements in the larger apologetic design of the *Commentaries*. In the context of discussing them, Pius consistently obscures papal weakness behind images of formidable strength, and he responds directly and forcefully to the powerful forces challenging papal authority, legitimacy, and relevance. In turn, this chapter has reminded us that many of the hallmarks of Pius's narrative – his vivid character sketches, his repeated references to his remarkable oratorical prowess, and the prominence of ceremonial display – reflect more than their author's stylistic preferences. They are also vital tools with which he constructs his defence. Together, the arguments presented here and in the preceding chapter leave the impression that while Pius's apology is not always fully coordinated, it is comprehensive: the *Commentaries* work on all levels to shield and strengthen the beleaguered authority of Pope Pius and the papal monarchy. The next chapter will further illuminate how apology permeates the *Commentaries* by examining still other defining features of the work: its sustained engagement with ancient authors and texts, and its conversations with contemporary humanist histories.

6 Portraits of Princes in the Portrait of Pius II

It was a sight worth seeing and one that future generations will scarcely believe. One of the most powerful princes of his age, feared by the French and the Italians, who was usually adorned in gold vestments, surrounded by courtiers, preceded by fasces and followed by armed cohorts and a crowd of powerful men, now welcomed the apostolic legate in cheap and common clothing, preceded by six hermits and followed by a few priests.[1]

In the above quotation, drawn from Book Seven of the *Commentaries*, Pope Pius II, then Aeneas Silvius Piccolomini, records in wide-eyed amazement his encounter in 1435 with Duke Amadeus of Savoy. En route to Arras with papal legate Cardinal Niccolò Albergati, Aeneas and the cardinal's retinue pay a visit to the duke at Thonon, near Lake Geneva. A few years earlier, the illustrious prince had abandoned his throne for a quiet hermitage there – a move, according to Aeneas, that clearly betrayed his ambition to become pope.[2] What strikes Aeneas immediately upon seeing Amadeus is the dramatic transformation in the duke's physical appearance and presentation: the symbols and spoils typically associated with the powerful *signori* of his day had been stripped away – so much so, in fact, that he is no longer recognizable as a prince. Looks, however, can be deceiving, as Pius goes on to note. Despite renouncing worldly goods and explicitly entrusting control of his duchy to his son, the duke insisted on handling the most important business of state, continued to control financial matters, and refused to relinquish his title of duke.[3] In short, though not immediately evident, the hermit Amadeus was, in fundamental ways, still a prince.

This scene offers a useful starting point for our final investigation of the *Commentaries* as a work of apology. It does so by directing us to certain features of Pius's self-portrait that are not easy to discern. To be sure, the Pius of the *Commentaries*, unlike Amadeus in the above passage, does not conceal his role as prince behind the robes he wears as a churchman. On the contrary, and as chapter 5 has elucidated, Pius's temporal rule is given a prominent place in this text. But in other ways, the presence of the prince in Pius's self-portrait is very much like the prince in the hermit Amadeus: it is not immediately apparent, even though it is fundamental to who he is.

This chapter will illuminate these more subtle ways in which the Pius of the *Commentaries* resembles a secular prince. It does so by comparing his self-portrait with representations of contemporary leaders in Italian politics. These figures found valuable tools for self-promotion in the texts of antiquity. They also did so by engaging with a set of contemporary texts – the portrayals of their political rivals. By undermining the flattering images of their opponents, these rulers were able to enhance their own. The *Commentaries*, this chapter argues, draw in similar ways on both ancient and contemporary texts to shape their image of Pope Pius II. For one, the text adopts from ancient authors the same genres and apologetic strategies used by the pope's contemporaries in secular politics. It also models his portrait on the same heroes of ancient literature that they did – and, indeed, on some of the very same features. In turn, the *Commentaries* participate in the same intertextual rivalries that defined the portraits of his secular contemporaries, and they do so, moreover, to the same end. By adopting these various features of secular political portraiture, the *Commentaries* do not simply make Pius look like a contemporary Italian signore. They also make him look stronger. Building on the arguments that concluded chapter 5, the following analysis illuminates how the language, imagery, and ideals of secular politics played an integral role in Pius's self-defence by shoring up his vulnerabilities as both a spiritual and a temporal monarch. The portraits of princes were, in short, one of the most powerful weapons in his arsenal as he launched his self-defence.

Literary and Historical Models

The literary and historical works of Roman antiquity play an essential role in Pius's *Commentaries*. Little attention, however, has been given to the pope's reception of classical literature in this, his magnum opus, and in particular, to how these texts functioned in the context of a political apology.[4] As with most humanists of his age, Pius's education was bound tightly to his political interests; and as ruler of Christendom and of the Papal States, these interests were as pressing as they were many. The author of the *Commentaries*, therefore, must be seen first and foremost as a political figure – and, thus, someone whose references to classical culture were likely to mean something more than simply a display of erudition or the product of individual literary tastes.

To understand fully how the *Commentaries* engage with antiquity, we must position the work in its larger political context, and not just in the conflicts, tensions, and dynamics of Pius II's own papacy. Equally vital is an understanding of how ancient texts were being put to political use by the pontiff's own contemporaries. The humanists at the courts of secular rulers were drawing on many of the same classical models that Pius used when shaping the prose, verse, and visual images of their rulers and other figures of temporal politics, most notably, the *condottieri*.[5] The appeal of such models was manifold. The revival of antiquity gave new lustre to figures and genres of ancient myth and history, lustre that could lend an aura of respectability to rulers of the fifteenth century. Such models held particular appeal for princes whose legitimacy was questioned or questionable, and the attraction was no coincidence. Many of the ancient figures at the centre of these portraits – the Trojan Aeneas, Julius Caesar, Augustus, Scipio Africanus – had faced similar challenges to their own authority; in fact, in many cases, their own images had been designed to remedy such problems. Through such associations, fifteenth-century rulers helped to shore up their credibility where they needed to the most. In short, at the secular courts that flourished during the pontificate of Pius II, the history and literature of classical culture were being honed and shaped into powerful tools to create, enhance, and defend the authority and legitimacy of temporal rule.

In the way they engage with antiquity, the *Commentaries* bear a striking resemblance to these representations of secular power. Like these rulers, Pius uses ancient texts to shape his values and attributes as a leader, to underscore the strength and scope of his command, and to defend his very claim to authority. He also, like them, found in the writings of Caesar and Virgil particularly useful models for self promotion. What separates Pius's image from that of his temporal counterparts is the expanded role he assigned to these ancient texts. In the *Commentaries*, the heritage of classical culture not only bolsters Pius's authority and legitimacy as a temporal prince: it also helps to strengthen and justify his position as supreme sovereign of Christendom.

Pope Pius II and Caesar

The generic framework Pius gave his self-portrait anchored it firmly in the political culture of his day.[6] The genre he adopted, that of the *commentarii*, was quickly becoming a popular one for this new political history.[7] The best-known fifteenth-century commentaries were written after Pius II completed his, but the pontiff was not the first in this period to adopt the genre.[8] Indeed, already by the mid-fifteenth century it had become an important form in which to praise military and political accomplishment. In 1452, King Alfonso of Naples sent poet Giannantonio de' Pandoni, known as Porcellio, to the camp of condottiere Jacopo Piccinino, who was then engaged on behalf of Naples's ally, Venice, in a war against Milan. Porcellio composed his *Commentaria comitis Jacobis Picininis* as a report from the front lines of battle. He dedicated the first ten books, which cover the campaigns of 1452, to Alfonso and the next nine books, on the second year of war, to Doge Francesco Foscari.[9] A few years later, Venetian humanist Francesco Contarini penned another history in Caesarean tradition and one that chronologically follows on the heels of Porcellio's. The focus of the *Commentarii Rerum in Hetruria Gestarum*, however, is considerably different. Contarini writes about his mission as Venetian ambassador to Siena (February 1453 to September 1455), and the central role he allegedly played in Sienese affairs; and while he, too, discusses a war involving Venice and Piccinino, in this conflict the condottiere and the republic were fighting on opposite sides.[10]

There is still a third text that must be considered alongside the histories of Porcellio and Contarini: Bartolomeo Facio's *Rerum gestarum Alfonsi regis libri*. Facio, who completed the work as Alfonso's official court historian, takes as his time frame a period of several decades (1420–55).[11] The first seven books recount Alfonso's conquest of the Kingdom of Naples, while the remaining three narrate his involvement in subsequent wars on the peninsula. On the surface, the *Gesta* seems an odd addition to the discussion at hand in that Facio did not identify it explicitly with Caesar's works. What justifies its inclusion in this discussion is that Pius II did: when describing Facio's history, he notes that it imitated Caesar "in his manner of speaking."[12] Pius, moreover, was not alone in finding connections between Caesar's and Facio's work:

his fellow humanists also drew such parallels, as have modern historians.[13] Together, they make a compelling case for including Facio's text in the analysis that follows.

The inspiration and model for all these works were the *Commentarii belli gallici* (*Gallic War*) and *Commentarii belli civilis* (*Civil War*) of Julius Caesar. Misattributed for much of the Middle Ages, these texts had been identified in the fourteenth century as the work of their protagonist, and their newly established authorship helped to win them considerable esteem in the eyes of fifteenth-century Italians – and, indeed, in the eyes of Pius himself.[14] It was not just the sanction of Caesar's name that made his writings such an attractive model: the very nature of the genre also made it an ideal fit with the political needs of fifteenth-century Italian princes, condottieri, and other political figures. The *Gallic War* and the *Civil War* are works of apology: they were written by a man who needed both to prove his military worth and to defend his political integrity against charges of unconstitutionality. They build their defence by illustrating Caesar's virtues and accomplishments both on the battlefield and in the political arena. Thus, Caesar's *Commentarii* offered humanist historians an attractive model for illustrating their protagonist's *virtus* through an account of his *res gestae*. This generic framework was particularly appealing to rulers who needed to defend political authority built on military conquest rather than on the law. More generally, it was useful for defending military or political actions that were in some way difficult to justify.[15]

To Pius II, Caesar's *Commentarii* would have held similar apologetic appeal. Like many of the princes attracted to the genre, Pius II's and, indeed, the papacy's claims to authority were insecure, in its spiritual as much as in its temporal realm. As chapter 1 has explained, those claims had been assaulted in myriad ways in the preceding decades – by conciliar theory, by the legal legacy of the councils of Constance and Basel, by the papacy's chronic failure to enact reform *in capite*, by papally approved concordats and agreements with Europe's princes, by challenges to the legal basis of its temporal authority, and by criticisms of how it exercised that power. Pope Pius II shared all these vulnerabilities and, indeed, had compounded them both in his pre-papal writings and during his own papacy. As a result, he found himself in a position very similar to rulers who had no legal claim to their authority: he needed means other than traditional ones for justifying his sovereign power. Under these circumstances, an emphasis on his *virtus* and his accomplishments, on his capabilities and his successes, was as valuable for him as it was for these rulers.

There is no question that Pius follows the basic apologetic blueprint of Caesar's *Commentarii* when writing his own. As the preceding two chapters have demonstrated, Pius consistently defends his claims to authority as both pope and prince on the basis of capability and proven success. It is on these grounds, for example, that he defends his right to direct church reform, to lead a crusade against the Turks, to serve as arbiter of Europe, to rule the Papal States, and to dominate the Italian League. These same criteria, in turn, permeate the *Commentaries* in still other ways. As much as they are the basis for legitimizing Pius's own rule, they are the primary grounds for delegitimizing the claims of those who are competing against his authority and that of the papacy more generally. It is because they are incapable of doing their job that the *Commentaries* disqualify the cardinals as co-sovereigns, the princes as crusade leaders and ecclesiastical authorities, and rebellious *signori* and *condottieri* as independent rulers. In contrast, Pius's *Commentaries* do little to develop traditional legal, biblical, theoretical, or philosophical defences of papal authority. While Pius repeatedly identifies his spiritual sovereignty using terms built on these arguments – terms like *vicarius Christi* and *successor Petri* – he, significantly, does not present those arguments explicitly.[16] Their absence from the text indicates the extent to which he embraced a very different way of defending the legitimacy of his rule. In adopting such an approach, Pius is aligning his self-portrait – and a crucial dimension of it – with portrayals of temporal leadership.

These rulers found more in Caesar's writings than a useful generic framework. An analysis of their own *commentarii* shows that they also adopted some of the same apologetic strategies that Caesar himself had employed. At the same time, they moulded their image as military leaders on the ancient general's own self-portrait. The relationship between these texts and Pius's *Commentaries* can, thus, be established still more clearly by determining how and to what extent the latter used these same tools. Investigating these parallels requires a complex comparative analysis: we must study these fifteenth-century *commentarii* in relation both to Caesar's writings and to one another. The results of such an analysis are telling. They confirm not just the strong Caesarean imprint on Pius's *Commentaries*. They also reveal how, in fundamental ways, Pius's self-portrait resembled contemporary humanist images of secular rule.

Caesar's strategies of self-defence have been documented by scholars of both ancient and Renaissance historiography. The most extensive, if at times overzealous, analysis can be found in Michel Rambaud's *L'Art de la déformation historique dans les "Commentaires" de César*.[17] Recent studies have extended Rambaud's line of inquiry, while at the same time refining and tempering his claims: rather than accusing Caesar of "deforming" – to use Rambaud's term – history with deliberate lies, scholars now characterize his apologetic techniques as the work of an "artful reporter."[18] The value of Rambaud's work for scholarship on Renaissance historiography has been illustrated by Gary Ianziti's study of humanist historiography in Milan.[19] Both implicitly and explicitly, his work signals the value of exploring how and to what extent earlier Renaissance *commentarii* drew, in turn, on Caesar as models for their apologetic techniques. It is with these important questions in mind that the following pages map out the debt Pope Pius II owed this ancient historian when penning his own *Commentaries*.

In terms of their overarching narrative strategy, Pius's *Commentaries* have much in common with Caesar's. In both the *Gallic War* and the *Civil War*, Caesar writes a *récit justificatif*, a narrative form of apology focused on offering explanations for questioned and questionable actions.[20] Caesar communicates such justifications through detailed outlines of his reasoning process and, especially in the *Gallic War*, through addresses, conversations, and debates. Pius relies heavily on the very same techniques. Indeed, much of his *Commentaries* reads less as a narrative and more as a collection of dialogues, both real and internal, and deliberative orations. The instances that Pius chooses to present in this way reveal how this strategy served him, as it did Caesar, as a critical form of self-defence – in his roles of both pope and prince. The *Commentaries* show Pius reasoning through the difficult decisions of forging peace between Ferrante of Naples and Sigismondo Malatesta, of personally leading the Christian army on crusade, and of postponing justice in the case of several egregious crimes.[21] They record orations he delivered in defence of the crusade and of the wars that had delayed this venture;[22] they document his debates with French ambassadors about rights to the crown of Naples, and with several cardinals about expanding the college;[23] and they record his exchanges with numerous legates who seek personal and political favours.[24] In each of these instances – and there are many others like them – Pius defends controversial decisions, including ones that had earned him considerable criticism and whose need for justification was particularly acute.

If Pius's *Commentaries* employ what might be described as Caesar's central narrative framework, they also draw on a range of his secondary apologetic devices. The use of the third person – a strategy that lends the work an aura of objectivity – is perhaps the most obvious parallel; indeed, it is the feature scholars traditionally point to when noting Pius's debt to Caesar.[25] In addition, Caesar routinely identifies himself by his own name, and in so doing enhances the apologetic import of his text. By repeating his name, Caesar emphasizes the strength and scope of his command, claims sole credit for notable (and often collective) achievements, and generally enhances his importance in the momentous events he describes.[26] A similar effect is produced by Caesar's regular reliance on a set of verbs that emphasize his command, both literal – imperare (to command), *iubere* (to order), *ducere* (to lead), *mittere* (to send) – and intellectual – *intelligere* (to understand), *existimare* (to consider), *arbitrari* (to make a decision), *judicare* (to judge), *instituere* (to establish), *decernere* (to decide), and *statuere* (to resolve).[27]

A close study of the language in Pius's *Commentaries* reveals similar patterns, but ones shaped to Pius's own apologetic needs. He frequently identifies the third person at the centre of his story as "Pius," as "praesul," as "vicarius Christi," and especially as "Pontifex." These repetitions do more than simply emphasize his prominence in the events of his day. At a time when papal sovereignty was being challenged in both theory and practice, these repeated references read as confident declarations of the supreme spiritual authority he both claimed and claimed to exercise. In the *Commentaries, Pius, praesul, vicarius Christi,* and *Pontifex* are repeated frequently in the context of ceremonial expressions of his power: at the Congress of Mantua, at the celebrations in Rome for the return of Saint Andrew's head, at the Corpus Christi festival in Viterbo, and in the reception he receives in towns and cities on his travels through Italy. They also appear frequently in his successful confrontations with cardinals and ambassadors, and at moments of significant spiritual triumphs, such as the appointment of new cardinals and the abolition of the Pragmatic Sanction of Bourges. In these and other similar instances, Pius, like Caesar, claims sole credit for success.[28]

Moreover, like Caesar, Pius also describes his thoughts and actions using words that draw particular attention to his prudence and judgment – *intelligere* (to understand), *existimare* (to consider), *censere* (to estimate), *meditari* (to think over), *animadvertere* (to perceive), and the expression *vicit pontificis sententia* (the pontiff's opinion triumphed) – and to his rule – *imperare* (to command), *statuere* (to resolve), *iubere* (to order), *monere* (to warn), *declarare* (to declare), and *decernere* (to decide). Significantly, the verb used most often to characterize Pius's interactions with others is *iubere*: the *Commentaries* show him continually giving orders to his cardinals, his legates, his allies, and his enemies. As it did for Caesar, this pronounced verbal emphasis on control, domination, and good judgment helped Pius II to create the impression that he exerted his authority over those who, in reality, challenged it persistently.

The above analysis suggests that Caesar's *Commentaries* offered Pius many valuable tools for fashioning his own apology, but were they the same ones used to construct the images of his contemporaries in secular politics? In other words, to what extent does Pius's Caesarean portrait resemble representations of secular rule? A survey of the histories written by Contarini and Facio reveals considerable common ground with the pope's. Both these authors rely heavily on the same verbs of intellectual and literal command that characterize the actions of Caesar and Pope Pius II.[29] Like Pius, moreover, they also follow Caesar in constructing their histories as a *récit justificatif*. From the beginning of the narrative to the end, Facio focuses as much on the reasons for Alfonso's actions as on the reporting of those actions. There are numerous examples of the king carefully working through decisions and then laying out his reasoning to others.[30] Contarini, in turn, is at pains to point out the motives behind his own actions.[31] Moreover – and again, in keeping with both Caesar and Pius II – he consistently underscores his own prominence in the events he recounts. While his name surfaces only a few times in the text, the title of "legatus," like Pius's many titles, appears frequently and at the centre of all the significant actions and decisions of the war.[32] Finally, like Pius and Caesar, too, Contarini makes that pre-eminence more plausible still by writing his account in the third person. In short, the mechanics of Pius's apology mirror those of contemporary secular rulers as much as they do the ancient *Commentarii* of Caesar.

The parallels between Pius's and Caesar's writings extend to the portrait of military leadership at the centre of these accounts, and for good reason. Caesar's emphasis in his *Commentarii* on military prowess and accomplishment would have held particular appeal for Pius. His papacy had been defined by war – ones he fought on the peninsula and the one he hoped to lead against the Turks, and it had also been damaged by his struggles on both fronts, especially to achieve credibility in military command. Casting himself in the mould of an esteemed Roman general was a useful strategy for shoring up these vulnerabilities. The kind of wars he was fighting would have made such a parallel still more attractive. Like Caesar, Pius was engaged in a *bellum gallicum* – and in the spiritual as much as the temporal realm. In the *Gallic War*, moreover, the Gauls suffer a resounding defeat at the hands of the Roman general. By casting himself as a second Caesar in his own French wars, Pius, thus, signals that his Rome will, in turn, triumph over its own Gallic enemy. Such reassurances would have had particular appeal as he began writing his *Commentaries*, a time when his victory over the French was anything but secure. Caesar the general was also a useful model for Pius in his other major military venture. As military leader of the crusade, he was taking on what had traditionally been an imperial responsibility. Caesar himself had, of course, never fought a crusade, but he was considered in the fifteenth century to be the founder of the Roman Empire.[33] By modelling his own portrait as military leader on Caesar's, Pius, thus, gave further sanction to his own imperial mission.

The parallels between Pius's and Caesar's military leadership are still more extensive. The particular features of Caesar's self-portrait as a general are imprinted on Pius's own. Caesar's actions reflect a leader who is first and foremost a master of *scientia rei militaris* (knowledge of military matters), and one whose expertise clearly exceeds that of his officers, allies, and opponents.[34] This vision of martial acumen as "an exercise of the mind" more than a matter of battlefield heroism was ideally suited to Pius's own needs. Both pope and priest, he had to demonstrate military expertise in a way that did not compromise his integrity as a spiritual authority. The *Commentaries* illustrate just such a delicate combination: Pius manages to maintain a dominating presence in his own accounts of war by presenting himself, like Caesar, as the foremost military mastermind. Pius's own display of martial acumen as primarily an intellectual activity has already been documented and discussed in chapter 5. What that analysis did not do, however, was illuminate the debt owed to Caesar. In dominating discussions of a crusade at the Congress of Mantua, in debating Francesco Sforza on the logistics of the Neapolitan war, and in offering expert analysis of battlefield action, Pius was not just being an effective military leader: he was also being a Caesarean one.

There are still other ways in which Caesar's images as a military commander seem to inform and defend Pius's self-portrait in his *Commentaries*. In the *Civil War*, especially, Caesar presents himself repeatedly as a reluctant warrior, pressing Pompey throughout his campaigns to put down arms and resolve their quarrel peacefully.[35] Pius casts himself in a similar role when discussing his involvement in the Neapolitan war. Throughout the *Commentaries* his constant refrain is like Caesar's: one of unwavering willingness to seek a peaceful, legal resolution to the dispute. He is quick to point out how many times he appealed to the French to make a legal case for their claim to the throne of Naples, and how he attempted to negotiate with his opponents at the eleventh hour. In short, like Caesar, Pius envisions himself an advocate of peace.

By shaping his portrait in these terms, the *Commentaries* were shoring up a series of vulnerabilities that both Pius and the papacy faced as spiritual and temporal rulers. For one, they challenged repeated accusations that the popes of the fifteenth century were warmongers – accusations that had been used to challenge the legitimacy of their authority in the Papal States. At the same time, they also shored up or concealed one of his most serious weaknesses as a spiritual sovereign. By insisting that Pius had repeatedly sought a peaceful resolution to the dispute over the Neapolitan crown, the *Commentaries* only further reinforce the impression they give elsewhere that the delays in Pius's crusade were the fault of the warmongering French. At the same time, by adopting the image of reluctant warrior, Pius serves to legitimize still further the role he establishes for himself in the *Commentaries* as arbiter of Europe.

Hand in hand with the image of Caesar as champion of diplomacy in peace is his image as a merciful victor, and Pius's self-portrait follows suit here, too.[36] While the *Commentaries* do not always characterize the pope this way, they routinely use the term "clementia" – considered one of Ceasar's chief virtues – to describe how he treats his prisoners of war. The account of his treatment of Tiburzio di Maso and six of his fellow Roman rebels is a case in point.[37] While the rebels are not spared a public execution, the emphasis in the *Commentaries* is not so much on their punishment as it is on Pius's *clementia* when meting it out. The pontiff's first act of clemency, the *Commentaries* tell us, comes when he prohibits papal officials from treating the rebels violently. When priests are then sent to confess the criminals, we learn, the clerics praise the pope's clementia – and for good reason: as the rebels are being executed, the *Commentaries* report, a tearful Pius lifts up a prayer to the heavens, calling on the prisoners' behalf for God's *misericordia* and *clementia* and promising by his own authority as St Peter's successor to open the gates of heaven to any of them who had truly repented of their sins.[38]

In similar ways, the *Commentaries* point up the abundant mercy Pius showed to the rebellious Jacopo Savelli, a Roman baron who had led a violent uprising in the Agro Romano.[39] According to Pius's account,

Savelli was paraded as a prisoner through the streets of Rome in the summer of 1461 and in a procession that Pius likens explicitly to an ancient Roman triumph.[40] The *Commentaries* record that when the procession ends and a weeping and repentant Savelli prostrates himself at Pius's feet, the pope cried along with him. As he does, he explains why compassion towards all who rebel against him is, in his eyes, so necessary: "What man is there who does not sin? No one is born wise. No one is given such wisdom that he does not still have something to learn."[41] The dramatic scene concludes with Pius's generous show of clementia to the contrite rebel: not only does the pope spare him his life, but also he allows him to retain control over some of his territory. As he did in the tale of the Roman rebels' execution, Pius chooses words here to emphasize his mercy. Responding to Savelli's repentance, the pontiff claims in a particularly memorable line: "My *clementia* is greater than your *dementia*" (emphasis added).[42]

These vivid vignettes of papal rule as mild and merciful were invaluable both for Pius and for the papacy more generally. For one, they countered directly the scathing contemporary portraits of the fifteenth-century popes as harsh and tyrannical. At the same time, they undermined the legitimacy of using such accusations to rebel against papal rule. In turn, the portrait of a merciful and compassionate Pius would have helped counter his reputation among Italian powers as a ruler who punished rebellious subjects with unnecessary severity. Pius had earned that reputation through the punishments he had inflicted on papal vicar Sigismondo Malatesta. The *Commentaries* make no attempt to hide these punishments – on the contrary, they defend them in the face of reported protests from Venetian and Florentine ambassadors. By maintaining that he took the very opposite approach to other rebels, however, and by suggesting compassion was inherent to his philosophy of rule, Pius makes his treatment of Malatesta the exception, not the rule.

The image of Caesar as general even seems to shape aspects of Pius's portrait that are not associated with war. The eighth and final book of the *Gallic War* describes Caesar's joyous welcome in Cisalpine Gaul as he celebrates a military triumph. The *Civil War* records his similarly enthusiastic reception in various towns on the peninsula after he crosses the Rubicon and makes his way south. Not only were the citizens of Italy willing to let him march through their towns and cities, but they also furnished him with troops and hailed him as their liberator.[43] When reading Pius's *Commentaries*, it is hard not to be reminded of these passages. The parallels are most striking in Pius's own excursions through the Papal States heading to and from the Congress of Mantua.[44] The pope's journey, like Caesar's, took him through towns that had been hostile to his authority. But the account in Pius's *Commentaries*, like that in Caesar's, reveals nothing of popular resentment and rebellion. In reporting his journey, Pius pauses to describe the crowds of people who poured into the streets to greet him as pope and prince and to hold festivities in his honour at each of the places he stopped.[45] His arrival in Rome is marked by still greater celebration. When the captured rebels are led through the streets, the Romans are said to have shouted, "Blessed be Pius, who has liberated us from such great danger."[46]

While the itinerary of Pius's journey to Mantua bears the closest resemblance to Caesar's own travels, there are numerous other instances in the *Commentaries* where Pius emphasizes a similar reception at the hands of his subjects. He writes of the warm reception he receives as both pope and prince in, among other places, Tivoli, Subiaco, Cripta, Todi, Terni, and Genzano.[47] By emphasizing the Caesarean popularity Pius enjoyed among his subjects, the *Commentaries* help to shore up several significant vulnerabilities. Not only do they conceal that his rule was insecure in many parts of the Papal States, but they also reinforce ideas expressed elsewhere in the text that his authority had the enthusiastic approval of his subjects. By reporting that those same subjects acknowledged him as pope as well as prince, Pius masks similar weaknesses in his spiritual sovereignty.

How do these Caesarean aspects of Pius's portrait compare with the images of military command in the works of Porcellio, Contarini, and Facio? The parallels are striking, and again especially in the latter two. Both Contarini and Facio characterize their protagonists as masters of *scientia ars militaris*. In his own self-portrait, Contarini leaves the impression that his military mind and diplomatic skills were the key to the campaign that he chronicles: among other accomplishments, he records how he plotted winning battlefield strategies, orchestrated major victories, and figured out how to rebuild seige engines from a heap of scrap.[48] Alfonso's military prowess is, in turn, framed in intellectual terms: he is shown frequently planning tactical manoeuvres, and his shrewd military mind is singled out as one of his greatest attributes.[49] Alfonso's parallels with both Caesar and Pius extend, however, beyond his skills as military strategist. Like Pius, Alfonso in the *Gesta* is painted as a reluctant warrior, one who exhausts every avenue of peaceful negotiation with his enemies before taking up arms against them.[50] Moreover, as did Pius and Caesar of themselves, Facio emphasizes

Alfonso's *clementia*, especially towards those whom he had defeated and captured.[51] In short, the Pius in the *Commentaries* – and in particular, Pius the military commander – looks not simply like Caesar: he bears a distinct resemblance to the Caesarean portrait of Alfonso of Naples.

The strong parallels between these images make sense when we look at the men behind them. Alfonso and Pius shared comparable vulnerabilities, albeit for different reasons. Like Pius, Facio wrote his history at a time when his protagonist's military reputation was vulnerable to attack. Documents reveal that in the wake of his conquest of Naples, Alfonso was perceived by other Italian states as a "king of war," who disrupted the peninsula's delicate equilibrium. Moreover, while recognized as a skilled condottiere, the king was known for his recklessness on the battlefield. He was also not considered much of a military mind.[52] Given these vulnerabilities, Caesar's image as a reluctant warrior, sophisticated strategist, and compassionate victor would, thus, have been as valuable for the king of Naples as it would for Pius.

These parallels might also be explained by Pius's personal connections with the humanists at Alfonso's court. In 1456, Aeneas visited Naples on a diplomatic mission at the very time Facio was completing his *Gesta*. In the several months he spent there, he became acquainted with official court histories and other works celebrating Alfonso, many of which drew parallels between the king and the historical figure of Julius Caesar. So engaged was he with this circle and with the Caesarean portraits of Alfonso that Pius wrote a commentary on Panormita's *De dictis et factis Alphonsi Regis Aragonum libri quatuor*. Perhaps most significantly, he formed a friendship with Facio. The brief correspondence between them indicates not only that Facio shared his historical writings with Aeneas, but also that Aeneas was one of several humanists to whom Facio circulated sections of his unfinished *Gesta*.[53] Recent scholarship has demonstrated that Aeneas knew the work well: he drew on it when writing his *De Europa* (1458).[54]

It is also likely Pius knew the other histories modelled explicitly on Caesar's writings. Porcellio had himself been part of Alfonso's humanist court and had dedicated the first seven books of his *Commentaries* to Alfonso. Pius's connection with the humanist continued during his papacy: Porcellio was one of the first to seek his patronage after Aeneas's election to the papal throne in 1458. Moreover, the pontiff's familiarity with and admiration of his work are attested to by the fact that seventeen of Porcellio's poems are included in the *Epaenetica*, a collection of poetry in celebration of Pius's papacy that the pontiff himself allegedly compiled.[55] Pius also had good reason to know Francesco Contarini as a prominent figure in Venetian politics during his pontificate; and when Pius had been bishop of Siena, Contarini had served as Venetian ambassador to the city.[56] Just as important, Pius would have had a personal interest in Contarini's work: Aeneas had been integrally involved in the peace negotiations that ended Piccinino's relentless assault on Siena – the military campaign at the heart of Contarini's book. Indeed, the diplomatic mission that sent him to Naples in 1456 was to negotiate peace among the Sienese, the condottiere, and his protector, King Alfonso. In short, the Neapolitan connections among all these works and Pius's own personal connections to political and humanistic circles in Naples make his familiarity with Contarini's and Porcellio's works seem likely.

Given his encounters and intellectual connections with all these historians, it is clear that, at the very least, Pius was aware that Caesar's *Commentaries* had become models for historians recording the deeds of contemporary political leaders. With this in mind, it seems fair to conclude that Pius must have himself recognized the claim at the centre of this chapter: that in modelling his own *Commentaries* on Caesar's, he shaped his portrait to conform with contemporary representations of secular rule.

Pope Pius II and Virgil

The kinship that Pius's *Commentaries* enjoyed with classical culture extended beyond Caesar to Virgil, and specifically to Virgil's *Aeneid*. That Pius would look to this text and its protagonist when designing his self-portrait is no surprise. Like many humanists of his day, the pontiff deemed Virgil the pre-eminent poet of ancient Rome; indeed, so admiring was he of Virgil's talents and accomplishments that he wrote two poems in his honour.[57] Pius had also engaged with Virgil's works in numerous other writings. His *Historia de duobus amantibus* (1444), for one, was rich with Virgilian allusions; and his epistolary treatise *De natura et cura equorum* (1444) drew heavily on the *Georgics* for both structure and content. Inspired in part by Book VI of the *Aeneid*, Pius had also written three times about dreams in which he visited the underworld.[58]

Pius II's vocal admiration for Virgil and his penchant for incorporating the poet's writings into his own work cannot alone explain the significant role he assigns Virgil in his *Commentaries*. As with Caesar, the interest Pius showed in Virgil in his self-portrait should be considered political as well as personal. By the time Pius had finished writing his *Commentaries*, eight other epic poems modelled at least in part on the *Aeneid* had been or were being written in celebration of contemporary Italian rulers. Francesco Filelfo seems to have started the trend, beginning with his *Sforziad* in 1451. At about the same time, Antonio Cornazzano began his own celebration of Francesco Sforza, the similarly entitled *Sforzeide* (finished in 1459). In 1455 Basinio Basini completed his *Hesperis* for Sigismondo Malatesta, while Matteo Zuppardo was working at about the same time on his *Alfonseis* and Giovan Pietro Arrivabene on his *Gonzagiad*.[59] Porcellio Pandoni shortly thereafter began work on his *Feltriad*, while Tito Vespasiano Strozzi started on his *Borsiad* in 1460. Gian Mario Filelfo completed his *Martiad* shortly before Pius had finished his *Commentaries*.[60]

While it is difficult to determine if Pius knew of the existence of all these poems, there is no doubt that he was familiar with some of them. Porcellio Pandoni was engaged in writing the *Feltriad* while residing in Rome and employed at the papal court.[61] Pius was still more directly connected to Filelfo's *Sforziad*. The pope was among the select group of humanists and statesmen to whom Filelfo circulated pieces of his manuscript. In January 1460, Filelfo sent Pius the beginning of Book XI of his *Sforziad*, which centred on the latter's visit to Milan years earlier as legate for Frederick III.[62] In short, by aligning himself with Virgilian epic and with Aeneas, its hero, Pius must have realized that his choice carried with it a political charge.

What was it about the *Aeneid* and about the figure of Aeneas that made them such attractive models for fifteenth-century rulers? Many of the same elements that drew them to the model of Caesar and his writings likely drew them to Virgil's epic. Like Caesar, Aeneas was a warrior prince and a stranger to the territory he sought as his own dominion. As did Caesar's *Commentarii*, the *Aeneid* points to the military prowess and political savvy of its hero as justification for his rule.[63] These features alone, however, cannot explain why the text offered a suitable blueprint for princes and would-be princes who were not military leaders, or for those whose claim to power rested on secure legal ground. For these rulers and others, there was something else about Virgil's work that made it an attractive model for their portrayal in works of history and literature. In fifteenth-century Italy, and indeed in much of the Middle Ages, Virgil's *Aeneid* was read and taught as a moral epic and as a work of epideictic rhetoric. Aeneas himself was seen to represent the morally perfect hero whose actions and decisions represented an allegorical tale of virtue triumphing over vice.[64] While Virgil celebrated the values of a pagan culture, his claims were considered compatible with the ethical ideals and teachings of Christianity. To model a prince on Virgil's Aeneas was, thus, to associate him with some very desirable characteristics. While it is not clear how significant this factor was to the authors of all the fifteenth-century "Aeneids," there is no question that they were well aware of the epic's moral valence when they set to work on their political portraits.[65]

It is likely that the contemporary ethical resonance of the *Aeneid* played some role in Pius's decision to use the text as a model for his own self-portrait. Indeed, the pope's explicit acknowledgment elsewhere in his writings of the epic's epideictic nature makes this inspiration still more likely.[66] Pius also could not have failed to notice how the *Aeneid*'s political narrative had significant apologetic value for the situation in which he found himself during his pontificate. Aeneas, like Caesar, was another ruler highly respected in fifteenth-century Italy and one whose claim to power rested solely – and comfortably – on his ability to rule effectively through arms and statesmanship. What is more, he appears in Virgil's epic as the founder of Rome and the king of the Italians – roles that Pius in some way fulfilled or hoped to fulfil as head of the restored Roman Church, as diplomatic leader of the peninsula, and as Italy's protector in the face of French expansionism. What must also be determined, though, is what drew Pius to incorporate numerous other features of Aeneas's experience and character into his own, and how the resulting image related to the Virgilian portraits of his contemporaries in secular politics.

The role of God in the *Commentaries* is an excellent place to begin this investigation. While Pius appears in the text to be predestined for the papal throne, he does not display the aura of holiness that surrounded his predecessor, Nicholas V, in his literary portraits. Moreover, the terms with which Pius records divine intervention are often obscured by references to "fortune" or by labels of "marvellous" or "incredible."[67] Indeed, as Luigi Totaro has noted, Pius seems to walk on "a more earthly plane": he compares himself rarely to biblical figures; he is clearly not a saint in the typical understanding of the term; and while he paints himself as a martyr, he never talks of martyrdom as a purifying sacrifice.[68] While it is clear, then, that the role Pius assigns to God in the *Commentaries* does not fit comfortably into Christian traditions of hagiography, martyrology, or papal historiography, it is not clear how exactly this role should be understood. Trying to squeeze Pius's anomalous image into these traditional categories serves only to obscure the very thing that makes him so different.

Further analysis of Pius's relationship to the divine helps to position the *Commentaries* in their larger intellectual context. The key to determining their position is to understand precisely in what way Pius walks on an "earthly plane." The absence of biblical models in the text is not the only reason he seems rooted to the ground. The depiction of his character and his actions also serves to create this impression. A brief comparison with the literary portraits of Pope Nicholas V reveals just how. God permeates all aspects of Nicholas's ventures and accomplishments. He is the source of the pope's virtues and the reason for his successes – so much so, in fact, that Nicholas appears to be simply a vessel for the divine.[69] The *Commentaries*, in contrast, never make such direct equations. Instead, it is Pius II's superiority to his fellow human beings, not his identification with God, that receives the greatest emphasis. Moreover, while Pius openly acknowledges divine intervention in his life, more often than not, he portrays this influence as secondary to his own.

Pius's election to the papacy is a case in point.[70] In their account of the conclave, the *Commentaries* focus first and foremost on how Pius personally convinced his fellow cardinals to choose him as pope. As discussed already in chapters 4 and 5, the account draws attention to Pius's remarkable powers of persuasion and to his clear moral superiority in relation to the other candidates for the papal throne. Divine intervention is shown to play a comparatively minimal role in the results of the election. While Pius notes more than once that it was God who chose him, it is difficult not to come away from his account thinking that the pontiff's own skills as an orator played a greater role in his election, and not only because of their impact in the context of this particular triumph.[71] The chapters leading up to the conclave read like a catalogue of Pius's oratorical accomplishments – accomplishments that, significantly, are not attributed to the hand of God.[72] In this larger context, Pius's election cannot help but seem another such success, a moment of glory for Pius as much as for God.

This is hardly the only occasion in which Pius credits success to his own virtues and talents. Consider how he presents the moment of epiphany when he realizes how he could convince the rulers of Europe to respond to his calls for a crusade. In a private consistory with a select group of cardinals, Pius explains how he wrestled for weeks and months with the problem of moving the princes to take up arms against the Turks, and how he pursued in his mind every possible avenue and strategy. These are his schemes and his ideas, not the designs of God.[73] Moreover, when Pius describes how he finally arrived at the solution, he emphasizes his own role in the discovery.[74] The cardinals who listen to Pius's explanation respond by pronouncing his ideas to be divinely inspired,[75] but their interpretation reads in the context merely as an afterthought. Indeed, their words lend support to what Totaro has said about the role of predestination in the *Commentaries*: rather than giving Pius an "image of holiness," it serves to validate his rule as pope.[76]

Elsewhere in the *Commentaries*, references to divine intervention come across more as a sign of Pius's piety than of God's active influence in the pontiff's life. For the most part, this is because it is Pius the character who recognizes God's role, rather than Pius the narrator. While the pontiff may claim to be part of a larger, divine plan, these claims are ultimately subjective in nature; they say more about Pius's view of God than they do about God's powers. Even while he acknowledges and appeals for God's help, however, Pius still positions his own virtues at centre stage. It is his reasoning that convinces the cardinals to add new members to the college, his wisdom and experience that allow him to re-establish control over Rome after the uprisings in his absence, and his decision to invest Ferrante with the Kingdom of Naples. In short, there is never any doubt that Pius's own virtues, skills, and talents are the main reasons behind his success.

The role Pius assigns to God in the *Commentaries*, a role of influence but not domination, is reminiscent of the one assigned to the divine in ancient epics and, significantly, one that was adopted in the portraits of the pontiff's contemporaries. Most fifteenth-century epics folded into their discussions the concept of the supernatural in terms of fatalism.[77] They seem, moreover, to have done so for the very same reason that Totaro identifies in the *Commentaries* – as sanction, not sanctification. The explanation for their choice is clear: God's approval and assistance would go a long way in justifying a ruler whose right to power had no legal or dynastic basis. This is precisely what Filelfo does in the *Sforziad* by emphasizing that the fates had chosen Francesco Sforza to rule the Duchy of Milan.[78] In the *Hesperis*, Basini, in turn, identifies divine intervention under Malatesta's rule in Rimini in the form of classical gods.[79] The same kind of predestination figures into portraits of secular rulers even outside the genre of epic: in their images of Ferrante of Naples, for example, both Bartolomeo Facio and Antonio Panormita note God sanctions his rule.[80]

While the power these rulers held was predetermined according to these texts, the divine is made to play a limited role both in their rise to power and in their subsequent leadership. In keeping with Virgil's *Aeneid* and other ancient epics, predestination and divine aid do not overshadow the independent *virtus* of the hero. Rather than controlling every move of their creation, the gods simply create opportunities for their heroes' own *virtus* to shine. For authors of political epics of the fifteenth century, striking this delicate balance between divine and human agency was of utmost importance. While heavenly sanction was certainly an asset to these rulers' campaigns of self-promotion, it was still more important to demonstrate their own capabilities as rulers. The humanists who wrote these works were, thus, careful to represent gods as assistants in a way that did not detract from the glory due their princes.[81]

It is this same pattern that Pius's image in the *Commentaries* follows. Pius is God's agent, but he is also very human; and it is his human *virtus* that is credited consistently and explicitly throughout the *Commentaries*. In Book One, divine intervention closely follows the classical epic pattern of opening the door to Pius's success, rather than determining that success for him. In his years as pope, there is no question that his own abilities are responsible for his triumphs. Pius does not show himself pausing to ask for divine grace or for the inspiration of the Holy Spirit when he makes decisions. The *Commentaries* show him turning instead to his own reason, experience, and the counsel of others.[82] Given that contemporary portraits of Francesco Sforza, Sigismondo Malatesta, and Ferrante of Naples assigned divine intervention the same limited role, Pius's decision to shape his relationship with God along similar lines cannot be understood simply in literary terms. It also meant that his portrait conformed to images of secular rule.

The emphasis in the *Commentaries* on Pius's *pietas* should be read in a similar way. The pope's devotion to religion, family, and *patria* features prominently in this text.[83] Certainly, the figure this virtue recalled most clearly was the pontiff's ancient namesake, *pius* Aeneas. In Pius II's day and age, however, this parallel also evoked the values and images of contemporary secular rulers. Filelfo underscores pietas as an essential trait in his portrait of Francesco Sforza; so does Basini in his image of Sigismondo Malatesta; and Facio does so, in turn, when recounting the deeds of Alfonso of Naples.[84] In making the classical pietas a defining element of his self-portrait, Pius depicted himself still more like a fifteenth-century Italian signore.

What makes Pius's presentation of this virtue fall in line still more with those images is the emphasis he gives to the element of *patria*. Devotion to one's patria was at the core of fifteeenth-century ethics.[85] It was also a defining feature of many political portraits, epic and otherwise, and for good reason: it was the prince's ability to protect and govern his patria that often served as the very basis for his power. Devotion to patria is essential to Basini's portrait of Sigismondo Malatesta in the epic the *Hesperis*, and to Giannantonio Campano's *res gestae* of the condottiere Braccio da Montone.[86] It was also a vital component of the public image of Cosimo de' Medici.[87] Pius's loyalty to his patria pervades Pius's *Commentaries* in part because he gave the term a variety of meanings. The pontiff considered his patria to be at once Rome, Siena, the Papal States, and Italy. He uses the term most frequently to describe Siena; in connection with the other geographical locations, the word patria itself appears only a few times.

To understand exactly how this emphasis on patria in the *Commentaries* served Pius's specific interests as pope requires an examination of the passages in which the term appears. The references to Siena are a good place to begin. Pius refers to the "sweet soil of his fatherland" often simply in passing, such as when he arrives and departs from the town. He also uses it when describing his intervention into its political and ecclesiastical affairs, an intervention that was both considerable and controversial.[88] By presenting his involvement in the Sienese church and government as a sign of his love for his patria, Pius could justify what to many appeared an inappropriate interest and investment. This interpretation finds support in a series of passages in the text where Pius explicitly connects such intervention to his concern for his patria. When, for example, the pope implores the Sienese government to readmit the nobles to power, he explains he is moved to do so out of love for his patria: "This is our advice, which we give to our most beloved patria."[89] When he elevates the church of Siena to a metropolitan church and promptly makes a member of the Piccolomini family the first archbishop, he explains: "So greatly did Pius strive to honour his patria."[90] When he transfers control of an area of Tuscany to his nephew Antonio, he again claims his motive is the welfare of Siena: "The pope entrusted Castiglione, the forts and the island of Giglio to his nephew Antonio, thinking not so much about how it would benefit him as it would his patria: Siena's coastal districts and public granaries were controlled by the town of Castiglione."[91] By casting these actions as expressions of civic virtue, Pius made more palatable the political and ecclesiastical ambitions he had for the Piccolomini family. At a time when the papacy had come under harsh attack for nepotism, and in a pontificate that saw significant positions of power in both temporal and ecclesiastical government distributed to Pius's relatives, it was more important than ever that these ambitions be masked.[92]

The term patria also has strategic significance elsewhere in the *Commentaries*. Pius's few references to Rome and the Papal States as his patria appear in the context of his return from Mantua, after a prolonged absence, and one that included a lengthy sojourn in Siena.[93] As chapter 3 explained, both Rome and the Agro Romano had been witness to violent uprisings. It was in Pius's best interests not only to repair his damaged relationship with the Roman citizens and those of the Papal States, but also to present that relationship as strong. If Pius's Caesarean emphasis on his warm reception by his subjects was one way of creating such an image, his equation of Rome and the Papal States with his patria was another. Pius's use of the term patria to define Italy is no different. The only place the pope makes the connection explicitly is in his account of the conclave and, more specifically, in the context of his conversations with other cardinals.[94] Here, Pius persuades more than one Italian member of the college not to elevate a Frenchman to the papal throne because of the consequences for their patria. Pius's use of the term in this context helps to underscore the idea already discussed in chapter 5 that, in the conclave, Pius proved himself the true leader of the Italian League. For this reason, too, the chief attribute of the Roman Aeneas serves as a valuable tool for defending the beleaguered Pope Pius.

In and of themselves, the Virgilian elements of Pius's self-portrait align it closely with contemporary images of secular rulers. Should they, however, be understood the same way in a text that is heavily interwoven with the features of an entirely different genre – the *Commentarii* of Julius Caesar? In mixing the more mythological and poetic features of an epic into a work of historical prose narrative, Pius might seem to be distancing himself from both the literary and historiographical traditions of his contemporary secular rulers. However, while some authors maintained a strict division of the two genres of writing, there were, in fact, many others who blended them in shaping their literary portraits. Porcellio's *Commentarii* on the wars between Venice and Milan, for example, were as much a work of mythology and imagination as they were a record of contemporary history. The entire text is explicitly modelled on the Punic Wars and it casts as the leaders of the two armies, Francesco Sforza and Jacopo Piccinino, as Hannibal and Scipio Africanus, respectively. Just as the genre of *commentarii* was tinged with what was customary to epic, so did the poetic celebrations of princes cross over into the realm of the prose historian. The epic that has received most attention for its hybrid status is Filelfo's *Sforziad*. Contemporaries and modern scholars alike have described this work as an uncomfortable fit with the epic genre. The poem is composed not so much from the poet's imagination, as it is the materials typically used in *commentarii* – dispatches, letters, speeches, and other official documents. Stylistically, moreover, it sheds the rhetorical flourishes and much of the mythologizing typical of epic poetry in favour of the more straightforward and analytical moves of a historian.[95] Rather than attempting to fit Filelfo's work into one or the other of the genres, we might do better to classify it as a historical narrative in epic clothing – or better yet, to recognize its hybrid nature as a distinct subgenre.[96]

By recognizing that the *Commentaries* share with Filelfo's *Sforziad* a hybrid approach to genre, we can position the work still more precisely in contemporary political culture. Pius's self-portrait resembles images of secular political rulers not simply by appropriating Caesarean and Virgilian features: it also does so by blending the genres of epic and *commentarii*. Pius's own particular mix of these genres, less overtly poetical than Porcellio's *Commentarii* and more faithful to the contemporary historical standards than Filelfo's epic, may, in fact, have grown out of his own sensitivity to how other generic hybrids had been received. There had been considerable backlash against Filelfo's work from contemporaries who viewed the *Sforziad's* attention to historical detail as "betraying" the poetic style of the genre – a backlash, significantly, that Pius himself seems to have supported.[97] The heavily mythologized *Commentarii* of Porcellio had also received a cold reception at the Neapolitan court.[98] By following more faithfully the standards of his chosen genre and by limiting the mythological elements of his account, Pius avoided the "errors" of his predecessors. These variations notwithstanding, his *Commentaries* must be classified alongside these texts and considered another version of the dual genre so common to the textual portraits of secular rulers of his day.

History as Polemic: Pius's *Commentaries* and Historiographical Rivalry

If histories of contemporary princes were defined by their adoption of classical models, they were also defined by an intertextual dialogue with one another. The literary portraits of Pius's contemporaries were not simply moulded by the political circumstances in which they were written. They also responded to a specific historiographical context, one that could prove as threatening as the political instability that so often prompted their composition. The humanists who celebrated their prince in prose and poetry did so at the expense of his enemies and, to a lesser extent, even his allies. His victories were best emphasized by exposing the failures of his rivals and by minimizing the accomplishments of his friends. Circulated in the right circles, such images could do significant damage; and the potential victims were well aware of this danger. Accordingly, the literary portraits they produced conversed with, corrected, and retaliated against the damaging ones created at other courts. In short, alongside military conflicts, the princes of fifteenth-century Italy were engaged in bitter and often dangerous historiographical wars.[99]

In his work on historiography at the Milanese court, Gary Ianziti uncovers some of these battlefields in the literary portraits of Francesco Sforza. He demonstrates how Lodrisio Crivelli's *De vita rebusque Francisci Sfortiae* (1461–62) responds to a pair of historical works written about two of Sforza's past rivals: Bartolomeo Facio's *Gesta* and Giannantonio Campano's *Bracii Perusini vita et gesta* (1450s).[100] As discusssed earlier, the first of these works centres on the character and accomplishments of King Alfonso of Naples. The second celebrates the deeds of Braccio da Montone, a Perugian exile and condottiere who in 1416 overthrew the ruling factions in his patria and went on to carve out a swathe of territory within the Papal States. Crivelli, familiar with the works of both Campano and Facio, includes in his history of Sforza some of the same episodes that appear in their writings. He does so, however, in a way that makes his patron shine to the detriment of both Alfonso and Braccio. In describing Alfonso's defeat at Naples in 1424, for example, Facio makes no mention of Sforza's role in the battle and chalks up the Aragonese loss to the defection of one of its commanders. He paints a disparaging portrait of Sforza's troops, moreover, by describing how they plundered the city. Crivelli's version tells a very different story. There Sforza appears as the mastermind behind the attack and receives full credit for the triumph. Far from pillaging Naples, his troops are described as treating its citizens with the utmost respect.[101]

Crivelli adopts the same revisionary tactics elsewhere in the text in discussing the exploits of Braccio da Montone. Whereas Campano had depicted Braccio as the saviour of Perugia, rescuing its citizens from violent factional struggle, Crivelli makes Braccio out to be a tyrant. While

Campano shapes the condottiere's attack on Rome into a defence of Christianity, Crivelli condemns him for preying on a papacy still weakened and wounded by years of schism.[102] By undermining the portrait of one of Sforza's greatest enemies, Crivelli indirectly builds up the image of his patron. In other places, the historian's tactics of praise are still more direct. The moment of Braccio's decisive defeat at the battle of L'Aquila is a case in point. In Campano's text, Braccio falls victim to overblown confidence in his *virtus* and to the overpowering force of *fortuna*. Crivelli revises this explanation. While reinforcing Campano's claim that Braccio can in part be blamed for his own downfall, he gives greater credit to something Campano had not mentioned: Francesco Sforza's superior virtus.[103]

What role did Pius play in these historiographical battles? By placing the *Commentaries* beside the literary portraits of some of the pope's enemies and allies – Braccio da Montone, Francesco Sforza, Alfonso of Naples, and Sigismondo Malatesta – it becomes clear that Pius was an active participant in this rivalry. The portraits he paints of these contemporary rulers are not simply pointed attacks on his political rivals: they also represent direct assaults on the literary defences of these figures. In constructing his self-portrait in these terms, Pius is embedding his work still more in the secular political culture of his day.

One of the clearest examples of Pius's attacks comes in his own discussion of Braccio da Montone. Though Braccio had long been dead by the time Pius came to power, his family and followers, including Jacopo Piccinino, continued to challenge his temporal authority throughout the Papal States. As a defence of the party's founder and the peaceful government he installed, Campano's *Vita Bracii* represented as much a menace to the present pope as it did a stain on the papacy's past. There were circumstances at Pius's own court, however, that made Braccio's portrait still more of a threat. Shortly after writing the work, Campano had come to Rome and had been welcomed into Pius's circle as court poet and close confidant. It was embarrassing enough that Campano's history discredited the papacy and exalted the enemy, but it was doubly awkward now that the same historian served at the papal court.[104] Campano himself reveals what a delicate dance such shifts in allegiance were in a letter he writes to Nicodemo Tranchedini. Here, however, he is talking about his earlier ambition to seek the patronage of Francesco Sforza and to write a history about the duke's rise to power. Campano's letter shows that he was not oblivious to the conflict of interest such a project would create. Were he to pursue a history of Sforza, he explains, he would have to abandon the idea of continuing his *Vita Bracii*. Campano's observations here help to underscore the uncomfortable situation he must have found himself in at the papal court.[105] They also make it still more reasonable to look for a response to Campano's work in Pius's text.

The image of Braccio that appears in the *Commentaries* directly undermines the one Campano puts forward. Far from the saviour of the church, Pius paints him as its archenemy: Braccio "invaded" rather than liberated Perugia; and he "subjugated," "snatched," and "tore away" other papal territories.[106] The pontiff reinforces this image still further by labelling Braccio repeatedly "enemy of the church" and by emphasizing his indifference to basic tenets of Christianity.[107] Just as Pius undermines Campano's image of Braccio's conquest, so does he challenge the image of his benevolent leadership. The pope uses his sojourn in Braccio's patria, Perugia, while en route to the Congress of Mantua as an opportunity to launch his counter-attack. According to Campano, Braccio was a just and generous statesman whose greatest concern was the welfare of his people. "In peace," Campano writes, "no one was more observant of justice and *aequitas*."[108] In Pius's account, nothing could be farther from the truth. In a rapid series of vignettes, the condottiere emerges in the *Commentaries* as a savage, irrational, and unpredictable leader, who was guided by a strong penchant for violence rather than by civic duty. As examples of his cruelty, Pius notes how Braccio laughed when he ordered people to be tortured, how he threw a messenger off a bridge who had brought him a hostile letter, how he crushed the testicles of eight subversive monks, and how he submerged a plaintive prisoner in boiling water.[109] Together, these comments not only condemned Braccio, the man – a point already noted in chapter 5: they also overturned his legitimizing historical memory as preserved in Campano's biography.

Campano's *Vita Bracii* is not the only contemporary history that Pius engages in conversation. In building his criticism of Braccio, the pontiff also echoes Crivelli's account in his *De vita* of the tyrant's death, and not just in the negative portrait the Milanese historiographer paints of Braccio. Pius notes that Braccio's defeat came "not without glory to Francesco Sforza," and in so doing, endorses one of the central features in Crivelli's description of the duke.[110] Pius's corroboration of this image seems fitting given that Sforza was one of the pope's most important allies, but it also reflects the uneasy nature of that alliance. Whereas Sforza was at the centre of the victory over Braccio in Crivelli's account,

Pius places him in the background. At one point in the text, the pope records that Braccio's defeat came at the hands of Pope Martin V's army, rather than singling out Sforza as had Crivelli; and at another point, the pontiff reports that Braccio's fellow countrymen captured the condottiere as he fled the battlefield. In both of these instances it is the papal forces that are given most credit for the victory, rather than Sforza. In framing the narrative in these terms, the *Commentaries* temper Crivelli's picture so that Sforza's authority and accomplishments would not overshadow those of the pope.[111] In so doing, they complete the image promoted elsewhere in the *Commentaries* of Pius's own dominance over the Milanese duke.

Pius responds in a similar way to Facio's portrait of Alfonso of Naples: he diminishes the glory of this ruler when it detracts from that of the papacy. In the tenth and final book of the *Gesta*, Facio presents the Neapolitan king as the best candidate to lead an expedition against the Turks. According to his account, it was the papal legate who, speaking on behalf of other Italian ambassadors, hailed the king in these terms and urged him to assume the role of crusade leader at their request: "Everyone believes that no one is better suited to this task. All are unanimous in proposing you as the commander."[112] Alfonso, Facio reports, obliges; and by declaring himself willing to risk his life to do so, he casts himself in the mould of a martyr.[113] The *Commentaries* paint a strikingly different portrait of Alfonso's attitude to the crusade. The references they make are short but damning. Twice Pius draws attention to the king's disinterest in an expedition against the Turks. He notes, for one, that Alfonso had been late sending his representatives to the Diet of Frankfurt (1454) – so late, in fact, that by the time they arrived, the assembly had adjourned.[114] Elsewhere, he observes that the king "did not so much impress the sign of the Cross on [his] heart as [he] sewed it into [his] clothes."[115] The *Commentaries* raise still other serious questions about Alfonso's ability to lead an expedition against the Turks. Describing the king's infatuation with a certain Lucrezia, Pius remarks, "A great king ... who had conquered many provinces in Italy and had defeated the most powerful generals in battle was, in the end, conquered by love, and like a prisoner of war, was enslaved to a weak woman."[116] These disparaging comments strike directly at Facio's image of Alfonso as both an ardent and capable crusade leader. In so doing, they help to reinforce the impression created elsewhere in the *Commentaries* that such expeditions were the rightful prerogative of the papacy. At the same time, they buttress the portrait of Pope Pius as the one best qualified for this task.

Pius engages in historiographical battle with figures far more dangerous to his own interests than Alfonso, Sforza, or Braccio. Of these, the most notorious was Sigismondo Malatesta, signore of Rimini. Unlike these princes, Malatesta could claim legitimate authority in his *signoria;* but like them, his power remained precarious for many of the same reasons. As papal vicar, Malatesta ultimately had no control over his legal and hereditary claims. His power was subject to the sovereignty of the pope; thus, the lands he ruled were effectively not his, nor was his title one he could pass down at will.[117] Like Francesco Sforza, Malatesta sought out the traditional sanctions of independent authority: he appealed to both pope and emperor for the grant of a dynastic title. And because his efforts were in vain, like Sforza, he turned to the humanist pen to buttress his claims. The aforementioned *Hesperis* by Basinio Basini is the most famous of this signore's literary portraits, but Roberto Valturio's treatise *De re militari* puts forward a very similar image.[118] Malatesta is hailed in these texts as a ruler of incomparable *virtus* and *pietas* who defends civil liberties and protects the public good. In short, argue Basini and Valturio, he has proven himself more than worthy of the power he requests.[119]

Malatesta emerges from these works as a blessing to much more than his patria: he is also made out to be the *defensor Italiae*, rescuing Italy from foreign domination. The *Hesperis* draws out this theme most fully. Centring on Malatesta's wars with Alfonso of Aragon in 1448 and again in 1452–53, the poem casts Malatesta as leader and protector of the "Latini," "Ausonii," and "Italii," battling the "barbarians," "Iberi," "Celti," and "Taraconii." Basini makes what were, in reality, relatively "modest ventures" into a turning point in Italian history, and Malatesta Italy's hero.[120] Indeed, so significant was this dimension of his image to his work that it gave shape to the title of the epic: calling the work the *Hesperis* was the equivalent of calling it the *Italiad*.

That Pius would seek to retaliate against such claims to power is not surprising given the nature of his relationship with Malatesta. Moreover, he had reason to fear Malatesta the image as well as Malatesta the man. Valturio's work, the *De re militari*, circulated heavily in the 1460s and precisely when the lord was trying to rally support in his war against the pope.[121] Moreover, there is evidence that Pius was at least partially aware of this circulation and its potential consequences. In 1461 the pontiff's men intercepted a copy of the text that was headed, significantly, for his greatest enemy: Mehmed II.[122] This discovery could not but have alarmed the pontiff and would have made the danger posed by such propaganda all too clear. It also would have made the image of Malatesta a particularly urgent target to attack.

While the disparaging portrait Pius paints of Malatesta in the *Commentaries* has long been a topic of scholarly discussion, its historiographical significance has yet to be fully appreciated. Scholars have recognized it as a strategic attack on one of the pontiff's greatest enemies, but they have not seen how it also represents an assault on this enemy's own historiographical ramparts. Even a cursory comparative analysis of the portraits of Malatesta in Basini's and Valturio's works and in Pius's *Commentaries* reveals how the pope systematically tears down the image put forward by the signore's two defenders, and in the process, his claim to rule. In Valturio's and Basini's portraits, for example, Malatesta was a man of great *virtus* and *pietas*. Pius targets this image from the beginning of the *Commentaries* to the end, introducing the duke as the "prince of all villainy" and reinforcing the image with the epithets of "master of wickedness" and "the worst of all men who ever lived and who will live."[123] While Malatesta's defenders had traced the signore's virtues back through his ancestors, Pius explicitly denies such heritage. "It was not through virtue that the Malatesta family become powerful," Pius insists, explaining that "the foundations of tyranny were laid in treachery," and he goes on to illustrate this pronouncement with a detailed and damning portrait of Malatesta rule down to when Sigismondo assumed power.[124] Pius undermines still more graphically the signore's claims to pietas. In a long chapter devoted to Malatesta, Pius presents a detailed list of his crimes against religion, his family, and his patria. Malatesta loathed the clergy and the religion they preached, Pius reports; he had no faith in the afterlife, and the church he built to San Francesco was reminiscent of a pagan shrine. His attitude towards his family was, according to Pius, equally despicable. He murdered his first two wives, committed incest with his children, and was both an incurable adulterer and a violent pedophile.[125] He was, in other words, hardly the paragon of pietas that his literary portraits conveyed.

Pius saves his most devastating attacks, however, for Malatesta the signore – and his choice of focus is significant. It was this aspect of pietas, love of patria, that Basini and Valturio had stressed the most in their portraits, and it was also the image that represented the greatest threat to Pius's authority. Malatesta appears in the *Commentaries* as the worst of all possible rulers. From Basini's and Valturio's leader, attentive to the needs of his people, he is transformed into a brutal tyrant who uses his power simply to fulfil his own desires. Pius reports how he crushed the poor, robbed the rich, cruelly punished both innocent and guilty, and menaced all with his insatiable lust.[126] His conclusion that "nobody lived safely under his rule" underscores the idea implicit in these images and strikes at the very heart of Malatesta's self-defence.[127] The pope finds in the signore's military ventures another opportunity to expose his civic neglect. More than once Pius blames the wartime sufferings of Malatesta's subjects on their "impious" leader.[128] And when the people pleaded with their signore to make peace with Federigo and Ferrante, the pontiff recounts, Malatesta dismissed their concerns in a statement that devastated his portrait as a benevolent ruler: "You will never have peace so long as I am alive."[129] In reporting his own involvement in the war as arbiter, moreover, Pius contrasts his own civic responsibility with Malatesta's chronic abuse of temporal power. He speaks explicitly at the negotiations of protecting the people of Malatesta's territories, and he explains how the certainty of their continued suffering compelled him to seek peace.[130] Pius's account thus not only underscores Malatesta's callous and selfish leadership, it also enhances the pope's own merits as a prince, and his image as a worthy and desirable ruler of the Papal States.

Pius retaliates against Basini and Valturio still more explicitly when he engages with their image of Malatesta as Italy's saviour. Admittedly, Pius spends little time discussing the wars that inspired such a title, but when he does, he erodes their portrait by explicitly dismissing these battles as "insignificant," and by attributing the signore's victories to *perfidia* and *deceptio*, rather then *virtus*.[131] Moreover, Pius's description of Malatesta as a man who "surpassed all barbarians with his cruelty" effectively upends Basini's claim that the signore was protecting Italy from barbarian invasion.[132] More than at the details of the wars themselves, Pius levels his attack against Malatesta's title of *defensor Italiae*, and he does so from the very first time the duke is mentioned: not only is Malatesta the "prince of all villainy," but he is also the "poison of all Italy."[133] Pius goes on to disparage his poor diplomatic relations by noting that he had tricked all the powers on the peninsula. Pius concludes his sketch by again repeating his danger to his neighbours, this time labelling him "the disgrace of Italy."[134] Even when describing Malatesta's wars with Federigo and Alfonso in the Marche, the pope makes a point of noting that the region devastated by their battles was "a territory renowned in all of Italy."[135] Perhaps most significant, however, is his formal pronouncement of Malatesta's crimes in a public consistory. Pius recounts how the author of the report, Andrea Benci, urged the pope not simply to save the desperate people of the Marche from Malatesta's tyranny, but also to "liberate Italy from a hideous and abominable monster."[136]

We have already seen these references in the context of studying Pius's own self-portrait as *defensor Italiae*, but here we see them in a different light. Historiographical precedents as well as historical pressures would have made it important for Pius to present himself in such terms. In fact, there is still a broader historiographical context within which these passages of the *Commentaries* should be read. Sigismondo Malatesta was not the only one of Pius's contemporararies to claim the title of defensor Italiae. Milanese historians had used the same image to describe Francesco Sforza and, as in Pius's case, the menacing foreigner was France. By bringing peace and stability to Lombardy, they argued, Sforza had helped to protect Italy from the very real threat north of the Alps.[137] Just as it had been for Malatesta, the title of defensor Italiae represented a valuable weapon with which Sforza could justify his questionable power in Milan. Just as Malatesta's had been for Pius, so did Sforza's heroic image threaten to overshadow the pope's ambitions to restore papal leadership in temporal politics on the peninsula.

What makes Pius's battle with these historical texts still more plausible is the fact that the pontiff was well connected with most of the figures who had written these texts. In 1461, Crivelli, out of favour at the Milanese court, had fled to Rome where he was awarded a papal secretaryship and began work on his own short history of Pius's crusade.[138] Campano was not only one of Pius's closest confidants: he also played a critical role in editing and correcting the *Commentaries*. Bartolomeo Facio's relationship with the pontiff and their communication about the latter's *Gesta* has already been noted. The pope's connections with Malatesta's defenders are not as clear, but, as mentioned above, he was certainly aware of the central elements their writings portrayed. In short, Pius was fully immersed in the contemporary culture of historical propaganda when he began composing his own self-portrait, and by participating in a historiographical rivalry, he firmly situated his *Commentaries* in the same political world.

The strength of Pius's self-portrait in the *Commentaries* is indebted in no small way to contemporary humanist portraits of secular rule. It is because of its strong resemblance to these representations that Pius appears still more effective as a crusade leader, still more capable and conscientious as a prince, and still more dominant in both spiritual and temporal realms. In short, the images of Pius's fellow signori did not just inform his own portrait of leadership: they defined it and strengthened it in essential ways. For this reason, Pius II's *Commentaries* stand as powerful evidence of the sea change scholars have identified in papal imagery of the fifteenth and sixteenth centuries. At the same time, this text suggests news ways of explaining why the language of secular politics might have held such appeal for popes of this age, and especially for those in the second half of the fifteenth century. Embattled sovereigns in both their spiritual and temporal realms, popes like Pius II would have found in the representations of these signori not just targets of attack. They would also have seen in them powerful weapons for fighting their own wars.

Conclusion

History is the witness of times past, the light of truth, the teacher of life, the messenger of antiquity.[1]

Eight years before his election as pope, Aeneas Silvius Piccolomini wrote these words to Juan de Carvajal. They appear at the beginning of his *De rebus Basiliae gestis commentarius*, the history of the Council of Basel that he addressed to the Spanish cardinal in 1450. Ciceronian in origin, Aeneas's claims about history would fit just as easily in the preface to the *Commentaries* he began writing twelve years later as Pope Pius II. From his perspective, that work exemplified this definition. The pope would have reached this conclusion in part because of how he understood the word "truth." For Pius the historian, truth did not consist of an impartial account of events. Truth meant *his* truth, and not simply his own subjective perceptions of the past: it meant a history that served a particular set of interests that he himself had defined. In the *Commentaries*, that truth was first and foremost the story of Pope Pius II's convincing triumphs as a spiritual and a temporal monarch; and it was the story of his tireless dedication to defending papal authority in the years before he reached the papal throne. That truth was also the tale of a papacy whose sovereign power was secure and whose leadership was indispensable both to the spiritual welfare and to the political stability of fifteenth-century Europe.

The historical truth Pius presents in the *Commentaries* is not the only one to which he subscribed over the course of his life and career. This book has argued that it reflects the one he embraced from the time he ascended the papal throne. To be sure, Aeneas began to align himself with papalist views a dozen years earlier when he abandoned conciliar doctrine and was reconciled with Eugenius IV. But the Aeneas who did these things would not have written the *Commentaries* in the same way that Pope Pius II did. Based on the position he held on councils, on the Bohemian Compacts and on Alfonso of Naples as peacemaker, his portrait of the papacy's temporal and spiritual authority would have looked considerably different from what Pius eventually wrote. By locating in his papacy Pius's full adherence to a papalist perspective, this book not only reconfigures traditional interpretations of his thought and career. It also distinguishes his *Commentaries* from his earlier writings, and in a significant way.

If on one level this text represents a break from Pius II's intellectual past, then on another it is integrally connected to it. The *Commentaries* bring together ideas, concerns, and criticisms that permeate his wide-ranging corpus of writings and that were fundamental to shaping his broader world view. These include his frustration with a Europe chronically ravaged by war; his bitter conviction that most people are driven by self-interest; his persistent faith in the universal authorities of papacy and empire, despite the fact that, in his day, popes and emperors struggled mightily to exercise that authority; his firm belief that a crusade should be Europe's top priority; and his insistence that a humanist education was the essential foundation for one to govern well. All these views are woven into the *Commentaries* and, still more importantly, into the apology this work represents. According to Pius's account, it is a pope, trained in the *studia humanitatis*, who can discipline the private interests of Europe's leaders and redirect them to public ends, who can restore peace to Europe, and who can turn back the Ottoman Turks from its shores.

The *Commentaries* are also, in many ways, the culmination of Pius's work as an apologist, and especially as an apologetic historian. This book has made the case that Pius II wrote this text by drawing from and building on a methodology he had begun to develop decades earlier and, ironically, in the context of defending some of the papacy's most dangerous opponents. More than fashioning new tools, he honed in the *Commentaries* ones he already had. In some cases, he turned them to very different tasks, such as when he characterized the college of cardinals in the same damning terms he had the council fathers at Basel. In other cases, he sharpened them: the colourful sketches of Pius's enemies in the *Commentaries* are far more venomous than those in his conciliar histories. In still other cases, he relied on them more heavily: in none of his earlier writings did Pius erase the historical record as extensively as he did here. In short, from a methodological perspective, the Pius who wrote the *Commentaries* is closely related to Aeneas the historian. They both used history to promote their own truths and they did so in similar ways. In the *Commentaries*, Pius simply does so on what was for him an unprecedented scale; and he does so more boldly, more systematically, and more confidently than ever before.

But was he right to have such confidence? In other words, are the *Commentaries* effective as a work of apology? The analysis of the text laid out in this book invites us to raise such a question. While it has been argued here that the *Commentaries* are consistently apologetic, it has also been maintained that this defence does not function consistently as a coherent whole. At several points in his account, Pius shores up one weakness in a way that exposes or even aggravates another. The resulting tensions and inconsistencies might easily be read as design flaws in the work's architecture, though ones that are understandable under the circumstances. Pius composed this vast and complex work in less than two years and in the crucible of a difficult papacy. He wrote it piecemeal, snatching time, and often late at night, to do so; and as he wrote his narrative, he had no clear sense of how it would end. Under these circumstances, it seems almost inevitable that the *Commentaries* would contain inconsistencies. But should they be understood as flaws – indeed, should they even be seen as inconsistencies? Answering that question requires knowing how Pius II intended the *Commentaries* to be read and used – and by whom. Those intentions, as the introduction to this book has explained, remain obscure. Based on what we do know, however, it is reasonable to think that Pius's text was meant to be read selectively, perhaps in the form of individual books, and to be viewed in their entirety only by the pope's closest confidants and advisers. In this scenario, the inconsistencies and tensions in the text become moot, and the apology therein anything but flawed.

Still another aspect of the *Commentaries* raises questions about its effectiveness as a work of apology. The preceding analysis has revealed how extensively and systematically the text conceals the liabilities of Aeneas's past, the struggles of Pius's pontificate, and the weaknesses of the fifteenth-century papacy. An extreme example of this broader pattern appears in Book One. There, in sharp contrast to reality, the conciliar movement poses no significant threat to papal sovereignty. Was Pius being naive or even reckless by misrepresenting history on the scale and to the degree that he did? It is unlikely that he would have characterized his composition of the text in these terms, and for good reason. While we do not know the intended audience of his work, it is unlikely that those who read it would have been equipped to detect many of the distortions of the text. Indeed, even with the tools and sources to do so, it is a difficult and painstaking process. If Pius did take a risk in writing the *Commentaries*, then, it was a conservative one. It was also one that paid off. A testament to his success as an apologist is the fact that his text was consistently read by distinguished nineteenth- and twentieth-century historians as a record of historical fact. It is preserved as such even today in what are deemed classic works of Renaissance history.[2]

Pius II's *Commentaries* were not always embraced so uncritically, however, and it is in this different attitude to the text that we can test for the last time its apologetic effectiveness. In 1584, Archbishop Francesco Bandini Piccolomini, a descendant of Pius II, published the work in a heavily censored form. Bandini's edition has yet to be examined in full, but an initial analysis of Book One suggests that he purged it of features that he deemed damaging to both papal authority and the Piccolomini family.[3] Given the nature and the extent of these changes, it appears that Bandini concluded that the *Commentaries* did not function well as a work of apology – indeed, the text seemed to him to serve the very opposite purpose. In reaching such a conclusion, Bandini was passing judgment not so much on the work itself, however, as he was on its resonances in his own day. In the political and religious climate of the late sixteenth century, those resonances would have been very different and more dangerous than what they had been in the mid- fifteenth century.

If anything, Bandini's version of the *Commentaries* must be read as a strong endorsement of Pius II's success as an apologetic historian. The approach he adopted when censoring it was the same one that Pius followed when he wrote it and when he effectively censored his own earlier history of the Basel council in the *De rebus*. Both editor and author assigned historical memory a fundamentally political function; and both agreed that that memory should be reshaped to meet changing political needs. Whether Pius would have approved of Bandini's version of his *Commentaries* is impossible to know. We can be sure, however, that he would have recognized in it the same kind of history that he himself had championed and that, by all accounts, he practised so well.

Notes

Introduction

1 "Non parcet Pio secundo pontifici maximo lingua dolosa, quae tot Christi vicariis et ipsi Christo non pepercit. Accusatur, reprobatur dum vivit inter nos Pius secundus; extinctus laudabitur … [V]era resurget fama, Piumque inter claros pontifices collocabit" (*Commentarii*, 1: 2–4).

2 "Interea nos de pontificatu suo historiam scribemus" (ibid., 1: 4).

3 For an extended discussion of the crisis of the fifteenth-century papacy, see chapter 1.

4 Paolo Prodi, *Il sovrano pontefice; un corpo e due anime: La monarchia papale nella prima età moderna* (Bologna: Il Mulino, 1982), and esp. 83–126. Prodi refers to the papacy's "reception of the terms of Renaissance political discourse on a religious and ecclesiastical plane" (93) and to how its temporal authority began "to take on the appearance of the modern *signoria*" (98).

5 See, e.g., Ernst Breisach, *Historiography: Ancient, Medieval, and Modern*, 2nd ed. (Chicago: University of Chicago Press, 1994), 153–6; and Donald J. Wilcox, *The Development of Florentine Humanist Historiography* (Cambridge, MA: Harvard University Press, 1969).

6 See, e.g., Gary Ianziti, *Humanistic Historiography under the Sforzas: Politics and Propaganda in Fifteenth-Century Milan* (Oxford: Clarendon, 1988); G. Ianziti, *Writing History in Renaissance Italy: Leonardo Bruni and the Uses of the Past* (Cambridge, MA: Harvard University Press, 2012); and Margaret Meserve, *Empires of Islam in Renaissance Historical Thought* (Cambridge, MA: Harvard University Press, 2008).

7 *Pii Secundi Pontificis Maximi commentarii rerum memorabilium, quae temporibus suis contigerunt, a R.D. Ioanne Gobellino vicario Bonnensi iam diu*

compositi, et a R.P.D. Francisco Bandino Piccolomineo Archiepiscopo Senensi ex vetusto originali recogniti (Rome: Basa, 1584). Giuseppe Cugnoni published the passages omitted from the sixteenth-century edition in *Aeneae Silvii Piccolomini Senensis qui postea fuit Pius II P.M. Opera inedita* (Rome: Salviucci, 1883), 496–549. For the first Italian translation, see Giuseppe Bernetti, ed., *I Commentarii*, 5 vols. (Siena: Cantagalli, 1972–76). The first English edition of the text was prepared by Leona C. Gabel and Florence A. Gragg, *The Commentaries of Pius II*, Smith College Studies in History, vol. 22, nos. 1 and 2; vol. 25, nos. 1–4, 30, 35, 43 (Northampton: Department of History of Smith College, 1937–57). For their abridged translation, see *Memoirs of a Renaissance Pope: The Commentaries of Pius II* (London: Allen and Unwin, 1960).

8 Ludwig von Pastor, *The History of the Popes* (London: Routledge and Kegan Paul, 1949), vol. 3. See also Jacob Burckhardt, *The Civilization of the Renaissance in Italy*, trans. S.G.C. Middlemore (1860; reprint, rev. and ed. by Irene Gordon, New York: New American Library, 1960); Georg Voigt, *Enea Silvio de' Piccolomini, als Papst Pius der Zweite und sein Zeitalter*, 3 vols. (Berlin: G. Reimer, 1856–63); William Boulting, *Aeneas Silvius (Enea Silvio de' Piccolomini – Pius II): Orator, Man of Letters, Statesman, and Pope* (London: Archibald Constable and Company, 1908); Cecilia Ady, *Pius II (Aeneas Silvius Piccolomini) the Humanist Pope* (London: Methuen, 1913); Leona C. Gabel, introduction to *The Commentaries of Pius II*; R.J. Mitchell, *The Laurels and the Tiara: Pope Pius II, 1458–1464* (London: Harvill, 1962); and Gioacchino Paparelli, *Enea Silvio Piccolomini: L'umanesimo sul soglio di Pietro* (Ravenna: Longo, 1978).

9 In Cor. 147, which is considered the final version of the manuscript, the text fills 428 folios.

10 "Multa me mutare oportet, quia non ille finis secutus est, quem putavi, atque idcirco periculosum est currentium rerum historiam texere" (Wolkan 2: 100); the letter is dated 9 Feb. 1450.

11 See Luigi Totaro, *Pio II nei suoi "Commentarii": Un contributo alla lettura della autobiografia di Enea Silvio Piccolomini* (Bologna: Pàtron, 1978). Totaro's is the only monograph that attempts a comprehensive study of the *Commentaries*. Published before he completed his edition of the text, this monograph ultimately focuses more on excerpting and summarizing than on analysing the *Commentaries*.

12 Luigi Totaro, ed., *I Commentarii*, 2 vols. (Milan: Adelphi, 1984; rev. ed., 2009); Adrianus Van Heck, ed., *Pii II Commentarii rerum memorabilium que temporibus suis contigerunt*, 2 vols. (Vatican City: Biblioteca Apostolica Vaticana, 1984); Ibolya Bellus and Iván Boronkai, eds., *Pii Secundi*

pontificis maximi "Commentarii": Textum recensuerunt atque explicationibus, apparatu critico indiceque nominum ornaverunt, 2 vols. (Budapest: Balassi Kiadó, 1993–94); and for Books One through Four, Margaret Meserve and Marcello Simonetta, eds., *Commentaries*, 2 vols. (Cambridge: Cambridge University Press, 2003 and 2007).

13 For a selection of these, please consult the bibliography.

14 See esp. Baldi; Baldi, *Il "cardinale tedesco": Enea Silvio Piccolomini fra impero, papato, Europa (1442–1455)* (Milan: Unicopli, 2012); Arturo Calzona, Francesco Paolo Fiore, Alberto Tenenti, and Cesare Vasoli, eds., *Il sogno di Pio II: Atti del convegno internazionale, Mantova, 13–15 aprile 2000* (Florence: Olschki, 2003); Anna Antoniutti and Marco Gallo, eds., *Enea Silvio Piccolomini: Arte, storia e cultura nell'Europa di Pio II* (Rome: Associazione Culturale Shakespeare 2, 2006); Fabrizio Nevola, ed., *Pio II Piccolomini, il Papa del Rinascimento a Siena: Atti del convegno internazionale di studi, 5–7 maggio 2005* (Siena: Protagon, 2009); Luisa Secchi Tarughi, ed., *Pio II Umanista Europeo: Atti del XVII convegno internazionale, Chianciano-Pienza, 18–21 luglio 2005* (Florence: Cesati, 2007).

15 See esp. Ianziti, *Humanistic Historiography*, and Gabriella Albanese, Daniela Pietragalla, Monia Bulleri, and Marco Tangheroni, "Storiografia come ufficialità alla corte di Alfonso il Magnanimo: I *Rerum gestarum Alfonsi regis libri X* di Bartolomeo Facio," in Gabriella Albanese, ed., *Studi su Bartolomeo Facio* (Pisa: ETS, 2000), 45–95.

16 See, e.g., Giannozzo Manetti, *De vita ac gestis Nicolai Quinti summi pontificis*, edited and translated by Anna Modigliani (Rome: Istituto Storico Italiano per il Medio Evo, 2005); Anthony F. D'Elia, "Stefano Porcari's Conspiracy against Pope Nicholas V in 1453 and Republican Culture in Papal Rome," *Journal of the History of Ideas* 68, no. 2 (2007): 207–31; Anna Modigliani, "Le ragioni del lusso e il rifiuto della povertà evangelica: I papi e la richezza terrena nel Quattrocento," in Thomas Ertl, ed., *Pompa sacra: Lusso e cultura materiale alla corte papale nel basso medioevo (1420–1527)* (Rome: Istituto storico germanico, 2010), 145–65.

17 Elizabeth McCahill, *Reviving the Eternal City: Rome and the Papal Court, 1420–1447* (Cambridge, MA: Harvard University Press, 2013); Luca Boschetto, *Società e cultura a Firenze al tempo del Concilio: Eugenio IV tra curiali, mercanti e umanisti (1434–1443)* (Rome: Edizioni di storia e letteratura, 2012).

18 See esp. Meserve, *Empires of Islam*; Meserve, "From Samarkand to Scythia: Reinventions of Asia in Renaissance Geography and Political Thought," in Zweder von Martels and Arjo Vanderjagt, eds., *Pius II "El Più Expeditivo Pontifice": Selected Studies on Aeneas Silvius Piccolomini (1405–1464)*

(Leiden: Brill, 2003), 13–39; Nancy Bisaha, *Creating East and West: Renaissance Humanists and the Ottoman Turks* (Philadelphia: University of Pennsylvania Press, 2004); Barbara Baldi, "Enea Silvio Piccolomini e il *De Europa*: Umanesimo, religione e politica," *Archivio Storico Italiano* 61 (2003): 619–83; and Emily O'Brien, "Aeneas Sylvius Piccolomini and the Histories of the Council of Basel," in Gerald Christianson, Thomas M. Izbicki, and Christopher Bellitto, eds., *The Church, the Councils, and Reform: A Fifteenth-Century Legacy Revisited* (Washington, DC: Catholic University Press, 2008), 60–81.

19 Adrianus Van Heck, "Amator vetusti ritus et observator diligens: Stile e modelli stilistici di Pio II," in Luisa Rotondi Secchi Tarugi, ed., *Pio II nella cultura del suo tempo: Atti del I convegno internazionale, 1989* (Milan: Guerini, 1991), 119–32; Mario Pozzi, "Struttura epica dei *Commentarii*," in Tarugi, ed., *Pio II nella cultura del suo tempo*, 151–62; Norbert Seeber, *Enea Vergilianus: Vergilisches in den "Kommentaren" des Enea Silvio Piccolomini (Pius II.)* (Innsbruck: Wagner, 1997); Emily O'Brien, "Arms and Letters: The *Commentaries* of Pope Pius II and the Politicization of Papal Imagery," *Renaissance Quarterly* 62 (2009): 1057–97; Claudia Märtl, "Wie schreibt ein Papst Geschichte? Zum Umgang mit Vorlagen in den 'Commentarii' Pius II," in R. Schieffer and J. Wenta, eds., *Die Hofgeschichtsschreibung im mittelalterlichen Europa* (Torun: Wydawn. Uniwersytetu Mikolaja Kopernika, 2006), 233–51.

20 Rossella Bianchi, *Intorno a Pio II: Un mercante e tre poeti* (Messina: Sicania, 1988).

21 Arnold Esch, "Enea Silvio Piccolomini als Papst Pius II.: Herrschaftspraxis und Selbstdarstellung," in Hartmut Boockmann, Bernd Möller, and Karl Stackmann, eds., *Lebenslehren und Weltentwurfe im Übergang vom Mittlelalter zur Neuzeit: Politik, Bildung, Naturkunde, Theologie* (Göttingen: Vandenhoeck and Ruprecht, 1989), 112–40; C. Märtl, "Les *Commentarii* d'Enea Silvio Piccolomini (Pie II, 1405/1458–1464)," in Pierre Monnet and Jean-Claude Schmitt, eds., *Autobiographies souveraines* (Paris: Publications de la Sorbonne, 2012), 221–45.

22 See, e.g., Patrick Gilli, *Au Miroir de l'humanisme: Les répresentations de la France dans la culture savante italienne à la fin du Moyen âge* (Rome: École Française de Rome, 1997); Anna Modigliani, "Pio II e Roma," in Calzona et al., *Il sogno di Pio II*, 77–108; Marco Pellegrini, "Pio II, il Collegio Cardinalizio, e la Dieta di Mantova," in ibid., 15–76; Marcello Simonetta, "Il Duca alla Dieta: Francesco Sforza e Pio II," in ibid., 247–85; M. Simonetta, "Pius II and Francesco Sforza: The History of Two Allies," in Martels and Vanderjagt, *Pius II – "Il Più Expeditivo Pontefice,"* 147–70;

Thomas M. Izbicki, "The Missing Antipope: The Rejection of Felix V and the Council of Basel in the Writings of Aeneas Sylvius Piccolomini and the Piccolomini Library," *Viator* 41, no. 1 (2010): 301–14; Corrado Vivanti, "I *Commentarii* di Pio II," *Studi Storici* 26 (1985): 443–62; Luigi Totaro, "Gli scritti di Enea Silvio Piccolomini sul concilio," in *Conciliarismo, stati nazionali, inizi dell'Umanesimo: Atti del XXV convegno storico internazionale, Todi, 9–12 ottobre 1988* (Spoleto: Centro di Studi sull'Alto Medioevo, 1990), 47–78; and Paola Ferenga, "'I Romani sono periculoso populo ...': Roma nei carteggi diplomatici," in Sergio Gensini, ed., *Roma Capitale (1447–1527)* (San Miniato: Pacini, 1994), 289–315.

23 Sara Honegger Chiari, "L'edizione del 1584 dei *Commentarii* di Pio II e la duplice revisione di Francesco Bandini (Analisi del libro primo)," *Archivio Storico Italiano* 149 (1991): 585–612; Adriano Prosperi, "Varia fortuna di Pio II nel Cinquecento," in Maria Antonietta Terzoli, ed., *Enea Silvio Piccolomini. Uomo di lettere e mediatore di culture: Atti del convegno internazionale di studi Basilea, 21–23 aprile 2005* (Basel: Schwabe: 2006), 357–76.

24 See, e.g., Eugenio Garin, *Ritratti di umanisti* (Milan: Bompiani, 1996), 9–39; John B. Toews, "Dream and Reality in the Imperial Ideology of Pope Pius II," *Medievalia et Humanistica* 16 (1964): 77–93.

25 See esp. Calzona et al., *Il sogno di Pio*; Baldi; Marco Pellegrini, "Unità europea, primato romano: Riflessi della teologia politica di Pio II Piccolomini," in Antoniutti and Gallo, *Enea Silvio Piccolomini: Arte, storia e cultura*, 423–32; Riccardo Fubini, introduction to Giovanni Battista Picotti, *La Dieta di Mantova e la politica de' Veneziani* (Trento: Università degli Studi di Trento, 1996); and Francesco Cardini, "La repubblica di Firenze e la crociata di Pio II," *Rivista di Storia della Chiesa in Italia* 33 (1979): 455–82.

26 Baldi.

27 See, e.g., E. Delaruelle, E.-R. Labande, and Paul Ourliac, *L'Église au temps du Grand Schisme et de la crise conciliare (1379–1449)*, 2 vols. (Paris: Bloud and Gay, 1962–64).

28 See, e.g., Francis Oakley, *The Conciliarist Tradition: Constitutionalism in the Catholic Church, 1300–1870* (Oxford: Oxford University Press, 2003); Aldo Landi, *Concilio e papato nel Rinascimento (1449–1516): Un problema irrisolto* (Turin: Claudiana, 1977).

29 See esp. Meserve, *Empires of Islam*, and "From Samarkand to Scythia."

30 Prodi, *Il sovrano pontefice*, 98.

31 For a fuller discussion of the manuscript tradition of the *Commentaries*, see esp. Giuseppe Bernetti, "Ricerche e problemi nei *Commentarii* di Enea Silvio Piccolomini," *La Rinascita* 7 (1939): 449–75; Giovanni Battista

Picotti, "Di un manoscritto bolognese de' 'Commentarii' di Pio II," in *Ricerche Umanistiche* (Florence: Nuova Italia, 1955), 239–56; G.B. Picotti "Su alcuni frammenti inediti dei 'Commentarii' di Pio II," in *Ricerche Umanistiche*, 257–74; Remo Ceserani, "Rassegna Bibliografica," *Giornale storico della letteratura italiana* 141 (1964): 265–82; Concetta Bianca, "La terza edizione moderna dei *Commentarii* di Pio II," *Roma nel Rinascimento* (1995): 5–16; and Totaro's introduction to his edition of the *Commentarii*, xlviii–li.

32 Totaro, ed., *I Commentarii*.

33 The editions of Meserve and Simonetta and of Bellus and Boronkai are also based on Cors. 147.

34 Cors. 147, 1–427.

35 Ibid., 147, 427–31v.

36 Reg. Lat. 1995, 1–584v. This manuscript is the basis of Van Heck's and Gragg's editions of the text.

37 On the different hands in the work, see Van Heck's introduction to his edition, 6–9.

38 Ceserani, "Rassegna bibliografica," 276–8.

39 Reg. Lat. 1995, 585–95v.

40 The differences that do exist have led scholars to conclude that there is a missing link: the manuscript on which Campano made his corrections and from which Gobellino worked (see Ceserani, "Rassegna bibliografica," 273; cf. Bianca, "La terza edizione," 15–16, who calls for a closer examination of the discrepancies between the two manuscripts.

41 Bianca, "La terza edizione," 10; she notes a precedent in works copied for Nicholas V.

42 See Ceserani, "Rassegna bibliografica," 275. The most complete list of manuscripts is in Giovanni Battista Picotti, "La pubblicazione e i primi effetti della 'Execrabilis' di Pio II," Archivio della R. Società Romana di Storia Patria 37 (1914), 18; and Van Heck, *Pii II Commentarii*, 13. Cf. Bianca ("La terza edizione," 11), who notes the need for a fuller investigation into the text's manuscript tradition.

43 Ianziti, *Humanistic Historiography*, 162–74; G. Ianziti,"A Humanist Historian and His Documents: Giovanni Simonetta, Secretary to the Sforzas," *Renaissance Quarterly* 34 (1981): 491–516; and G. Ianziti, "I *Commentarii*: Appunti per la storia di un genere storiografico quattrocentesco," *Archivio Storico Italiano* 150, no. 4 (1992): 1056–7.

44 See esp. Giulio Zimolo, "Il Campano e il Platina come biografi di Pio II," in Domenico Maffei, ed., *Enea Silvio Piccolomini, Papa Pio II: Atti del convegno per il quinto centenario della morte e altri scritti raccolti da Domenico*

Maffei (Siena: Accademia senese degli intronati, 1968), 401–11; Rossella Bianchi, "Cultura umanistica intorno ai Piccolomini fra Quattro e Cinquecento: Antonio da San Severino ed altri," in Elisabetta Cioni and Daniela Fausti, eds., *Umanesimo a Siena: Letteratura, arti figurative, musica* (Florence: Nuova Italia, 1994), 29–88; R. Bianchi, *L'"Eversana Deiectio" di Jacopo Ammannati Piccolomini* (Rome: Edizione di Storia e Letteratura, 1984); Amedeo De Vincentiis, *Battaglie di memoria: Gruppi, intellettuali, testi e la discontinuità del potere papale alla metà del Quattrocento, con l'edizione del regno di Leodrisio Crivelli* (Rome: Roma nel Rinascimento, 2002); Concetta Bianca, "I poeti e la Dieta di Mantova," in Calzona et al., *Il sogno di Pio II*, 579–90; and Anna Maria Corbo, *Pio II Piccolomini: Un papa umanista (1458–1464)* (Rome: Edilazio, 2002). Despite the wealth of new publications on this topic, the connections between Pius's *Commentaries* and the works of his followers have yet to be fully explored.

45 Honegger Chiari, "L'edizione del 1584," 591; and Emily O'Brien, "The Politics of Painting: Cardinal Francesco Todeschini Piccolomini, Pope Pius II, and the Frescoes of the Piccolomini Library," in Diogo Ramada Curto, Eric R. Dursteler, Julius Kirshner, and Francesca Trivellato, eds., *From Florence to the Mediterranean and Beyond: Essays in Honor of Anthony Molho* (Florence: Olschki, 2009), 427–44.

1. An Institution in Crisis

1 "Christianitas nullum habet caput, cui parere omnes velint. Neque summo sacerdoti, neque Imperatori quae sua sunt dantur. Nulla reverentia, nulla obedientia est. Tanquam ficta nomina, picta capita sint, ita Papam Imperatoremque respicimus" (*Opera Omnia*, 656).

2 This tradition was not fully established until the eleventh century. For an overview of the origins and development of papal absolutism, see esp. Walter Ullmann, *Medieval Papalism: The Political Theories of the Medieval Canonists* (London: Methuen, 1949); and W. Ullmann, *A Short History of the Papacy in the Middle Ages*, 2nd ed. (London: Routledge, 2003); Karl August Fink, *Chiesa e papato nel Medioevo* (Bologna: Mulino, 1981); Agostino Paravicini-Bagliani, *Il trono di Pietro: L'universalità del papato da Alessandro III a Bonifacio VIII* (Rome: Carocci, 1996); and Claudio Azzara, *Il papato nel Medioevo* (Bologna: Mulino, 2006).

3 Scholarship on the conciliar movement is vast. Useful introductions include Giuseppe Alberigo, *Chiesa conciliare: Identità e significato del conciliarismo* (Brescia: Paideia, 1981); Francis Oakley, *The Western Church in the Later Middle Ages* (Ithaca, NY: Cornell University Press, 1979); and Antony Black,

"Popes and Councils," in Christopher Allmand, ed., *The New Cambridge Medieval History*, vol. 7 (Cambridge: Cambridge University Press, 1998), 65–86. On both the history and the historiography of fifteenth-century conciliarism, see esp. Francis Oakley, *The Conciliarist Tradition*; and Nelson H. Minnich, "Councils of the Catholic Reformation: A Historical Survey," in Christianson et al., *The Church, the Councils, and Reform*, 27–59.

4 For an overview of fourteenth-century visions of ecclesiastical reform, see Christopher M. Bellitto, "The Reform Context of the Great Western Schism," in Joëlle Rollo-Koster and Thomas M. Izbicki, eds., *A Companion Guide to the Great Western Schism (1378–1417)* (Leiden: Brill, 2009), 303–31.

5 On the Avignon papacy, see esp. G. Mollat, *The Popes at Avignon* (New York: Harper Torchbooks, 1963); and Bernard Guillemain, *La cour pontificale d'Avignon* (Paris: E. de Boccard, 1962).

6 On the Great Schism, see the survey of scholarship above n3 and also Walter Ullmann, *The Origins of the Great Schism: A Study in Fourteenth-Century Ecclesiastical History* (London: Burns Oates and Washbourne, 1948); Walter Brandmüller, *Papst und Konzil im Großen Schisma (1378–1431): Studien und Quellen* (Paderborn: Schöningh, 1990); and Rollo-Koster and Izbicki, *A Companion Guide to the Great Western Schism.*

7 On the origins of conciliar ideas, see esp. Brian Tierney's ground-breaking *Foundations of the Conciliar Theory: The Contribution of the Medieval Canonists from Gratian to the Great Schism*, rev. ed. (Leiden: Brill, 1998).

8 This line of conciliar thought was developed in the context of the Council of Basel; see esp. Antony Black, *Monarchy and Community: Political Ideas in the Later Conciliar Controversy, 1430–1450* (Cambridge: Cambridge University Press, 1970), 7–52.

9 Oakley, *Conciliarist Tradition*, 31, 67–71. The cardinals had long served as the pope's chief advisers and, since the eleventh century, as his electors. Their influence over church policy and their share of ecclesiastical revenues expanded significantly over the course of the fourteenth century. They had sought to safeguard these powers in electoral capitulations or pacts that were to be binding on the newly elected pope. On the evolution of the cardinals' power, see Giuseppe Alberigo, *Cardinalato e collegialità* (Florence: Vallechi, 1969); Paravicini-Bagliani, *Il trono di Pietro*, 51–68; and Philip H. Stump, *The Reforms of the Council of Constance, 1414–1418* (Leiden: Brill, 1994), 109–18. On the capitulations, see esp. Walter Ullmann, "The Legal Validity of the Papal Electoral Pacts," *Ephemerides Iuris Canonici* 12 (1956): 3–35; and J. Lulvès, "Päpstliche Wahlkapitulationen: Ein Beitrag zur Entwicklungsgeschichte des Kardinalats," *Quellen und Forschungen aus italianischen Archiven und Bibliotheken* 12 (1909): 212–36.

10 The vast recent scholarship on the Council of Constance is documented in Ansgar Frenken, "Die Erforschung des Konstanzer Konzils (1414–1418)," *Annuarium Historiae Conciliorum* 25 (1993): 1–512. See esp. Walter Brandmüller, *Das Konzil von Konstanz, 1414–1418*, 2 vols. (Paderborn: Schöningh, 1991–99).

11 For a discussion of the council's reforms, see esp. Stump, *Reforms of the Council of Constance.*

12 The decrees are printed in Giovanni Domenico Mansi, *Sacrorum conciliorum nova et amplissima collectio*, vol. 27 (Paris: H. Welter, 1901–27), coll. 590–1, col. 1159; and Giuseppe Alberigo, P.P. Joannou, C. Leonardi, P. Prodi, and H. Jedin, eds., *Conciliorum oecumenicorum decreta* (Bologna: Istituto per le scienze religiose, 1973), 409–10 and 438–42. For English translations, see C.M.D. Crowder, *Unity, Heresy and Reform, 1378–1460: The Conciliar Response to the Great Schism* (New York: St Martin's, 1960), 82–3, 128–9. For a survey of the differing scholarly readings of the decree, see esp. Oakley, *Conciliarist Tradition*, 81–99.

13 Between the Constance and Basel assemblies, Martin V had summoned the short-lived Council of Pavia-Siena (1423–24). On this council, see esp. Walter Brandmüller, *Das Konzil von Pavia-Siena, 1423–24*, 2 vols. (Munster: Aschendorff, 1964, 1974). On the Basel assembly, see esp. the wide-ranging and detailed analysis of Joachim Stieber, *Pope Eugenius IV, The Council of Basel and the Secular and Ecclesiastical Authorities in the Empire: The Conflict over Supreme Authority and Power in the Church* (Leiden: Brill, 1978); Johannes Helmrath, *Das Basler Konzil, 1431–1449* (Cologne: Böhlau, 1987); Black, *Monarchy and Community*; and Antony Black, *Council and Commune: The Conciliar Movement and the Fifteenth-Century Heritage* (London: Burns and Oates, 1979).

14 On the Council of Ferrara-Florence, see Joseph Gill, *The Council of Florence* (Cambridge: Cambridge University Press, 1959); Giuseppe Alberigo, ed., *Christian Unity: The Council of Ferrara-Florence, 1438/9–1989* (Leuven: Leuven University Press, 1991); and Paolo Viti, ed., *Firenze e il Concilio del 1439* (Florence: Olschki, 1994). The reunion agreement, promulgated as the decree *Laetantur Coeli* (6 July 1439), was a short-lived victory for Eugenius: it was quickly rejected by the Byzantine church.

15 For several years, Milan, Aragon, Naples, and Poland all acknowledged the legitimacy of both the Basel assembly and its pope, Felix V.

16 See esp. Black, *Monarchy and Community*, 85–130.

17 For a discussion of the Pragmatic Sanction and the *Acceptatio*, see Stieber, *Pope Eugenius IV*, 64–71, 132–54. On the idea of the "third council," see

Stieber, *Pope Eugenius IV*, 218, 231–2, 237–42, 266–72; and Black, *Monarchy and Community*, 113–23.

18 Stieber, *Pope Eugenius IV*, 276–322.

19 On the ideological limits of Eugenius's victory, see Oakley, *Conciliarist Tradition*, 46, 50; and Black, "Popes and Councils," who concludes the papal monarchy ultimately won "by default" (83). For a full discussion of why Europe's princes threw their support to Eugenius, see the next section of this chapter.

20 Of these defences, the most important were Juan de Torquemada's *Summa de ecclesia* (1453); and Pietro del Monte's *Contra impugnantes sedis apostolicae auctoritatis* (1447–51). On Torquemada, see esp. Thomas M. Izbicki, *Protector of the Faith: Cardinal Johannes de Turrecremata and the Defense of the Institutional Church* (Washington, DC: Catholic University Press, 1981); and Black, *Monarchy and Community*, 53–84. On Pietro del Monte, see M. Zanchin, *Il primato del romano pontefice in un'opera inedita di Pietro del Monte del secolo XV* (Vigodarzere [Padua]: Progetto Ed. Mariano, 1997). For a general introduction, see esp. Marco Pellegrini, *Il papato nel Rinascimento* (Bologna: Il Mulino, 2010), 29–36.

21 See esp. Giannozzo Manetti, *De Vita ac Gestis*; Michele Canensi, *Ad Beatissimum Dominum Nostrum Nicolaum V Pontificem Maximum Michael Canensis de Viterbio Humillimus Servulus de Ipsius Laudibus et Divina Electione*, in Massimo Miglio, ed., *Storiografia pontificia del Quattrocento* (Bologna: Patròn, 1975), 205–43; and Jean Jouffroy, *Oratio Episcopi Atrebatensis habita Rome in funeralibus Nicolai pape quinti*, in Laura Onofri, ed., "'Sicut fremitus leonis ita et regis ira'": Temi neoplatonici e culto solare nell'orazione funebre per Niccolò V di Jean Jouffroy," *Humanistica Lovaniensia* 32 (1982): 1–28 (for the oration, see 21–8).

22 On France, see below on the Pragmatic Sanction of Bourges.

23 See Black, "Popes and Councils," 83; Oakley, *Conciliarist Tradition*, 51, 53–4. For a detailed discussion of conciliar support in Germany after 1447, see esp. Stieber, *Pope Eugenius IV*, 331–47.

24 On the Concordat of Vienna, see esp. John B. Toews, "Formative Forces in the Pontificate of Nicholas V, 1447–1455," *Catholic Historical Review* 54 (1968): 261–84; J.B. Toews, "Pope Eugenius IV and the Concordat of Vienna (1448) – An Interpretation," *Church History* 34 (1965), 178–94; Stieber, *Pope Eugenius IV*, 312–22, 333, 342; and *Defensorium*, 12–13.

25 Black, "Popes and Councils," 73; Landi, *Concilio e papato*, 33.

26 On the capitulations as an expression of conciliar doctrine, see esp. Baldi, 82–3; and Pellegrini, "Pio II e la Dieta," 35–6.

27 The electoral capitulations are in Odoricus Raynaldus, *Annales Ecclesiastici* 29 (Lucca: Leonardo Venturini, 1753), 159–61.

28 The college had been more resolved than ever to check papal *plenitudo potestatis* after what it considered an egregious abuse of such authority by Calixtus III. On the 1458 capitulations, see esp. Pellegrini, "Pio II e la Dieta," 35–6; and Baldi, 82–3.

29 Negotiated at the Council of Basel in 1433, the agreement was finally ratified by the Bohemian estates in 1436. See esp. Frederick Heymann, *George of Bohemia: King of Heretics* (Princeton: Princeton University Press, 1965), 6–12. An extensive bibliography is given in Stieber, *Pope Eugenius IV*, 117–18.

30 On the Pragmatic Sanction, see esp. Noël Valois, *Histoire de la Pragmatique Sanction de Bourges sous Charles VII* (Paris: Alphonse Picard et fils, 1906). A useful overview is offered in Stieber, *Pope Eugenius IV*, 64–71.

31 On Pope Nicholas V's efforts to pressure Charles VII to revoke the Pragmatic Sanction, see Landi, *Concilio e papato*, 34–5. For the pope's Bohemian policy, see esp. Heymann, *George of Bohemia*, 33–40, 64–80.

32 See, e.g., the writings of Gregor Heimburg, discussed in chapter 2.

33 It was on the basis of *Haec Sancta* that the Council of Constance had deposed the rival claimants to the papal throne and had elected Martin V. See Oakley, *Conciliarist Tradition*, 42, 97, 113; and Thomas M. Izbicki, "The Papalist Reaction to the Council of Constance: Juan de Torquemada to the Present," *Church History* 55, no. 1 (1986): 8.

34 See Francis Rapp, "Le rétablissement de la papauté: Une victoire imparfaite et coûteuse," in J.-M. Mayeur, Ch. and L. Pietri, A. Vauchez, and M. Venard, eds., *Histoire de Christianisme*, vol. 7 (Paris: Desclée, 1994), 121–35.

35 During Eugenius's battle with the Basel assembly, papal apologists had vociferously refuted the validity of both decrees, and the pope had himself denounced them in the bulls *Moyses Vir* (1439) and *Etsi non dubitemus* (1441). See Izbicki, "Papalist Reaction," 10–11. Martin V's attitude to *Haec Sancta* in particular remains the subject of debate. See Oakley, *Conciliarist Tradition*, 42–3; and Pellegrini, *Il papato*, 11–12.

36 *Defensorium*, 12.

37 See, e.g., Eugenius's brief *Ad ea ex debito* (5 Feb. 1447). For the text of this brief, see Angelo Mercati, *Raccolta di concordati su materie ecclesiastiche e le autorità civili* (Rome: Tipografia Poliglotta Vaticana, 1919), 168–9. For a fuller discussion of this document, see chapter 2.

38 Izbicki, "Papalist Reaction," 12. At the same time, Juan de Torquemada continued to argue the illegitimacy of *Haec Sancta* in *Summa de Ecclesia* (1453) (ibid., 11).

39 Appeals were repeatedly made or were threatened in Germany and France during the reigns of Nicholas V and Calixtus III. On these appeals and papal reaction to them, see esp. J.L. Gazzaniga, "L'appel au concile dans la politique gallicane de la monarchie de Charles VII et Louis XII," *Bulletin de littérature ecclésiastique* 85 (1984): 111–29. See also Landi, *Concilio e papato*, 47–8; and Baldi, *Il "cardinale tedesco,"* 186.
40 Black, "Popes and Councils," 73; see also Stieber, *Pope Eugenius IV*, 331–47.
41 For an analysis of Eugenius's pledge, see chapter 2. See also Stieber, *Pope Eugenius IV*, 299; and Black, "Popes and Councils," 73. On Nicholas V's pledge to call a council, see Gill, *Council of Florence*, 340; and Stieber, *Pope Eugenius IV*, 310, 326, 329.
42 The most prominent of these was Nicholas of Cusa. See esp. Morimichi Watanabe, "Nicholas of Cusa and the Tyrolese Monasteries: Reform and Resistance," in Thomas M. Izbicki and Gerald Christianson, eds., *Concord and Reform: Nicholas of Cusa and Legal and Political Thought in the Fifteenth Century* (Aldershot: Ashgate, 2001), 133–53; and Brian Pavlac, "Reform," in Christopher M. Belitto, Thomas M. Izbicki and Gerald Christianson, eds., *Introducing Nicholas of Cusa: A Guide to a Renaissance Man* (New York: Paulist, 2004), 59–112.
43 Black is still more extensive: "Most informed opinion continued to see a truly general and representative council as the best and indeed, the only means by which the universally accepted need for church reform could be fulfilled" ("Popes and Councils," 73). See also Stieber, *Pope Eugenius IV*, 331–47.
44 *Defensorium*, 14–15.
45 For the reception of Nicholas of Cusa's reform legation in Germany, see esp. Watanabe, "Nicholas of Cusa and the Tyrolese Monasteries," 133–53; and Pavlac, "Reform," 59–112.
46 German princes, including several imperial electors, and prelates gathered at a series of diets held between Aug. 1456 and March 1457 (see esp. Pastor, *History of the Popes*, 2: 413–18; and Baldi, 30–1).
47 On this subject, see esp. John A.F. Thomson, *Popes and Princes: Politics and Polity in the Late Medieval Church, 1417–1517* (London: Allen and Unwin, 1980), esp. 29–53.
48 The princes and Emperor Sigismund in particular were largely responsible for orchestrating and directing the Council of Constance. Their support was also crucial to the subsequent Council of Basel, though because of the different organization of this assembly, princely influence was sharply reduced. On the structure of the Basel council,

see Black, "Popes and Councils," 70. In turn, conciliar efforts to restore self-government to local churches were not always in the best interests of secular powers.

49 The centralizing machinery of the fourteenth-century church had met with sharp resistance from secular princes. In the context of the Great Schism, moreover, secular rulers had succeeded in restricting papal authority in their territories. See Stephen Ozment, *The Age of Reform, 1250–1550* (New Haven: Yale University Press, 1980), 182–90; Oakley, *Conciliarist Tradition*, 30–1, 52; and Oakley, *Western Church*, 71–2.

50 For an overview of these developments, see esp. Thomson, *Popes and Princes*; Denys Hay, *Europe: The Emergence of an Idea* (Edinburgh: Edinburgh University Press, 1957); and Martin Wight, *Systems of States* (Leicester: Leicester University Press, 1977).

51 Through the Statutes of Provisors (1351 and 1390) and *Praemunire* (1353–93), e.g., the king of England controlled provisions to benefices and judicial appeals to Rome. On England, see Thomson, *Popes and Princes*, 151–3. On France and Germany, see above on the Pragmatic Sanction of Bourges and the Concordat of Vienna.

52 Thomson, *Popes and Princes*, 78–113.

53 See Black, *Monarchy and Community*, 124–8; and Stieber, *Eugenius IV*, 304–22, 325–9. For Italy in particular, see Giorgio Chittolini, "Papato, corte di Roma e stati italiani dal tramonto del movimento conciliarista agli inizi del Cinquecento," in Gabriele De Rosa and Giorgio Cracco, eds., *Il Papato e l'Europa* (Catanzaro: Rubbettino, 2001), 191–217.

54 For the example of Naples, see Alan Ryder, *Alfonso the Magnanimous: King of Aragon, Naples, and Sicily, 1396–1458* (Oxford: Clarendon, 1990), 255–6, 260–2, 283.

55 On Sforza's appeal to "il principio giuridico della 'consuetudine,'" in the context of a cardinal appointment, see Riccardo Fubini, "Niccolò V, Francesco Sforza e la lega italica: Un memoriale adespoto di Giovanni Castiglioni, vescovo di Coutances (Milano, 12 settembre 1451)," in Eliana M. Vecchi, ed., *Papato, stati regionali e Lunigiana nell'età di Niccolò V: Atti delle giornate di studio. La Spezia, Sarzana, Pontremoli, Bagnone, 25–28 Maggio 2000* (La Spezia: Accademia lunigianese di scienze Giovanni Capellini, 2004), 180. On the king of France's defence of the Pragmatic Sanction as Gallican liberties, see Stieber, *Pope Eugenius IV*, 66–70.

56 For example, when Calixtus III refused to consent to Alfonso's candidates for a series of bishoprics, the king promptly appealed to a council; and after the pope's threat that "your majesty should know that a pope can depose kings," an undaunted Alfonso stopped the pope's advance with

his own threat: "your holiness should know that should we wish, we shall find a way of deposing a pope" (see Ryder, *Alfonso the Magnanimous*, 420). Also see Alan Ryder, *The Kingdom of Naples under Alfonso the Magnanimous* (Oxford: Oxford University Press, 1976), 39–41.

57 After Nicholas V had overridden Duke Sigismund of Austria's candidate for bishop of Brixen, the angry duke allegedly orchestrated the assassination of the pope's own choice, Nicholas of Cusa, and drove the bishop into hiding. See esp. Watanabe, "Nicholas of Cusa and the Tyrolese Monasteries"; Pardon E. Tillinghast, "Nicholas of Cusa vs. Sigmund of Habsburg: An Attempt at Post-conciliar Church Reform," *Church History* 36 (1967): 371–90; Brian A. Pavlac, "Nicholas Cusanus as Prince-Bishop of Brixen (1450–64): Historians and a Conflict of Church and State," *Historical Reflections/Reflexions historiques* 21 (1995): 131–54; and Pavlac, "Reform," 87–91, 95–7.

58 See Nicholas V's remark on the impotence of spiritual weapons in the face of temporal powers in Riccardo Fubini, *Italia quattrocentesca: Politica e diplomazia nell'età di Lorenzo il Magnifico* (Milan: Francoangeli, 1994), 202. Also see Ozment, *Age of Reform*, 180.

59 There is an extensive and growing literature on the Ottoman Turks and crusading in the fifteenth century. See, e.g., Norman Housley, *Crusading and the Ottoman Threat, 1453–1505* (Oxford: Oxford University Press, 2012); N. Housley, ed., *Crusading in the Fifteenth Century: Message and Impact* (London: Palgrave Macmillan, 2004); Bisaha, *Creating East and West*. On the humanists and the crusades, see James Hankins, "Renaissance Crusades: Humanist Crusade Literature in the Age of Mehmed II," *Dumbarton Oaks Papers* 49 (1995): 111–207; and Meserve, *Empires of Islam*. For an overview of recent scholarship, see Housley, *Crusading and the Ottoman Threat*, 1–6.

60 Fubini, *Italia quattrocentesca*, 171.

61 See Thomson, *Popes and Princes*; 173–4; Pastor, *History of the Popes*, 2: 378, 381; Kenneth M. Setton, *The Papacy and the Levant, 1204–1571*, 2: 190; and Landi, *Concilio e papato*, 48. On Alfonso of Naples's concerted efforts to thwart Calixtus III's crusade, see Ryder, *Alfonso the Magnanimous*, 411–18.

62 Setton, *Papacy and the Levant*, 2: 188–9.

63 Fubini, *Italia quattrocentesca*, 197.

64 Landi, *Concilio e papato*, 41.

65 Pastor, *History of the Popes*, 2: 126–31.

66 Concetta Bianca, "Alla corte di Napoli: Alfonso, libri e umanisti," in Amadeo Quondam, ed., *Il Libro a Corte* (Rome: Bulzoni, 1994), 177–201, esp. 191.

67 Patrick Gilli, *Au Miroir de l'humanisme*, 169–223; and Marjorie Reeves, *The Influence of Prophecy in the Later Middle Ages: A Study of Joachimism* (Oxford: Clarendon, 1969), 323–8.
68 An English translation can be found in Gerald Strauss, ed., *Manifestations of Discontent in Germany on the Eve of the Reformation* (Bloomington: Indiana University Press, 1971), 3–34. See also Reeves, *Influence of Prophecy*, 341; and Thomas A. Brady, *German Histories in the Age of Reformations, 1400–1650* (Cambridge: Cambridge University Press, 2009), 132–4.
69 These ideas were most fully developed first in the early fourteenth-century *Vaticinia de summis pontificibus*, a collection of fifteen prophecies represented in both text and images. See Marjorie Reeves, *Influence of Prophecy*, 304; M. Reeves, "The *Vaticinia de Summis Pontificibus*: A Question of Authority," in Lesley Smith and Benedicta Ward, eds., *Intellectual Life in the Middle Ages: Essays Presented to Margaret Gibson* (London: Hambledon, 1992), 145–56; M. Reeves, "The Medieval Heritage," in Marjorie Reeves, ed., *Prophetic Rome in the High Renaissance Period* (Oxford: Clarendon, 1992), 9–13; and Bernard McGinn, "The Angel Pope and the Papal AntiChrist," *Church History* 47, no. 2 (1978): 155–73. According to McGinn, angel popes were regular figures in fifteenth-century prophetic texts.
70 The figure of the Second Charlemagne first appeared in the late thirteenth century and early fourteenth century (see Reeves, *Influence of Prophecy*, 313–14, 321). It was prophesied that the French king would precede his own imperial coronation by defeating a series of anti-Christs, including a heretical German emperor and an antipope (see Reeves, "Medieval Heritage," 10; and Reeves, *Influence of Prophecy*, 320–4, 416–17).
71 Reeves, *Influence of Prophecy*, 309–11, 332, 424. For other prophecies of the emperor, see ibid., 332–46.
72 There were manuscripts in Italy, France, and Germany in the fifteenth century. Prophecies of the emperor as reformer were circulating in Italy in popular verse in the first part of the fifteenth century. There are approximately fifty-five known fifteenth-century manuscripts of the *Vaticinia de summis pontificibus*. See Reeves, "Medieval Heritage," 13, 16. In the years leading up to Pius II's papacy, Charles VII was presented with a prophetic program that established him as a Second Charlemagne (see Reeves, *Influence of Prophecy*, 342). According to one account, Nicholas V discussed with Frederick III his concerns about the parallels between the pope and the anti-Christ (see Reeves, "Medieval Heritage," 19; and Reeves, *Influence of Prophecy*, 334–5).
73 Fubini, *Italia quattrocentesca*, 189–91, 196–7, 207n78; and Fubini, "Niccolo V, Francesco Sforza," 189.

74 Fubini, "Niccolò V, Francesco Sforza," 192.

75 Colette Beaune, *The Birth of an Ideology: Myths and Symbols of Nation in Late-Medieval France*, trans. Susan Ross Huston (Berkeley: UCLA Press, 1991), 173–93; Jacques Krynen, *L'idéal du prince et pouvoir royal de France à la fin du Moyen âge (1380–1440): Etude de la littérature politique du temps* (Paris: Picard, 1981), 228–39; and J. Krynen, *L'Empire du Roi: Idées et croyances politiques en France XIIIe–XVe siècles* (Paris: Gallimard, 1993), 345–6, 376–82.

76 Vincent Ilardi, "France and Milan: The Uneasy Alliance, 1452–1466," in *Studies in Italian Renaissance Diplomatic History* (London: Variorum Reprints, 1986), 418. Gilli, *Au Miroir de l'humanisme*, 22; Fubini, *Italia quattrocentesca*, 207.

77 On French pretensions to empire, see Riccardo Fubini's introduction to Giovanni Battista Picotti, *La Dieta di Mantova e la politica de' Veneziani*, xv–xviii.

78 For French interests in Italy, see esp. Fubini, "Niccolò V, Francesco Sforza." For a discussion of Italian humanist and diplomatic concerns about French intervention in Italy, see Gilli, *Au Miroir de l'humanisme*, 225–65. The French already controlled the County of Asti, the Duchy of Savoy, and the Marquisates of Saluzzo and Monferrato (see Ilardi, "France and Milan," 418).

79 Ilardi, "France and Milan," 426–7.

80 Anti-Aragonese sentiment came in part from Alfonso's expansionist policies and ambitions; pro-French sentiment was strong in, among other places, Ferrara and Florence (see Ilardi, "France and Milan," 415–47). In the Kingdom of Naples, the prince of Taranto was threatening in August 1458 to appeal to the French for help in his own battle with Alfonso's successor, his illlegitimate son Ferrante (see Baldi, 17–18).

81 Ilardi, "France and Milan," 225; Fubini, "Niccolò V, Francesco Sforza," 184, 207; and Baldi, 17–20.

82 On the background to Aeneas's election, see chapter 3.

83 On the origin and growth of the Patrimony of St Peter during the Middle Ages, see esp. Peter Partner, *The Lands of St Peter: The Papal State in the Middle Ages and the Early Renaissance* (London: Methuen, 1972); P. Partner, *The Papal State under Martin V: The Administration and Government of the Temporal Power in the Early Fifteenth Century* (London: British School at Rome, 1958); and Daniel Waley, *The Papal State in the Thirteenth Century* (London: Macmillan, 1961).

84 Peter Partner, "The 'Budget' of the Roman Church in the Renaissance Period," in E.F. Jacob, ed., *Italian Renaissance Studies* (London: Faber and Faber, 1960), 256–78.

85 On the transformation of the Patrimony of St Peter into a principate, the essential reference remains Prodi, *Il sovrano pontefice*. See also Mario Caravale and Alberto Caracciolo, *Lo stato pontificio da Martino V a Pio IX* (Turin: UTET, 1978), 3–80; Pellegrini, *Il papato*, 69–89; Thomson, *Popes and Princes*.

86 See Caravale and Caracciolo, *Lo stato pontificio*, 4–16.

87 Serena Ferente, *La sfortuna di Jacopo Piccinino: Storia dei bracceschi in Italia, 1423–1465* (Florence: Olschki, 2005).

88 Fubini, *Italia quattrocentesca*, 89–196.

89 Ibid., 187–93.

90 See below on Nicholas V.

91 On Calixtus III, see esp. *Enciclopedia dei Papi*, 2: 658–62; Caracciolo and Caravale, *Lo stato pontificio*, 76–8; and Pellegrini, *Il papato*, 84–9.

92 On Sigismondo Malatesta, see esp. P.J. Jones, *The Malatesta of Rimini and the Papal State: A Political History* (London: Cambridge University Press, 1974); and Giovanni Soranzo, *Pio II e la politica italiana nella lotta contro i Malatesti (1457–1463)* (Padua: Fratelli Drucker, 1911).

93 On Nicholas V and the Italian League, see esp. Fubini, *Italia quattrocentesca*, 185–206; and R. Fubini, "Aux origines de la balance des pouvoirs: Le système politique en Italie au XVe siècle," in Lucien Bély, ed., *L'Europe des traités de Westphalie: Esprit de la diplomatie et diplomatie de l'esprit* (Paris: PUF, 2000), 111–21.

94 Fubini, *Italia quattrocentesca*, 186–204.

95 In recognizing Sforza and Alfonso of Aragon as legitimate rulers of Milan and Naples, respectively, the Italian League effectively dismissed French claims to both states. On Milan's pre-eminence in the League, see esp. Vincent Ilardi, "The Italian League, Francesco Sforza, and Charles VII," *Studies in the Renaissance* 6 (1959): 129–66; Ilardi, "France and Milan," 417–46; and V. Ilardi, "The Banker-Statesman and the Condottiere-Prince (1450–1464): Cosimo de' Medici and Francesco Sforza," in Craig Hugh Smyth and Gian Carlo Garfagnini, eds., *Florence and Milan. Comparisons and Relations: Acts of Two Conferences at Villa I Tatti in 1982-1984* (Florence: La Nuova Italia Editrice, 1989), 217–39. Cosimo de' Medici regarded Sforza as "sole rudder and stabilizer not only of Florence but of Italy as a whole" (see Ilardi, "Banker-Statesman," 231).

96 For a detailed discussion of Alfonso's relationship with Calixtus III, see esp. Ryder, *Alfonso the Magnanimous*, 407–21.

97 Ianziti, *Humanistic Historiography*, 204; Ilardi, "Banker-Statesman," 231; and Helen Shahrokh Ettlinger, "The Image of a Renaissance Prince:

Sigismondo Malatesta and the Arts of Power," doctoral dissertation, University of California at Berkeley (1988), 157, 163–4.

98 Lorenzo Valla, *On the Donation of Constantine*, edited by G.W. Bowersock (Cambridge, MA: Harvard University Press, 2007), 155.

99 Pellegrini, *Il papato*, 69–72, 74–80; D.S. Chambers, *Popes, Cardinals and War: The Military Church in the Renaissance and Early Modern Europe* (London: I.B. Tauris, 2006); and John E. Law, "Giovanni Vitelleschi, 'prelato guerriero,'" in *Renaissance Studies* 12 (1998): 40–66.

100 Valla, *On the Donation*, 141.

101 Ibid., 155–61.

102 See, e.g., the fifteenth-century continuations of the *Liber Pontificalis*, a vast collection of papal histories begun in the sixth century and considered to be the first example of official papal historiography. For unflattering pictures of Martin V and Nicholas V, see esp. Louis Duchesne, ed., *Liber Pontificalis: Texte, Introduction et Commentaire*, (Paris: E. De Boccard, 1886–1892), 2: 546–60. For other criticisms of fifteenth-century popes in their role as temporal princes, see D'Elia, "Stefano Porcari's Conspiracy," 207–31; and Modigliani, "Le ragioni del lusso," 152–65.

103 D'Elia, "Stefano Porcari's Conspiracy," 207–31.

104 See Riccardo Fubini, "Conciliarismo, regalismo, impero nelle discussioni tre e quattrocentesche sulla Donazione di Costantino," in Giorgio Bonamente, Giorgio Cracco and Klaus Rosen, eds., *Costantino il Grande: Tra medioevo ed età moderna* (Bologna: Mulino, 2009), 133–58.

105 On Nicholas of Cusa, see Riccardo Fubini, "Contestazioni quattrocentesche della Donazione di Costantino: Niccolò Cusano, Lorenzo Valla," in Giorgio Bonamente and Franca Fusco, eds., *Costantino il Grande: Dall'antichità all'umanesimo* (Macerata: Università di Studi di Macerata, 1992), 1: 385–431. Essential works on Valla's invective include Domenico Maffei, *La donazione di Costantino nei giuristi medievali* (Milan: Giuffrè, 1964); and Giovanni Antonazzi, *Lorenzo Valla e la polemica sulla donazione di Costantino* (Roma: Storia e Letteratura, 1985).

106 Arguably, it was not the most dangerous either. On the limited effect Valla's argument had on the papacy's claim to temporal authority, see Prodi, *Il sovrano pontefice*, 28–40.

107 Valla, *On the Donation*, 155.

108 Ibid., 159.

109 Ibid., 147.

110 Louis Pascoe, "Gerson and the Donation of Constantine: Growth and Development within the Church," *Viator* 5 (1974): 469–85; for the quotation, see 476.

111 Brady, *German Histories*, 132–4. In the empire far more than in France and England, prelates were princes. See Francis Rapp, *Les origines medievales de l'Allemagne moderne* (Paris: Aubier, 1989), 220.

112 These included John Wycliffe, John Hus, Marsilius of Padua, and Lorenzo Valla. The church condemned the first three as heretics.

113 Apocalyptic prophecy, the *Reformatio Sigismundi*, and the reform programs of Hus and Wycliffe all envisioned a reformed church as a poor church. For a fuller survey of this topic, see Scott Hendrix, "In Quest of the *Vera Ecclesia*: The Crises of Late Medieval Ecclesiology," *Viator* 7 (1976): 347–78; Gerald Strauss, "Ideas of *Reformatio* and *Renovatio* from the Middle Ages to the Reformation," in Thomas Brady, Heiko Oberman, and James Tracy, eds., *Handbook of European History, 1400–1600: Late Middle Ages, Renaissance, Refomation* (Leiden: Brill, 1994), 2: 1–30; and Christopher Bellitto, *Renewing Christianity: A History of Church Reform from Day One to Vatican II* (New York: Paulist, 2001).

114 For the German princes' vision of the ideal church as a poor church, see Baldi, 85.

2. The Conciliar Crisis and Aeneas Silvius Piccolomini

1 "Nondum sedati sunt Basilienses fluctus, sub aqua luctantur ventuli et ad nos usque fistulis latentibus perflant ... Indutias belli, non pacem habemus ... Campus expectatur, ubi rursus de majoritate certetur" (see Wolkan 2: 72). The letter is dated 25 Nov. 1448.

2 "Tu, si pugnandum est, illic decerne, ubi nec venti noceant nec sol adversetur nec loci contra te pugnet iniquitas" (see Wolkan, 2: 72).

3 See, e.g., Ady, *Pius II*, 245; and Totaro, "Gli scritti di Enea Silvio sul concilio," 47–78.

4 See, e.g., Pellegrini, *Il papato*, 38–43; and Landi, *Concilio e papato*, 54–74.

5 "Nec quasi unus ex infimis fui, sed elatus animo, superbus mente, plenus vento inter primiores bella ciebam ... Nec parvum erat inter hostes Romane curie nomen Enee" (see Wolkan, 2: 55). The letter, addressed to the rector of the University of Cologne, is dated 13 Aug. 1447.

6 Aeneas also served as the council's ambassador on several diplomatic missions and, according to his own account, sat on one of the assembly's major deputations (the Deputation of the Faith) and its Commission of Twelve, which, among other things determined the council's membership. For a fuller overview of Aeneas's positions at Basel, see *Reject Aeneas, Accept Pius: Selected Letters of Aeneas Sylvius Piccolomini (Pope Pius II)*, introduced and translated by Thomas M. Izbicki, Philp Krey, and

Gerald Christianson (Washington, DC: Catholic University Press, 2006), 14–26. On the structure and responsibilities of the council's committees, see Black, "Popes and Councils," 70.

7 Aeneas was enlisted to write letters promoting the emperor's plan and served as imperial envoy to the Diet of Nuremberg (Aug. to Oct. 1444) where this plan was discussed; see esp. Wolkan, 1: 156–7, 165–6, 251–62. Also see Baldi, *Il "cardinale tedesco,"* 58, 67–8, 72–3, 103–10.

8 Aeneas expressed interest in selling this post in a letter dated 18 Apr. 1444; see Wolkan 1: 312–14.

9 See, e.g., his two letters to the council president, Louis d'Aleman (Sept. and Oct. 1443), and his letters to Giovanni Peregallo (1 June 1444) and to Juan de Segovia (6 June 1444) in Wolkan, 1: 192–4, 202–4, 331–3, 336–7.

10 See his letters to a friend at Basel (Oct. 1443), Juan de Carvajal (23 Oct. 1443), and to the imperial chancellor, Kaspar Schlick (11 Dec. 1443), in Wolkan, 1: 195–6, 208–11, 240–4. In making his inquiries, Aeneas casts himself explicitly as an ally of the Basel council; see ibid., 1: 163, 332.

11 *In minoribus*, 148–64. For an English translation, see *Reject Aeneas, Accept Pius*, 392–406. Towards the beginning of the bull, Aeneas writes: "plus scripto, quam facto nocuimus" (see *In minoribus*, 150).

12 Piccolomini, Aeneas Silvius, *Libellus dialogorum de generalis concilii auctoritate et gestis Basileensium*, in Adam F. Kollar, ed., *Analecta monumentorum omnis aevi Vindobonensia*, vol. 2 (Vienna: Ioannis T. Trattner, 1762), coll. 691–790. On this work, see esp. Simona Iaria, "Diffusione e recezione del *Libellus dialogorum* di Enea Silvio Piccolomini," *Italia Medioevale e Umanistica* 44 (2003): 65–114. See also Totaro, "Gli scritti di Enea Silvio," 63–7; O'Brien, "Aeneas Sylvius Piccolomini," 60–81.

13 The interlocutors are Nicholas of Cusa, papal envoy to the council; Stefano della Caccia, lawyer and secretary to Felix V; Martin LeFranc, a Franciscan and provost of Lausanne; and Aeneas himself.

14 *De gestis*, 2–255. For discussions of this text, see Totaro, "Gli scritti di Enea Silvio," 51–63; and Totaro, "Enea Silvio e il Concilio di Basilea," in Maria Antonietta Terzoli, ed., *Enea Silvio Piccolomini. Uomo di lettere e mediatore di culture: Atti del convegno internazionale di studi, Basilea, 21–23 aprile 2005* (Basel: Schwabe, 2006), 82–90. For the debate over whether this work is unfinished, see Totaro, "Gli scritti di Enea Silvio" 50–1, 63–4; and the introduction to *De gestis*, xxviii–xxix.

15 Wolkan, 1: 105–10; and *Reject Aeneas*, 125–31. Aeneas addressed the letter to Juan de Segovia, who himself would go on to write a history of the Basel council. On this letter, see esp. Izbicki, "Missing Antipope," 301–14.

16 Aeneas states the thesis of his argument thus: "papam in omni re inferiorem esse concilio" (see Wolkan, 1: 134). This claim to ecclesiastical sovereignty differed from the more restrictive one established by the Council of Constance, which declared supremacy only in matters of schism, heresy, and reform. See Black, *Monarchy and Community*, 7. The letter is in Wolkan, 1: 132–44, and in an English translation in *Reject Aeneas*, 137–49. Aeneas also promotes the idea of conciliar supremacy in the context of his *Pentalogus*, another dialogue he composed in 1443 at the imperial court (see *Pentalogus*, 136).

17 "In multas inciderunt manus, et vulgo leguntur" (see *In minoribus*, 150).

18 "Verendum est ne talia nostris aliquando successoribus objiciantur" (see ibid., 150).

19 The fullest discussions to date are Totaro, "Gli scritti di Enea Silvio," and O'Brien, "Aeneas Sylvius Piccolomini." The following analysis both revises and expands significantly on my previous consideration of these texts.

20 Throughout the *De gestis*, Aeneas draws attention to the oratorical skills of his speakers, pausing at times to note how eloquence plays a crucial role in their argument. Several of the dialogues in the *Libellus*, moreover, are written as a defence of humanistic learning and in particular of oratorical skill. See esp. dialogue three and the beginning of dialogue four in *Libellus*, coll. 706–10.

21 See Gerald Christianson, "Aeneas Sylvius Piccolomini and the Historiography of the Council of Basel," in Walter Brandmüller, Herbert Immenkötter, and Erwin Iserloh, eds., *Ecclesia Militans: Studien zur Konzilien- und Reformationsgeschichte: Remigius Baumer zum 70. Geburtstag gewidmet* (Paderborn: Schöningh, 1988), 157–84, and esp. 168–70; Stieber, *Pope Eugenius IV*, 27–8; Black, *Monarchy and Community*, 93, 100, 103, 104, 118; and Crowder, *Unity, Heresy and Reform*, 172–7.

22 This is one of Black's chief arguments in *Monarchy and Community* (see esp. 85–129). On the influence of this argument in scholarship on conciliar thought, see Oakley, *Conciliarist Tradition*, 74.

23 See, e.g., John of Segovia: "Nam in concilio convenit magna multitudo sapientum," *Decem Advisamenta*, quoted in Black, *Monarchy and Community*, 142. On the council's good judgment and the virtue and wisdom of its members, see ibid., 19, 20, 26, 33, 37, 44, 45. Conciliarists also maintained that, in addition to wisdom and virtue, the council fathers were guided by the Holy Spirit (see ibid., 21–2, 37, 91).

24 "Quod ubi sunt homines liberi pollentes ingenio et virtute, melius est regi communitatem a pluribus sapientibus virtuosis quam ab uno" (*Decem*

Advisamenta, quoted in ibid., 141). Also see ibid., 44; for a similar reference to Aristotle, see ibid., 147.

25 This lack of education is sometimes identified explicitly: Eugenius claimed they were "without degrees" (see Stieber, *Pope Eugenius IV*, 28). And Torquemada stated they did not know Latin (see Christianson, "Aeneas Sylvius," 169). Other times it is implicit in the professions of the men they claim make up the council – notaries, copyists, cooks (see ibid., 169–70).

26 "Illius sententia in rebus omnibus est preferenda, qui omnibus melius discernit et auctoritate potitur majori, que duo in conciliis generalibus invenies, in Romanis pontificibus non invenies, quod mox probo" (see Wolkan 1: 134).

27 Like other conciliarists, Aeneas moves from this premise to an Aristotelian argument: "papa unus est, concilium multorum est peritorum congregatio, unde plus vident oculi quam oculus et omnes omnia sciunt, nemo omnia" (Wolkan, 1: 134; see Aristotle, *Politics*, III, xi, 1287b). For his reference in the *Libellus*, see col. 773; earlier in this text, his pro-papal interlocutor had accused the Basel assembly of being "fatua" (col. 705).

28 From *De gestis*, 164: "nullam rem unquam aut maturius aut diligentius fuisse expeditam"; the translation is Hay and Smith's. For similar remarks, see ibid., 16, 18, 106.

29 "Congregati adinuicem diutius inter se disputarunt, aliis negativam, aliis affirmativam sententiam defendentibus, scientes hanc fuisse veterem et Socraticam rationem contra alterius opinionem disserendi. Nam ita facillime quid verisimillimum esset inveniri posse Socrates arbitrabatur … [T]andem sententia vicit ut haereticus atque relapsus Eugenius diceretur" (see ibid., 16).

30 Ibid., 30–2.

31 Ibid., 20–94.

32 Juan de Segovia, a leading voice in the debates, is "theologiae peritissimus" (see ibid., 22). Louis d'Aleman, council president and the cardinal of Arles, is "praelatus cum multis virtutibus insignis" (see ibid., 18). Also see ibid., 16, 92–4.

33 Ibid., 112, 120, 122–4, 174, 176, 178. For similar references, see ibid., 16, 18, 22–4.

34 For a comparison of the council fathers to martyrs, see ibid., 128. This parallel is echoed in Book Two, when the council fathers remain in plague-ridden Basel to continue preparing for the conclave, thereby risking their lives for the *bonum ecclesiae* (see ibid., 198). On Aeneas's

ongoing and explicit emphasis on Segovia and Aleman's strong leadership, see ibid., 106, 132–4, 140, 198.

35 "Ubinam gentium talis patrum est chorus, ubi tantum scientiae lumen, ubi prudentia, ubi bonitas est, quae horum patrum aequari virtutibus queat?" (see ibid., 238). Also see ibid., 190, 200–2, 204, 208, 210–20, 226–8, 240.

36 From ibid., 188: "sapientissimus."

37 Ibid., 244–6.

38 See esp. ibid., 228, 232, and more generally 221–54.

39 The ambassadors of Castile, Aragon, and Lombardy also opposed the council fathers. Since Eugenius did not recognize the legitimacy of the council during this period, he had no official presence at the assembly. In several places, however, Aeneas explicitly identifies the ambassadors as Eugenius's defenders; see, e.g., ibid., 18, 20, 96, 148. In their efforts to stall the vote, the ambassadors adopted as their central argument the same one papalists had employed against the council – that only bishops should be allowed to vote; see, e.g., ibid., 98, 102.

40 Ibid., 112, 122, 148.

41 See ibid., 26, 28, 96, 104, 108, 112, 138, 152 160, 172, 182–4. Aeneas's characterization here has some merit: both Pontano and Panormitanus had been strong and vocal advocates of conciliarism and of the Council of Basel.

42 "Plus quoque in vulgus de Panormitano relatum est, illum scilicet, postquam domum venit, in cubiculum se recepisse, secumque de rege suo questum, quod eum adversus veritatem pugnare compelleret, et suam famam suamque animam ire perditum; mediasque inter lachrymas obdormivisse" (see ibid., 152); the translation is Hay and Smith's.

43 "Saepiusque illum ego in sua bibliotheca de suo principe vidi conquestum, qui aliorum monita sequeretur" (see ibid., 172); the translation is Hay and Smith's.

44 See Black, *Monarchy and Community*, 85–108.

45 On the authority of the University of Cologne, see Stieber, *Pope Eugenius IV*, 73–5. On its position on the legitimacy of the assembly at Basel, post-1437, see Iaria, "Diffusione," 80–2. For the letter addressing the rector, see *Libellus*, coll. 691–3.

46 Cusanus was in Germany from the end of March 1438 to the beginning of September 1440. During this period, he defended Eugenius in both an official and an unofficial capacity; see Iaria, "Diffusione," 83. On Cusanus's role, see Black, *Monarchy and Community*, 97, 103; and Paul Sigmund, *Nicholas of Cusa and Medieval Political Thought* (Cambridge, MA: Harvard University Press, 1963), 261–5.

47 "Hercules … omnium Eugenianorum." *De gestis*, 14.

48 Cusanus's opponent in the dialogue does, however, draw on some of the arguments Cusanus had himself employed in defence of conciliar power in his *De Concordantia Catholica*; see Iaria, "Diffusione," 100.

49 "Nimium multis jaculis confossus sum; aut nimis multa es eloquentia; aut verum non est, quod defendere institueram. Nihil jam mihi restat, quo meae partis Decretum tueri sciam. Itaque do victam manum, nisi mihi campum in aliud certamen servas" (see *Libellus*, col. 733). "Non potui ostendere transtulisse legitime se Concilium" (ibid., col. 738). Also see coll. 775–6. Stefano della Caccia, it should be noted, did not have the same stature among conciliarists that Cusanus had among papalists – a fact that only seems to underscore the significance of Cusanus's surrender.

50 *Libellus*, col. 733; also see his comparison to Marcus Marcellus in ibid., col. 738.

51 In its range, the debate in the *Libellus* covers similar ground to the mock debate that Eugenius staged in the fall of 1439 in defence of papal sovereignty. In this debate, entitled *Oratio synodalis de primatu*, Juan de Torquemada defends the papalist position and Cesarini plays the part of the conciliarist – until he yields to the papalist position at the end. See Izbicki, *Protector of the Faith*, 13; and Pellegrini, *Il papato*, 28. For the English translation of the debate, see Juan de Torquemada, *A Disputation on the Authority of the Pope and Council*, trans. Thomas M. Izbicki (Oxford: Oxford University Press, 1988). On some level, Aeneas's *Libellus* might be seen as a response to this papal debate.

52 "Oranti mihi, sive divina inspiratio fuit, sive aliud quicquam, Stephane, mutata mens mutatusque animus est, ne iam ille sum, quo paulo ante loquebar tecum. Nescio unde hoc est; jam omnia, quae disputata abs te sunt, vera, et quae contra objeci, falsa videntur" (see *Libellus*, col. 787).

53 The *Dialogue against the Amedeists* is found in its original Latin and in English translation, edited by Thomas M. Izbicki, *Nicholas of Cusa: Writings on Church and Reform* (Cambridge, MA: Harvard University Press, 2008), 272–333.

54 For a discussion of Keck, and of the manuscript tradition and circulation of his treatise, see Iaria, "Diffusione," 97–114. For religious orders' support for Basel, see Stieber, *Pope Eugenius IV*, 92–113.

55 See Iaria, "Diffusione," 74, 94, 99.

56 For a full discussion of this, see Stieber, *Pope Eugenius IV*, 305–11. The alliance had formally begun 28 June 1447; see Pastor, *History of the Popes*, 2: 34–7.

57 See Iaria, "Diffusione," 100–1; *Reject Aeneas*, 44; and Baldi, *Il "cardinale tedesco,"* 143. Aeneas was clearly being attacked for switching sides; see the letter of 13 Aug. 1447, in Wolkan, 2: 55.

58 Wolkan, 2: 54–65; the letter is dated 13 Aug. 1447.

59 "Quis tam hebetis est ingenii, quis tam obtusi intellectus, quis tam ceci judicii, ut propter annatas conturbari universam arbitretur ecclesiam?" (see ibid., 2: 59). "Arelatensis et que cum eo plebs erat Sabaudiam, que necessaria minime dabat, et Avinionem, que non erat in decreto comprehensa, insulsis et fatuis consiliis elegerunt" (see ibid., 2: 60). Writing of his decision to support the Basel fathers' endorsement of Avignon as the location for the council, Aeneas writes: "congratulator ego mihi, quoniam huic dementie non consensi" (see ibid., 2: 60). He also writes "insaniunt rursus mei Basilienses" (see ibid., 2: 62). "Ego vero nolui amplius cum Basiliensibus delirare" (see ibid., 2: 64–5). And he concludes that what they did was "horribilia deliramenta" (see ibid., 2: 57).

60 "Nemo apud Basilienses audiebatur, qui sedis apostolice jura defenderet, qui Romanam curiam commendaret, qui laudi Eugenium daret" (see ibid., 2: 56).

61 See Ady, *Pius II*, 286; *Reject Aeneas*, introduction, 44; Iaria, "Diffusione," 67; Christianson, "Aeneas Sylvius," 166; and Baldi, *Il "cardinale tedesco,"* 143.

62 Aeneas's language reinforces this characterization consistently: "loquebar inepte, scribebam ineptius"; "ignorans peccavi"; "calligantes … oculos"; "stultus factus sum, illorum stultitia stultior coinquinatus sum" (see Wolkan, 2: 55–6). He does not, however, use the language of madness to characterize his own behaviour. He underscores this portrait still further with explicit parallels to the conversion of Saul, and with his claim that Jesus nourished him with "scientia et doctrina" (see ibid., 2: 57). It is worth noting, too, that Aeneas's description of both himself and the Basel fathers as blind directly undermines conciliarist claims (and ones Aeneas had himself pointed out in the *Libellus*) that the council fathers illustrated the Aristotelian principle that many eyes see better than one eye; see Wolkan, 1: 134; and Aristotle, *Politics*, III, xi, 1287b.

63 "Existimabam vera, que dicebantur, et audita non probata scribebam" (see Wolkan, 2: 55). "Adhibui fidem dicentibus" (see ibid., 2: 56).

64 Aeneas even grounds this approach to learning in the same Socratic authority that he had associated with the Basel fathers in his *De gestis*: "Socratis est sententia, ex disputationibus in utramque partem factis veritatem facilius elucescere" (ibid., 2: 56).

65 "Adhibui aures fierique studui magnorum, qui adventabant, virorum sapientia doctior" (see Wolkan, 2: 56–7).

66 "Incipio meditari, examinare que dicebantur" (see ibid., 2: 57); "perscrutatus sum omnia diligenter" (see ibid., 2: 58).

67 "Sed nihil est horum, quod Eugenio vera vox imputet. Hereticum illum propterea dixere Basilienses, quia sinistra de generalium conciliorum auctoritate sentiret. Falsum hoc esse reperi. Fungebar namque apud Eugenium legatione regia, dum Constantiense concilium ac eius decreta recepit" (see ibid., 2: 58).

68 "Intelligo quomodo acta est res, est et judicata" (see ibid., 2: 60).

69 "Aspice nunc ecclesiam universam et vide, quam multi ex orbe toto cum Basiliensibus sentiant. Nec papa nec prelati nec principes nec populi quippiam auscultavit eis … Hoc mihi plenissime constat. Namque cum jussu regio per universam Christianitatem scripsissem atque ad restinguendum schismatis incendium prelatos et principes invitassem, responderunt omnes, unum se habere pontificem Eugenium, ex cuius obedientia nec recessissent unquam nec recedere cogitarent … ex quo fit, ut neque concilium faciant, quia non est concilium, quod non representat ecclesiam" (see ibid., 2: 62).

70 For the full Latin text, see ibid., 2: 164–228; for an English translation, see *Reject Aeneas*, 321–87.

71 Aeneas undercuts the good judgment of the council fathers in the same way he does in his 1447 letter of retraction to Jordan Mallant: they are unlearned, unreasonable, and driven by madness (see Wolkan, 2: 175, 189, 190, 192–4). Also see O'Brien, "Aeneas Sylvius Piccolomini," 73–8.

72 Wolkan, 2: 187–8.

73 Ibid., 2: 190–2.

74 Ibid., 2: 189.

75 "Adversus concilii dignitatem mutire aliquid, crimen haeresis fuit. Una omnium vox concilium Eugenio praeferebat" (*In minoribus*, 155); see also 153–4.

76 The full quotation reads: "Quid ageremus? Audire potuimus, et non discere? Rude nimis ingenium est, quod per singulos dies audita et inculcata non capit … Didicimus ergo quae audivimus" (ibid., 155).

77 Ibid., 153.

78 "Tu, si sapias, idem facies" (ibid., 159).

79 Aeneas echoes this idea with the very final words of the bull, referring to his writings as "juvenilis animi parum pensata iudicia" (see ibid., 164).

80 Seeing a conversation between these two texts makes sense by looking at their recipients as well as their content: both were addressed to the rector of the University of Cologne.

81 From *In minoribus*, 151: "quae supremam apostolicae sedis auctoritatem quovis pacto elidunt aut aliquid astruunt, quod sacrosancta Romana non amplectitur ecclesia."
82 From ibid., 152: "aliis opusculis."
83 From ibid: "seni magis, quam juveni credite; nec privatum hominem pluris facite, quam pontificem. Aeneam rejicite, Pium recipite."
84 Both Stieber and Baldi set the date in May 1445; see Stieber, *Pope Eugenius IV*, 282; Baldi, *Il "cardinale tedesco,"* 103–11.
85 Marco Pellegrini describes Aeneas's "conversion to the Eugenian party" and his subsequent role as "invaluable champion" of the "papal cause" in Germany; see Marco Pellegrini, "Pio II," in *Enciclopedia dei Papi* (Rome: Treccani, 2000), 3: 666. During his service at the imperial court, Aeneas is typically referred to as a "papal diplomat" (*Defensorium*, 11) or "papal agent" (Ady, *Pius II*, 84) and as an "ecclesiastical agent for the papacy" (Boulting, *Aeneas Sylvius*, 182).
86 It is also to assume that the papacy engineered all of these ecclesiastical promotions. On the emperor's role in Aeneas's promotion to bishop of Trieste, see Baldi, *Il "cardinale tedesco,"* 133. Baldi has begun to illuminate some of these tensions more generally.
87 Aeneas was not the only papalist to preserve an important role for councils. On Juan de Torquemada's views on the role of councils, see Izbicki, *Protector of the Faith*, 95–106; and Pellegrini, *Il papato*, 30–1. The major difference between Torquemada and Aeneas was that the former spoke in theoretical terms only.
88 See, e.g., his 1452 oration *Adversus Austriales* in *Orationes*, 1: 182–248. Both this oration and his *Germania* offered strong and extended defences of papal sovereignty in the face of conciliarist challenge.
89 For a discussion of Aeneas's deep understanding of German politics during this period and his primary commitment to the emperor, see Baldi, *Il "cardinale tedesco."*
90 See *Orationes*, 1: 108–20.
91 See Baldi, *Il "cardinale tedesco,"* 122–4.
92 On these and other details of the electors' proposal of March 1446, see Stieber, *Pope Eugenius IV*, 278–80.
93 The final version of the proposal is published in Wilhelm Rossmann, *Betrachtungen über das Zeitalter der Reformation* (Jena: F. Mauke, 1858), 389–93. Eugenius's written instructions to his legates are published in *Annales Ecclesiastici*, edited by Augustin Theiner (Barri-Ducis: Guérin, 1864), 28: 460–1.
94 *Orationes*, 1: 114.

95 Aeneas refers in his oration to the council's responsibilities of reform: "Concilium sane propterea petitur, quia plurima necessario sunt reformanda, nedum in populo, sed etiam in clero" (see *Orationes*, 1: 114). His written proposal refers to its responsibility in negotiating the *Acceptatio*, see Rossman, *Betrachtungen*, 389.

96 Eugenius's legates apparently made such promises at the Diet of Frankfurt in 1446; see Stieber, *Pope Eugenius IV*, 287, 290. Aeneas implies as much in this oration delivered a few months later; see *Orationes*, 1: 114–15.

97 Eugenius does not seem to have issued oral instructions about calling a council. Eugenius instructs his legates that he will confirm the *Acceptatio* "proviso tamen ante omnia, quod in recompensam gravaminum … debita fiat per nationem ipsam ac eius praelatos nobis et ipsi Apostolicae Sedis provisio … super qua cum praelatis et principibus ipsius nationis tractanda, concludenda, recipienda" (see Theiner, *Annales Ecclesiastici*, 28: 461).

98 "Generalia Concilia Constantiense ac Basileense ab ejus initio usque ad translationem per nos factam, absque tamen praejudicio juris, dignitatis, et praeeminentiae sanctae sedis apostolicae" (see ibid.).

99 "Scimus, Pater Beatissime, in ea te Sede sedere, quae cardo et caput Ecclesiae, ut factum est, a Domino, et non ab alio constituta est. Et sicut cardine ostium regitur, sic huius Sanctae Sedis auctoritate omnes Ecclesiae, Domino disponente, reguntur" (see *Orationes*, 1: 115). "Nihil ad nos attinet, Beatissime Pater, de tuarum sententiarum viribus disputare, cum primae sedis solius Dei judicio reserventur" (see ibid., 1: 117).

100 Aeneas phrases this all-important condition as follows: "professio potestatis, auctoritatis, et praeeminentiae generalium Conciliorum catholicam militantem ecclesiam repraesentantium per tuos oratores Franchfordiae facta, tuis literis approbetur" (see ibid., 1: 114). On the papacy's use of the term *praeeminentia*, see Stieber, *Pope Eugenius IV*, 295. Curiously, the written proposal uses "eminence" ("eminenciam") instead of "pre-eminence" – a term that did not imply sovereignty. Stieber does not discuss the discrepancy between the written text of the provisions and Aeneas's oration.

101 The proposal asked that the pope profess "auctoritatem, honorem, potestatem et eminenciam sacrorum generalium Conciliorum prout in decrete Frequens, et aliis Constanciencis Concilii decretis Basilee tempore que inibi indubitatum per orbem Concilium reputabatur" (see Rossmann, *Betrachtungen*, 389).

102 For a slightly different reading of the significance of some of these terms, see Stieber, *Pope Eugenius IV*, 135.

103 For an excerpt of the original letter, dated 23 Jan. 1447, see Pastor, *History of the Popes*, 1: 403.
104 "In tractatu cardinalium maxime difficultates contentionesque fuerunt. Grave videbatur cardinalibus … conciliumque convocare … Circa professionem major difficultas fuit" (Wolkan, 2: 244–5).
105 Eugenius issued his response in three bulls and a brief, dated 5–7 Feb. 1447; for a summary of their contents, see Stieber, *Pope Eugenius IV*, 298–300.
106 For the text of this brief, see Angelo Mercati, *Raccolta di concordati su materie ecclesiastiche*, 168–9. On the choice of the brief, see Stieber, *Pope Eugenius IV*, 310n60.
107 Stieber concludes he had no intention of calling a new council; see ibid., 299.
108 See Mercati, *Raccolta*, 169–70. Eugenius gives preference to this option in his bull.
109 Ibid., 176.
110 For Aeneas's understanding of peace with Eugenius as a means of stabilizing and strengthening the empire, see Baldi, *Il "cardinale tedesco,"* 109–10, 119–20. For her analysis of the *De ortu et auctoritate imperii Romani*, written in the middle of this crisis, see ibid., 125–32.
111 Aeneas envisioned Germany's reunion with the Roman church as crucial both to stability in Germany and to the strength of the empire as a whole (see ibid., 109–10).
112 Stieber, *Pope Eugenius IV*, 301–2.
113 "Eius orationis complurimi postea copiam petivere, non tam propter ornatum quam propter materiam" (Wolkan, 2: 241).
114 For the classification of the *De rebus* as "papalist," see, e.g., Pellegrini, "Pio II," in *Enciclopedia dei Papi*, 3: 665; and O'Brien "Aeneas Silvius Piccolomini," 74–5. For different interpretations, and ones that diverge from the one argued here, see Totaro, "Gli scritti di Enea," 71–4; and Baldi, *Il "cardinale tedesco,"* 167–72.
115 Wolkan, 2: 206–25.
116 On the dating of the two versions of the proposal, see Stieber, *Pope Eugenius IV*, 291, 293.
117 "Interea et Bononiensis Francfordiam venit, qui auditis omnibus, ut res se habuerant, dicebat se libenter abfuisse; namque si presens interfuisset, nunquam super decreto *Frequens* ad ea descendisset" (see Wolkan, 2: 218–19).
118 "Nolebant auctoritatem conciliorum juxta decretum Constantie ullo pacto recipi" (see ibid., 2: 219).

119 See ibid., 2: 210–17.

120 "Nam si de auctoritate dissensisset, turbata omnia verisimiliter fuissent" (see ibid., 2: 219).

121 Aeneas makes a point of noting that the papal legates went so far as to praise Aeneas for handling these matters faithfully: "legati apostolici ad regem reversi gratias agebant, quia oratores sui fideliter et bene res gessissent" (see ibid., 2: 220). See also the remarks that Aeneas reports the bishop of Bologna made as they travelled together to the Diet of Frankfurt: "tu tamen me senior es et sensu melior; te equum est consulere, me sequi, que monueris" (see ibid., 2: 213).

122 After listening to Aeneas's 1447 oration, Eugenius "benignus fuit: gratias regi Romanorum egit, qui fideliter res ageret ecclesiasticas" (see ibid., 2: 220). In contrast to his official report to Frederick in 1447, Aeneas leaves vague the cardinals' objections to the proposal: "multe difficultates in tractatibus fuerunt." Also obscured is how those objections were resolved. Aeneas describes the successful conclusion of the negotiations in the passive voice, leaving it unclear if the envoys had to make further concessions: "tandem omnia sunt obtenta, que petebantur" (see ibid.).

123 At the same time, he seems to reassure Carvajal that this compromise was ultimately a small one to make: the opening of the *De rebus* seems to undermine *Frequens* or any conciliar law as sacrosanct; see ibid., 2: 164 and Baldi, *Il "cardinale tedesco,"* 168.

124 On the particular nature of his objections, see chapter 3.

125 Several of Aeneas's letters attest to Carvajal's role as Aeneas's channel to Eugenius. See the letter he wrote Carvajal shortly after Nicholas's election in Wolkan, 2: 46; also see ibid., 2: 101 (9 Feb. 1450); 3: 22 (21 Aug. 1451); 3: 369 (Dec. 1453); and 3: 311 (16 Oct. 1453).

126 "Tu quoque et pars tua unionem velles, sed modo tuo, maneat papa tuus pontifex et unio sit. Idem etiam pars altera cupit. Nemo pacem, nemo unionem aspernatur, nemo tamen pacem amplectitur, que sibi detrahit. Omnes volunt vincere, nemo se flectit. Dure cervicis homines!" (see ibid., 1: 210).

127 "Ob quam causam rogo, precor, obsecro, ne quid innovari permittatis sine litteris regiis. Nolite principem offendere … Si vultis apud nos, apud Gerse nostramque Viennam bene recipi, curate, ne quid Rome contra nos fiat et omnia, que petimus, fiant" (see ibid., 2: 45–6). The letter is dated 9 Apr. 1447.

128 Aeneas's depiction of Eugenius as embracing the German proposals wholesale seems to offer a useful model of how the pope should act under these circumstances.

129 See Wolkan, 2: 217: "dura, aspera, auditu horrida."
130 See *Orationes*, 1: 139–49.
131 "Diffident Christiani Principes quammulti, concordia quaerenda est. Labascunt Cleri et populi mores, investiganda modestia; oppressam Ecclesiam quamplurimi lacesssunt, recuperanda libertas." He goes on: "Ad quas res licet tua satis sit auctoritas, non tamen executio sine conventu Praelatorum ... facile potest haberi" (ibid., 1: 147).
132 "Ad quas res licet tua satis sit auctoritas" (see ibid., 1: 147). After characterizing this council as one "in quo nullum sit membrum, quod suo capiti non consentiat" and "quod non de clavibus summi Pastoris disputet," Aeneas goes on to quote the biblical passages traditionally used in defence of papal absolutism (see ibid., 1: 147–8).
133 "Non tamen executio sine conventu Praelatorum ... facile potest haberi" (see ibid., 1: 147). "De Concilio namque generali deque loco conventus habendi dicendum est nobis, ex quibus Rebus magna potest utilitas redundare" (see ibid.). "Habes, sanctissime Pater, quae sit petitio Caesaris, nobis et admodum justa videtur, et utilis" (see ibid., 1: 149).
134 "Plurima tamen, sunt, propter quae necessaria videtur conventio Episcoporum generalis" (see ibid., 1: 147). Aeneas expounds at length on why the council should be held in Germany (see ibid., 1: 148–9).
135 See Aeneas's letter to Carvajal, 13 Oct. 1449 in Wolkan, 2: 88–93; and his letter to Bishop Johann von Eichstädt, 23 July 1450 in ibid., 2: 162–3. In the first of these letters, he writes: "Quid faciunt orbis capita? Nunc ex Alamania recessit Johannes legatus, quando erat admodum necessarius!" (see ibid., 2: 91).
136 "Si pacem inter Christifideles componere, si frugalitatem bonosque mores serere, si libertatem Ecclesiasticam vendicare, si partem unionem servare cupis ... generale Concilium ... convocabis" (see *Orationes*, 1: 149).
137 Just how dangerous, however, has yet to be determined. It is not clear whether or not Aeneas actually delivered this oration. He wrote another version in which he leaves out any reference to a council. For this alternate version, see *Orationes*, 1: 152–61. It is more likely, some scholars have reasoned, that Aeneas decided to deliver the latter version, given how "invisam" his request would have been to the pope and at a time when he needed Nicholas's good favour in the context of making requests regarding the imperial coronation. See Mansi's analysis of these orations in ibid., 1: 150–1. And yet, while helping to underscore still further the distance between Aeneas and Nicholas, this argument sidesteps an important question: if Aeneas believed that asking for a council would jeopardize his other requests, why did he even bother

to write an oration that made such request? It was hardly because he had only just learned of Nicholas's aversion to councils; indeed, he had known of it for years. The best explanation is that he wrote that oration because he believed he was going to deliver it. As the above analysis of the *De rebus* argues, Aeneas was not afraid of defending his own very different position on councils and conciliar authority to the papal curia – indeed, he sent the *De rebus* to Nicholas's inner circle at the very time that he was preparing for his embassy to the papal court. It seems more likely, then, that in choosing which version of his 1450 oration to deliver, Aeneas was guided not so much by his broader mission as by how receptive he judged the pontiff would be to such a petition at the time of his audience – a judgment that has not survived the passage of time. There is, however, indirect evidence that suggests that he did, in fact, deliver the version requesting a council. Two years later, in another address he made before Nicholas and Frederick on the occasion of the latter's coronation, Aeneas makes a point of stating explicitly that the emperor had not come to Rome to request a new council; and the reasons he gives unravel the very arguments he had used when advocating for one in 1450: "Alius fortasse vel generale Concilium, vel reformationis decreta petivisset, sed quod maius Concilium potest, quam tuae Sanctitatis, tuique sancti Senatus praesentia: frustra Concilium petit, qui Romani Pontificis mandata non recipit. Ubi tua Sanctitas est, ibi Concilium, ibi Reges, ibi mores, ibi decreta salubrisque reformatio" (see ibid., 1: 181).

138 Ibid., 1: 335–49.

139 Ibid., 1: 350–85.

140 On those discussions and on Aeneas's speech, see the brief remarks by Heymann, *George of Bohemia*, 129–30, 164–5; and Howard Kaminsky, "Pius Aeneas among the Taborites," *Church History* 28, no. 3 (1959): 297–300.

141 See Wolkan, 3: 22–57; the letter is dated 21 Aug. 1451. Aeneas reports his conversation with Podiebrad, written in dialogue form (see ibid., 3: 29–36). The rest of the letter describes Aeneas's encounters and debates with the Taborites.

142 Ibid., 2: 22, 28–9.

143 For a similar interpretation, see Kaminsky, "Pius among the Taborites," 287–8.

144 For a discussion of Carvajal's mission, see Heymann, *George of Bohemia*, 36–40.

145 Aeneas became legate at the same time (18 Apr. 1452) to Moravia, Silesia, Austria, Styria, Carinthia, and Carniola.

146 See the letter, dated 8 Sept. 1452, from Nicholas V to Aeneas in Wolkan 3: 102–3. Nicholas V does not elaborate on Aeneas's recommendations, other than they were different from the pontiff's current approach. That approach included relying on his other legate to Bohemia, Nicholas of Cusa, to meet with Hussite leaders; and dispatching Franciscan John of Capistrano to Bohemia to preach. On the results of their efforts, and esp. on Capistrano's violent attacks on the Compacts, see Heymann, *George of Bohemia*, 69–80. By the spring of 1452, the moderate Hussites had defeated the radical Taborites and subdued the once powerful Catholic factions. On 27 Apr. 1452, Podiebrad was elected governor of Bohemia by Catholics and Hussites alike.

147 See Aeneas's letter to Nicholas V, dated 12 Nov. 1453, in Wolkan 3: 362–4. Aeneas's efforts both to negotiate with Podiebrad and to insert himself into the peace process are documented in several letters from this period. See his letters to Bohemian chancellor, Procop von Rabenstein (15 Nov. and 12 Dec. 1453); his letter to Podiebrad (22 Jan. 1453); and his letter to Carvajal (4 Mar. 1454) in Wolkan, 3: 357–9, 376–8, 425–7 and 453–5, respectively.

148 Aeneas's frustration with Nicholas V comes through explicitly in a letter to Carvajal dated 16 Oct. 1453: "hoc scripsi pridem dignationi vestre, que suo ex more nunquam mihi nisi truncate respondet et ad pauca que vult non ad omnia" (see ibid., 3: 311). On the particular source of his frustration, see the related letters of July and Oct. 1453 in ibid. 3: 216–18, 218–20, 297–9.

149 Aeneas to Procop von Rabenstein (12 Dec. 1454) in ibid., 3: 376–8.

150 See in particular Aeneas's letters to Nicholas V and Carvajal on 7 June, 10 June, 16 Oct., 24 Nov., and esp. 10 Dec. 1453, in ibid., 3: 372–3, 189–202 (esp. 197–8), 302–1, 362–7, and 367–71, respectively. That sense of urgency subsides momentarily once Ladislaus's commitment to Catholicism seems confirmed. See Aeneas's letter to Carvajal, 1 June 1454, in ibid., 3: 490–1. It suggests Aeneas has given up on Nicholas as the one who will reunite Bohemia with the Roman church: "Spero si vixerit hic adolescens et virilem etatem attigerit, regnum Bohemie reformabitur et ad unionem redibit ecclesiasticam, quod jam heretici reformidant."

151 See Kaminsky, "Pius Aeneas," 300–1; and Heymann, *George of Bohemia*, 165–6.

152 See Heymann, *George of Bohemia*, 160–72, and esp. 167–8. Also see Pastor, *History of the Popes*, 1: 442.

153 *Germania*, 143–6.

154 "Neque enim generales conventus sine magna universalis ecclesie novitate, sine gravamine, sine tumultu, sine vexatione coguntur" (see ibid., 146).

155 Aeneas writes: "Incertum est an ea per concilium geri potuerint, in quo tot solent esse sententie quot capita, nec facile multitudinem unius voluntatis invenias: periculum erat ne dum patres in synodo verba trivissent, strictus in viscera nostra Turchorum gladius penetrasset" (see ibid., 149).

156 "Quinimo quamvis liberrima sit Apostolicae sedis autoritas, nullisque debebat pactionum vinculis coerceri, ex mera tamen liberalitate nostra, ex zelo quem gerimus ad pacem, ex charitate qua te tuamque nationem prosequimur, concordatis ipsis locum esse voluimus" (see *Opera Omnia*, 841).

157 See Pastor, *History of the Popes*, 2: 413–18.

158 For a summary, see ibid., 2: 417–422. Many of his letters, dating from July and including those to papal legate Rovarella, are in his *Opera Omnia*; see esp. 793, 794, 828, 809, 810, 811, 813, 821–2, 829.

159 The letters, directed to the chancellor of the archbishop of Mainz, are in *Opera Omnia*, 836–9 (8 Aug. 1457); 801–3 (11 Sept. 1457); 822–4 (20 Sept. 1457). The *Germania* was written between Nov. 1457 and Feb. 1458. See *Germania*, 26.

160 Mair's letter is itself not extant, but its content and approximate date can be deduced from Aeneas's response to the chancellor on 8 Aug. 1457; see *Opera Omnia*, 836–9. Mair's acccusations also emerge clearly in the letter that prefaces the *Germania*. Though presented as the one Mair himself wrote to Aeneas, it appears to be Aeneas's own synopsis of that letter; it is also dated 31 Aug. – several weeks after Aeneas wrote his reply to Mair (see *Germania*, 20). Aeneas controlled reservations to benefices worth about 2,000 ducats in Mainz, Trier, and Cologne (see ibid., 11).

161 Aeneas is already expressing concern in a letter dated 22 July 1457 that he is one of the cardinals being targeted because of his authority over such lucrative benefices (*Opera Omnia*, 831–2).

162 See, e.g., his letter to Frederick III in *Opera Omnia*, 763. It is incorrectly dated 22 Dec. 1457 (the year should be 1456): "Conabor tamen tum spiritus hoc regit artes ita me genere ut omnes intelligant … meque Theutonicum magis quam Italicum Cardinalum esse." Aeneas makes similar pledges to work for the empress; see ibid., 764, 781. In his letter to the archbishop of Cologne dated Feb. 1457, he writes: "Nam ego qui tuus clericus, praesbiter, et episcopus fui, tuus quoque cardinalis esse non desinam. Utatur igitur dignatio tua neque mihil ullo intempore ullo inlabore ignoscat" (see ibid., 775). Also see ibid., 809, 832.

163 See the letter dated 8 Aug. 1457 in ibid., 836–9. Aeneas sums up his time in Germany this way: "nihil nobis antiquius fuit quam nationi vestre nostra obsequia consecrare."

164 For a discussion of curial reform under Pius II, see Pastor, *History of the Popes*, 3: 269–75; and Carol M. Richardson, *Reclaiming Rome: Cardinals in the Fifteenth Century* (Leiden: Brill, 2009), 89–93. For Cusanus's program, see Morimichi Watanabe, "Nicholas of Cusa and the Reform of the Roman Curia," in Thomas M. Izbicki and Gerald Christianson, eds., *Concord and Reform: Nicholas of Cusa and Legal and Political Thought in the Fifteenth Century* (Aldershot: Ashgate, 2001), 169–85; and Morimichi Watanabe and Thomas Izbicki, "Nicholas of Cusa: A General Reform of the Church," in ibid., 187–216. For a modern edition of Cusanus's *Reformatio generalis* (1459) and an English translation, see Nicholas of Cusa, *Nicholas of Cusa: Writings on Church and Reform*, 550–91. For Domenichi's *Tractatus de reformationibus Romanae curiae* (1458), see Cesare Di Pietro, *Domenico de' Domenichi (1416–1478): Vescovo riformatore* (Rome: Pontificia Universitaria Gregoriana, 2010).

165 On *Pastor aeternus*, see Rudolf Haubst, "Reformentwurf Pius des Zweiten," *Römische Quartalschrift* 49 (1954): 188–242 (for the text of the bull, see 205–36). For an overview, selected excerpts, and partial English translation of the bull, see Pastor, *History of the Popes*, 3: 397–404. For a contextualization of the bull and the reasons for its late appearance, see ibid., 3: 275–6, and Baldi, 249.

166 On Pius's nepotism, see Richard B. Hilary, "The Nepotism of Pope Pius II, 1458–1464," *Catholic Historical Review* 64, no. 1 (1978): 33–5; and Wolfgang Reinhard, "Papa Pius: Prolégomènes à une histoire sociale de la papauté," in Robert Descimon, ed., *Papauté, confessions, modernité* (Paris: EHESS, 1998), 43–8. Domenico de' Domenichi's program of reform explicitly condemned nepotism (see Pastor, *History of the Popes*, 3: 272).

167 Baldi, 189. On at least one occasion, Pius did, in fact, use them to fight the French in northern Italy (see Baldi, 193). In March 1462, the king of Hungary explained to Pius that he refused to collect crusade tithes in his territories because he thought they would be put to this very purpose – to fight the French, not the Turks (Baldi, 209).

168 See *Defensorium*, 23; and Pastor, *History of the Popes*, 3: 176.

169 See Pastor, *History of the Popes*, 3: 199; and *Defensorium*, 29.

170 For Pius's relationship with the college of cardinals, see esp. Pellegrini, "Pio II, il Collegio Cardinalizio e la Dieta," 15–76.

171 On the capitulations, see chapter 1.

172 See Pellegrini, "Pio II … e la Dieta," 40.

173 The phrasing of Pius's oath was the first indication of the position he would take towards the capitulations (see Baldi, 84). Pius violated two capitulations almost immediately when he made the unilateral decision

to assemble a congress of princes at Mantua. The capitulations forbade him from moving the curia from Rome and from making decisions of such importance without first consulting the college. For these and other violations, see Pellegrini, "Pio II … e la dieta," 50–2, 75–6.

174 Pius's greatest enemies in the college were d'Estouteville, Coetivy, Trevisan – all of whom had strong French sympathies – Borgia, Barbo, and Tebaldi. His allies, though not in all matters, were Torquemada, Carvajal, Cusa, Colonna, Kiev, and Bessarion. For an overview of the French cardinals in the college and their relationship to the French crown, see Pellegrini, "Pio II … e la Dieta," 31–3.

175 See ibid., 55–73; and Picotti, *La Dieta*, 105–11, 145.

176 Pellegrini, "Pio II … e la Dieta," 64–5.

177 The cardinals had warned that Rome was likely to erupt in conflict with the departure of the curia. They were right. They also predicted accurately that the congress would be poorly attended. See ibid., 48, 52–3, 55–6.

178 Ibid., 52.

179 Ibid., 49, 55, and also 47, where Pellegrini describes the clash as "permanent."

180 "Quotidianum compendiosum ecclesiae concilium" (see Nicholas of Cusa, *Nicholas of Cusa: Writings on Church Reform*, 578–9); the translation is Izbicki's.

181 Ibid., 574–7. On this parallel, also see Watanabe, "Nicholas of Cusa and the Reform," 177.

182 Pellegrini, "Pio II … e la Dieta," 56. For the need for such a defence after his death, see De Vincentiis, *Battaglie di memoria.*

183 For a fuller account of Louis's abrogation of the Pragmatic and of Pius's response, see esp. Baldi, 195–7, 200–15. See also chapter 3.

184 Heymann, *George of Bohemia*, 168–72.

185 Cardinal Juan de Carvajal interpreted the oath to mean that Podiebrad had already renounced the Compacts.

186 See *Defensorium*, 23.

187 See Heymann, *George of Bohemia*, 258–78.

188 For the Latin version of the bull, with an English translation, see *Defensorium*, 224–7; the translation is reprinted in *Reject Aeneas*, 391–2. The fullest study of *Execrabilis* remains Giovanni Battista Picotti, "La pubblicazione," 5–56.

189 The fact that Pius drew up the bull at the end of the Congress of Mantua suggests that he did so in anticipation of imminent resistance to his own tithes (see Pellegrini, *Il papato*, 39). It should be noted,

however, that Pius was well aware that other matters could trigger such appeals: he had heard of two appeals to future councils (Nov. 1458 and Aug. 1459) on very different grounds; on those appeals, see Baldi, 110, 129.

190 It should also be understood as an assault on *Frequens* (see Pellegrini, *Il papato*, 39).

191 See chapter 1. For Pius's own equivocations on *Haec Sancta*, see, e.g., his 1447 Letter of Retraction in which he vaguely says that Eugenius "Constantiense concilium ac ejus decreta recepit" (see Wolkan, 2: 58). Also see his 1452 oration *Adversus Austriales*, in which he explicitly sidesteps the question of whether the councils of Constance and Basel were correct in stating the pope can be judged by a council under certain circumstances: "Nolumus hoc disputationis ingredi pelagus, neque hos grypos aggredi. Anceps quaestio et in utramque partem a prudentibus viris arbitratum est" (see *Orationes*, 1: 231). He takes a similar approach in his *Germania* (1457–58) where he again avoids addressing the question of whether the council is superior to the pope: "Nolumus hanc modo questionem ingredi, que longiorum tractatum requiret et aliud ingenium quam nostrum est" (see *Germania*, 273).

192 See Picotti, "La pubblicazione," 7; *Defensorium*, 4; and Pellegrini, *Il papato*, 40.

193 For an excellent overview of these two instances, and a collection of related documents, see *Defensorium*.

194 On the long-standing clashes between Sigismund and Cusanus, see Watanabe, "Nicholas of Cusa and the Tyrolese Monasteries," 133–54; and Pavlac, "Reform," 59–112.

195 It was issued in the bull *Infructuosos Palmites*, printed in Picotti, "La pubblicazione," 50–6. For Sigismund's excommunication and his first appeal, see M. Freher and B.G. Struve, eds., *Rerum Germanicum Scriptores varii, qui res in Germania ...* (Strasbourg, 1717), 197–202, 203–306.

196 As archbishop of Mainz, Diether's ecclesiastical authority extended over twelve bishoprics. His political power was also extensive: he controlled vast territory as a temporal prince and claimed the titles of elector and archchancellor of Germany. See *Defensorium*, 20.

197 The bull forms part of the sentence of deposition that Pius issued to Diether on 21 Aug. 1461; for the text of this document, see ibid., 228–47.

198 Diether, e.g., reissued his appeal in October 1461 and again in March 1462. Sigismund's chancellor, Gregor Heimburg, renewed the duke's appeal in March 1461 after putting forward his own two months earlier. The University of Vienna, Albert of Austria, and the Count Palatine all

joined Sigismund in his appeal. See ibid., 28; Landi, *Concilio e papato*, 67; Baldi, 208; and Pastor, *History of the Popes*, 3: 206.

199 Adolph even agreed to pay the annates Diether owed Pius (see *Defensorium*, 40–1).

200 See ibid., 41; and Pastor, *History of the Popes*, 3: 210.

201 This is not something that scholarship has emphasized. In recent years, scholars have focused on the limited effect of *Execrabilis*, not its aggravating power.

202 See Pellegrini, "Pio II," in *Enciclopedia dei Papi*, 3: 680. Heimburg also penned Sigismund's first appeals (Aug. and Sept. 1460) and glossed his own bull of excommunication. See Freher and Struve, *Rerum Germanicum*, 210. He also wrote Diether's appeal of Feb. 1461; Sigismund's renewed appeals of Mar. (undated in ibid., 193–7) and May 1461; a lengthy response to Teodore Laelio, a papalist who had penned a vitriolic response to Heimburg's Jan. *Appellatio* (ibid., 231–55); an invective against Sigismund's arch nemesis, Nicholas of Cusa (ibid., 255–65); and Diether's Oct. 1461 manifesto (*Defensorium*, 248–81).

203 On the extent of their circulation, see *Defensorium*, 26; Pastor, *History of the Popes*, 3:192; Creighton, *History of the Papacy*, 414; Landi, *Concilio e papato*, 63; and Baldi, 194.

204 See, e.g., Sigismund's first appeal in Freher and Struve, *Rerum Germanicum*, 206. The most explicit reference to these decrees is in Sigismund's March appeal, penned by Heimburg: "Nos autem edocti sumus, quod magna Synodus Constantiensis decrevit, universale Concilium a Christo immediate potestatem super Papam, in his quae fidei, reformationis et pacis esse dignoscuntur, quae etiam sacra Basiliensis Synodus innovavit, et Eugenius ac Nicolaus Romani Pontifices recognoverunt. Unde Papa Pius auctoritatem usurpavit, ut superiori suo, scilicet universali Concilio, manum clauderet, cui et ipse tenetur obedire? … Hoc enim scitur, quod ex decretis magnae Synodi Constantiensis de decennio in decennium perpetuis temporibus concilia habent celebrari" (see ibid., 194). On both Diether's and Heimburg's use of the decrees, see *Defensorium*, 43.

205 See *Defensorium*, 32, 36–7, 42–3; and Pastor, *History of the Popes*, 3: 203. The tracts dwelled in particular on the fact that Pius had censured Diether and Sigismund without a trial. Pius and papalists argued that manifest crimes did not require one.

206 Heimburg pits legal studies against oratory in particular: "Ipse in numero sit illorum, qui putant haec omnia vi et artificio Rhetorum contineri" (see Freher and Struve, *Rerum Germanicum*, 213). Drawing a sharp

distinction between his rhetoric and Pius's, he says: "at non ita, ut civilis et Canonicae traditionis praecepta contempserim: quae ille ne unquam quidem olfecit, nuda verbositate contentus" (see ibid.).

207 "Veruntamen suam potestatem ... nihil profecto suis machinationibus in hisce partibus ... obstare posse rebatur, nisi fortasse totius Orbis Christiani conventus cieretur, quod universale Concilium nuncupamus" (see ibid., 212). Compare with Diether's Oct. 1462 defence, where he makes a similar argument about papal tyranny in general terms (see *Defensorium*, 265).

208 "Quod si Papa hoc tale tantumque asylum interceperit, hoc roboris vallum fortasse demolitus fuerit seu obruerit, antequam emineat seu oriatur, vos abiecto clypeo exarmati tandem, precii venalitate, hoc est tributorum pensitatione, animas vestras cogemini redimere: pecuniaque vestra sub velamento militaris expeditionis adversus Turcas instaurandae" (see Freher and Struve, *Rerum Germanicum*, 212). The English translation is from Pastor, *History of the Popes*, 3: 189–90.

209 See Pastor, *History of the Popes*, 3: 199; and Landi, *Concilio e papato*, 63. On the possibility that the French would join the German princes in their opposition to the pope, see Pastor, *History of the Popes*, 3: 197; and Baldi, 189.

210 "This broadside is believed to be the oldest printed act of diplomacy and the first piece of printed political propaganda" (see *Defensorium*, 36n127).

211 The text is edited in *Defensorium*, 66–223.

212 De Vincentiis, *Battaglie di memoria*, 29. Laelio did not finish the text until after Pius had died. Laelio had previously written a lengthy response to Heimburg's *Appellatio*, printed in *Defensorium*, 282–347.

3. Papal Sovereignty and the Challenge of Princes

1 "Nemo est enim, cui magis tanti mali fama, quam vestre pietati sit obfutura. Nam scriptores omnes, qui apud Latinos Romanorum pontificum gesta referent, cum ad vestrum tempus fuerit ventum ... Pulchra hec et decora de vestro nomine predicabuntur, sed illud omnia funestabit, cum in fine adjicietur: at huius tempore urbs regia Constantinopolis a Turchis capta direptaque est ... Nihil est, quod vestre clementie possit impingi, sed tamen impinget hoc vestro nomini posteritas rerum ignara, cum vestro tempore Constantinopolim amissam didicerit" (see Wolkan, 3: 200–1).

2 See Fubini's introduction to Picotti, *La Dieta di Mantova*, xiv–xix; and Baldi, 88–92.

3 Baldi, 93; and Pellegrini, "Pio II," in *Enciclopedia dei Papi*, 3: 671.

4 Pellegrini, *Il papato*, 89–92; Caravale and Caracciolo, *Lo Stato Pontificio*, 80–8; Ceserani, "Note sull'attività di scrittore," 105–6.

5 On this text, see in particular Barbara Baldi, "Un Umanista alla corte di Federico III: Il *Pentalogus* di Enea Silvio Piccolomini," *Cahiers d'études italiennes* 13 (2011): 161–71; and Baldi, *Il "cardinale tedesco,"* 35–48. Baldi's readings are somewhat different from the ones I offer here.

6 "Eugenio si faveas, rex, aperteque illum amplectaris, totam Almaniam nationemque tuam videris erroris arguere, que post sententiam Basiliensis concilii neutralem se fecit … Nunc si illi obedientia restitueretur, vitio levitatis argui tua natio posset" (*Pentalogus*, 108).

7 "Vocandi michi videntur, rogandique omnes christianitatis principes, ut aliquem ad locum oratores suos destinare velint simulque divini et humani juris peritos ad tractandum super nonnullis imperii et christianae reipublice negotiis maximeque ad consulendum paci ecclesiastice tollendumque schisma … Illi postquam congregati essent, vellem te quoque regem adesse, proponere rem ecclesie, ostendere pericula, rogare, ut omissis affectionibus in medium consulerent" (ibid., 114).

8 "Ibi ex communi consilio rursus vocarentur partes, que de pontificio certant, ut dature pacem ecclesie aut venirent, aut mitterent mandatum plenum. Quod si facerent, aperta via ad concordiam esset. Si minus, ex communi consilio episcoporum presentium, et oratorum, qui adessent concilium indicere posses, et congregationem eandem concilium nuncupare tumque rogare patres, qui illic forent, ut providere vellent, ne respublica christiana aliquid detrimenti pateretur, offerreque ipsis sententiarum executionem … Post hec procederent illi adversus rebellem partem; et, si utraque pars retrograda esset, utramque deponerent, et saluti ecclesie cum alio consulerent" (ibid., 116).

9 "Quomodo enim absque auctoritate apostolice sedis concilium rex congregabit, cum regula apud canonistas sit notissima, nullam synodum ratam esse, quam sedis predicte non confirmaverit auctoritas?" (ibid., 132).

10 Ibid., 132–40.

11 "Etenim quid aliud est convocare concilium, quam convocare prelatos? Quis prohibere vult, ne certum ad locum rex vocet prelatos?" (ibid., 138).

12 "Hoc non est judicare, sed judices accersire" (ibid., 138–40). For his alternative suggestion, see ibid., 140–2.

13 "Memini enim cum … [de] hac ipsa re sereremus sermonem, quonam pacto pacari ecclesia quiret, dixisse paternitatem vestram: ego si cesaris essem loco, vellem cunctos rogare principes, unum ut in locum mitterent

oratores, qui plenam potestatem haberent res ecclesie componendi. Nam quod principes facerent, et populus sequeretur et clerus" (Wolkan, 1: 249).

14 "Velint nolintque illi [papa et concilium], convenire principes possunt seque in hanc vel illam partem declarare" (see ibid.).

15 "Si etiam reges omnes absque ulteriori prelatorum declaratione unam partem amplecterentur, semper tamen rubigo maneret in hominum mentibus, et alii hoc, alii illud tenerent" (*Pentalogus*, 108–10).

16 "At non erit hoc concilium" (Wolkan, 1: 249).

17 "Non sit, quid ad nos? ... Satis est, si scisma de medio auferatur, vocetur quocunque nomine, qui aufert" (ibid., 1: 249–50).

18 "Nec papa vel concilium reniti posssent, tanquam hoc absque ipsis fieri nequiret, licet enim principibus secularibus conveniret, invito clero, et tamen illic fieri unio posset. Nam ille papa indubitatus esset, cui omnes principes obedirent ... Omnes hanc fidem habemus, quam nostri principes, qui si colerent idola et nos etiam colerumus et non solum papam sed Christum etiam negaremus seculari potestate urgente" (ibid., 1: 255).

19 It is worth emphasizing the distinction between these two proposed solutions – the third council and Aeneas's assembly of princes. In some scholarship, these solutions are incorrectly elided, thereby clouding Aeneas's thought on this important issue.

20 "Sed non habuimus venalem animam nec res synodales nutu principum sed jussu dei agendas putabamus" (see Wolkan, 2: 191).

21 "Regis Francie scriptura erat, relinquendum esse concilii nomen; convenire principes bonum esse et in rebus ecclesie sese aperire atque componere; nihil se dubitare, ubi essent principes, quin illic ecclesia esset, conventumque illorum nullum prohibere posse" (ibid, 2: 205).

22 Aeneas writes: "Nec consentaneum est, ubi plures sunt principes, ibi res bene disponi" (see ibid.). Aeneas's criticisms of the French are threaded throughout the text. He refers, e.g., to the "insania" of the French prelates (ibid., 2: 194).

23 The proposal only asks the pope to recognize the authority of the decrees until a more permanent resolution is reached regarding Germany's grievances with the Roman church; but significantly, it gives a future council the authority to make this settlement (see Rossmann, *Betrachtungen*, 489).

24 See the brief Eugenius issued in response to the proposal in Mercati, *Raccolta*, 162–3; and Pastor, *History of the Popes*, 1: 403. Aeneas's official report to the emperor about this mission records: "Grave videbatur cardinalibus annatas remittere, collationem beneficiorum amittere" (Wolkan, 2: 244).

25 According to Aeneas, Carvajal "horruit," and then he said: "Nihil fiet … etiam hodie in primis terminis sumus" (Wolkan 2: 219).

26 "Sed erat Rome inter cardinales duplex factio: una fidem respiciebat, altera curie pinguedinem. Cum … secundis [erat] Johannes [Carvajal]"; those in this faction "deplumari sedem apostolicam annatarum sublatione et aliis decretis dolebant" (ibid.).

27 "Indignatus autem Eneas, nemo, inquit, vobis satisfacere potest" (see ibid.).

28 *Orationes*, 1: 115–16.

29 For the terms of the Concordat of Vienna (1448), Germany's final settlement with the papacy and a very different agreement than the one envisioned by the imperial compromise, see chapter 1.

30 Aeneas's awareness of and concerns about these developments are reflected in his correspondence (see, e.g., *Opera Omnia*, 810, 813).

31 *Germania*, 225.

32 Ibid., 225.

33 That suffering is defined primarily as destructive conflicts among Germany's princes (see ibid., 216).

34 "Quod si feceritis, haud dubium quin vetus nomen recuperantes multis et magnis gentibus leges dicatis" (ibid., 217).

35 For a discussion of the limited results of the diets, see Baldi, *Il "cardinale tedesco,"* 201–8; Setton, *Papacy and the Levant*, 2: 150–4; and Pastor, *History of the Popes*, 2: 304–5.

36 "Puto tamen etiam si Cicero aut Demostenes hanc causam agerent, dura haec pectora movere non possent" (Piccolomini, *Opera Inedita*, 103). On the limits of crusading oratory in the context of these diets, see Johannes Helmrath, "The German *Reichstage* and the Crusade," in Norman Housley, ed., *Crusading in the Fifteenth Century: Message and Impact* (London: Palgrave Macmillan, 2004), 53–69.

37 On those strained relations and the papacy's limited participation in the imperial diets, see Baldi, *Il "cardinale tedesco,"* 201.

38 "Ecce dominus noster sanctissimus Christanorum summus Pater Nicolaus Papa V … omnibus qui hanc expeditionem sequentur delicta remittit, culpas abluit, veniam praebet, coelum promittit" (*Orationes*, 1: 284); see also ibid., 1: 270–1.

39 "Isti Papam, illi Imperatorem calumniabantur" (Piccolomini, *Opera Inedita*, 105).

40 *Opera Omnia*, 656.

41 "Dum imperare singuli volumus, omnes imperium amittemus. De proprio commodo sumus anxii, rei publice nulla cura est, privatis

affectibus inservimus. Hinc rex Alfonsus et Veneti, inde Florentini et Mediolanenses suas injurias prosequuntur" (see Wolkan, 3: 279).

42 "Exhortati sumus reges et principes ... magna cum instantia commonuimus ut nobiscum concurrentes pro dei honore, pro tutela fidei Catholice ... Sed non responderunt illi desiderio nostro, neque in tanta reipublice necessitate que speravimus auxilia prebuerunt. Sive quod aliis occupati negotiis, res privatas publicis anteponerent" (Piccolomini, *Opera Inedita*, 131).

43 *Dialogus*. On the dating of this work, see Riccardo Fubini, "Enea Silvio Piccolomini nei suoi rapporti con la cultura umanistica del suo tempo," in Nevola, 131–44.

44 For the text, see Wolkan, 3: 492–563. For a recent analysis of this work, see Baldi, *Il "cardinale tedesco,"* 202–7.

45 In his letter to Benvoglienti, he writes: "avaritie omnes studemus, libidinem sequimur, voluptati servimus" (Wolkan, 3: 281). In the *Dialogus*, see esp. 184–91.

46 "Rogasse se ... terre ad tuendam patriam demorari; sed plus apud se caesaris mandata quam subditorum postulata valuisse; preposuisse majora minoribus et privatis publica" (see Wolkan, 3: 531). Aeneas had reported earlier in the text that the duke received the following advice before deciding to attend the diet: "Si quod te dignum est efficere cupis, non tam tuum negocium quam dei curabis. Que te domi premit, tua causa est; quod Ratisponam vocaris, dei res est" (ibid., 3: 510).

47 For Aeneas's opinion of the emperor, see ibid., 3: 495–500.

48 Wolkan, 2: 6–24. For an English translation, see *Three Tracts on Empire: Engelbert of Adamont, Aeneas Silvius Piccolomini and Juan de Torquemada*, edited by Thomas M. Izbicki and Cary J. Nederman (Bristol: Thoemmes, 2000), 95–112. For an analysis of this text, see Cary J. Nederman, "Humanism and Empire: Aeneas Silvius Piccolomini, Cicero, and the Imperial Ideal," *Historical Journal* 36 (1993): 499–515; and Baldi, *Il "cardinale tedesco,"* 125–32.

49 Baldi, 17–20; Pellegrini, "Pio II ... e la Dieta," 31–2; and Fubini, "Niccolo V, Francesco Sforza," 169–94.

50 Some sources suggest that Castiglioni was Aeneas's main rival; see Fubini, "Niccolò V, Francesco Sforza," 183–5.

51 Baldi, 19.

52 On Pius's crusade efforts, see esp. Baldi; Norman Housley, "Pope Pius II and Crusading," *Crusades* (2012): 209–47; and Nancy Bisaha, "Pope Pius II and the Crusade," in Housley, *Crusading in the Fifteenth Century*, 39–52.

53 On the significance of the crusade for Pius II, see Riccardo Fubini's introduction to Picotti, *La Dieta di Mantova*, xiv–xix; Fubini,

"Conclusioni," in Calzona et al., *Il sogno di Pio II*, 592–5; Baldi, 88–92; Pellegrini, "Unità Europea, primato romano," 424; Pellegrini, "Pio II … e la Dieta," 44–5; and Francesco Cardini, "La repubblica di Firenze e la crociata di Pio II," 456. On Pius's crusade plans as an effort to defend himself against conciliarism, see Landi, *Concilio e papato*, 90.

54 Pellegrini, "Pio II … e la dieta," 31–4; and Fubini's introduction to Picotti, *La Dieta di Mantova*, xiv–xix.

55 Pius officially announced his plans to convene a congress of princes on 13 Oct. 1458. On the Congress of Mantua, see Picotti, *La Dieta di Mantova*; Calzona et al., *Il Sogno di Pio*; and Setton, *Papacy and the Levant*, 2: 201–14. For a positive assessment of the congress's outcome for Pius, see Baldi, 147–70.

56 The first official session of the congress took place on 26 Sept. 1459. Ambassadors were still arriving in December. Pius left Mantua on 19 Jan. 1460.

57 For the role Pius envisioned for the emperor, see Fubini's introduction to Picotti, *La Dieta di Mantova*, xiv–xix; and Pellegrini, "Unità Europea, primato romano," 424. For the reasons why the emperor rejected this vision, see Pellegrini, "Pio II … e la dieta," 43–5.

58 On the reasons for their hesitation, see Picotti, *La Dieta di Mantova*, 119–30, 146, 212–13, 241, 275–9.

59 On this document, the *Instrumentum in causa defensionis fidei*, see Picotti, *La Dieta di Mantova*, 197–202. The *Instrumentum* is transcribed in the appendix (437–44).

60 Ibid., 187–9, 197–217, 260–81, 286–95; Pastor, *History of the Popes*, 3: 72, 95; and Baldi, 165–8.

61 Picotti, *La Dieta di Mantova*, 234, 362–72; Setton, *Papacy and the Levant*, 2: 221, 245–7, 264; Baldi, 176–8; and Pellegrini, "Pio II … e la Dieta," 55.

62 For an overview of these diplomatic efforts, see Baldi, 179–82; also see Pastor, *History of the Popes*, 3: 157–62.

63 For more on this war and its implications for Pius, see below in this chapter, "Further Liabilities: Pius as Prince."

64 Baldi, 232–3.

65 Even if he had joined the ships, his intention was to go no further than Albania (Baldi, 251, 259).

66 *Defensorium*, 22–3; and Baldi, 189.

67 Traditionally, this was the role of the emperor, in his capacity of *protector ecclesiae* (Pellegrini, "Pio II … e la Dieta," 43–5).

68 Baldi, 225, 234–5, 244; and Fubini, "Conclusioni," 595.

69 Baldi, 189.

70 For a full explanation of the origin of the league and of its design, see Heymann, *George of Bohemia*, 298–320; J. Kejř, I. Dvořák, L.P. Mozhanskaya, E.V. Tarabrin, K. Jelinek, and E. Šimková, editors and translators, *The Universal Peace Organization of King George of Bohemia: A Fifteenth-Century Plan for World Peace 1462–1464* (Prague: Czechoslovak Academy of Sciences, 1964); and Heymann, "George of Podiebrad's Plan for an International Peace League," in *The Czechoslovak Contribution to World Culture* (The Hague: Mouton, 1964), 224–44.

71 Heymann, "George of Podiebrad's Plan," 214–15.

72 For a useful summary of Pius's achievements as a temporal prince, see Pellegrini, "Pio II," in *Enciclopedia dei Papi*, 3: 676–8.

73 *Pentalogus*, 160–244.

74 Ibid., 150–2.

75 "Nempe, quod pastori quondam, de quo est apud Iustinum: Canis aliquando partu gravida locum a pastore precario petiit, ut sibi educare eodem in lodo catulos liceret. Ad postremum adultis catulis, fulta domestico presidio, proprietatem loci excluso pastore sibi vendicavit" (ibid., 152).

76 "In patrimonio tamen beati Petri, sicuti canones asserunt, libere potest apostolica sedes nedum summi pontificis auctoritatem exercere, sed etiam summi principis exequi potestatem" (Wolkan 2: 12).

77 *Dialogus*, 72–80.

78 *Germania*, 225.

79 Aeneas Silvius Piccolomini, *Enee Silvii Piccolominei: Postea PII PP. II De Europa*, edited by Adrianus Van Heck (Vatican City: Biblioteca Apostolica Vaticana, 2001). On the *De Europa* and its relationship to political developments in fifteenth-century Europe, see Barbara Baldi, "Enea Silvio Piccolomini e il *De Europa*," 619–83. See also Nancy Bisaha's introduction to Aeneas Silvius Piccolomini, *Europe (c. 1400–1458)* (Washington, DC: Catholic University Press, 2013), 3–35.

80 See chapter 1.

81 See, e.g., the characterization of the peace treaty between Eugenius IV and Alfonso in Piccolomini, *De Europa*, 271. For a fuller and more accurate description of this agreement, see Ryder, *Alfonso the Magnanimous*, 255–6.

82 See, e.g., Piccolomini, *De Europa*, 231–2, 255, 271.

83 See, e.g., ibid., 272–3, 275.

84 Baldi, 107–14. For a fuller discussion of the peace agreement, see Gino Franceschini, "Quattordici brevi di Pio secondo a Federico da Montefeltro," in Maffei, *Enea Silvio Piccolomini, Papa Pio II: Atti del Convegno*, 137–41. See also David Abulafia, "The Inception of the Reign of King Ferrante of

Naples: The Events of the Summer 1458 in the Light of Documentation from Milan," in David Abulafia, ed., *The French Descent into Renaissance Italy: Antecedents and Effects* (Brookfield, VT: Ashgate, 1995), 71–89.

85 For a detailed account of these events, see Baldi, 122–7, 173–5.

86 See Baldi, 187–9; and Pellegrini, "Pio II," in *Enciclopedia dei Papi*, 3: 676–7. Pius left Rome in January 1459. In the first few months of 1460, the papal government in Rome had appealed for military support after violence and disorder had made power untenable. Tiburzio was the nephew of Stefano Porcari, who had made an unsuccessful assassination attempt a few years before on Nicholas V. On the Porcari conspiracy, see Anna Modigliani, *Congiurare all'antica: Stefano Porcari, Niccolò V, Roma 1453* (Rome: Roma nel Rinascimento, 2013).

87 Franceschini, "Quattordici Brevi," 148–9.

88 On these events and on Pius's turbulent relationship with the Romans during his papacy, see Farenga, "'I Romani sono periculoso populo,'" 297–310; and Modigliani, "Pio II e Roma," 77–92.

89 On Malatesta's war with Pius II, see Giovanni Soranzo, *Pio II e la politica italiana nella lotta contro i Malatesta*; Franceschini, "Quattordici brevi," 133–76; and Jones, *The Malatesta of Rimini and the Papal State*.

90 Baldi, 132–3, 173–4, 182–3, 189, 193, 212–18.

91 Ibid., 116–17, 184.

92 Ibid., 144. On Pius's complicated relationship with Ferrante, see esp., 107–27.

93 Pius's relationship with Sforza is a central theme in Baldi's analysis of the pope's pontificate (see Baldi, 129–46). Baldi describes Sforza as the "central pivot" of the Italian League (ibid., 242).

94 Ibid., 116–17, 125, 166–7.

95 On these events, see ibid., 220–4, 239–40; and Soranzo, *Pio II e la politica italiana*, 342–4, 379–93, 444–62.

96 Baldi, 189, 214–15, 226.

97 Ibid., 110, 189, 196–206, 251–2.

98 Ibid., 194–5, 213–15, 220–3, 226.

99 So concerned was the pontiff about the threat d'Anguillara posed that he considered launching an attack against him in the winter of 1463–64 (see Bianchi, *L' "Eversana Deiectio,"* 16).

100 Modigliani "Pio II e Roma," 99. For a series of other moves Pius made that suggest his fear of disorder and revolt in the city, see ibid., 98–9. On chronic violence in Rome throughout the fifteenth century, see Farenga, "'I Romani sono periculoso populo,'" 291–3.

101 Farenga, "I Romani sono periculoso populo," 309.

102 The battles of Senigallia (16 Aug.) and Troia (18 Aug.).

103 See above on the vicariate of Cervia. For a more general discussion of the continued disorder in the Papal States during this period, see also Partner, *Lands of St Peter*, 417–18.

104 Baldi, 205–8.

105 For a detailed discussion of this issue, see Albano Sorbelli, *Francesco Sforza a Genova (1458–1466): Saggio sulla politica italiana di Luigi XI* (Bologna: Zanichelli, 1901).

106 Ferenga, "I Romani sono periculoso populo," 290–1.

4. Pius II and the Triumph over Conciliarism

1 "Scio multa de me tuis auribus inculcata esse, neque bona neque digna relatu. Sed neque mentiti sunt qui me tibi detullerunt. Plurima ego dum Basileae fui adversus te dixi, scripsi et feci. Nihil inficior. At non tam tibi nocere quam Dei Ecclesiae prodesse mens mea fuit. Nam cum te persequerer, obsequium me Deo praestare putabam … Nunc apud te sum, et quia ignorans peccavi mihi ut ignoscas oro" (*Commentarii*, 1: 58–60).

2 Wolkan, 2: 72–7; a quotation from this letter appears at the beginning of chapter 2.

3 Wolkan, 2: 72.

4 *Commentarii*, 1: 10–86. As the following analysis will explain, not all of this discussion is devoted to the events of the council itself. In his analysis of this section of the *Commentaries*, Luigi Totaro makes some similar points, but he draws different conclusions from them; see Totaro, *Pio II nei suoi Commentarii*, 36–44.

5 "Hoc tempore Basilienses Eugenium papam suis decretis e summo pontificatu deiecerant" (*Commentarii*, 1: 46).

6 "Forte fortuna tunc affuit Dominicus Capranicus, vir et animi et sensus altioris, quem Martinus papa quintus ad cardinalatus honorem vocaverat, successor Eugenius quartus repudiaverat" (ibid., 1: 10). See also ibid., 1: 12.

7 Ibid., 1: 30–2.

8 See n5 above.

9 *Commentarii*, 1: 10–14.

10 Ibid., 1: 18–30.

11 Ibid., 1: 34.

12 Immediately after reporting the favourable response to his oration, the *Commentaries* observe: "Abhinc Aeneae … Concilium gratius fuit." This is followed by a summary of all the positions he held at the council. Ibid., 1: 34.

13 Ibid., 1: 38–40.
14 Ibid., 1: 42–6.
15 Ibid., 1: 66.
16 "Nam cum placuisset ad reformandam Ecclesiae pacem aliud Concilium convocare in quod et Eugenius et Basilienses consentirent, urbs Constantia provinciae Maguntinae pro loco Concilii nominata est, quae ab Eugenio remotissima erat, Basiliensibus propinqua" (ibid., 1: 54).
17 Ibid., 1: 56–64.
18 Stieber, *Pope Eugenius IV*, 178–280.
19 *Commentarii*, 1: 64–6.
20 "auctoritatem Conciliorum, ut Constantiae declarata fuerat" (ibid., 1: 66).
21 Here is how Aeneas summarizes these demands: "Nisi Eugenius irritam depositionem hanc decerneret, nationis onera tolleret et auctoritatem Conciliorum, ut Constantiae declarata fuerat, profiteretur; se suam depositionem in Basilea factam amplexuros" (ibid.).
22 Stieber, *Pope Eugenius IV*, 278.
23 From *Commentarii*, 1: 74: "auctoritas conciliorum generalium non conculcaretur."
24 From *Commentarii*, 1: 74: "omni … veneno quod Eugenius obhorrebat."
25 *Commentarii*, 1: 156–60.
26 See esp. Wolkan, 2: 54–65, 182–204; and *In minoribus*, 148–59.
27 Parentucelli's criticism, in full, reads: "'Quid vos,' inquit 'Concilium commendatis? Non hic Concilium neque Ecclesiam quisquam esse dixerit mente sanus. Synagogam Sathanae non Synodum agitis, perditi homines et mancipia daemonum!" (*Commentarii*, 1: 32).
28 Ibid., 1: 32.
29 Ibid., 1: 58–60.
30 *Commentarii*, 1: 32, 52.
31 Cf. Totaro, *Pio II nei suoi Commentarii*, 42–3.
32 *Commentarii*, 1: 10–12.
33 Ibid., 1: 14, 32. The *Commentaries* obscure just what the bishop had done to earn papal censure, and for good reason: he was involved in a plot, along with the duke of Milan and Niccolò Piccinino, to kidnap the pope. Aeneas's own relationship to the plot remains obscure.
34 "Qui cum Senas venisset, unanimi propinquorum voce prohibebatur Romam petere, qui Basileae infensus Eugenio fuisset" (ibid., 1: 56).
35 "Plurima ego dum Basileae fui adversus te dixi, scripsi et feci. Nihil inficior. At non tam tibi nocere quam Dei Ecclesiae prodesse mens mea fuit. Nam cum te persequerer, obsequium me Deo praestare putabam" (ibid., 1: 58).

36 "'Scimus te,' inquit, 'in nos graviter deliquisse'" (ibid., 1: 60).

37 In his Letter of Retraction, e.g., Aeneas writes: "Non eribui … insulsis sermonibus Romani pontificis auctoritati detrahere" (Wolkan, 2: 55). The bull *In minoribus* describes the writings that it condemns as those "quae supremam apostolicae sedis auctoritatem quovis pacto elident"; see *In minoribus*, 151. For other explicit references to defending the authority of the council, see esp. his reported conversation with the cardinal of Arles in the *De rebus* in Wolkan, 2: 218. All of these texts do, however, share one thing in common with the *Commentaries*: they all emphasize that Aeneas's errors were not motivated by malice. His intent was always pure: to do what was best for the church.

38 The *Commentaries* simply refer to the "res Ecclesiae" that Aeneas discussed with Eugenius (*Commentarii*, 1: 60).

39 Ibid., 1: 64.

40 Ibid., 1: 62.

41 Pius reports: "detersa est omnis rubigo simulatis, et amicitia quae olim fuit aut eo maior innovata est" (ibid., 1: 64).

42 "In omne officium Thomae praestandum tanto sese magis voluntarium exhibuit" (ibid.).

43 Wolkan, 2: 218–19

44 *Commentarii*, 1: 64.

45 Ibid., 1: 104.

46 "Hominem magis dominandi cupiditate, quam haeresis errore deceptus existimavit" (Ibid., 1: 110).

47 Ibid., 1: 230.

48 "Germani omnes principes Aeneae per epistolas congratulati sunt, tanquam in eo et Germania ipsa decorata fuisset" (Ibid., 1: 180).

49 "Nec decepti; nam Aeneas Germanorum semper et laudator et defensor extitit, non modo in cardinalatu verum etiam in pontificatu maximo" (ibid., 1: 180–2).

50 Ibid., 1: 182–8.

51 Ibid., 1: 200.

52 The *Commentaries* report that "sententias omnis extendit, per quas … auctoritas conciliorum generalium non conculcaretur" (ibid., 1: 74). In so doing, they make Aeneas out to be a more zealous defender of German interests than the *De rebus* does. There, Aeneas writes that in formulating the compromise proposal he included only some of the princes' demands: "recipiam ego scripta, que facta ab altera parte. Ex his recipiam, que sunt honesta et factibilia" (see Wolkan 2: 217). Also, instead of promising to amplify their demands regarding the authority of councils, he says in

the *De rebus* simply that he will preserve those demands: "auctoritatem conciliorum conservabimus" (see ibid.).

53 *Commentarii*, 1: 1120–2.

54 Ibid., 1: 1120.

55 Pius does not give the name of either decree, nor does he mention that they were first promulgated at Constance: "Tunc de Conciliis per decennia celebrandis statuta lex est, et Universali Synodo subiectum esse Romanum praesulem declaratum in his quae vel fidem concernerent vel sublationem scismatis aut Universalis Ecclesiae reformationem" (see ibid., 1: 1120–2). The second of these omissions is particularly significant. The entire point of this section of Book Six is to emphasize that the decrees of Basel were inherently invalid. By defining *Haec Sancta* and *Frequens* as Basilean legislation only, Pius obscures from view the much stronger claim to legitimacy these decrees had as products of the Council of Constance.

56 From ibid., 1: 1120: "[multitudo] semper inimica principi popularem asserit libertatem."

57 He writes that at Basel, "decreta praeter bonum et aequum edita sunt" (ibid.).

58 A very similar set of tensions emerges when Book Seven and Book One are put side by side. The latter, which discusses the election of Amadeus of Savoy as Felix V, also diverges sharply from the neutral presentation in Book One. Like the portrait of the council fathers in Book Six, the one in Book Seven draws heavily on Pius's familiar representation of them as lacking in good judgment. The portrait of Amadeus does this to an extreme, labelling him bluntly and repeatedly as a man of exceptional stupidity: "sapientiam aliena stultitia praebuit" (see ibid., 2: 1398); also see ibid., 1: 1410. In so doing, Pius is directly undercutting the lengthy and flattering portrait of Amadeus in Book Two of the *De gestis*, one that portrayed him first and foremost as a man of incomparable wisdom. See *De gestis*, 188, 244-6.

59 *Commentarii*, 1: 20, 26–8.

60 Ibid., 1: 160–2.

61 "Quomodo relevabit inopem Ecclesiam inops …?" (ibid., 1: 200); also see ibid., 1: 204.

62 In addition to bribing several cardinals to cast their votes for him, the cardinal of Rouen explains that he will be a good leader because he has friends in high places and plenty of money. In this context, the cardinal's pledge that he will abandon simony once on the papal throne should be read as evidence of his hypocrisy (see ibid., 1: 200).

63 Ibid., 1: 202–12.

64 "Atque his dictis Philippum terruit ne Rhotomagensi accederet" (ibid., 1: 206). "Audivit patienter ab amico Vicecancellarius seque admodum cohibuit" (ibid.). See also the description of the cardinal of Pavia's reaction to Pius's words: "obstupuit his auditis" and "victus his" (ibid., 1: 210, 212).
65 The *Commentarii* are quick to note Pius finds simony particularly repugnant: "Nam simoniacam pravitatem praecipuo insectabatur odio" (ibid., 1: 258).
66 Pius reports: "Ac per hunc modum et facilis expeditio rerum erat, et incorrupta" (ibid.).
67 Ibid., 1: 258, 260, 270.
68 Ibid., 1: 258.
69 Ibid., 1: 670.
70 Ibid., 1: 674–8; 2: 1442–4.
71 "Intellexerunt omnes Pio praesuli gratam esse virtutem, atque hinc multi postea probitati ardentius incubuerunt. Nulla res adeo virtutem excitat quam spes ipsa praemii, qui est honor" (ibid., 1: 678–80).
72 "Fuitque in omnium vultibus et gravitas et religio et devotio, neque ullus affuit gestis indecorus; adeoque modeste incessit cardinalium ordo ut supra modum astantis turbae commoverentur ad religionem animi" (ibid., 2: 1530).
73 "At Pius etiam in paupere virtutem censuit honorandam, haud ignarus primos Ecclesiae principes, pro mundi consuetudine ignobiles pauperesque fuisse. Quaesivit etiam in adbitis monachorum excellentem animum nec inopiam auri in eo contempsit, quem bonarum artium copia illustrasset" (ibid., 1: 678).
74 Ibid., 1: 356–8, 996–8.
75 "Si liberales fuistis, nunc opes in rebus honestis profundite et maxime in alendos pauperes" (ibid., 1: 682).
76 Speaking to the college on the eve of his first new appointments, he observes: "Convivia opulentiora quam deceat instruitis; vestimentis utimini nimium preciosis; auro et argento abundatis; equos et famulos plures quam satis est alitis" (ibid., 1: 670).
77 See, e.g., ibid., 1: 818; 2: 1584, 1624, 1948.
78 Ibid., 2: 2442–4.
79 Ibid., 1: 1120–2. Pius characterizes these reforms as "full of poison" ("plena … veneno").
80 Ibid., 1: 162–4, 178–80. Included in these appointments were several cardinals whom Pius singles out for attack elsewhere in the *Commentaries*: Rodrigo Borgia, cardinal of San Niccolò; Jacopo Tebaldi, cardinal of

Santa Anastasia; Jacopo da Castiglione, cardinal of Pavia; and James of Portugal, cardinal of San Eustachio.

81 "Nec Callistus infamia caruit, qui carnis affectum Ecclesiae praetulit utilitati" (ibid., 1: 164).

82 *Commentarii*, 1: 196, 222. He had, in fact, qualified his support of them.

83 "Absit a nobis iuramenti violatio. Nihil est quod tam formidemus" (ibid., 2: 1434).

84 "Capitula quaedam" is used both times the capitulations are mentioned by name (see ibid., 1: 196, 222).

85 Ibid.

86 "Et iuratis quibusdam capitulis nudiustertius in Collegio editis, in altari positus, rursus a cardinalibus adoratus est pedes eius et manus et ora exosculantibus" (ibid., 1: 222). On Eugenius IV and the role of papal ceremony, see McCahill, *Reviving the Eternal City*, 137–67.

87 For a brief analysis of this passage in the *Commentaries*, see Sigmund, *Nicholas of Cusa and Medieval Political Thought*, 299–301.

88 "Si aliquando in consistorio de reformatione facio verba, irrideor" (*Commentarii*, 2: 1432).

89 "Nec tibi nec cardinalibus Ecclesiae cura est" (ibid., 1: 1432).

90 "Cardinalis est ea consulere quae putet reipublicae convenire; si auditur consilium, gratias agere Deo quod recte consulit; si reiicitur, suam potius quam principis ignorantiam accusare … Nobis, non tibi, commissa est Petri navicula. Tibi necesse est recte consulere; at nos sequi consilium tuum, nisi optimum videatur, nulla necessitas urget … Cardinalem te scito esse, non papam" (ibid., 2: 1436–8).

91 "Flebat, loquente Pontifice, Nicolaus et ab imo pectore aegra trahebat suspiria. Post finem tacitus assurgens, moerore ac rubore plenus, per medios cardinales qui erant in anteriori cubiculo nihil locutus et flenti similis in domum suam se recepit. Deinceps mitiorem imbuit animum multumque stulti rigoris amisit; nec inutilem prorsus Pontificis correctionem ostendit" (ibid., 2: 1438–40).

92 *Commentarii*, 1: 260–8.

93 "Clarum te Sedes Apostolica facit, non tu illi decus affers" (ibid., 1: 264); and "Deo tantum et sacris litteris subiecta est auctoritas nostra" (ibid., 1: 268). The sun-moon analogy adapts the one developed first by Pope Innocent III to describe the papacy's relationship to secular authorities. For similar comments expressed to James of Portugal, see also ibid., 1: 264.

94 The full quotation is as follows: "Cardinalis plenus irarum domum concessit, et paulo post, repetens verba Pontificis, ad se reversus amare

flevit. Nec multos moratus dies, Praesulem adiens, errati veniam petit" (ibid., 1: 264). See also Barbo's reaction to Pius's words in ibid., 1: 268.

95 For an account of his successful battle with the cardinals for his first round of appointments, see ibid., 1: 666–78. For the battle over his second distribution of red hats, see ibid, 2: 1418–44.

96 "Nec deinceps dubitandum sibi esset quin pro sua voluntate Senatum duceret" (ibid., 2: 1444).

97 Ibid., 1: 672–6.

98 Pellegrini, "Pio II … e la dieta," 35.

99 See *Commentarii*, 1: 342, 430.

100 "Statura parvis, sapientia minor" (ibid., 1: 428). On Tebaldo, see ibid., 1: 180, 430; and 2: 1430. On Trevisan, see esp. ibid., 1: 426–30, 672; and 2: 1526, 1574, where he criticizes his leadership of the crusade under Calixtus III.

101 Ibid., 1: 238–40, 340–4.

102 For a similar analysis, see Pellegrini, "Pio II … e la dieta," 49–50, 54.

103 Ibid., 1: 164, 178, 182–8.

104 Ibid., 1: 262; and 2: 2330–6.

105 Ibid., 1: 164, 178, 186–8, 262, 462, 606, 672, 914–16, 958, 970–2; and 2: 2042–8, 2470–82.

106 Ibid., 1: 194–226.

107 Ibid., 1: 202–10.

108 Ibid., 1: 200, 204, 220.

109 Ibid., 1: 202.

110 Ibid., 1: 214.

111 Ibid., 1: 218. The *Commentaries* even condemn the decision-making process of the cardinal who casts this deciding vote. According to Pius's account, he was driven by pure self-interest – the thought that he would become famous as the one who chose a pope. See ibid.

112 In a single speech, Pius labels Cardinal Borgia twice "stulte iuvenis" and also "inexperte iuvenis" when he learns of his plans to vote for Rouen as pope (see ibid., 1: 206). He says something similar to the cardinal of Pavia: "Adeone rudes es, ut non intelligas hoc pacto perpetuum imponi iugum nationi tuae" (see ibid., 1: 210). He underscores the ignorance of the cardinal who assumes he is equal in importance to the pope: "Desipis. Clarum et Sedes Apostolica facit, non tu illi decus affers" (see ibid., 1: 264). Those who gave him advice about the Congress of Mantua he describes as drawing on "stultam prudentiam" (see ibid., 1: 342). Pius is particularly critical of the intellectual faculties of the cardinal of Sant'Anastasia, Jacopo Tebaldi, who undermined his crusade

plans, and also Cardinal Cusanus. Of Tebaldi, he writes: "statura parva, sapientia minor, nulla rerum experientia praeditus, nec doctrina nec moribus excellens" (see ibid., 1: 428). He also notes that he abandons his attempts to convince Tebaldi that more cardinals should be added to the college, observing "est incapax stultitia rationis," and that the cardinal "prae ceteris … fuerat … minus prudens" (see ibid., 2: 1430, 1440). Pius condemns Cusanus's reasoning in the same circumstances. He mocks him for his advice about the congress: "Sapis, qui tuae nationi cum nostra infamia demere ignominiam studes" (see ibid., 1: 344). He is still more blunt in his criticisms when Cusanus objects to his appointment of new cardinals: Pius says to him directly "nec boni nec prudentis viri officium imples," and "putavimus hactenus sapientem. Esse hodie tui dissimilis visus es, et animo inconstanti ac multivolo" (see ibid., 2: 1436–8). In contrast, he emphasizes himself and those supporting him as wise and prudent (see ibid., 2: 1444, 2454).

113 Upon hearing that Capranica supports Rouen for pope, Pius exclaims "ubi hominis mens?" (ibid., 1: 210). He labels Tebaldi "quasi alienum a mente," while he says to Cusanus "delirare et insanire prorsus, qui propterea fugiendam Curiam arbitraris" (see ibid., 2: 1430, 1436). For a similar criticism of Cusanus, see ibid., 2: 2496–8. Jean Jouffroy, cardinal of Arras, is repeatedly described as insane: "ad insaniam usque proruperat" (see ibid., 2: 2456). Also see ibid., 2: 2458, 2478.

114 The cardinal of San Eustachio, e.g., is so angry with Pius that he cannot find words to articulate his objections (see ibid., 1: 262). Cusanus is described as being driven by "furor" (see ibid., 2: 1438). For references to the cardinals acting out of self-interest, see ibid., 1: 154, 178, 958; and 2: 2454, 2456. For their arrogance, see ibid., 1: 186, 262–4, 462; and 2: 1436, 2456.

115 Of Pius's many portraits of the council fathers, the one the cardinals bear the closest resemblance to is the one that appears alongside them in Book Six, see ibid., 1: 1120–6. In the *Commentaries*, the council and cardinals alike are as lacking in virtue as they are in wisdom.

116 "Ita enim vivitis, ut non ad Rem Publicam gubernandam electi, sed ad voluptates perfruendas vocati videamini" (ibid., 2: 670).

117 "Nos eos cardinales quaerimus, qui nobis et Ecclesiae consulant" (ibid., 1: 674).

118 Ibid., 1: 676–8, 1442–4.

119 Later, they make the less probable assertion that Pius had been entirely oblivious to his evil ways before he appointed him cardinal; see ibid., 2: 2470.

120 Ibid., 2: 2470–82; the anecdotes appear on 2474.
121 He refers to Arras's "gallicas vanitates" and "artes Gallicas" (ibid., 2: 1464, 2472).
122 Ibid., 2: 2470–2, 2478–82. Pius's many efforts to reform him are described as ineffective (ibid., 2: 2480).
123 Ibid., 1: 634.
124 "Paucissimi tamen ausi sunt eius appellationi consentire, Mantuani decreti censuram formidantes" (ibid., 1: 890).
125 Ibid., 1: 1018; 2: 1558.
126 "Totum virus evomens" (ibid., 1: 888). Pius notes that while some thought him wise, others considered him "insanum" (ibid., 1: 890).
127 "Cum accepisset aliquando gladium esse in Austria, quo duae humanae cervices uno ictu amputatae fuissent, quiescere non potuit donec, adnitente Iohanne, Imperatoris quaestore, eo potitus" (ibid., 1: 630). For a fuller portrait of Sigismund's savagery, see ibid., 1: 626–30.
128 "Divina et humana iura contemnens" (see ibid., 1: 1034). "Exulat universa civitas. Clerici alter alterum invitant, eamque diem esse fatentur qua tandem saevae tyrannidis excusserint iugum" (see ibid., 1: 1040). Also see ibid., 1: 1022, where Diether is criticized by papal legate Rudolph of Worms for violating canon law; and see ibid., 1: 1034, 1048.
129 Ibid., 1: 1022, 1028.
130 Ibid., 2: 2492–8.
131 "Convenitque tandem inter eos ut Dyetherus, iure quo in ecclesia Maguntina sibi competere asseruerat prorsus dimisso, Adolfo tanquam dominum suuum et archiepiscopum a Romano pontefice rite institutum veneraretur … et humiliatus, flexo genu, ab apostolico nuncio veniam petens, absolutus est et tanquam privatus praetorium exiit" (ibid., 2: 2496).
132 Ibid., 1: 1016–32.
133 *Defensorium*, 29.
134 *Commentarii*, 1: 1020.
135 For Rudolph's response, see ibid., 1: 1022–32. Pius reports the following reaction to the legate's oration: "Constat conventum, eius oratione persuasum, nihil eorum fecisse quae Dyetherus efflagitaverit, Gregoriumque inde confusum abiisse, ac testes qui pro Dyethero producti fuerant adversus eum deposuisse" (ibid., 1: 1032).
136 *Commentarii*, 2: 1474–6, and 1784–8.
137 Ibid., 2: 1476–8, 1786, 1798.
138 The mysterious messenger is not identified ("ignotus obvoluto capite"). Pius writes about the contents of the briefcase: "In eo Fantinus quinque et viginti aureos repperit et complures Basiliensis et Constantiensis

Concilii bullas, quas postera die in conventu publice recitavit, quoniam et Communionem utriusque speciei damnabant, et quomodo indulta fuissent Compactata manifestabant, erroresque Rochezanae et Hussitarum omnium viris rationibus evincebant" (see ibid., 2: 1802–4).

139 Ibid., 2: 1460–6.

140 Ibid., 2: 1466.

141 "Tanto res videri dignior atque admirabilior quanto minus sperata fuisset. Neque enim quisquam erat qui post quattuor et viginti amnos inveteratum Pragmaticae morbum sub Pio pontifice auferri posse consideret. Satis consultum iri Apostolicae Sedi existimabant omnes si malum non ingravesceret" (ibid., 2: 1466).

142 "Ludovicus … ex animo Pontifici deditissimo visus est paululum cecidisse" (ibid., 2: 2342).

143 "Non tam religiosus abolita Pragmatica Sanctione visus quam huiuscemodi decretorum editione sacrilegus" (ibid., 2: 2344).

144 Ibid., 2: 1778–1804.

145 "Corpus mihi, Rex … auferre potes; animam non potes. Si vitam perdidero temporalem, acquiram aeternam, pro veritate moriens: atque utinam tanto me facias honore dignum!" (ibid., 2: 1790).

146 "Apostolica Sede[s] est porta coeli: mori praestat quam illi contra ire" (ibid., 2: 1798).

147 From ibid., 2: 1804: "ad martyrium pro veritate."

5. The Triumph over the Princes and the Triumph of a Prince

1 "Vos … audiam et quanto quotiens placebit. Verum scitote ultimum verbum in ore nostro remansurum, nec miremini si puncti estis qui pupugistis. Non est haec Sedes quae cuiquam cedat, quamvis maximo regi" (*Commentarii*, 1: 608).

2 Ibid., 1: 52.

3 On these conditions and on Aeneas's role in shaping the imperial compromise proposal, see chapter 2.

4 The phrase he uses is "nationi provideretur" (*Commentarii*, 1: 74).

5 "Tertia die ad Eugenium vocati in consistorio secreto auditi sunt, quo in loco nomine omnium Aeneas oravit, quem cum Papa tum cardinales mirum in modum laudaverunt" (ibid., 1: 78).

6 Ibid., 1: 138–52.

7 "At cum in contionem itum est, mirabile dictu, locuto Aenea, omnium repente animi in priorem belli gerendi ardorem rediere" (ibid., 1:148); see also ibid., 1: 142-4, 150.

8 "Non placuit divinae pietati per id tempus excindi Turchorum imperium: ad correctionem nostrarum iniquitatum diutius conservatur" (ibid., 1: 152).
9 Ibid., 1: 156–60.
10 Ibid., 1: 228.
11 Ibid., 1: 122, 174.
12 Ibid., 1: 198–210.
13 For the full account of the Congress of Mantua, see *Commentarii*, 1: 422–638 (Book Three).
14 "Maximo Pio pontifici vita"(ibid., 420). For the full account of Pius's formal entry into Mantua, see ibid., 1: 416–20.
15 Ibid., 1: 506–10.
16 Ibid., 1: 514.
17 "'En quia sublimis et excellentissima est Romani praesulis auctoritas ac maiestas, ad cuius deobsculandos pedes tantus princeps advenit'" (ibid., 1: 506). For examples of this ritual elsewhere in the text, see ibid., 1: 268, 808, 902; and 2: 1462.
18 See, e.g., ibid., 1: 422, 464, 634, 638.
19 Pius delivered the first oration at the congress's official opening in June 1459. He delivered a second when proceedings finally got underway in September, and a third at the assembly's closing in January 1460. For the account of these orations in the *Commentaries*, see ibid., 1: 422–6, 570–2, 634–8.
20 Ibid., 1: 426, 572, 638.
21 Ibid., 1: 478–86, 574–6, 626.
22 Ibid., 1: 594–614.
23 "Idem nobis accidit: viso et audito Pio pontifice, cecidit omnis furor" (ibid., 1: 612); see also ibid., 1: 610.
24 "Speravimus, fratres ac filii, hanc urbem adeuntes, frequentes qui praecessissent regum legatos invenire. Pauci adsunt, ut videmus; decepti sumus" (ibid., 1: 422).
25 Ibid., 1: 292–4, 510–14, 586–92, 624.
26 "Non est religionis cura apud Christianos quantam credidimus" (see ibid., 1: 422). "Pudet nos tantam esse Christianorum negligentiam. Alii delitiis indulgent, alios avaritia retinet" (ibid., 1: 424).
27 He tells the Venetians: "Non est, ut videmus, in animo vestro, Veneti, religionem tueri" (ibid., 1: 590).
28 "Regem vestrum Christanissimum appellatis, neque labenti christianae religioni subvenire curatis" (ibid., 612). See also Pius's reprimand of Frederick III and his criticism of the French and Germans in ibid., 1: 292–4, 482.

29 See, e.g., his opening oration: "'Reliquimus Ecclesiae Patrimonium non sine periculo, ut fidei catholicae subveniremus'" (*Commentarii*, 1: 424); see also ibid., 1: 454, 456, 464, 568–570, 574, 598, 600.
30 Ibid., 1: 638.
31 Ibid., 1: 422–4.
32 The legates are "rei militaris peritissimi" (ibid., 1: 476). The discussion is found in ibid., 1: 476–86.
33 Ibid., 1: 576–92.
34 "Vos, si melius aliquid cogitastis, proponite in medium … Placuit omnibus sententia Pontificis" (ibid., 1: 586).
35 Ibid., 1: 432–4, 444–8.
36 "Laudaverunt … animum ac propositum eius et in coelum extulerunt, qui unus esset omnium salvandae relgionis curiosus" (ibid., 1: 240).
37 "Christiani reges, principes ac populi colla subiiciant, tibi oboediant, tuis iussi ut dominicis mandatis obtemperent" (ibid., 2: 1548). For the account of the ceremony, see ibid., 2: 1494–1558. For the reference to the canopy, see ibid., 2: 1532.
38 Ibid., 2: 2442–4, 2452.
39 "Tu pater religionis es ac magister fidei. Te decet in primis curare ne christianus cultus imminuatur" (ibid., 2: 1390). See also what the legates from Monovasia say to Pius when they arrive at the papal court: "'Respice nos, Pie pontifex,' dixere. 'Nisi manum porrigis, praeda Turchorum sumus'" (ibid., 1: 734). The duke of Burgundy also gives Pius's crusade leadership powerful endorsement (ibid., 2: 1742).
40 "Quoniam sunt omnes reges avarissimi … de suo ingenio metiuntur nostrum. Nihil difficilius est quam extorqueri aurum ab avaro" (ibid., 2:1484). Commenting on those at the Congress of Mantua, Pius writes: "pauciores fuere quibus religio potior quam voluptas videretur" (ibid., 2: 806). For other similar comments, see 1: 648; and 2: 2026, 2176, 2280–2, 2360.
41 Indeed, he notes how legates are turned away from other courts when they solicit help for the crusade (ibid., 1: 904).
42 See, e.g., what Pius writes about the French fighting the Turks in the fourteenth century (ibid., 2: 2352).
43 Ibid., 1: 1124–6.
44 "Multas in hunc modum ineptias Pragmatica Sanctio peperit, quae ab ingrato rege aut iussa fuerunt aut permissa" (ibid., 2: 1126).
45 "De religione, de Deo nihil sentiens; mundum casu regi et mortales animas dicitans hominum aeque ac iumentorum" (ibid., 1: 280). On Malatesta, he observes: "Sacerdotes odio habuit, religionem contempsit.

De venturo saeculo nihil credidit et animas perire cum corpore existimavit" (ibid., 1: 366).

46 He observes that "nonnullos principes" are guided by their desires (ibid., 1: 512). About popular governments, he states: "sed in populari dominatu nihil religiosum, nihil sanctum" (ibid., 1: 552). For additional references, see above.

47 The historical excursus scattered throughout the text focuses overwhelmingly on wars fought among European powers. See, e.g., *Commentarii*, 1: 530–68, 1048–60, 1066–72, 1074–80, 1082–1112, 1126–52; and 2: 1332–56, 1678–86, 1804–18, 1960–2, 2042–4, 2140–8, 2152–6. Pius's discussion of the Neapolitan war also consumes much of the *Commentaries*.

48 Wolkan, 2: 6–18.

49 "Inter saeculi principes nulla caritas est, nec tanta propinquitas usquam pereritur quae tollat invidia" (*Commentarii*, 2: 1410).

50 On the popes' traditional role as arbiters and peacemakers, see Michael Wilks, *The Problem of Sovereignty in the Later Middle Ages* (Cambridge: Cambridge University Press, 1962), 445–7; and Antony Black, *Political Thought in Europe, 1250–1450* (Cambridge: Cambridge University Press, 1992), 89–92.

51 See, e.g., *Commentarii*, 1: 382–4, 434–44, 446, 466–76, 478–80, 632.

52 Ibid., 1: 434–42. Pius writes of the effects of the ambassadors' speech: "His commoti, principes paulo post concordiam iniere" (ibid., 1: 442).

53 Ibid., 1: 12–16.

54 Ibid., 1: 52, 88, 158, 132–3, 134–8.

55 See, e.g., ibid., 1: 382–4, 434–44, 466–76.

56 "Nisi Papa succurreret, alium esse neminem qui tantum ignem restinguere posset" (ibid., 1: 436).

57 Ibid., 1: 534, 556, 1118; see also, ibid., 1: 12–16, 470.

58 The savagery of Europe's secular rulers, especially at war, is a theme that runs throughout the *Commentaries*. See e.g., ibid., 1: 280, 286, 388, 394–6, 440, 630, 862, 960; 2: 1346, 1352, 1366, 1480, 1818, 2156, 2226.

59 Ibid., 1: 818–22, 840, 962, 976–80.

60 Ibid., 1: 962–6; 2: 2490–2.

61 "Sigismundus hic ego sum Malatesta, filius Pandulfi, rex proditorum, Deo atque hominibus infestus, sacri censura senatus igni damnatus" (ibid., 2: 1448–50).

62 Ibid., 1: 372–4, 278.

63 Ibid., 1: 248–52.

64 "Picininum meretriculae nomen mereri … si se aliquando Asisio … extrudi sineret" (ibid., 1: 278).

65 "Quem qui laudant non pugnandi sed fugiendi peritum dicunt, et nos quidem fugacem magis quam fortem esse fatemur" (ibid., 1: 690). Pius also notes in this context that Piccinino was afraid of papal troops (ibid., 1: 686). For other examples of Piccinino's fears on the battlefield, see 1: 166, 746, 824, 1844.

66 Ibid., 1: 2452.

67 See, e.g., ibid., 1: 950, 692; and 2: 1914, 2194.

68 Pius rejects Federigo da Montefeltro's advice not to enter a potentially rebellious Tivoli (see ibid., 1: 970–2). He points out a flaw in Sforza's military strategy (see ibid., 2: 1930–2). And he convinces both Cosimo de' Medici and Francesco Sforza of his own idea on how to organize troops in battle (see ibid., 1: 950).

69 Ibid., 1: 828.

70 Ibid., 1: 868, 526.

71 Pius refers to the well-fortified citadels and/or walls of Spoleto, Narni, Sora, Orvieto, Viterbo, Civita Castellana, Assisi, Radicofani, Civitavecchia, Vicovaro, Subiaco, Soriano, Capodimonte, Cripta, Rocca dei Papi, and Rome itself.

72 His entry into Rome in 1460 is one of these exceptions (see ibid., 1: 818–22).

73 See, e.g., the account of his journey to the Congress of Mantua (ibid., 1: 272–420).

74 Ibid., 1: 232, 290. See also ibid., 1: 822, where his pallium is torn to shreds by adoring Romans as he returns to the city after a long absence.

75 Ibid., 1: 646, 656–62; 2: 1974–94, 2008–10, 2174–86.

76 "'Nunc,' inquit 'libet de pace loqui quando mediator accessit quem diligimus.' Moxque tractatum iniit" (ibid., 1: 170).

77 Ibid., 1: 584–6.

78 For Malatesta's suggestions and Pius's criticism of them, see ibid., 1: 580–4. For the pontiff's disparagement of *condottieri*, see ibid., 1: 582. For his correction of Venetian estimates, see ibid., 1: 578–80, 584.

79 "Tueri se Italiam, dum Ferdinandum tueretur" (ibid., 1: 660).

80 "En genus italicum … Ego te quantum potero adiuvabo, ne tam crudeles patiare dominos" (ibid., 1: 750).

81 "Totius Italiae virus" (ibid., 1: 166).

82 "Purgaret tandem Italiam teterrimo et abhominabili monstro" (ibid., 1: 908).

83 "Et quid est nostra Italia absque Romano praesule?" (ibid., 1: 208).

84 Ibid., 1: 646. Pius writes: "Aut ibit in Galliam pontifex gallus, et orbata est dulcis patria nostra splendore suo, aut manebit inter nos, et serviet regina gentium Italia extero domino, erimusque mancipia Gallicae gentis" (ibid., 1: 208–10).

85 "Siccine fidem servatis? Piccininus … timuisset infamiam, timuisset populi voces, timuisset proditoris nomen. At Venetos nihil horum movet. Inanimis est Respublica, non verecundatur, non erubescit, non pallet, non titubat" (ibid., 2: 2180).
86 "Laudavit Cosmas Pontificis animum, verumque fassus est popularem multitudinem nihil honesti facere nisi cogat utilitas aut metus" (ibid., 1: 660).
87 "Horriguit ea cum audisset legatus Venetus … sperare se dixit senatum Venetum quod impraesentiarum malefecisset, in posterum erga Romanam Ecclesiam … repensaturum" (ibid., 2: 2186).
88 Ibid., 1: 276.
89 Ibid., 2: 1974–94, 2008–10.
90 Ibid., 1: 316–30, 518–24, 812–22.
91 Ibid., 1: 950–2; 2: 1930–2; 1: 736–8.
92 "Delitiis iam praesentibus devinctus animus futuras contempsit" (ibid., 2: 2484).
93 Ibid., 1: 506.
94 See esp. ibid., 1: 118–22.
95 Ibid., 1: 242.
96 Ibid., 1: 822. For further analysis of Rome and the Romans in the *Commentaries*, see Farenga, "'I Romani sono periculoso populo,'" 297–310; and Modigliani, "Pio II e Roma," 77–92.
97 *Commentarii*, 1: 806–12. For similar comments in his subsequent address to the Roman people, see ibid., 1: 854–74.
98 *Commentarii*, 1: 808. One of the criticisms Valla makes is that the popes oppressed the Romans with excessive taxes (see Valla, *On the Donation*, 152). For a discussion of similar defences of papal rule, see D'Elia, "Stefano Porcari's Conspiracy," 223–9.
99 "Viri sane et probi et prudentes estis, qui vestro domino constanter servitis, quamvis vestra servitus regnum est" (*Commentarii*, 1: 808).
100 "Et quae civitas reperitur Roma liberior?" (ibid., 808).
101 *Commentarii*, 1: 958, and 2: 2274, 2018.
102 Ibid., 1: 280
103 Ibid., 1: 302.
104 Ibid., 1: 366, 960.
105 "Forsitan experti Genuenses iniusta esse regimina saecularia, atque inde tot mutationes oriri putantes" (ibid., 2: 2136).
106 "Non eadem sacerdotalis et saecularis imperii norma. Paternam et omni clementia plenam esse pontificalem administrationem oportet, non tyrannicam" (ibid., 2: 2136).

107 "Multa in saeculari principe ferunt homines quae abhorrent in ecclesiastico. Quae in laico pusilla et levia existimantur delicta, in clerico maxima et gravissima iudicantur" (ibid.).

108 Ibid., 2: 2406–10.

109 "Principes saeculi et rectores urbium quocunque tandem modo sua tueantur imperio non curant, dum tueantur. Atque iccirco saepe ius gentium violant et moribus adversantur honestis" (ibid., 2: 2410).

110 "At nos, si vel minima negligentia in his utimur quae sunt fidei, mox omnium Christianorum vocibus laceramur. 'En' inquiunt 'Christi vicarium siccine defensionem fidei postponere decet? Concilio opus est, in quo negligentia puniatur et melior eligatur!" (ibid., 2: 2410–12).

111 "Maior erit nostra clementia quam vestra perfidia" (ibid., 1: 2222).

112 "Discite inter ecclesiasticum et saeculare imperium quantum intersit. Nemo qui regem quempiam offenderit quemadmodum vos Ecclesiam offendistis, ab illo eam gratiam reportasset quam vos hodie refertis a nobis" (ibid., 2: 2222–4).

113 "Admirati sunt omnes liberalitatem Praesulis: nam supra centum milia ovium ea die donavit Aquilanis" (ibid., 2: 2224).

114 *Liberalitas* was a trademark of the Renaissance prince. See Quentin Skinner, *The Foundations of Modern Political Thought* (Cambridge: Cambridge University Press, 1978), 1: 126–8.

115 *Dialogus*, 92–3.

116 See, e.g., *Commentarii*, 1: 274–6, 292, 422, 456, 460, 806.

117 "Sin pergimus, nutat temporale regnum Ecclesiae; at hoc saepe amissum est et saepe recuperatum. Spirituali si semel exciderimus, incertum est an vendicari aliquando poterit. Pereant haec fluxa, dum solidiora illa retineamus" (ibid., 1: 274–6).

118 Ibid., 2: 1484.

119 Ibid., 1: 640, 862.

120 From ibid., 1: 862: "expeditionem contra Turchos impedivit."

121 "Existimabatis ex animo nostro zelum fidei penitus decidisse, nec ullam nobis esse curam tuendae religionis" (ibid., 2: 2426).

122 "Pro Christo pugnavimus cum Ferdinandum defendimus. Turchis intulimus bellum cum Sigismundi concussimus agros" (ibid., 2: 2428).

123 *Commentarii*, 2: 1450–8.

124 "Hodie … tibi victoriam de Turcho affero" (ibid., 2: 1452).

125 "Licebit iam tibi adversus Turchos bellum instruere. Haec tibi minera nervos belli administrabit et auferet Turcho, hoc est pecuniam" (ibid., 2: 1454).

126 "Romanos pontifices ad ferenda christianae religionis onera non parum adiuvabit" (ibid., 2: 1456).

127 Ibid. 1: 812–22.

128 "Quod si occulto aliquo divino iudicio decretum est hostiles nos manus incidere, aut impio ferro cadere, non recusamus pro Roma et in Roma mori. Mortem oppetere pro Patrimonio Petri gloriosum est, effugere miserum" (ibid., 1: 816).

129 "Quomodo enim pacari provincie et amicitie vel conflari vel integrari possent, nisi facundia foret, quam poesis alit? ... Rex regi per litteras conciliatur, civitates federa percutiunt ... orationes senatum regunt, populos ducunt, leges suadent. Sed quis haec bene agat, nisi poeticis et oratoriis imbutus disciplinis?" (Wolkan 1: 329).

130 See esp. *Pentalogus*, 60–72; and Baldi, *Il "cardinale tedesco,"* 37–8. For a modern Latin edition and English translation of his educational treatise, see Craig Kallendorf, ed., *Humanist Educational Treatises* (Cambridge, MA: Harvard University Press, 2002), 126–259.

6. Portraits of Princes in the Portrait of Pius II

1 "Spectaculo digna res et quam vix posteri credant. Princeps saeculi potentissimus, Gallis atque Italis metuendus, quem aureis vestibus ornatum purpurati admodum multi cicumsistere consuessent et secures praeire atque armatorum sequi cohortes et turba potentum; nunc, sex tantum eremitis praecedentibus et paucis sequentibus sacerdotibus, in veste vili et abiecta legatum apostolicum excipit" (*Commentarii*, 2: 1402).

2 Ibid., 2: 1398–1402; see also 1: 16.

3 Ibid., 2: 1402.

4 See, e.g., Seeber, *Enea Vergilianus*; Totaro, *Pio II nei suoi "Commentarii,"* 96–164; Pozzi, "Struttura epica," 151–62; and Van Heck, "Amator vetusti ritus," 127–30. None of these discussions explores the political or apologetic resonances of Pius's engagement with ancient texts. For a brief discussion of the political resonances of Caesar's *Gallic War* in Pius's *Commentaries*, see Marziano Guglielminetti, *Memoria e scrittura: L'autobiografia da Dante a Cellini* (Torino: Einaudi, 1975), 210–25.

5 The bibliography on this subject is immense. For a discussion of how classical culture is incorporated into the humanist texts sponsored by Alfonso of Aragon, Cosimo de' Medici, Sigismondo Malatesta, Jacopo Piccinino, and Francesco Sforza, see citations below.

6 For an extended version of this discussion, see O'Brien, "Arms and Letters."

7 Gary Ianziti has written extensively on the genre of the *commentarii* in fifteenth-century Italy, with particular attention to Milan. See

esp. "I *Commentarii*: Appunti per la storia di un genere storiografico quattrocentesco," *Archivio Storico Italiano* 150, no. 4 (1992): 1029–63; "Storiografia come propaganda: Il caso dei 'Commentarii' Rinascimentali," *Società e Storia* 22 (1983): 909–18; and *Humanistic Historiography*.

8 These include Giovanni Simonetta's *De rebus gestis Francisci Sfortiae commentarii*; Pierantonio Paltroni's *Commentarii della vita et gesti dell'illustrissimo Federico Duca d'Urbino*; and Francesco Filelfo's *Commentarii de vita et rebus gestis Federicii Comitis urbinatis*.

9 The full titles of these two sets of books are *Commentaria comitis Jacobi Picinini vocati Scipionis Aemiliani edita per P. Porcelium et missa Alphonso Regi Aragonum* and *Commentaria secundi anni de gestis Scipionis Picinini in Annibalem Sfortiam ad Serenissimum Principem Franciscum Foscari Venetorum Ducem per Porcellium*. For a discussion of Porcellio's *Commentaries*, see Ugo Fritelli, *Giannantonio de' Pandoni detto 'il Porcellio': Studio critico* (Florence: Paravia, 1900), 104–10; and Picotti, *Ricerche Umanistiche*, 179–203.

10 The complete title is *Historia Hetruriae seu Commentariorum de rebus in Hetruria a Senensibus gestis cum adversus Florentinos, tum adversus Ildebrandum Ursinum Petilianiensium comitem libri tres*. For a modern edition of Book Three, see Renata Fabbri, ed., *Per la memorialistica veneziana in latino del Quattrocento: Filippo da Rimini, Francesco Contarini, Coriolano Cippico* (Padua: Antenore, 1988), 75–137. This edition is the only reliable printed edition of any part of Contarini's text. For a discussion of the work, see ibid., 1–26, 41–67; and Agostino Pertusi, "Gli inizi della storiografia umanistica del Quattrocento," in Agostino Pertusi, ed., *Storiografia veneziana fin al secolo XVI: Aspetti e problemi* (Florence: Olschki, 1970), 304–5. According to Pertusi, Contarini began his *Commentaries* in 1457.

11 Bartolomeo Facio, *Rerum gestarum Alfonsi regis libri*, edited by Daniela Pietragalla (Alessandria: Edizioni dell'Orso, 2004). Facio spent a decade writing the *Gesta*. He completed the work by 1456, but it was not formally presented to Alfonso until 1457 (ibid., xx).

12 "Bartholomaeum Facium, qui gesta regis scribit, non miror imitatum esse in genere dicendi C. Caesarem, quando eius commentaria regi tantopere placent" (*Opera Omnia*, 480).

13 See Paul Oskar Kristeller, *Studies in Renaissance Thought and Letters II* (Rome: Edizioni di storia e letterature, 1950), 274; and Francesco Tateo, *I miti della storiografia umanistica* (Roma: Bulzoni, 1990), 152.

14 Virginia Brown, "Caesar," in F.E. Cranz and P.O. Kristeller, eds., *Catalogus Translationum et Commentariorum: Medieval and Renaissance Latin*

Translations and Commentaries, vol. 3, 87–139 (Washington, DC: Catholic University of America Press, 1976). Through much of the Middle Ages, Caesar's *Commentarii* were believed to be the work of Giulio Celso.

15 Ianziti, *Humanistic Historiography*, 176; and Ianziti, "Un genere storiografico," 1058–60, 1032–3.

16 See, e.g., *Commentarii*, 1: 264, 268, 598, 818, 846; 2: 1438, 1486, 1548, 1552. In one instance, Pius does refer implicitly to the passage from Matthew 16 traditionally used as the biblical basis for papal supremacy (ibid., 1: 854).

17 Michel Rambaud, *L'Art de la déformation historique dans les "Commentaires" de César* (Paris: Belles Lettres, 1953).

18 Kathryn Welch and Anton Powell, eds., *Julius Caesar as Artful Reporter: The War Commentaries as Political Instruments* (London: Duckworth, 1998).

19 Ianziti, *Humanistic Historiography*, 176–209.

20 Rambaud, *L'Art de la déformation*, 111–51.

21 *Commentarii*, 1: 368–74, 518–24; 2: 1480–90; 1: 474–6, 880.

22 Ibid., 1: 424–6, 572, 854–74; 2: 2422–54.

23 Ibid., 1: 254–6, 604–9, 610–12, 666–76; 2: 1418–44.

24 Ibid., 2: 1634–44, 1664–8, 1892–4, 2412–22.

25 See, e.g., Guglielminetti, *Memoria e scrittura*, 212.

26 Rambaud, *L'Art de la déformation*, 196–8.

27 Ibid., 250.

28 *Commentarii*, 1: 422, 450, 464; 2: 1594–1622, 1514; 1: 288–90, 300, 308, 312, 316, 328–30, 662–4, 394–6, 406–8, 418–20, 786–8, 790, 800, 262–8, 598, 608, 666–80; 2: 1418–44, 1446, 1462–6.

29 Facio typically places these verbs in clear sequence in his narrative of the king's actions: Alfonso first learns, perceives, or decides something – *cernere* (to determine), *animadvertere* (to perceive), *existimare* (to consider), *convertere animum* (to direct attention), *cognoscere* (to notice), *intelligere* (to understand) – and on the basis of this information he takes command – *instituere* (to establish), *obducere* (to lead against), *mandare* (to deliver), *imperare* (to command), *decernere* (to decide). See Sondra Dall'Oco, "Bartolomeo Facio e la tecnica dell' 'excursus' nella biografia di Alfonso d'Aragona," *Archivio Storico Italiano* 154, no. 2 (1996): 239, who notes a similar pattern in verbs of command but not their connection to Caesar's *Commentaries*. Contarini creates the impression that he masterminded the military campaign at the centre of his history by routinely employing the same or similar verbs of judgment and command.

30 See, e.g., Facio, *Rerum gestarum*, 12, 26, 30, 34, 42.

31 See, e.g., Fabbri, *Per la memorialistica*, 83, 84, 88, 92, 98, 101, 132–3.

32 Ibid., 83, 84, 88, 92–3, 99, 100, 102, 108 115, 132, 136.

33 Hans Baron, *The Crisis of the Early Italian Renaissance: Civic Humanism and Republican Liberty in an Age of Classicism and Tyranny* (Princeton: Princeton University Press, 1966), 61–2. For Pius's own identification of Caesar in these terms, see Wolkan, 1: 330; 2: 10.
34 Frank Adcock, *Caesar as Man of Letters* (Cambridge: Cambridge University Press, 1956), 52–4.
35 Caesar, *The Gallic War*, translated by H.J. Edwards (Cambridge, MA: Harvard University Press, 1917), 10, 16–18, 36–8, 40–1, 114–18, 208–10, 220–2 (1.5, 9, 24, 26, 85; 3.10, 18).
36 Caesar's *clementia* was to become a hallmark of his character in the works of other authors, including Cicero, Sallust, Suetonius, Plutarch, and St Augustine.
37 *Commentarii*, 1: 840–8.
38 Ibid., 1: 846–8.
39 Ibid., 1: 962–6.
40 "Victus tandem Sabellus, cum periculi magnitudinem non ignoraret, se ac sua in manu Pontificis … mediam Romam veluti captivus in triumpho ductus, ad pontificem venit" (ibid., 1: 962).
41 "Sed quis homo est et non peccat? Nemo sapiens nascitur. Nulli tanta prudentia est cui non supersit aliquid discere" (ibid., 1: 964).
42 "Maior erit nostra clementia quam tua dementia" (ibid., 1: 966).
43 Rambaud, *L'art de la déformation*, 272–83; Caesar, *The Gallic War*, 584 (8.15); Caesar, *The Civil War*, translated by A.G. Peskett (Cambridge, MA: Harvard University Press, 1914), 22–4, 26 (1.15, 18).
44 See Guglielminetti, *Memoria e scrittura*, 15–16, who notes a parallel between the Romans' reaction to Pius's election and Caesar's reception in Cisalpine Gaul in *De Bello Gallico*. Aside from this connection, Guglielminetti draws no other parallels between Caesar's and Pius's popular receptions.
45 Pius records a jubilant reception from the people of Cività Castellana (*Commentarii*, 1: 288–90); of Spoleto (1: 290); of Perugia (1: 300, 308); of Corsignano (1: 312); of Siena (1: 316, 328–30, 662–4, where he describes himself entering the town "quasi triumphans"); of Bologna (1: 394); of Ferrara (1: 408); of Mantua (1: 418–420); of Proceno (1: 786–8); of Orvieto, and of Bagnoreggio (1: 790, 800).
46 "Benedictus Pius, qui nos ex tanto periculo liberavit" (ibid., 1: 840).
47 Ibid., 1: 976, 1172–4; 2: 1632, 1996, 2012, 2242.
48 Fabbri, *Per la memorialistica*, 86–7, 101–13, 116, 92, 97–8, 82–3, 128–9, 123–4, 130.
49 See, e.g., Facio, *Rerum gestarum*, 68, 90, 150, 174, 224, 246, 288, 306, and 538, where his "summam … belli scientiam" is explicitly identified.

50 See, ibid., 34, 76, 80, 420, and esp. 542, where Alfonso speaks at length of his preference for peace over war.

51 Ibid., 52, 58, 70, 270, 300, 308.

52 Giacomo Ferraù, "Il 'Il *De rebus* ab Alphonso Primo Gestis' de Bartolomeo Facio," *Studi Umanistici* 1 (1990): 60–113.

53 For this correspondence, see *Opera Omnia*, 788–9. On Pius's access to the *Gesta*, see Albanese et al., "Storiografia come ufficialità," 52. For his commentary on Panormita's text, see *Opera Omnia*, 472–97. On this work see Tateo, *I miti*, 121–35.

54 Bisaha, introduction to Piccolomini, *Europe (c. 1400–1458)*, 20–2.

55 For Porcellio's contributions to the *Epaenetica*, see Rino Avesani, "*Epaeneticorum* ad Pium II Pont. Max. Libri V," in Maffei, *Enea Silvio Piccolomini, Papa Pio II*, 15–97.

56 Fabbri, *Per la memorialistica*, 47–8. For Contarini's role at the Congress of Mantua, see Picotti, *La Dieta di Mantova*.

57 Adrianus Van Heck, ed., *Enea Silvii Piccolominei postea Pii PP. II Carmina* (Vatican City: Biblioteca Apostolica Vaticana, 1994), 5–6.

58 Wolkan, 1: 343–53; 2: 88–93; and *Dialogus*.

59 Kristen Lippincott, "The Neo-Latin Historical Epics of North Italian Courts," *Renaissance Studies* 3, no. 4 (1989), 417.

60 For an overview of these epics, see esp. ibid., 415–28; and Zabughin, *Vergilio nel Rinascimento italiano: Da Dante a Torquato Tasso* (Bologna: Zanardelli, 1921), 1: 281–301. The epic continued to be a popular genre for the celebration of quattrocento princes after Pius had completed his *Commentarii*. Among those written after 1464 were Gian Mario Filelfo's *Lorenziad*, *Cosmiad*, and *Amaryis*; and Naldo Naldi's *Volterrais*.

61 Rossi, *Il Quattrocento*, reprint with revisions by Rosella Bessi (Padua: Vallardi, 1992), 380.

62 Guglielmo Bottari, "La 'Sphortias,'" in *Francesco Filelfo nel quinto centenario della morte: Atti del XVII convegno di studi Maceratesi* (Padua: Antenore, 1986), 464–6.

63 Diana Robin, in *Filelfo in Milan: Writings, 1451–1477* (Princeton: Princeton University Press, 1991), 61–2, describes the *Aeneid* as "a workable model for the representation of the legitimacy of [Francesco Sforza's] claims to the throne, his military campaigns and his expansionist policy."

64 Craig Kallendorf, *In Praise of Aeneas: Virgil and Epideictic Rhetoric in the Early Italian Renaissance* (Hanover, NH: University of New England Press, 1989).

65 It is clear, e.g., that Filelfo read Virgil this way (see Robin, *Filelfo in Milan*, 53–5).

66 *Opera Omnia*, 596, 943.

67 See, e.g., *Commentarii*, 1: 10–12, 148, 504.
68 Totaro, *Pio II nei suoi "Commentarii,"* 27n41, and 187n387.
69 See, e.g., Canensi, *Ad Beatissimum Dominum Nostrum*, 207, 211, 213, 224, 225–6, 227–8; Jean Jouffroy, *Oratio*, 21, 23, 25–6, 27.
70 *Commentarii*, 1: 194–226.
71 Ibid., 1: 202–4, 220.
72 In Book One of the *Commentaries*, there are references to more than twenty separate instances in which Pius calls on his talents as an orator.
73 "Quaerimus hoc efficere. Investigamus vias: nulla occurrit idonea … Vertimus in omnes partes aciem mentis: nihil certum, nihil solidum invenimus; nihil non vanum occurrit … Perplexa et nimis anxia diu mens nostra fuit et renuit consolari anima nostra, cum in deterius prolabi omnia cerneremus, nec vel minima spes rei bene gerendae daretur" (ibid., 2: 1482–4).
74 "At cum dies noctesque taciti magis huc animo ferimur ut de communi salute consilium inquiramus, unum tandem remedium in mentem venit, nostro iudicio valentissimum" (ibid., 2: 1482).
75 Ibid., 2: 1490.
76 Totaro, *Pio II nei suoi "Commentarii,"* 27n41.
77 Zabughin, *Vergilio nel rinascimento*, 1: 301.
78 Bottari, "La 'Sphortias,'" 475.
79 Ibid., 475; and Otto Pächt, "Giovanni da Fano's Illustrations for Basinio's Epos 'Hesperis,'" *Studi Romagnoli* 2 (1951): 91–2.
80 Tateo, *I miti*, 158.
81 In some cases, God's role was completely eliminated so as to ensure that the hero's responsibility would not be obscured. Leodrisio Crivelli, e.g., decided to strip away all evidence of predestination in his history of Francesco Sforza as a way to give added glory to the duke (see Ianziti, *Humanistic Historiography*, 104–6).
82 For a different reading of the role of God in the *Commentaries*, see Pozzi, "Struttura epica dei *Commentarii*," 151–62.
83 For a detailed catalogue of examples of Pius's pietas, see Totaro, *Pio II nei suoi "Commentarii,"* 95–164; on Pius and pietas, see also Reinhard, "Papa Pius," 41–8.
84 Robin, *Filelfo in Milan*, 62, 78; Helen Shahrokh Ettlinger, "The Image of a Renaissance Prince: Sigismondo Malatesta and the Arts of Power," 169; Facio, *Rerum gestarum*, 580.
85 Baron, *The Crisis of the Italian Renaissance*, *passim*.
86 Ettlinger, "Image of a Renaissance Prince," 169; and R. Valentini, "'De gestis et Vita Bracii,' di A. Campano: A proposito di storia della

storiografia," *Bollettino della R. Deputazione di Storia Patria per l'Umbria* 27 (1924): 188–96; Ianziti, *Humanistic Historiography*, 55–6.

87 See, e.g., Alison M. Brown, "The Humanist Portrait of Cosimo de' Medici, Pater Patriae," *Journal of the Warburg and Courtauld Institute* 24 (1961): 186–221.

88 On Pius's relationship to Siena, see Irene Polverini Fosi, "'La Comune, dolcissima patria': Siena e Pio II," in Daniella Rugiadini, ed., *I Ceti dirigenti nella Toscana del Quattrocento: Atti del V e VI convegno, Firenze, 10–11 dicembre 1982; 2–3 dicembre 1983* (Monte Oriolo: Impruneta Papafava ed., 1987), 509–21.

89 "Hoc est consilium nostrum, quod amantissimae damus patriae" (*Commentarii*, 1: 324).

90 "Tantopere suam decorare patriam Pontifex adnitebatur patria" (ibid., 1: 330).

91 "Pontifex Castrum Leonis et arces et Insulam Lilii nepoti Antonio tradidit, non tam ei quam patriae consulturus, cuius maritima loca et horrea civitatis hoc oppido clauduntur" (ibid., 1: 766).

92 On Pius's ambitions for his nephew Francesco Todeschini Piccolomini and for how such ambitions clashed with specific conciliar legislation and concerns, see A. Strnad, "Pio II e suo nipote Francesco Todeschini Piccolomini," *Atti e memorie della deputazione di storia patria per le Marche*, 8th ser., vol. 4, no. 2 (1964–65): 37–84.

93 To the Roman ambassadors who met him outside of the city in October 1460, Pius explains: "Flentem … et admodum dolentem flentes ipsi et vehementer dolentes Urbem reliquimus, quae patria nostra est non minus quam Senae" (*Commentarii*, 1: 804). See also ibid., 1: 810, 816, 872.

94 Totaro, *I Commentarii*, 1: 1208–12.

95 Bottari, "La 'Sphortias,'" 468–73, 486, 489, 490; and Zabughin, *Vergilio nel Rinascimento*, 1: 297.

96 To date, scholarship has not created such a category, with the result that the epics and *commentarii* of Filelfo, Porcellio, and Cornazzano appear as poor cousins to the texts truer to their generic standards.

97 Pius's attitude to the *Sforziad* seems to have been one of marked indifference rather than explicit criticism (see Bottari, "La 'Sphortias,'" 473).

98 Picotti, *Ricerche umanistiche*, 180.

99 Ianziti, *Humanistic Historiography*, 118–26; Ianziti, "La storiografia umanistica a Milano nel Quattrocento," in Anita di Stefano et al., eds., *La Storiografia umanistica*, vol. 1 (Messina: Sicania, 1992), 324–5.

100 Giannantonio Campano, *Bracii Perusini vita et gesta*, edited by Roberto Valentini, in *Rerum Italicarum Scriptores*, 2nd ser., vol. 19, no. 4 (Bologna: Zanichelli, 1929).

101 Ianziti, *Humanistic Historiography*, 119–20.

102 Valentini, "'De gestis et Vita Bracii.'" See also Ianziti, *Humanistic Historiography*, 123–4; and Tateo, *I miti*, 109.

103 Ianziti, *Humanistic Historiography*, 125–6. For a discussion of the roles *virtus* and *fortuna* play in Campano's *Vita Bracii*, see Tateo, *I miti*, 117–20; and Claudio Finzi, "Una 'Vita' di Braccio di Giannantonio Campano," in Maria Vittoria Baruti Ceccopieri, ed., *Braccio da Montone e I Fortebracci: Atti del convegno internazionale di studi, Montone 23–25, Marzo 1990* (Narni: Pubblicazioni del Centro Studi Storici, 1993), 55–9.

104 Campano's decision to accept employment by the enemy of his former patron was not unusual in a day when humanists peddled their talents and skills regularly to different regimes.

105 Ianziti, *Humanistic Historiography*, 56–8.

106 *Commentarii*: "invasisset" (1: 302); "obsessam tenebat" (1: 492); "eripuit" (2: 1998); and "ademerat" (1: 492).

107 Ibid., 1: 302, 304, 398, 490.

108 As quoted in Finzi, "Una 'Vita' di Braccio," 54: "pace … iustitiae et aequitatis observantior nemo."

109 *Commentarii*, 1: 302–4.

110 From ibid., 1: 302: "non sine gloria Francisci Sfortiae." *Virtus* and *gloria* are the two qualities that Crivelli constantly associates with Sforza and that he uses to defend the duke's right to rule (see Ianziti, *Humanistic Historiography*, 104–18, and esp. 108 and 117).

111 *Commentarii*, 1: 302, 306. The *Commentarii* toe the Sforza party line more closely when doing so is of use to the papacy. In his biographical sketch of Francesco, e.g., Pius explicitly supports an element of Milanese propaganda – promoted by Crivelli, Filelfo, and others – that represented a lynchpin of Pius's own foreign policy: that the duke's talents and abilities earned him the right to rule Milan (*Commentarii*, 1: 502–4, 506, 508).

112 "Te autem uno neminem aptiorem ad tantum imperium gerendum arbitrantur omnes, ad te summo consensu hanc praefecturam deferunt" (Facio, *Gesta*, 536).

113 "Statui enim pro illius religione defendenda vitam exponere, qui pro humano genere conservando vitam exponere non dubitavit" (ibid., 544).

114 *Commentarii*, 1: 146.

115 Pius is criticizing here both Alfonso of Naples and Alfonso of Portugal. He writes: "Nullum adhuc inventum qui se offerret, quamvis Alfonsi duo, alter Aragonum rex alter Portusgalliae, signum crucis non tam corde impresserint quam vesti consuerint" (*Commentarii*, 1: 486).

116 "Rex magnus … qui plurimas Italiae provincias sibi subiecerat viceratque potentissimos in armis duces, ad extremum, victus amore, quasi captivus mulierculae serviebat" (ibid., 1: 172).

117 Partner, *Papal State*, 186–92; Jones, *Malatesta of Rimini and the Papal State.*

118 Valturio's work, which was published in many editions, has been studied mostly for its discussion of real and imaginary military inventions and strategies. It has been almost entirely ignored as a work of political promotion for Malatesta. For a discussion of Malatesta's role in these literary projects, see esp. Pächt, "Giovanni da Fano," 89; Ettlinger, "Image of a Renaissance Prince," 153–4, and 162; Angela Donati, ed., *Il Potere, le arti, la guerra: Lo splendore dei Malatesta* (Milan: Electa, 2001), 312–14. For other humanist portraits of Malatesta, see Anthony F. D'Elia, "Heroic Insubordination in the Army of Sigismondo Malatesta: Petrus Parleo's *Pro milite*, Machiavelli, and the Uses of Cicero and Livy," in Christopher S. Celenza and Kenneth Gouwens, eds., *Humanism and Creativity in the Renaissance: Essays in Honor of Ronald G. Witt* (Leiden: Brill, 2006), 31–60.

119 Ettlinger, "Image of a Renaissance Prince," 153–70.

120 Ibid., 157, 163–4; *Dizionario Biografico degli Italiani, s.v.* "Basinio da Parma."

121 Ettlinger, "Image of a Renaissance Prince," 160. On the significance of the numerous copies of the *De Re Militari* produced at Malatesta's court, see Donati, *Il Potere, le arti, la guerra*, 58.

122 G. Soranzo, "Una missione di Sigismondo Pandolfo Malatesta a Maometto II nel 1461," *La Romagna* (1909); "Ancora sulla missione di Sigismondo Pandolfo Malatesta a Maometto II e Matteo de' Pasti," *La Romagna* (1910).

123 "Totius nequitate principem" (*Commentarii*, 1: 166); "magister scelerum" (1: 874); "hominum qui unquam fuerunt quique futuri sunt pessimus" (1: 368); "Barbaros omnis crudelitate vicit" (1: 366).

124 "Nec per virtutem crevit: prima tyrannidis fundamenta in proditione iacta fuerunt" (ibid., 2: 1874). See 2: 1866–1914 for the disparaging portraits of Malatesta's ancestors.

125 Ibid., 1: 366–8.

126 Ibid., 1: 366.

127 "Nemo sub eius imperio securus vixit" (ibid); for a similar comment, see ibid., 1: 908.

128 Malatesta is described as "impio superbiente" and "tyranno impiissimo" (ibid., 1: 370). See also 1: 874–6 for an illustration of his "impietas."

129 "Nunquam me vivo pacem habebitis" (ibid., 1: 368).

130 Ibid., 1: 372, 520.

131 Ibid., 1: 368, 502.

132 "Barbaros omnis crudelitate vicit" (ibid., 1: 366).
133 From ibid., 1: 166: "totius nequitiae principem"; "totius Italiae virus."
134 From ibid., 1: 368: "dedecus Italiae."
135 "Vastabatur ager tota Italia nobilis" (ibid., 1: 370).
136 From ibid., 1: 908: "purgaret tandem Italiam teterrimo et abhominabili monstro."
137 Ianziti, *Humanist Historiography*, 204.
138 Ibid., 127–9. See also L.F. Smith, "Lodrisio Crivelli of Milan and Aeneas Silvius," *Studies in the Renaissance* 9 (1962): 31–63.

Conclusion

1 "Historia testis temporum, lux veritatis, magistra vite, nuntia vetustatis" (Wolkan, 2: 164). Aeneas repeats this line elsewhere in his writings. See, e.g., his June 1444 letter to Wilhelm Von Stein, in ibid., 1: 329.
2 Burckhardt's *The Civilization of the Renaissance in Italy* is the most obvious example. Scholars continue to draw on Pius's *Commentaries* as a reliable record of the past. See, e.g, Arthur White, *Plague and Pleasure: The Renaissance World of Pius II* (Washington, DC: Catholic University Press, 2014).
3 Honegger Chiari, "L'edizione del 1584."

Bibliography

Manuscripts

Rome, Biblioteca dell'Accademia dei Lincei, Corsiniano 147.
Vatican City, Biblioteca Apostolica Vaticana, Reginense Latino 1995.

Printed Primary Sources

Alberigo, G., P.P. Joannou, C. Leonardi, P. Prodi, and H. Jedin, eds. *Conciliorum oecumenicorum decreta*. Bologna: Istituto per le scienze religiose, 1973.

Caesar, Julius. *The Civil War*. Translated by A.G. Peskett. Cambridge, MA: Harvard University Press, 1914.

–. *The Gallic War*. Translated by H.J. Edwards. Cambridge, MA: Harvard University Press, 1917.

Campano, Giannantonio. *Bracii Perusini vita et gesta*. In *Rerum Italicarum Scriptores*, 2nd ser., vol. 19, no. 4. Edited by R. Valentini. Bologna: Zanichelli, 1929.

Canensi, Michele. *Ad Beatissimum Dominum Nostrum Nicolaum V Pontificem Maximum Michael Canensis de Viterbio Humillimus Servulus de Ipsius Laudibus et Divina Electione*. In *Storiografia pontificia del Quattrocento*, ed. Massimo Miglio, 205–43. Bologna: Pàtron, 1975.

De Pandoni, Porcellio. *Commentaria comitis Jacobi Picinini vocati Scipionis Aemiliani edita per P. Porcelium et missa Alphonso Regi Aragonum*. In *Rerum Italicarum Scriptores*, vol. 20. Milan, 1731.

–. *Commentaria secundi anni de gestis Scipionis Picinini in Annibalem Sfortiam ad Serenissimum Principem Foscari Venetorum Ducem per Porcellium*. In *Rerum Italicarum Scriptores*, vol. 35, no. 1. Milan, 1751.

Del Monte, Pietro. *Il primato del romano pontefice in un'opera inedita di Pietro del Monte del secolo XV.* Edited by Mario Zanchin. Padua: Progetto Editoriale Mariano, 1997.

Di Pietro, Cesare. *Domenico de' Domenichi (1416–1478): Vescovo riformatore.* Rome: Pontificia Universitaria Gregoriana, 2010.

Duchesne, Louis, ed. *Liber Pontificalis: Texte, Introduction, et Commentaire*, vol. 2. Paris: E. De Boccard, 1886–1892.

Fabbri, Renata, ed. *Per la memorialistica veneziana in latino del Quattrocento: Filippo da Rimini, Francesco Contarini, Coriolano Cippico.* Padua: Antenore, 1988.

Facio, Bartolomeo. *Rerum gestarum Alfonsi regis libri.* Edited by Daniela Pietragalla. Alessandria: Edizioni dell'Orso, 2004.

Fea, C. *Pius II Pont. Max. a calumniis vindicatus.* Rome, 1823.

Franco, S., and A. Dalmazzo, eds. *Bullarium diplomatum et privilegiorum sanctorum Romanorum pontificum*, vol. 5. Turin, 1860.

Freher, M., and B.G. Struve. *Rerum Germanicarum scriptores varii, qui res in Germania et Imperio sub Friderico III, Maximilano I, Impp. memorabiliter gestas illo aevo litteris prodiderunt.* Vol. 2 of *Rerum Germanicarum scriptores aliquot insignes.* Strasbourg, 1717.

Jouffroy, Jean. *Oratio Episcopi Atrebatensis habita Rome in funeralibus Nicolai pape quinti.* In "'Sicut fremitus leonis ita et regis ira': Temi neoplatonici e culto solare nell'orazione funebre per Niccolò V di Jean Jouffroy." *Humanistica Lovaniensia* 32 (1982): 21–8, edited by Laura Onofri.

Kallendorf, Craig, ed. *Humanist Educational Treatises.* Cambridge, MA: Harvard University Press, 2002.

Kejř, J., and I. Dvořák, L.P. Mozhanskaya, E.V. Tarabrin, K. Jelínek, and E. Šimková, editors and translators. *The Universal Peace Organization of King George of Bohemia: A Fifteenth-Century Plan for World Peace, 1462–1464.* Prague: Czechoslovak Academy of Sciences, 1964.

Manetti, Giannozzo. *De vita ac gestis Nicolai Quinti summi pontificis.* Edited and translated by Anna Modigliani. Rome: Istituto Storico Italiano per il Medio Evo, 2005.

Mansi, Giovan Domenico. *Sacrorum conciliorum nova et amplissima collectio*, vols. 35 and 37. Florence and Venice, 1759–98.

–. *Sacrorum conciliorum nova et amplissima collectio*, vol. 27. Paris: H. Welter, 1901–27.

Mercati, Angelo. *Raccolta di concordati su materie ecclesiastiche e le autorità civili.* Rome: Tipografia Poliglotta Vaticana, 1919.

Nicholas of Cusa. *Nicholas of Cusa: Writings on Church and Reform.* Edited by Thomas M. Izbicki. Cambridge, MA: Harvard University Press, 2008.

Oberman, Heiko, Daniel E. Zerfoss, and William J. Courtenay, eds. *Defensorium Obedientiae Apostolicae et Alia Documenta*. Cambridge, MA: Belknap Press of Harvard University Press, 1968.

Pez, Bernard. *Thesaurus anecdotorum novissimus*, vol. 4, pt. 3. Augsburg, 1723.

Piccolomini, Aeneas Silvius. *Aeneae Silvii Piccolomini Senensis qui postea fuit Pius II P.M. Opera inedita*. Edited by Giuseppe Cugnoni. Rome: Salviucci, 1883.

–. *Der Briefwechsel des Eneas Silvius Piccolomini*. Edited by Rudolf Wolkan. Fontes Rerum Austriacarum: Diplomataria et Acta, 2nd ser., vols. 61, 62, 67, 68. Vienna, 1909–18.

–. *The Commentaries of Pius II*. Edited by Leona C. Gabel and translated by Florence A. Gragg. Smith College Studies in History, vol. 22, nos. 1 and 2; vol. 25, nos. 1–4, 30, 35, 43. Northampton: Department of History of Smith College, 1937–57.

–. *I Commentarii*. 5 vols. Edited by Giuseppe Bernetti. Siena: Cantagalli, 1972–76.

–. *I Commentarii*. 2 vols. Edited and translated by Luigi Totaro. Rev. ed. Milan: Adelphi, 2009.

–. *Commentaries*. Edited by Margaret Meserve and Marcello Simonetta. I Tatti Renaissance Library, vols. 12 and 29. Cambridge: Cambridge University Press, 2003 and 2007.

–. *De educatione liberorum*. In *Humanist Educational Treatises*, edited and translated by Craig Kallendorf. Cambridge, MA: Harvard University Press, 2002.

–. *Dialogus*. Edited by Duane R. Henderson. Hannover: Hahnsche Buchhandlung, 2011.

–. *Enee Silvii Piccolominei Epistolarium seculare: Complectens De duobus amantibus, De naturis equorum, De curialium miseriis*. Edited by Adrianus Van Heck. Vatican City: Biblioteca Apostolica Vaticana, 2007.

–. *Enee Silvii Piccolominei postea PII PP. II Carmina*. Edited by Adrianus Van Heck. Studi e Testi, vol. 364. Vatican City: Biblioteca Apostolica Vaticana, 1994.

–. *Enee Silvii Piccolominei. Postea PII PP. II De Europa*. Edited by Adrianus Van Heck. Studi e Testi, vol. 398. Vatican City: Biblioteca Apostolica Vaticana, 2001.

–. *De gestis concilii Basiliensis commentariorum, libri II*. Edited by Denys Hay and W.K. Smith. Oxford: Clarendon, 1978.

–. *Germania*. Edited by Maria Giovanna Fadiga. Florence: Sismel-Edizioni del Galluzzo, 2009.

–. *Libellus dialogorum de generalis concilii auctoritate et gestis Basileensium*. In *Analecta monumentorum omnis aevi vindobonensia*, vol. 2, ed. Adam F. Kollar, coll. 691–790. Vienna: Ioannis T. Trattner, 1762.

–. *Memoirs of a Renaissance Pope: The Commentaries of Pius II*. An Abridgment. Translated by Florence A. Gragg. Edited by Leona C. Gabel. London: Allen and Unwin, 1960.

–. *Opera Omnia*. Basel, 1551.

–. *Pentalogus*. Edited by Christoph Schingnitz. Hanover: Hahnsche Buchhandlung, 2009.

–. *Pii Secundi Pontificis Maximi commentarii rerum memorabilium, quae temporibus suis contigerunt, a R.D. Ioanne Gobellino vicario Bonnenensi iam diu compositi, et a R.P.D. Francisco Bandino Piccolomineo Archiepiscopo Senensi ex vetusto originali recogniti*. Rome: Basa, 1584 and 1589.

–. *Pii Secundi pontificis maximi "Commentarii": Textum recensuerunt atque explicationibus, apparatu critico indiceque nominum ornaverunt*. 2 vols. Edited by Ibolya Bellus and Iván Boronkai. Budapest: Balassi Kiadó, 1993–94.

–. *Pii II Commentarii rerum memorabilium que temporibus suis contigerunt*. Edited by Adrianus Van Heck. Studi e Testi, vols. 312 and 313. Vatican City: Biblioteca Apostolica Vaticana, 1984.

–. *Pii II P.M. olim Aeneae Sylvii Piccolominei Senensis orationes politicae et ecclesiasticae*, vol. 1. Edited by J.D. Mansi. Lucca, 1755–59.

–. *Reject Aeneas, Accept Pius: Selected Letters from Aeneas Sylvius Piccolomini (Pope Pius II)*. Introduced and translated by Thomas M. Izbicki, Gerald Christianson, and Philip Krey. Washington, DC: Catholic University Press, 2006.

–. *Three Tracts on Empire: Engelbert of Adamont, Aeneas Silvius Piccolomini and Juan de Torquemada*. Edited and translated by Thomas M. Izbicki and Cary Nederman. Bristol: Thoemmes, 2000.

Raynaldus, Odoricus, ed. *Annales Ecclesiastici*, vol. 29. Lucca: Leonardo Venturini, 1753.

Simonetta, Giovanni. *De rebus gestis Francisci Sfortiae commentarii*. In *Rerum Italicarum Scriptores*, 2nd ser., vol. 31, pt. 2. Edited by G. Soranzo. Bologna, 1901.

Theiner, Augustin, ed. *Annales Ecclesiastici*, vol. 28. Barri-Ducis: Guérin, 1864.

Torquemada, Juan de. *A Disputation on the Authority of Pope and Council*. Translated by Thomas M. Izbicki. Oxford: Oxford University Press, 1988.

Tuccia, Niccolò della. *Cronache e statuti della città di Viterbo*. Edited by I. Ciampi. Florence: M. Cellini, 1872.

Valla, Lorenzo. *On the Donation of Constantine*. Edited by G.W. Bowersock. I Tatti Studies, vol. 24. Cambridge, MA: Harvard University Press, 2007.

Secondary Sources

Abulafia, David. "The Inception of the Reign of King Ferrante of Naples: The Events of the Summer 1458 in the Light of Documentation from Milan." In *The French Descent into Renaissance Italy: Antecedents and Effects*, ed. David Abulafia, 71–89. Brookfield, VT: Ashgate, 1995.

Adcock, Frank. *Caesar as Man of Letters*. Cambridge: Cambridge University Press, 1956.

Ady, Cecilia. *Pius II (Aeneas Silvius Piccolomini) the Humanist Pope*. London: Methuen, 1913.

Albanese, G., D. Pietragalla, M. Bulleri, and M. Tangheroni. "Storiografia come ufficialità alla corte di Alfonso il Magnanimo: I *Rerum gestarum Alfonsi regis libri X* di Bartolomeo Facio." In *Studi su Bartolomeo Facio*, ed. Gabriella Albanese, 45–95. Pisa: ETS, 2000.

Alberigo, Giuseppe. *Cardinalato e collegialità*. Florence: Vallechi, 1969.

–. *Chiesa conciliare: Identità e significato del conciliarismo*. Brescia: Paideia, 1981.

Alberigo, Giuseppe, ed. *Christian Unity: The Council of Ferrara-Florence, 1438/9–1989*. Leuven: Leuven University Press, 1991.

Antonazzi, Giovanni. *Lorenzo Valla e la polemica sulla donazione di Costantino*. Rome: Storia e Letteratura, 1985.

Antoniutti, Anna, and Marco Gallo, eds. *Enea Silvio Piccolomini: Arte, storia e cultura nell'Europa di Pio II*. Rome: Associazione Culturale Shakespeare 2, 2006.

Avesani, Rino. "Epaeneticorum ad Pium II Pont. Max. Libri V." In *Enea Silvio Piccolomini, Papa Pio II: Atti del convegno per il quinto centenario della morte e altri scritti raccolti da Domenico Maffei*, ed. Domenico Maffei, 15–97. Siena: Accademia senese degli intronati,1968.

Azzara, Claudio. *Il papato nel Medioevo*. Bologna: Mulino, 2006.

Baldi, Barbara. "Enea Silvio Piccolomini e il *De Europa*: Umanesimo, religione e politica." *Archivio Storico Italiano* 61 (2003): 619–83.

–. *Pio II e le trasformazioni dell'Europa cristiana*. Milan: Unicopli, 2006.

–. "Un Umanista alla corte di Federico III: Il *Pentalogus* di Enea Silvio Piccolomini." *Cahiers d'études italiennes* 13 (2011): 161–71.

–. *Il "cardinale tedesco": Enea Silvio Piccolomini fra impero, papato, Europa (1442–1455)*. Milan: Unicopli, 2012.

Baron, Hans. *The Crisis of the Early Italian Renaissance: Civic Humanism and Republican Liberty in an Age of Classicism and Tyranny*. Princeton: Princeton University Press, 1966.

Beaune, Colette. *The Birth of an Ideology: Myths and Symbols of Nation in Late-Medieval France*. Translated by Susan Ross Huston. Berkeley: UCLA Press, 1991.

Bellitto, Christopher M. "The Reform Context of the Great Western Schism." In *A Companion Guide to the Great Western Schism (1378–1417)*, ed. Joelle Rollo-Koster and Thomas M. Izbicki, 303–31. Leiden: Brill, 2009.

–. *Renewing Christianity: A History of Church Reform from Day One to Vatican II*. New York: Paulist, 2001.

Bernetti, Giuseppe. "Ricerche e problemi nei *Commentarii* di Enea Silvio Piccolomini." *La Rinascita* 7 (1939): 449–75.

–. *Saggi e studi sugli scritti di Enea Silvio Piccolomini, Papa Pio II (1405–1464).* Florence: Tipolitografia STIAV, 1971.

Bianca, Concetta. "Alla corte di Napoli: Alfonso, libri e umanisti." In *Il Libro a Corte*, ed. Amadeo Quondam, 177–201. Rome: Bulzoni, 1994.

–. "I poeti e la Dieta di Mantova." In *Il sogno di Pio II e il viaggio da Roma a Mantova: Atti del convegno internazionale, Mantova, 13–15 aprile 2000*, ed. Arturo Calzona, Francesco Paolo Fiore, Alberto Tenenti, and Cesare Vasoli, 579–90. Florence: Olschki, 2003.

–. "La terza edizione moderna dei *Commentarii* di Pio II." *Roma nel Rinascimento* (1995): 5–16.

Bianchi, Rossella."Cultura umanistica intorno ai Piccolomini fra Quattro e Cinquecento: Antonio da San Severino ed altri." In *Umanesimo a Siena: Letteratura, arti figurative, musica*, ed. Elisabetta Cioni and Daniela Fausti, 29–88. Florence: Nuova Italia, 1994.

–. *L'"Eversana Deiectio" di Jacopo Ammannati Piccolomini*. Rome: Edizione di Storia e Letteratura, 1984.

–. *Intorno a Pio II: Un mercante e tre poeti*. Messina: Sicania, 1988.

Bisaha, Nancy. *Creating East and West: Renaissance Humanists and the Ottoman Turks*. Philadelphia: University of Pennsylvania Press, 2004.

–. "Pope Pius II and the Crusade." In *Crusading in the Fifteenth Century: Message and Impact*, ed. Norman Housley. London: Palgrave Macmillan, 2004.

–. Introduction to *Europe (c. 1400–1458)*, by Aeneas Silvius Piccolomini. Washington, DC: Catholic University Press, 2013.

Black, Antony. *Council and Commune: The Conciliar Movement and the Fifteenth-Century Heritage.* London: Burns and Oates, 1979.

–. *Monarchy and Community: Political Ideas in the Later Conciliar Controversy, 1430–1450*. Cambridge: Cambridge University Press, 1970.

–. "Popes and Councils." In *The New Cambridge Medieval History*, ed. Christopher Allmand, vol. 7, 65–86. Cambridge: Cambridge University Press, 1998.

–. *Political Thought in Europe, 1250–1450*. Cambridge: Cambridge University Press, 1992.

Boschetto, Luca. *Società e cultura a Firenze al tempo del Concilio: Eugenio IV tra curiali, mercanti e umanisti (1434–1443)*. Rome: Edizioni di storia e letteratura, 2012.

Bottari, Guglielmo. "*La 'Sphortias.'*" In *Francesco Filelfo nel quinto centenario della morte: Atti del XVII convegno di studi Maceratesi*, 459–83. Padua: Antenore, 1986.

Boulting, William. *Aeneas Silvius (Enea Silvio de' Piccolomini – Pius II): Orator, Man of Letters, Statesman, and Pope*. London: Archibald Constable and Company, 1908.

Brady, Thomas A. *German Histories in the Age of Reformations, 1400–1650*. Cambridge: Cambridge University Press, 2009.

Brandmüller, Walter. *Das Konzil von Konstanz, 1414–1418*. 2 vols. Paderborn: Schöningh, 1991–99.

–. *Das Konzil von Pavia-Siena, 1423–24*. 2 vols. Munster: Aschendorff, 1964, 1974.

–. *Papst und Konzil im Großen Schisma (1378–1431): Studien und Quellen*. Paderborn: Schöningh, 1990.

Breisach, Ernst. *Historiography: Ancient, Medieval, and Modern*. 2nd ed. Chicago: University of Chicago Press, 1994.

Brown, Allison M. "The Humanist Portrait of Cosimo de' Medici, Pater Patriae." *Journal of the Warburg and Courtauld Institute* 24 (1961): 186–221.

Brown, Virginia. "Caesar." In *Catalogus Translationum et Commentariorium: Medieval and Renaissance Latin Translations and Commentaries*, vol. 3, 87–139, ed. F.E. Cranz and P.O. Kristeller. Washington, DC: Catholic University of America Press, 1976.

Burckhardt, Jakob. *The Civilization of the Renaissance in Italy*. Translated by S.G.C. Middlemore. 1868. Reprint, revised and edited by Irene Gordon. New York: New American Library, 1960.

Calzona, Arturo, Francesco Paolo Fiore, Alberto Tenenti, and Cesare Vasoli, eds. *Il sogno di Pio II e il viaggio da Roma a Mantova*. Florence: Olschcki, 2003.

Caravale, Mario, and Alberto Caracciolo. *Lo Stato Pontificio da Martino V a Pio IX*. Vol. 14 of *Storia d'Italia*. Turin: UTET, 1978.

Cardini, Franco. "La repubblica di Firenze e la crociata di Pio II." *Rivista di storia della Chiesa in Italia* 33 (1979): 455–82.

Celenza, Christopher. *Renaissance Humanism and the Papal Curia: Lapo da Castiglionchio the Younger's "De curiae commodis."* Vol. 31 of Papers and Monographs of the American Academy in Rome. Ann Arbor: University of Michigan Press, 1999.

Ceserani, Remo. "Note sull'attività di scrittore di Pio II." In *Enea Silvio Piccolomini, Papa Pio II: Atti del convegno per il quinto centenario della morte e altri scritti raccolti da Domenico Maffei*, ed. Domenico Maffei, 99–115. Siena: Accademia senese degli intronati, 1968.

–. "Rassegna bibliografica." *Giornale storico della letteratura italiana* 141 (1964): 265–82.

Chambers, D.S. *Popes, Cardinals and War: The Military Church in the Renaissance and Early Modern Europe*. London: I.B. Tauris, 2006.

Chittolini, Giorgio. "Papato, corte di Roma e stati italiani dal tramonto del movimento conciliarista agli inizi del Cinquecento." In *Il Papato e l'Europa*, ed. Gabriele De Rosa and Giorgio Cracco, 191–217. Catanzaro: Rubbettino, 2001.

Christianson, Gerald. "Aeneas Sylvius Piccolomini and the Historiography of the Council of Basel." In *Ecclesia Militans Studien zur Konzilien- und Reformationsgeschichte Remigius Bäumer zum 70. Geburtstag gewidmet*, ed. Walter Brandmüller, Herbert Immenkötter, and Erwin Iserloh, 157–84. Paderborn: Schöningh, 1988.

Corbo, Anna Maria. *Pio II Piccolomini: Un papa umanista (1458–1464)*. Rome: Edilazio, 2002.

Crowder, C.M.D. *Unity, Heresy and Reform, 1378–1460: The Conciliar Response to the Great Schism.* New York: St Martin's, 1960.

D'Elia, Anthony F. "Heroic Insubordination in the Army of Sigismondo Malatesta: Petrus Parleo's *Pro milite*, Machiavelli, and the Uses of Cicero and Livy. In *Humanism and Creativity in the Renaissance: Essays in Honor of Ronald G. Witt*, ed. Christopher S. Celenza and Kenneth Gouwens, 31–60. Leiden: Brill, 2006.

–. "Stefano Porcari's Conspiracy against Pope Nicholas V in 1453 and Republican Culture in Rome." *Journal of the History of Ideas* 68, no. 2 (2007): 207–31.

Dall'Oco, Sondra. "Bartolomeo Facio e la tecnica dell' 'excursus' nella biografia di Alfonso d'Aragona." *Archivio Storico Italiano* 154, no. 2 (1996): 207–51.

De Vincentiis, Amedeo. *Battaglie di memoria: Gruppi, intellettuali, testi e la discontinuità del potere papale alla metà del Quattrocento, con l'edizione del regno di Leodrisio Crivelli*. Rome: Roma nel Rinascimento, 2002.

Delaruelle, Étienne, E.R. Labande, and P. Ourliac. *L'Église au temps du Grand Schisme et de la crise conciliaire, 1379–1449*. 2 vols. Paris: Bloud and Gay, 1962–64.

Donati, Angela, ed. *Il potere, le arti, la guerra: Lo splendore dei Malatesta*. Milan: Electa, 2001.

Esch, Arnold. "Enea Silvio Piccolomini als Papst Pius II.: Herrschaftspraxis und Selbstdarstellung." In *Lebenslehren und Weltentwurfe im Übergang vom Mittlelalter zur Neuzeit: Politik, Bildung, Naturkunde, Theologie*, ed. Hartmut Boockmann, Bernd Möller, and Karl Stackmann, 112–40. Göttingen: Vandenhoeck and Ruprecht, 1989.

Ettlinger, Helen Shahrokh. "The Image of a Renaissance Prince: Sigismondo Malatesta and the Arts of Power." Doctoral dissertation, University of California at Berkeley, 1988.

Ferenga, Paola. "'I Romani sono periculoso populo …': Roma nei carteggi diplomatici." In *Roma Capitale (1447–1527)*, ed. Sergio Gensini, 289–315. San Miniato: Pacini, 1994.

Ferente, Serena. *La sfortuna di Jacopo Piccinino: Storia dei bracceschi in Italia, 1423–1465*. Florence: Olschki, 2005.

Ferraù, Giacomo. "Il 'Il *De rebus* ab Alphonso Primo Gestis' de Bartolomeo Facio." *Studi Umanistici* 1 (1990): 60–113.

Fink, Karl August. *Chiesa e papato nel Medioevo*. Bologna: Mulino, 1981.

Finzi, Claudio. "Una 'Vita' di Braccio di Giannantonio Campano." In *Braccio da Montone e i Fortebracci: Atti del convegno internazionale di studi, Montone, 23–25 marzo 1990*, ed. Maria Vittoria Baruti Ceccopieri, 147–70, Narni: Pubblicazioni del Centro Studi Storici, 1993.

Fosi, Irene Polverini. "'La Comune, dolcissima patria': Siena e Pio II." In *I Ceti dirigenti nella Toscana del Quattrocento: Atti del V e VI convegno, Firenze, 10–11 dicembre 1982; 2–3 dicembre 1983*, ed. Daniella Rugiadini, 509–21. Monte Oriolo: Impruneta Papafava ed., 1987.

Franceschini, Gino. "Quattordici brevi di Pio secondo a Federico da Montefeltro." In *Enea Silvio Piccolomini, Papa Pio II: Atti del convegno per il quinto centenario della morte e altri scritti raccolti da Domenico Maffei*, ed. Domenico Maffei, 133–64. Siena: Accademia senese degli intronati, 1968.

Frenken, Ansgar. "Die Erforschung des Konstanzer Konzils (1414–1418)." *Annuarium Historiae Conciliorum* 25 (1993): 1–512.

Frittelli, U. *Giannantonio de' Pandoni detto 'il Porcellio': Studio critico*. Florence: Paravia, 1900.

Fubini, Riccardo. "Conciliarismo, regalismo, impero nelle discussioni tre e quattrocentesche sulla Donazione di Costantino." In *Costantino il Grande: Tra medioevo ed età moderna*, ed. Giorgio Bonamente, Giorgio Cracco, and Klaus Rosen, 133–58. Bologna: Mulino, 2009.

–. "Contestazioni quattrocentesche della Donazione di Costantino: Niccolò Cusano, Lorenzo Valla." In *Costantino il Grande: Dall'antichità all'umanesimo (Colloquio sul Cristianesimo nel mondo antico, Macerata, 18–20 dicembre 1990)*, ed. G. Bonamente and F. Fusco, 385–431. Macerata: Università degli Studi di Macerata, 1992.

–. *Italia quattrocentesca: Politica e diplomazia nell'età di Lorenzo il Magnifico*. Milan: Francoangeli, 1994.

–. Introduction to *La Dieta di Mantova e la politica de' Veneziani*, by Giovanni Battista Picotti. Trento: Università degli Studi di Trento, 1996.

–. "Niccolò V, Francesco Sforza e la lega italica: Un memoriale adespoto di Giovanni Castiglioni, vescovo di Coutances (Milano, 12 settembre 1451)." In *Papato, stati regionali e Lunigiana nell'età di Niccolò V : Atti delle giornate di studio. La Spezia, Sarzana, Pontremoli, Bagnone, 25-28 Maggio 2000*, ed. Eliana M. Vecchi, 169–204. La Spezia: Accademia lunigianese di scienze Giovanni Capellini, 2004.

–. "Aux origines de la balance des pouvoirs: Le système politique en Italie au XVe siècle." In *L'Europe des traités de Westphalie: Esprit de la diplomatie et diplomatie de l'esprit*, ed. Lucien Bély, 11–121. Paris: Presses Universitaires de France, 2000.

–. "Enea Silvio Piccolomini nei suoi rapporti con la cultura umanistica del suo tempo." In Fabrizio Nevola, ed., *Pio II Piccolomini, il Papa del Rinascimento a Siena: Atti del convegno internazionale di studi, 5–7 maggio 2005*, 131–44. Siena: Protagon, 2009.

Garin, Eugenio. *Ritratti di umanisti*. Milan: Bompiani, 1996.

Gazzaniga, J.L. "L'appel au concile dans la politique gallicane de la monarchie de Charles VII et Louis XII." *Bulletin de littérature ecclésiastique* 85 (1984): 111–29.

Gill, Joseph. *The Council of Florence*. Cambridge: Cambridge University Press, 1959.

Gilli, Patrick. *Au Miroir de l'humanisme: Les représentations de la France dans la culture savante italienne à la fin du Moyen âge*. Rome: École française de Rome, 1997.

Guglielminetti, Marziano. *Memoria e scrittura: L'autobiografia da Dante a Cellini*. Turin: Einaudi, 1975.

Guillemain, Bernard. *La cour pontificale d'Avignon*. Paris: E. de Boccard, 1962.

Hankins, James. "Renaissance Crusades: Humanist Crusade Literature in the Age of Mehmed II." *Dumbarton Oaks Papers* 49 (1995): 111–207.

Haubst, Rudolf. "Reformentwurf Pius des Zweiten." *Römische Quartalschrift* 49 (1954): 188–242.

Hay, Denys. *Europe: The Emergence of an Idea*. Edinburgh: Edinburgh University Press, 1957.

Helmrath, Johannes. *Das Basler Konzil, 1431–1449*. Cologne: Böhlau, 1987.

–. "Pius II. und die Türken." In *Europa und die Türken in der Renaissance*, ed. Bodo Guthmüller and W. Kühlmann, 79–137. Tübingen: Max Niemeyer, 2000.

–. "The German *Reichstage* and the Crusade." In *Crusading in the Fifteenth Century: Message and Impact*, ed. Norman Housley, 53–69. London: Palgrave Macmillan, 2004.

Hendrix, Scott. "In Quest of the *Vera Ecclesia*: The Crises of Late Medieval Ecclesiology." *Viator* 7 (1976): 347–78.

Heymann, Frederick. *George of Bohemia: King of Heretics*. Princeton: Princeton University Press, 1965.

–. "George of Podiebrad's Plan for an International Peace League." In *The Czechoslovak Contribution to World Culture*, 224–44. The Hague: Mouton, 1964.

Hilary, Richard B. "The Nepotism of Pope Pius II, 1458–1464." *Catholic Historical Review* 64, no. 1 (1978): 33–5.

Honegger Chiari, Sara. "L'edizione del 1584 dei *Commentarii* di Pio II e la duplice revisione di Francesco Bandini (Analisi del libro primo)." *Archivio Storico Italiano* 149 (1991): 585–612.

Housley, Norman. *Crusading and the Ottoman Threat, 1453–1505*. Oxford: Oxford University Press, 2012.

–. "Pope Pius II and Crusading." *Crusades* 11 (2012): 209–47.

Housley, Norman, ed. *Crusading in the Fifteenth Century: Message and Impact*. London: Palgrave Macmillan, 2004.

Ianziti, Gary. "I *Commentarii*: Appunti per la storia di un genere storiografico quattrocentesco." *Archivio Storico Italiano* 150, no. 4 (1992): 1029–63.

–. "A Humanist Historian and His Documents: Giovanni Simonetta, Secretary to the Sforzas." *Renaissance Quarterly* 34 (1981): 491–516.

–. *Humanistic Historiography under the Sforzas: Politics and Propaganda in Fifteenth-Century Milan*. Oxford: Clarendon, 1988.

–. "Storiografia come propaganda: Il caso dei 'Commentarii' Rinascimentali." *Società e Storia* 22 (1983): 909–18.

–. "La storiografia umanistica a Milano nel Quattrocento." In *La Storiografia umanistica*, vol.1, ed. Anita di Stefano et al., 311–32 Messina: Sicania, 1992.

–. *Writing History in Renaissance Italy: Leonardo Bruni and the Uses of the Past*. Cambridge, MA: Harvard University Press, 2012.

Iaria, Simona. "Diffusione e recezione del *Libellus dialogorum* di Enea Silvio Piccolomini." *Italia Medioevale e Umanistica* 44 (2003): 65–114.

Ilardi, Vincent. "The Banker-Statesman and the Condottiere-Prince (1450–1464): Cosimo de' Medici and Francesco Sforza." In *Florence and Milan. Comparisons and Relations: Acts of Two Conferences at Villa I Tatti in 1982-1984*, ed. Craig Hugh Smyth and Gian Carlo Garfagnini, 217–39. Florence: La Nuova Italia Editrice, 1989.

–. "France and Milan: The Uneasy Alliance, 1452–1466." In *Studies in Italian Renaissance Diplomatic History*, 415–47. London: Variorum Reprints, 1986.

–. "The Italian League, Francesco Sforza, and Charles VII." *Studies in the Renaissance* 6 (1959): 129–66.

Izbicki, Thomas M. "The Papalist Reaction to the Council of Constance: Juan de Torquemada to the Present." *Church History* 55, no. 1 (1986): 7–20.

–. *Protector of the Faith: Cardinal Johannes de Turrecremata and the Defense of the Institutional Church*. Washington, DC: Catholic University Press, 1981.

–. "The Missing Antipope: The Rejection of Felix V and the Council of Basel in the Writings of Aeneas Sylvius Piccolomini and the Piccolomini Library." *Viator* 41, no. 1 (2010): 301–14.

Jones, P.J. *The Malatesta of Rimini and the Papal State: A Political History*. London: Cambridge University Press, 1974.

Kallendorf, Craig. *In Praise of Aeneas: Virgil and Epideictic Rhetoric in the Early Italian Renaissance*. Hanover, NH: University of New England Press, 1989.

Kaminsky, Howard. "Pius Aeneas among the Taborites." *Church History* 28, no. 3 (1959): 281–309.

Kramer, Hans. "Untersuchungen über die *Commentarii* des Papstes Pius II." *Mitteilungen des Oesterreichischen Instituts für Geschichtsforschung* 158 (1934): 58–92.

Kristeller, Paul Oskar. *Studies in Renaissance Thought and Letters II*. Rome: Edizioni di storia e letteratura, 1950.

Krynen, Jacques. *L'Empire du Roi: Idées et croyances politiques en France XIIIe–XVe siècles*. Paris: Gallimard, 1993.

–. *L'idéal du prince et pouvoir royal de France à la fin du Moyen âge (1380–1440): Etude de la littérature politique du temps*. Paris: Picard, 1981.

Landi, Aldo. *Concilio e papato nel Rinascimento (1449–1516): Un problema irrisolto*. Turin: Claudiana, 1997.

Law, John E. "Giovanni Vitelleschi, 'prelato guerriero.'" *Renaissance Studies* 12 (1998): 40–66.

Lippincott, Kristen. "The Neo-Latin Historical Epics of North Italian Courts." *Renaissance Studies* 3, no. 4 (1989): 415–28.

Lulvès, J. "Päpstliche Wahlkapitulationen: Ein Beitrag zur Entwicklungsgeschichte des Kardinalats." *Quellen und Forschungen aus italianischen Archiven und Bibliotheken* 12 (1909): 212–36.

Maffei, Domenico. *La donazione di Constantino nei giuristi medievali*. Milan: Giuffrè, 1964.

Mallett, Michael. *The Borgias: The Rise and Fall of a Renaissance Dynasty*. London: Bodley Head, 1969.

Märtl, Claudia. "Wie schreibt ein Papst Geschichte? Zum umgang mit Vorlagen in den 'Commentarii' Pius II." In *Die Hofgeschichtsschreibung im mittelalterlichen Europa*, ed. R. Schieffer and J. Wenta, 233–51. Torun, Wydawn. Uniwersytetu Mikolaja Kopernika, 2006.

–. "Les *Commentarii* d'Enea Silvio Piccolomini (Pie II, 1405/1458–1464)." In *Autobiographies souveraines*, ed. Pierre Monnet et Jean-Claude Schmitt. Paris: Publications de la Sorbonne, 2012.

McCahill, Elizabeth. *Reviving the Eternal City: Rome and the Papal Court, 1420–1447*. Cambridge, MA: Harvard University Press, 2013.

McGinn, Bernard. "The Angel Pope and the Papal AntiChrist." *Church History* 47, no. 2 (1978): 155–73.

Meserve, Margaret. "From Samarkand to Scythia: Reinventions of Asia in Renaissance Geography and Political Thought." In *Pius II – "El Più Expeditivo Pontifice": Selected Studies on Aeneas Silvius Piccolomini (1405–1464)*, ed. Zweder von Martels and Arjo J. Vanderjagt, 13–39. Leiden: Brill, 2003.

–. *Empires of Islam in Renaissance Historical Thought.* Cambridge, MA: Harvard University Press, 2008.

Minnich, Nelson H. "Councils of the Catholic Reformation: A Historical Survey." In *The Church, the Councils, and Reform: The Legacy of the Fifteenth Century*, ed. Gerald Christianson, Thomas M. Izbicki, and Christopher M. Bellitto, 27–59. Washington, DC: Catholic University Press, 2008.

Mitchell, R.J. *The Laurels and the Tiara: Pope Pius II, 1458–1464.* London: Harvill, 1962.

Modigliani, Anna. "Pio II e Roma." In *Il sogno di Pio II e il viaggio da Roma a Mantova: Atti del convegno internazionale, Mantova, 13–15 aprile 2000*, ed. Arturo Calzona, Francesco Paolo Fiore, Alberto Tenenti, and Cesare Vasoli, 77–108. Florence: Olschki, 2003.

–. "Le ragioni del lusso e il rifiuto della povertà evangelica: I papi e la richezza terrena nel Quattrocento." In *Pompa sacra: Lusso e cultura materiale alla corte papale nel basso medioevo (1420–1527): Atti della giornata di studio*, ed. Thomas Ertl, 145–65. Rome: Istituto storico germanico, 2010.

–. *Congiurare all'antica: Stefano Porcari, Niccolò V, Roma 1453.* Rome: Roma nel Rinascimento, 2013.

Mollat, G. *The Popes at Avignon.* New York: Harper Torchbooks, 1963.

Monaco, Michele. *Dalla fine del Grande Scisma alla Pace di Cateau-Cambrésis (1417–1559).* Vol. 1 of *Lo Stato dela Chiesa.* Lecce: Milella, 1971.

Nederman, Cary J. "Humanism and Empire: Aeneas Silvius Piccolomini, Cicero, and the Imperial Ideal." *Historical Journal* 36 (1993): 499–515.

Nevola, Fabrizio, ed. *Pio II Piccolomini, il Papa del Rinascimento a Siena: Atti del convegno internazionale di studi, 5–7 maggio 2005.* Siena: Protagon, 2009.

Oakley, Francis. *The Conciliarist Tradition: Constitutionalism in the Catholic Church, 1300–1870.* Oxford: Oxford University Press, 2003.

–. *The Western Church in the Later Middle Ages.* Ithaca, NY: Cornell University Press, 1979.

O'Brien, Emily. "Arms and Letters: The *Commentaries* of Pope Pius II and the Politicization of Papal Imagery." *Renaissance Quarterly* 62 (2009): 1057–97.

–. "Aeneas Sylvius Piccolomini and the Histories of the Council of Basel." In *The Church, the Councils, and Reform: a Fifteenth-Century Legacy Revisited*, ed.

Gerald Christianson, Thomas M. Izbicki, and Christopher Bellitto, 60–81. Washington, DC: Catholic University Press, 2008.

–. "The Politics of Painting: Cardinal Francesco Todeschini Piccolomini, Pope Pius II, and the Frescoes of the Piccolomini Library." In *From Florence to the Mediterranean and Beyond: Essays in Honor of Anthony Molho*, ed. Diogo Ramada Curto, Eric R. Dursteler, Julius Kirshner, and Francesca Trivellato, 1: 427–44. Florence: Olschki, 2009.

Ozment, Stephen. *The Age of Reform, 1250–1550*. New Haven: Yale University Press, 1980.

Pächt, Otto. "Giovanni da Fano's Illustrations for Basinio's Epos 'Hesperis.'" *Studi Romagnoli* 2 (1951): 91–111.

Paparelli, Gioacchino. *Enea Silvio Piccolomini: L'umanesimo sul soglio di Pietro*. Ravenna: Longo, 1978.

Paravicini-Bagliani, Agostino. *Il trono di Pietro: L'universalità del papato da Alessandro III a Bonifacio VIII*. Rome: Carocci, 1996.

Partner, Peter. "The 'Budget' of the Roman Church in the Renaissance Period." In *Italian Renaissance Studies*, ed. E.F. Jacob, 256–78. London: Faber and Faber, 1960.

–. *The Lands of St Peter: The Papal State in the Middle Ages and the Early Renaissance*. London: Methuen, 1972.

–. *The Papal State under Martin V: The Administration and Government of the Temporal Power in the Early Fifteenth Century*. London: British School at Rome, 1958.

Pascoe, Louis. "Gerson and the Donation of Constantine: Growth and Development within the Church." *Viator* 5 (1974): 469–85.

von Pastor, Ludwig. *The History of the Popes*, vols. 2 and 3. (London: Routledge and Kegan Paul, 1949).

Pavlac, Brian A. "Nicholas Cusanus as Prince-Bishop of Brixen (1450–64): Historians and a Conflict of Church and State." *Historical Reflections/Reflexions historiques* 21 (1995): 131–54.

–. "Reform." In *Introducing Nicholas of Cusa: A Guide to a Renaissance Man*, ed. Christopher M. Belitto, Thomas M. Izbicki, and Gerald Christianson, 59–112. New York: Paulist, 2004.

Pellegrini, Marco. "Pio II." In *Enciclopedia dei Papi*, 3: 663–85. Rome: Treccani, 2000.

–. *Il Papato nel Rinascimento*. Bologna: Mulino, 2010.

–. "Pio II, il Collegio Cardinalizio e la Dieta di Mantova." In *Il sogno di Pio II e il viaggio da Roma a Mantova: Atti del convegno internazionale, Mantova, 13–15 aprile 2000*, ed. Arturo Calzona, Francesco Paolo Fiore, Alberto Tenenti, and Cesare Vasoli, 15–76. Florence: Olschki, 2003.

–. "Unità Europea, primato romano: Riflessi della teologia politica di Pio II Piccolomini." In *Enea Silvio Piccolomini: Arte, storia e cultura nell'Europa di Pio II*, ed. Anna Antoniutti and Marco Gallo, 423–32. Rome: Associazione Culturale Shakespeare 2, 2006.

Pertusi, Agostino. "Gli inizi della storiografia umanistica del Quattrocento." In *Storiografia veneziana fin al secolo XVI: Aspetti e problemi*, ed. Agostino Pertusi, 269–332. Florence: Olschki, 1970.

Picotti, Giovanni Battista. *Ricerche umanistiche*. Florence: Nuova Italia, 1955.

–. *La Dieta di Mantova e la politica de' Veneziani*. 1912. Reprint, with an introduction by Riccardo Fubini. Trento: Università degli Studi di Trento, 1996.

–. "La pubblicazione e i primi effetti della 'Execrabilis' di Pio II." *Archivio della R. Società Romana di Storia Patria* 37 (1914): 5–56.

Pozzi, Mario. "Struttura epica dei *Commentarii*." In *Pio II nella cultura del suo tempo: Atti del I convegno internazionale, 1989*, ed. Luisa Rotondi Secchi Tarugi, 151–62. Milan: Guerini, 1991.

Prodi, Paolo. *Il sovrano pontefice; un corpo e due anime: La monarchia papale nella prima età moderna*. Bologna: Il Mulino, 1982.

Prosperi, Adriano. "Varia fortuna di Pio II nel Cinquecento." In *Enea Silvio Piccolomini. Uomo di lettere e mediatore di culture. Atti del convegno interazionale di studi Basilea, 21-23 aprile 2005*, ed. Maria Antonietta Terzoli, 357–76. Basel: Schwabe, 2006.

Rambaud, Michel. *L'Art de la déformation historique dans les "Commentaires" du César*. Paris: Les Belles Lettres, 1953.

Rapp, Francis. *Les origines medievales de l'Allemagne moderne*. Paris: Aubier, 1989.

–. "Le rétablissement de la papauté: Une victoire imparfaite et coûteuse." In *Histoire de Christianisme*, vol. 7, ed. J.-M. Mayeur, Ch. and L. Pietri, A. Vauchez, and M. Venard, 79–144. Paris: Desclée, 1994.

Reinhard, Wolfgang. "Papa Pius: Prolégomènes à une histoire sociale de la papauté." In *Papauté, confessions, modernité*, ed. Robert Descimon, 41–67. Paris: EHESS, 1998.

Reeves, Marjorie. *The Influence of Prophecy in the Later Middle Ages: A Study of Joachimism*. Oxford: Clarendon, 1969.

–. "The Medieval Heritage." In *Prophetic Rome in the High Renaissance Period*, ed. Marjorie Reeves, 3–21. Oxford: Clarendon, 1992.

–. "The *Vaticinia de Summis Pontificibus*: A Question of Authority." In *Intellectual Life in the Middle Ages: Essays Presented to Margaret Gibson*, ed. Lesley Smith and Benedicta Ward, 145–56. London: Hambledon, 1992.

Richardson, Carol M. *Reclaiming Rome: Cardinals in the Fifteenth Century*. Leiden: Brill, 2009.

Robin, Diana. *Filelfo in Milan: Writings, 1451–1477*. Princeton: Princeton University Press, 1991.

Rollo-Koster, Joëlle, and Thomas M. Izbicki, eds. *A Companion Guide to the Great Western Schism (1378–1417)*. Leiden: Brill, 2009.

Rossi, Vittorio. *Il Quattrocento*. 1933. Reprint, with revisions by Rosella Bessi. Padua: Piccin Nuova Libreria, 1992.

Rossmann, Wilhelm. *Betrachtungen über das Zeitalter der Reformation*. Jena: F. Mauke, 1858.

Ryder, Alan. *Alfonso the Magnanimous: King of Aragon, Naples, and Sicily, 1396–1458*. Oxford: Clarendon, 1990.

–. *The Kingdom of Naples under Alfonso the Magnanimous*. Oxford: Oxford University Press, 1976.

Seeber, Norbert. *Enea Vergilianus: Vergilisches in den "Kommentaren" des Enea Silvio Piccolomini (Pius II.)*. Vol. 30 of Commentationes Aenipontanae. Innsbruck: Wagner, 1997.

Setton, Kenneth M. *The Papacy and the Levant, 1204–1571*. 4 vols. Philadelphia: American Philosophical Society, 1976–84.

Sigmund, Paul. *Nicholas of Cusa and Medieval Political Thought*. Cambridge, MA: Harvard University Press, 1963.

Simonetta, Marcello. "Il Duca alla Dieta: Francesco Sforza e Pio II." In *Il Sogno di Pio II e il viaggio da Roma a Mantova: Atti del convegno internazionale, Mantova, 13–15 aprile 2000*, ed. Arturo Calzona, Francesco Paolo Fiore, Alberto Tenenti, and Cesare Vasoli, 247–85. Florence: Olschki, 2003.

–. "Pius II and Francesco Sforza: The History of Two Allies." In *Pius II – "El Più Expeditivo Pontifice": Selected Studies on Aeneas Silvius Piccolomini (1405–1464)*, ed. Zweder von Martels and Arjo J. Vanderjagt, 147–70. Leiden: Brill, 2003.

Skinner, Quentin. *The Foundations of Modern Political Thought*. 2 vols. Cambridge: Cambridge University Press, 1978.

Smith, L.F. "Lodrisio Crivelli of Milan and Aeneas Silvius." *Studies in the Renaissance* 9 (1962): 31–63.

Soranzo, G. "Ancora sulla missione di Sigismondo Pandolfo Malatesta a Maometto II e Matteo de' Pasti." *La Romagna* (1910).

–. "Una missione di Sigismondo Pandolfo Malatesta a Maometto II nel 1461." *La Romagna* (1909).

–. *Pio II e la politica italiana nella lotta contro i Malatesti, 1457–1463*. Padua: Fratelli Drucker, 1911.

Sorbelli, Albano. *Francesco Sforza a Genova (1458–1466): Saggio sulla politica italiana di Luigi XI*. Bologna: Zanichelli, 1901.

Stieber, Joachim. *Pope Eugenius IV, the Council of Basel and the Secular and Ecclesiastical Authorities in the Empire: The Conflict over Supreme Authority and Power in the Church*. Leiden: Brill, 1978.

Stinger, Charles. *The Renaissance in Rome*. Bloomington: Indiana University Press, 1985.

Strauss, Gerald. "Ideas of *Reformatio* and *Renovatio* from the Middle Ages to the Reformation." In *Handbook of European History, 1400–1600: Late Middle Ages, Renaissance, Reformation*, ed. Thomas Brady, Heiko Oberman, and James Tracy, vol. 2, 1–30. Leiden: Brill, 1994.

Strauss, Gerald, ed. *Manifestations of Discontent in Germany on the Eve of the Reformation*. Bloomington: Indiana University Press, 1971.

Strnad, Alfred A. "Pio II e suo nipote Francesco Todeschini Piccolomini." *Atti e memorie della deputazione di storia patria per le Marche*, 8th ser., vol. 4, no. 2 (1964–65): 37–84.

Stump, Philip H. *The Reforms of the Council of Constance, 1414–1418*. Leiden: Brill, 1994.

Tarughi, Luisa Secchi, ed. *Pio II Umanista Europeo: Atti del XVII convegno internazionale, Chianciano-Pienza, 18–21 luglio 2005*. Florence: Cesati, 2007.

Tateo, Francesco. *I miti della storiografia umanistica*. Rome: Bulzoni, 1990.

Thomson, John A.F. *Popes and Princes, 1417–1517: Politics and Polity in the Late Medieval Church*. London: George Allen and Unwin, 1980.

Tierney, Brian. *Foundations of the Conciliar Theory: The Contribution of the Medieval Canonists from Gratian to the Great Schism*. Rev. ed. Leiden: Brill, 1998.

Tillinghast, Pardon E. "Nicholas of Cusa vs. Sigmund of Habsburg: An Attempt at Post-conciliar Church Reform." *Church History* 36 (1967): 371–90.

Toews, John B. "Dream and Reality in the Imperial Ideology of Pope Pius II." *Medievalia et Humanistica* 16 (1964): 77–93.

–. "Formative Forces in the Pontificate of Nicholas V." *Catholic Historical Review* 54 (1968): 261–84.

–. "Pope Eugenius IV and the Concordat of Vienna (1448): An Interpretation." *Church History* 34 (1965): 178–94.

Totaro, Luigi. *Pio II nei suoi "Commentarii": Un contributo alla lettura della autobiografia di Enea Silvio Piccolomini*. Bologna: Pàtron, 1978.

–. "Gli scritti di Enea Silvio Piccolomini sul concilio." In *Conciliarismo, stati nazionali, inizi dell'Umanesimo: Atti del XXV convegno storico internazionale, Todi, 9–12 ottobre 1988*, 47–78. Spoleto: Centro di Studi sull'Alto Medioevo, 1990.

–. "Enea Silvio e il Concilio di Basilea." In *Enea Silvio Piccolomini. Uomo di lettere e mediatore di culture: Atti del convegno internazionale di studi, Basilea, 21–23 aprile 2005*, ed. Maria Antonietta Terzoli, 82–90. Basel: Schwabe, 2006.

Ullmann, Walter. "The Legal Validity of the Papal Electoral Pacts." *Ephemerides Iuris Canonici* 12 (1956): 3–35.

–. *Medieval Papalism: The Political Theories of the Medieval Canonists*. London: Methuen, 1949.

–. *The Origins of the Great Schism: A Study in Fourteenth-Century Ecclesiastical History*. London: Burns Oates and Washbourne, 1948.

–. *A Short History of the Papacy in the Middle Ages*. 2nd ed. London: Routledge, 2003.

Valentini, R. "'De gestis et vita Bracii' di A. Campano: A proposito di storia della storiografia." *Bollettino della R. Deputazione di Storia Patria per l'Umbria* 27 (1924): 153–96.

Valois, Noël. *Histoire de la Pragmatique Sanction de Bourges sous Charles VII*. Paris: Alphonse Picard et fils, 1906.

Van Heck, Adrianus. "Amator vetusti ritus et observator diligens: Stile e modelli stilistici di Pio II." In *Pio II nella cultura del suo tempo: Atti del convegno internazionale, 1989*, ed. Luisa Rotondi Secchi Tarugi, 119–32. Milan: Guerini, 1991.

Viti, Paolo, ed. *Firenze e il Concilio del 1439*. Florence: Olschki, 1994.

Vivanti, Corrado. "I *Commentarii* di Pio II." *Studi Storici* 26 (1985): 443–62.

Voigt, Georg. *Enea Silvio de' Piccolomini, als Papst Pius der Zweite und sein Zeitalter*. 3 vols. Berlin: G. Reimer, 1856–63.

Waley, Daniel. *The Papal State in the Thirteenth Century*. London: Macmillan, 1961.

Watanabe, Morimichi. "Nicholas of Cusa and the Tyrolese Monasteries: Reform and Resistance." In *Concord and Reform: Nicholas of Cusa and Legal and Political Thought in the Fifteenth Century*, ed. Thomas M. Izbicki and Gerald Christianson, 133–53. Aldershot: Ashgate, 2001.

–. "Nicholas of Cusa and the Reform of the Roman Curia." In *Concord and Reform: Nicholas of Cusa and Legal and Political Thought in the Fifteenth Century*, ed. Thomas M. Izbicki and Gerald Christianson, 169–85. Aldershot: Ashgate, 2001.

Watanabe, Morimichi, and Thomas Izbicki. "Nicholas of Cusa, a General Reform of the Church." In *Concord and Reform: Nicholas of Cusa and Legal and Political Thought in the Fifteenth Century*, ed. Thomas M. Izbicki and Gerald Christianson, 187–216. Aldershot: Ashgate, 2001.

Welch, Kathryn, and Anton Powell, eds. *Julius Caesar as Artful Reporter: The War Commentaries as Political Instruments*. London: Duckworth, 1998.

White, Arthur. *Plague and Pleasure: The Renaissance World of Pius II.* Washington, DC: Catholic University Press, 2014.
Wight, Martin. *Systems of States*. Leicester: Leicester University Press, 1977.
Wilcox, Donald J. *The Development of Florentine Humanist Historiography.* Cambridge, MA: Harvard University Press, 1969.
Wilks, Michael J. *The Problem of Sovereignty in the Later Middle Ages.* Cambridge: Cambridge University Press, 1962.
Zabughin, Vladimiro. *Vergilio nel rinascimento italiano: Da Dante a Torquato Tasso.* 2 vols. Bologna: Zanardelli, 1921.
Zanchin, M. *Il primato del romano pontefice in un'opera inedita di Pietro del Monte del secolo XV*. Vigodarzere [Padua]: Progetto Ed. Mariano, 1997.
Zimolo, Giulio. "Il Campano e il Platina come biografi di Pio II," In *Enea Silvio Piccolomini, Papa Pio II: Atti del convegno per il quinto centenario della morte e altri scritti raccolti da Domenico Maffei*, ed. Domenico Maffei, 401–12. Siena, Accademia senese degli intronati,1968.

Index